Everyday Revolutions

Remaking Gender, Sexuality and
Culture in 1970s Australia

Everyday Revolutions

Remaking Gender, Sexuality and Culture in 1970s Australia

Edited by Michelle Arrow
and Angela Woollacott

PRESS

Published by ANU Press
The Australian National University
Acton ACT 2601, Australia
Email: anupress@anu.edu.au

Available to download for free at press.anu.edu.au

ISBN (print): 9781760462963
ISBN (online): 9781760462970

WorldCat (print): 1113935722
WorldCat (online): 1113935780

DOI: 10.22459/ER.2019

This title is published under a Creative Commons Attribution-NonCommercial-NoDerivatives 4.0 International (CC BY-NC-ND 4.0).

The full licence terms are available at
creativecommons.org/licenses/by-nc-nd/4.0/legalcode

Cover design and layout by ANU Press

This edition © 2019 ANU Press

Contents

Contributors vii

1. Revolutionising the everyday: The transformative impact of the sexual and feminist movements on Australian society and culture 1
   Michelle Arrow and Angela Woollacott

Everyday gender revolutions: Workplaces, schools and households

2. Of girls and spanners: Feminist politics, women's bodies and the male trades 23
   Georgine Clarsen

3. The discovery of sexism in schools: Everyday revolutions in the classroom. 37
   Julie McLeod

4. Making the political personal: Gender and sustainable lifestyles in 1970s Australia. 63
   Carroll Pursell

Feminism in art and culture

5. How the personal became (and remains) political in the visual arts 85
   Catriona Moore and Catherine Speck

6. Subversive stitches: Needlework as activism in Australian feminist art of the 1970s. 103
   Elizabeth Emery

7. Women into print: Feminist presses in Australia 121
   Trish Luker

8. 'Unmistakably a book by a feminist': Helen Garner's *Monkey Grip* and its feminist contexts 139
   Zora Simic

Redrawing boundaries between public and private

9. A phone called PAF: CAMP counselling in the 1970s 163
   Catherine Freyne
10. Discomforting politics: 1970s activism and the spectre
    of sex in public. 183
    Leigh Boucher
11. Creative work: Feminist representations of gendered
    and domestic violence in 1970s Australia. 199
    Catherine Kevin
12. 'Put on dark glasses and a blind man's head':
    Poetic defamation and the question of feminist privacy
    in 1970s Australia. 223
    Nicole Moore

Re-gendering language, authority and culture

13. Changing 'man made language': Sexist language
    and feminist linguistic activism in Australia 241
    Amanda Laugesen
14. 'A race of intelligent super-giants': The Whitlams, gendered
    bodies and political authority in modern Australia 261
    Bethany Phillips-Peddlesden
15. *Cleo* magazine and the sexual revolution 279
    Megan Le Masurier
16. Male chauvinists and ranting libbers: Representations
    of single men in 1970s Australia. 295
    Chelsea Barnett

Index 313

Contributors

Michelle Arrow is Associate Professor in Modern History at Macquarie University. Her books include *The Seventies: The Personal, The Political and the Making of Modern Australia* (NewSouth Publishing, 2019) and *Friday on Our Minds: Popular Culture in Australia Since 1945* (NewSouth Publishing, 2009). Together with Catherine Freyne and Timothy Nicastri, Michelle won the 2014 NSW Premier's Multimedia History Prize for the radio documentary 'Public Intimacies: The 1974 Royal Commission on Human Relationships'. Michelle has previously held fellowships at the National Library of Australia and the National Archives of Australia. Together with Leigh Boucher and Kate Fullagar, she is currently editing the Australian Historical Association's journal, *History Australia*. She is currently a Chief Investigator (with Leigh Boucher, Barbara Baird and Robert Reynolds) on the ARC-funded project 'Gender and Sexual Politics: Changing Citizenship in Australia since 1969'.

Chelsea Barnett is a Chancellor's Postdoctoral Research Fellow in the Australian Centre for Public History at the University of Technology Sydney. Her first book, *Reel Men: Australian Masculinity in the Movies, 1949–1962*, was published by Melbourne University Press in 2019. She is currently working on a cultural history of single men in twentieth-century Australia.

Leigh Boucher is a Senior Lecturer in Modern History at Macquarie University. His research centres on the construction and representation of difference in liberal democratic political and popular cultures. This has produced work that investigates a wide variety of historical contexts and representations. This includes research on the dynamic of settler-colonialism and changing constructions of manhood in nineteenth-century Victoria, anthropological constructions of the 'Aborigine' in nineteenth-century Australia, sexuality in contemporary historical films, contestations over masculinity in the representation of the AFL, and the impact of changing ideas about sexuality on the operation of citizenship in late modern Australia. He is currently a Chief Investigator (with Michelle Arrow, Barbara Baird and Robert Reynolds) on the ARC-funded project 'Gender and Sexual Politics: Changing Citizenship in Australia since 1969'. He is currently co-editor, together with Michelle Arrow and Kate Fullagar, of the Australian Historical Association's journal, *History Australia*.

Georgine Clarsen teaches Australian history in the Faculty of Law, Humanities and the Arts at the University of Wollongong. She has published in the area of women's engagements with automobile technology and the role of automobility in the creation of settler identities and space in twentieth-century Australia. Georgine picked up a spanner in the 1970s and became a qualified car mechanic. She worked for many years as the production manager of the Australian performing company Circus Oz.

Elizabeth Emery is a feminist scholar, artist and educator working at the intersection of textiles history, feminist theory and activist politics. Her work as an artist and researcher centres on the subversive use of textiles as a creative strategy of resistance within the history of women's domestic labour and in feminist movements. Elizabeth is currently sessional lecturer of Art History and Textiles Studio at the University of South Australia School of Art, and is a PhD candidate in Women's Studies at Flinders University.

Catherine Freyne is an award-winning historian and media producer. As a PhD candidate at University of Technology Sydney, she is combining history, family memoir and sexuality studies in a research project called 'The Family as Closet: Gay Married Men in Sydney, 1970–2000'.

Catherine Kevin is an Associate Professor in History at Flinders University. She has published on the histories of pregnancy and miscarriage, feminism, post–World War Two refugee women and the making of the film *Jedda* (1955). Her work has appeared in a range of journals including *Women's History Review* and *Australian Feminist Studies*. She is currently collaborating with Ann Curthoys and Zora Simic on a history of domestic violence in Australia since 1788.

Amanda Laugesen is a historian and lexicographer, and currently Director of the Australian National Dictionary Centre and Chief Editor of the *Australian National Dictionary*. She has published widely in American and Australian history. Her most recent monograph is *Globalizing the*

Library: Librarians and Development Work, 1945–1970 (Routledge, 2019). She is currently working on a book tracing the history of offensive language in Australia.

Megan Le Masurier is a Senior Lecturer in the Department of Media and Communications at the University of Sydney. Her research focuses on magazines, journalism and feminism. She has published in a wide range of journals including *The International Journal of Cultural Studies, Angelaki, Feminist Media Studies, Australian Feminist Studies, MIA, Text, Digital Journalism, Journalism Practice* and *Journalism: Theory, Practice, Criticism*. Her edited collection *Slow Journalism: An Introduction to a New Research Paradigm* was published in 2018. She is currently completing a book for Routledge, *Independent Print Magazines in a Digital Age*.

Trish Luker is based in the Faculty of Law, University of Technology Sydney. Her research focus is in interdisciplinary studies of law and humanities, particularly in relation to documentary practices, legal decision-making, court processes and evidence law. She is co-editor of three collections: *The Court as Archive* (with Ann Genovese and Kim Rubenstein) (ANU Press, 2019); *Evidence and the Archive: Ethics, Aesthetics, and Emotion* (with Katherine Biber) (Routledge, 2017); and *Australian Feminist Judgments: Righting and Rewriting Law* (with Heather Douglas, Francesca Bartlett and Rosemary Hunter) (Hart Publishing, 2014). Trish was a member of Sybylla Feminist Press during the 1980s.

Julie McLeod researches in the history and sociology of education, with a focus on curriculum, youth, gender and educational reform. She is Professor of Curriculum, Equity and Social Change, University of Melbourne, Graduate School of Education. She was an editor of the journal *Gender and Education* (2011–16) and currently co-edits the *History of Education Review* (2018–22). Publications include *Uneven Space-Times of Education: Historical Sociologies of Concepts, Methods and Practices* (Routledge, 2018); *Rethinking Youth Wellbeing: Critical Perspectives* (Springer, 2015); *The Promise of the New and Genealogies of Educational Reform* (Routledge, 2015); *Researching Social Change: Qualitative Approaches* (Sage, 2009); *Making Modern Lives: Subjectivity, Schooling, and Social Change* (Springer, 2006).

Catriona Moore is a Senior Lecturer in Art History and Film Studies at the University of Sydney. Over the past 40 years, Catriona has written many articles, reviews and catalogue essays on feminism in the visual arts. Her work has helped to pioneer Australian feminist scholarship in this area, through early books like *Indecent Exposures: Australian Feminist Photography 1970–1990* (Allen & Unwin, 1994) and her editorial work on *Dissonance: Twenty Years of Australian Feminist Art Writing* (Allen & Unwin, 1994) (from which her introductory chapter 'Once Upon a Time' was reprinted in Amelia Jones (ed.), *Feminism and Visual Culture Reader*, 2nd ed., Routledge, 2009). More recent work includes co-editing (with Jacqueline Millner and Georgina Cole) a special edition of *Australian and New Zealand Journal of Art: Art and Feminism: Twenty-First Century Perspectives* (2015). Her most recent research, *Contemporary Art and Feminism* (with Jacqueline Millner), is currently under consideration by Bloomsbury Academic.

Nicole Moore is completing a biography of the Australian writer Dorothy Hewett, funded by an ARC Future Fellowship. Her research interests encompass Australian literature, especially women's writing, comparative and postcolonial literatures, and book history. Recent books investigate the history of print censorship internationally and comparative accounts of the cultural Cold War. Professor in English and Media Studies at UNSW Canberra, her current role as Associate Dean Special Collections gives her oversight of the university's manuscript and rare book collections. With Katherine Bode, she is editor of the Anthem Studies in Australian Literature and Culture Series.

Bethany Phillips-Peddlesden is an Australian History PhD candidate and research assistant at the University of Melbourne. Her thesis examines the intersections of power and gender in the lives of Australian prime ministers. She has published on this topic in *Australian Historical Studies*; her article won a School of Historical and Philosophical Studies Fellows Group Annual History Essay Prize. She has been submissions manager on the Australian Women's Health Network's *Lilith*; a postgraduate representative for the Australian Historical Association; a National Library of Australia summer scholar; and received a National Archives of Australia postgraduate scholarship. She is also currently executive officer for the Australian Historical Association.

Carroll Pursell is a Distinguished Honorary Professor of History at The Australian National University and the Adeline Barry Davee Professor (Emeritus) at Case Western Reserve University, Ohio, USA. His latest book is *From Playgrounds to PlayStation: The Interaction of Technology* *and Play* (John Hopkins University Press, 2015). He is currently working on a book, *When Small Was Beautiful*, covering the rise and fall of the appropriate technology movement in the United States during the 1970s.

Zora Simic is Senior Lecturer in History and convener of Women's and Gender Studies in the School of Humanities and Languages at the University of New South Wales. She has published widely on the past and present of Australian feminism and teaches and researches post-war Australian migration history.

Catherine Speck is a feminist art historian and Professor of Art History at the University of Adelaide. Her publications include 'Forging Culture: Australian Art in the Nineteenth Century', in Michelle Facos (ed.), *A Companion to Nineteenth-Century Art* (Wiley Blackwell, 2019); *Heysen to Heysen: Selected Letters of Hans Heysen and Nora Heysen* (National Library of Australia, 2011; 2nd ed., Wakefield Press, 2019); *Australian Art Exhibitions: A New Story*, with Joanna Mendelssohn, Catherine De Lorenzo and Alison Inglis (Thames and Hudson, 2017); *Beyond the Battlefield: Women Artists of the Two World Wars* (Reaktion, 2014); *Painting Ghosts: Australian Women Artists in Wartime* (Craftsman House/Thames and Hudson, 2004). She is a member of the Fay Gale Centre for Research into Gender, the JM Coetzee Centre for Creative Practice and the Adelaide Critics Circle.

Angela Woollacott is the Manning Clark Professor of History at The Australian National University. Her latest book *Settler Society in the Australian Colonies: Self-Government and Imperial Culture* (Oxford University Press, 2015) was shortlisted for the Queensland Literary Awards—University of Southern Queensland History Book Award. Her biography of the transformative premier of South Australia in the 1960s–70s, *Don Dunstan: The Visionary Politician who Changed Australia*, (Allen & Unwin, 2019), was funded by an Australian Research Council Discovery Grant.

CHAPTER 1
Revolutionising the everyday: The transformative impact of the sexual and feminist movements on Australian society and culture

Michelle Arrow and Angela Woollacott

> I don't know if you've seen photographs of it, from that time, and everyone from Margaret Whitlam on through, all the women of that time, there's a look on the face. That wide-eyed sort of bright and hopeful look, and it was that feeling, you know. There was a feeling of incredible anger, of course, when you're understanding all the ways ... in which women are oppressed. But at the same time, this sense of joy and power coming from this working together and working it out and the scales being taken from the eyes.
>
> Sue Jackson, interview with Ruth Ford, 1997[1]

From our contemporary vantage point, it's the sense of excitement and possibility embodied by the 1970s women's and gay liberation movements that is most striking. Activists in these liberation movements weren't just campaigning for equal pay or decriminalisation of homosexuality— though both of these campaigns were essential to achieving equal rights for women and gay men. Many of these activists wanted to remake their world, to transform society. Fundamental to this was a new understanding

---

1   Sue Jackson, interview with Ruth Ford, 3 November 1997, p. 4, cited in Susan Magarey, '1970: When It Changed: The Beginnings of Women's Liberation in Australia', in *Turning Points in Australian History*, ed. Martin Crotty and David Andrew Roberts (Sydney: UNSW Press, 2009), 185.

of the divide between the public and the private spheres, and a new understanding of politics that took the inequalities and oppressions of the private sphere and everyday life seriously. 'The personal is political' has become a truism, but it remains a resonant way to comprehend the outlook of these social movements, and to understand just how radical their project was.

The rise of women's liberation and gay liberation created seismic change in Australian public and private lives. Gay men and lesbians made the personal political by gradually embracing and asserting their sexual identity publicly. 'Coming out' as gay or lesbian was integral to 1970s homosexual politics. Dennis Altman declared in *Homosexual: Oppression and Liberation* that his homosexuality was 'an integral part of my self-identity and that to hide it can only make my life, if less precarious, more difficult'.[2] Making the personal political was also a cornerstone of women's liberation. Previously private experiences of oppression were given political meaning by being shared publicly through consciousness-raising. For example, by mid-1972 in suburban Diamond Valley, Melbourne, women had formed two consciousness-raising groups. While many of them informed their discussions by reading Germaine Greer, Kate Millett, Shulamith Firestone and Friedrich Engels, others articulated their frustrations with their families, and the drudgery and boredom of a life of housework:

> There was a feeling of having been duped. Most of us had looked forward to milestones in our lives such as getting married and having children but found the reality was quite different. We enjoyed the opportunity to whinge.[3]

Through these confessional discussions, women not only felt the catharsis of the 'whinge' but supported each other to help change their situation: whether it was making major life changes or working out ways to share their domestic chores. While for many women, participation in the group was transitory, its effect was to make life 'more meaningful'. One woman recalled the buzz of consciousness-raising: 'women's lib was seven days a week, twenty-four hours a day'.[4] Understanding that the personal was political could help people transform their lived experience into politics.

---

2   Dennis Altman, *Homosexual: Oppression and Liberation* (Sydney: Angus and Robertson, 1972), 1.
3   Robyn Hartley and Dianne Parsons, 'Women's Liberation in Diamond Valley', in *Worth Her Salt: Women at Work in Australia*, ed. Margaret Bevage, Margaret James and Carmel Shute (Sydney: Hale and Iremonger, 1982), 383.
4   Ibid., 384.

Sue Bellamy, an active participant in the Women's Liberation movement since its earliest years, recalled that the movement's actions and perspectives were built on four core principles. 'These principles were: (1) sisterhood is powerful; (2) consciousness raising; (3) the personal is political; and (4) direct action. However, we struggled about them, we didn't always agree on what they meant.'[5] These core principles would act as a springboard for social, political and cultural transformation across the 1970s and beyond. The women's and gay and lesbian movements transformed Australian politics through wide-ranging law and policy reforms. Indeed, the 'femocrat'—the feminist bureaucrat—was internationally recognised as an innovative response to the challenge of working with the state to achieve change.[6] The women's and gay and lesbian movements created their own social services to respond to the needs of their distinctive communities: women's refuges, phone-a-friend and telephone counselling services, rape crisis centres, and places to meet and gather and foster a sense of community. These projects put 'the personal is political' into action.

The women's and gay and lesbian movements not only transformed Australian politics and social policy, they sparked far-reaching cultural and social changes. The notion that 'the personal is political' began to transform long-held ideas about masculinity and femininity, both in public and private life. Women's and gay liberationists also sought to remake the everyday, to transform ways of living, working, practices of childbirth, childrearing and motherhood.[7] Gay men and women started to live openly with their same-sex partners, forging new kinds of intimate relationships in emerging gay communities that were both political and commercial, like the bar scene in

---

5 Suzanne Bellamy, 'Sexual Politics: The Women's Liberation Movement', in *A Turbulent Decade: Social Protest Movements and the Labour Movement, 1965–1975*, ed. Beverly Symons and Rowan Cahill (Sydney: Australian Society for the Study of Labor History, 2005), 31.
6 Hester Eisenstein, *Inside Agitators: Australian Femocrats and the State* (Philadelphia: Temple University Press, 1996).
7 Kerreen Reiger, *Our Bodies, Our Babies: The Forgotten Women's Movement* (Melbourne: Melbourne University Press, 2001); Catherine Kevin, 'Maternity and Freedom: Australian Feminist Encounters with the Reproductive Body', *Australian Feminist Studies* 20, no. 46 (2005): 3–15, doi.org/10.1080 /0816464042000334492; Isobelle Barrett Meyering, '"There Must Be a Better Way": Motherhood and the Dilemmas of Feminist Lifestyle Change', *Outskirts* 28 (May 2013), www.outskirts.arts.uwa. edu.au/volumes/volume-28/isobelle-barrett-meyering; and Isobelle Barrett Meyering, 'Liberating Children: The Australian Women's Liberation Movement and Children's Rights in the 1970s', *Lilith* 19 (2013): 60–75. On lesbian mothers, see Rebecca Jennings, 'Lesbian Mothers and Child Custody: Australian Debates in the 1970s', *Gender and History* 24, no. 2 (2012): 502–17, doi.org/10.1111/ j.1468-0424.2012.01693.x.

Sydney.[8] Numerous experiments in communal living, shared households, non-monogamy and rural self-sufficiency were shaped by the new feminist and sexual politics, as Carroll Pursell and Zora Simic's chapters in this volume demonstrate. Some lesbians lived out a separatist politics on female-only, utopian rural communities like Amazon Acres, in northern New South Wales.[9] These communities represented a wholehearted embrace of the everyday revolutions of the era; others attempted to live out these new ideas in more tentative ways, as 'lifestyle change'.[10] In the spaces between official discourses and everyday experience, many Australian men and women sought to revolutionise their lives, experimenting with new quotidian ways to be self-consciously egalitarian.

The surge in vegetarianism reflected concern with animal rights, and renewed interest in gardening and alternative agriculture. Negotiations over housework were part of contested sexual politics, and the move in group households towards individual bedrooms, even for those in couples, expressed desires for personal autonomy.

Some 'everyday revolutions' were made in public spaces and ordinary interactions across Australian towns and cities. Women in what were traditionally men's jobs, like car mechanics, or women insisting on chopping wood or using hammers and screwdrivers, challenged notions of women's abilities as circumscribed. Men who cooked, participated in childcare or took up 'women's' jobs like fashion or hairdressing, similarly pushed gender boundaries. Women who kept their own names when they married or demanded to be addressed as 'Ms', along with heated debates about sexism in language as discussed in Amanda Laugesen's chapter in this volume, brought ideas of change into kitchens, lounge rooms, offices, classrooms and pubs. In shops, streets, houses and yards, small acts and daily work heralded gender and social change, even as the counter-culture trumpeted it in publications and iconography.

---

8   On lesbian social spaces, see Rebecca Jennings, 'A Room Full of Women: Lesbian Bars and Social Spaces in Postwar Sydney', *Women's History Review* 21, no. 5 (2012): 813–29. doi.org/10.1080/0961 2025.2012.658185. The growth of gay male community spaces in 1970s Sydney is discussed in Garry Wotherspoon, *Gay Sydney: A History* (Sydney: NewSouth Publishing, 2016); and Scott McKinnon discusses the role of cinema in fostering gay community and activism in 'The Activist Cinema-Goer: Gay Liberation at the Movies', *History Australia* 10, no. 1 (2013): 125–43, doi.org/10.1080/144908 54.2013.11668449.
9   Rebecca Jennings, 'Creating Feminist Culture: Australian Rural Lesbian Separatist Communities in the 1970s and 1980s', *Journal of Women's History* 30, no. 2 (2018): 88–111, doi.org/10.1353/jowh. 2018.0015.
10 Meyering, '"There Must Be a Better Way"'.

The women's and gay and lesbian movements were both interwoven with, and sometimes in opposition to, the broader changes in sexual cultures and behaviour that are broadly referred to as the sexual revolution. The sexual revolution is a deeply contested concept and its origins and causes are much debated, but it seems clear that changes to sexual morality, attitudes and practices became visible in the West in the late 1960s and early 1970s. Old taboos about sex began to break down, and a new emphasis on sexuality as a form of self-expression and as a source of pleasure began to be articulated across many sites. Women's liberation and gay liberation each had their own, radical sexual politics, but new ideas about sex were also discussed in the mass media and in popular culture. As Donald Horne remarked, 'an open discussion on the right to sexual enjoyment was being accepted as a recognised item on the mass media menu'.[11] Yet remarkably, when one considers the body of scholarship on the sexual revolution in other nations, there has been no comprehensive historical account of Australia's 'sexual revolution', especially as it impacted on heterosexuality.[12] Lisa Featherstone's important history of sexuality in Australia ends with the advent of the contraceptive pill, often regarded as the beginning of the sexual revolution.[13] Frank Bongiorno's *The Sex Lives of Australians* traces the many changes in Australians' ideas about sex from the 1960s onwards, including the introduction of the contraceptive pill, the slow introduction of sex education, women's liberation's construction of male heterosexuality and the struggle to decriminalise abortion, prostitution and homosexuality, suggesting that on balance, the sexual revolution offered many Australians a new sense of 'freedom, pleasure and belonging'.[14]

---

11   Donald Horne, *Time of Hope: Australia 1966–72* (Sydney: Angus and Robertson, 1980), 21.
12   On the sexual revolution elsewhere, see, for example, Hera Cook, *The Long Sexual Revolution: English Women, Sex, and Contraception: 1800–1975* (Oxford: Oxford University Press, 2004); and Matt Cook, 'Sexual Revolution(s) in Britain', in *Sexual Revolutions*, ed. Gert Hekma and Alain Giami (Basingstoke: Palgrave Macmillan, 2014), doi.org/10.1057/9781137321466_7. There is a large literature on the sexual revolution in the United States, see Beth Bailey, *Sex in the Heartland* (Cambridge: Harvard University Press, 2002); Elaine Tyler May, *The Pill: A History of Promise, Peril, and Liberation* (New York: Basic Books, 2010); Alice Echols, *Shaky Ground: The Sixties and Its Aftershocks* (New York: Columbia University Press, 2002); and John Heidenery, *What Wild Ecstasy: The Rise and Fall of the Sexual Revolution* (New York: Simon & Schuster, 1997).
13   Lisa Featherstone, *Let's Talk about Sex: Histories of Sexuality in Australia from Federation to the Pill* (Newcastle Upon Tyne: Cambridge Scholars Publishing, 2011).
14   Frank Bongiorno, *The Sex Lives of Australians: A History* (Collingwood: Black Inc., 2012), 258.

Some smaller-scale studies have shed light on the ways that Australian (hetero)sexual cultures began to change, like Yorick Smaal's study of sex in the 1960s, based on oral history interviews with people who were teenagers and young adults in the 1960s. Smaal found that while the availability of the pill may have increased public discussion about sex, most people still had little access to sexual knowledge, and pieced together this knowledge from fragments available in the wider culture.[15] The interviewees in the Australian Lives project conducted recently at Monash University offered evidence of changes in attitudes to sex, as well as revealing a greater frankness in talking about it.[16] Stephen Angelides has also addressed the question of teen sexuality in the 1960s, as changing sexual mores produced a transnational moral panic around teenage sexuality.[17] Some of the best work on changing sexualities in the 1970s has been found in the now extensive scholarship on the emergence of homosexual cultures in the decade, as noted above. Explicit discussions of how gay and lesbian sexual cultures emerged in the decade, however, have been sparser, though Clive Moore has outlined the long history of homosexual beat sex in Queensland, and Kimberly O'Sullivan has examined the ways in which understandings of lesbianism as a political and/or a sexual identity began in the 1970s, though her work focuses on the 1980s, as does Sophie Robinson's significant work on lesbian sex radicalism in the 1980s.[18] Much of the work on gay and lesbian sexual cultures documents and analyses the period from the 1980s onwards; more work needs to be done on tracing the emergence of these subcultures in the 1970s.

---

15   Yorick Smaal, 'Sex in the Sixties', in *The 1960s in Australia: People, Power and Politics*, ed. Shirleene Robinson and Julie Ustinoff (Newcastle Upon Tyne: Cambridge Scholars Publishing, 2012), 79.

16   Anisa Puri and Alistair Thomson, 'Intimate Relations', in their *Australian Lives: An Intimate History* (Clayton, Vic.: Monash University Publishing, 2017), 249–65.

17   Stephen Angelides, 'The "Second Sexual Revolution", Moral Panic, and the Evasion of Teenage Sexual Subjectivity', *Women's History Review* 21, no. 3 (2012): 831–47, doi.org/10.1080/09612025.2012.658169.

18   See, for example, Wotherspoon, *Gay Sydney*; Reynolds, *From Camp to Queer*; Clive Moore, 'Poofs in the Park: Documenting Gay "Beats" In Queensland, Australia', *GLQ* 2, no. 3 (1995): 319–39, doi.org/10.1215/10642684-2-3-319; Kimberly O'Sullivan, 'Dangerous Desire: Lesbianism as Sex or Politics', in *Sex in Public: Australian Sexual Cultures*, ed. Jill Julius Matthews (St Leonards, NSW: Allen & Unwin, 1997), 114–26; and Sophie Robinson, '"The New Lesbian Sexual Revolution": Lesbian Sex Radicals in Sydney during the 1980s and 1990s', *Australian Historical Studies* 49, no. 4 (2018): 475–92, doi.org/10.1080/1031461X.2018.1522654.

Some of the most thoughtful work on the ways that the sexual revolution transformed heterosexuality in Australia has emerged outside histories of sexuality: Megan le Masurier's careful readings of *Cleo* magazine (including in her chapter in this volume) have revealed the broader purchase of new ideas about sex amongst heterosexual men and women.[19] Many scholars agree that popular culture, in the early 1970s in particular, was one of the most potent sites for discussing and showing new cultures of sex. Alan McKee argues that the notorious 1970s television soap *Number 96* was an 'important part of the trickle down [of the new permissiveness] in Australia, bringing the ethos (if not the explicitness) of the R rating in to the homes of Australia'.[20] Several critics have read the films of the Australian film revival of the 1970s not through a lens of nationalism, but as commentaries on the strained and dysfunctional state of heterosexual relationships in 1970s Australia.[21] Nicole Moore's comprehensive history of literary censorship in Australia offers another way to trace changes in attitudes towards sex and its literary representation, particularly the ways that Australia's censorship apparatus was gradually dismantled by the early 1970s and replaced by a system of classification for film.[22] These works examine cultural production (and the regulation of this culture) as a site where we can observe changes in sexual cultures, attitudes and conduct. Historians writing histories of the sexual revolutions of the 1970s need to take culture into account.

The women's and gay and lesbian movements were not just social and political, they also had profound cultural manifestations. In 2004, Susan Magarey suggested that women's liberation was a 'cultural renaissance', committed to 'disorderly rule-breaking' and change.[23] Margaret Henderson extended this analysis a few years later, arguing that the women's movement was a rebirth of women's cultural production that can be best characterised as avant garde. Thinking of the women's movement as a cultural avant garde, Henderson suggests, has the potential to expand

---

19 Also see Megan Le Masurier, 'Reading the Flesh: Popular Feminism, the Second Wave and *Cleo*'s Male Centrefold', *Feminist Media Studies* 11, no. 2 (2011): 215–29, doi.org/10.1080/14680777.2010. 521628.
20 Alan McKee, 'Number 96: Speaking Sex and Showing Sex', in his *Australian Television: A Genealogy of Great Moments* (Melbourne: Oxford University Press, 2001), 105.
21 See, for example, Meghan Morris, 'Personal Relationships and Sexuality', in *The New Australian Cinema*, ed. Scott Murray and Peter Beilby (West Melbourne: Nelson, 1980), 133–51; Jack Clancy, 'Australian Films and Fantasies', *Meanjin* 38, no. 2 (July 1979): 193–205; and Catharine Lumby, *Alvin Purple* (Sydney: Currency Press, 2008).
22 Nicole Moore, *The Censor's Library* (St Lucia: University of Queensland Press, 2012).
23 Susan Magarey, 'Feminism as Cultural Renassance', *Hecate* 30, no. 1 (2004): 236, 244.

our understanding of the feminist project. 'It is more than legislative or campaign defeats or victories; indeed, it is a force that used an expansive range of tactics to attempt a social revolution—a project in which cultural activism was intrinsic.'[24] Magarey and Henderson drew scholarly attention to the scale and scope of cultural activities happening beyond the political world of demonstrations and organising in the 1970s. Women in the women's movement created performances, music, writing and art about their experiences.[25] Culture was important: feminists believed it could raise consciousness. The National Advisory Committee for Australia's celebrations of International Women's Year in 1975 funded numerous cultural and creative activities as part of their commemorations. Indeed, Elizabeth Reid's three key aims for International Women's Year were to change attitudes towards women, to lessen areas of discrimination and to encourage women's creativity.[26]

Women in the women's movement produced newspapers and periodicals like *Mejane*, *Refractory Girl* and *Vashti's Voice*, which contained poems, drawings and other creative works.[27] They made films, picked up spanners and established printing presses.[28] Activists saw film as a tool,

---

24 Margaret Henderson, 'Wonders Taken for Signs: The Cultural Activism of the Australian Women's Movement as Avant-Garde Reformation', *Lilith* 17/18 (2012): 116.
25 See, for example, on performance, Suzanne Spunner, 'Since Betty Jumped: Theatre and Feminism in Melbourne', *Meanjin* 38 (September 1979): 368–77; and Claire Dobbin, 'Women's Theatre and the APG—Australian Performing Group', *Meanjin* 43, no. 1 (1984): 129–39; on music, Kathy Sport, 'Below the Belt and Bleeding Fingertips: Feminist and Lesbian Music in the late 1970s', *Australian Feminist Studies* 22, no. 53 (July 2007): 343–60, doi.org/10.1080/08164640701364703; on writing, see Ann Vickery and Margaret Henderson, 'Manifesting Australian Literary Feminisms: Nexus and Faultlines', *Australian Literary Studies* 24, nos 3–4 (2009): 1–19; Ann Vickery, 'The Rise of "Women's Poetry" in the 1970s', *Australian Feminist* Studies 22, no. 53 (2007): 265–85, doi.org/10.1080/08164640701378596; and Zora Simic, '"Women's Writing" and "Feminism": A History of Intimacy and Estrangement', *Outskirts* 28 (May 2013), www.outskirts.arts.uwa.edu.au/volumes/volume-28/zora-simic; on art, see Janine Burke, *Field of Vision: A Decade of Change, Women's Art in the Seventies* (Ringwood: Viking, 1990); Sandy Kirby, *Sight Lines: Women's Art and Feminist Perspectives in Australia* (Roseville, NSW: Craftsman House, 1992); and Emery and Moore and Speck's chapters in this volume.
26 Hon. E. G. Whitlam, *International Women's Year: Priorities and Considerations*, statement prepared for the information of the Parliament and tabled by the Prime Minister, 4 December 1974, p. 18.
27 Mary Spongberg, 'Australian Women's History in Australian Feminist Periodicals 1971–1988', *History Australia* 5, no. 3 (2008): 73.1–73.16; Paula Byrne, 'Mabelled', *Hecate* 22, no. 2 (1996): 87–100.
28 On feminist filmmaking in the 1970s, see Annette Blonski, Barbara Creed and Freda Freiberg, eds, *Don't Shoot Darling: Women's Independent Filmmaking in Australia* (Richmond: Greenhouse Publications, 1987); and Mary Tomsic, *Beyond the Silver Screen: A History of Women, Filmmaking and Film Culture in Australia, 1920–1990* (Melbourne: Melbourne University Publishing, 2017). On women's entry into male-dominated occupations, see Georgine Clarsen's chapter in this volume. On feminist presses, see Diane Brown and Susan Hawthorne, 'Feminist Publishing', in *Paper Empires: A History of the Book in Australia 1946–2005*, ed. Craig Munro and Robyn Sheehan-Bright (St Lucia: University of Queensland Press, 2006); as well as Trish Luker's chapter in this volume.

and made historical documentaries and feature films not only to counter a heterosexual male screen culture, but also to advance women's culture and history. Popular feminism also operated in a cultural realm, as shown by le Masurier's convincing argument about *Cleo*, and Michelle Arrow has suggested that Helen Reddy's anthem 'I Am Woman' spoke to women outside and beyond the organised women's movement.[29] Feminists worked within educational institutions to challenge sexist stereotypes and to teach feminist perspectives in women's studies courses.[30] Women's liberationists challenged 'man-made' norms and masculinist language both within and beyond the academy, and they sought to recover lost histories of female achievement and cultural endeavour. These acts of recovery would animate and transform a range of academic disciplines into the 1980s, 1990s and beyond, especially history, literary studies and art history.[31] Recovering women's long history of cultural production, and challenging the relative obscurity in which it had long languished, became one of the most powerful legacies of the 1970s women's movement. Restoring the forgotten women of the past to history was part of women's liberation from the very beginning.[32]

While the cultural dimensions of the Australian gay and lesbian movement were perhaps not as wide-ranging in the 1970s, gay men and lesbians sought to foster community identity through producing specialist gay and lesbian magazines, and the commercial bar scene, in Sydney, was a particular focus of gay social life (and, later, political life)

---

29   Megan Le Masurier, 'My Other, My Self: *Cleo* Magazine and Feminism in 1970s Australia', *Australian Feminist Studies* 22, no. 53 (July 2007): 191–211, doi.org/10.1080/08164640701361766; and Michelle Arrow, '"It Has Become My Personal Anthem": "I Am Woman", Popular Culture and 1970s Feminism', *Australian Feminist Studies* 22, no. 53 (July 2007): 213–30, doi.org/10.1080/08164640701361774.
30   On education, see Julie McLeod's chapter in this volume, and Lyn Yates, 'Feminism's Fandango with the State Revisited: Reflections on Australia, Feminism, Education and Change', *Women's Studies International Forum* 22, no. 5 (1999): 555–62, doi.org/10.1016/S0277-5395(99)00061-8. On the growth of women's studies in Australian universities, see Alison Bashford, ed., 'The Return of the Repressed: Feminism in the Quad', special issue of *Australian Feminist Studies* 13, no. 27 (1998).
31   For example, works such as Drusilla Modjeska's *Exiles at Home: Australian Women Writers, 1925–1945* (Sydney: Angus & Robertson, 1981) and Joan Kerr's, *Heritage: The National Women's Art Book* (Sydney: Art and Australia/Craftsman House, 1995) stimulated scholarship in their respective fields.
32   See Spongberg, 'Australian Women's History in Australian Feminist Periodicals'. There were also four key works of feminist history published in Australia by the mid-1970s: Anne Summers, *Damned Whores and God's Police* (Ringwood: Penguin, 1975); Anne Conlon and Edna Ryan, *Gentle Invaders: Australian Women at Work* (Ringwood: Penguin, 1975); Beverly Kingston, *My Wife, My Daughter and Poor Mary Ann: Women at Work in Australia* (West Melbourne: Thomas Nelson, 1977); and Miriam Dixson, *The Real Matilda: Women and Identity in Australia 1778 to 1975*, (Ringwood: Penguin, 1976).

from the 1970s onwards.[33] Lesbians were, of course, a crucial part of the feminist cultural renaissance and there was considerable crossover between women's liberation and lesbian and gay liberation, particularly in the early years.[34] Even if there was not a large gay and lesbian film-making scene in Australia in the 1970s, films like the One in Seven collective's *Witches, Faggots, Dykes and Poofters* (Digby Duncan, producer), a 1979 documentary with a particular focus on the lesbian experience in Australia, was a ground-breaking cultural intervention, particularly valued today for its footage of the very first Gay Mardi Gras in 1978.[35] Music was an important site of lesbian feminist cultural production, and feminist and lesbian dances were crucial for both fundraising and socialising.[36]

Gay and lesbian writing began to emerge in the late 1970s, flourishing as a subgenre of literature by the 1980s in Australia.[37] Similarly, gay theatre companies and plays with gay themes became increasingly common by the mid-1980s.[38] The Sydney Gay and Lesbian Mardi Gras, which began in 1978, always incorporated costumes, music, dance and other cultural expression. Celebrating gay and lesbian identity through culture was a political act. Gay artists like David McDiarmid and William Yang also started to make art that explored their sexuality in the 1970s, though both these men, and many others, would become more prominent in the context of the HIV/AIDS epidemic in the 1980s and beyond. The cultural responses to this crisis, rather than gay culture in the previous decade,

---

33   On gay and lesbian magazines, see Bill Calder, *Pink Ink: The Golden Era for Gay and Lesbian Magazines* (Newcastle Upon Tyne: Cambridge Scholars Publishing, 2016); and Garry Wotherspoon, 'Telling It Like It Is: The Emergence of Australia's Gay and Lesbian Media', in *Acts of Love and Lust*, ed. Lisa Featherstone, Rebecca Jennings and Robert Reynolds (Newcastle Upon Tyne: Cambridge Scholars Publishing, 2015).
34   Rebecca Jennings, *Unnamed Desires: A Sydney Lesbian History* (Melbourne: Monash University Publishing, 2015), ch. 4; Sophie Robinson, 'Bar Dykes and Lesbian Feminists: Lesbian Encounters in 1970s Australian Feminism', *Lilith* 22 (2016): 52–65.
35   Scott McKinnon, '*Witches, Faggots, Dykes and Poofters*', in *Making Film and Television Histories: Australia and New Zealand*, ed. James E. Bennett and Rebecca Beirne (London: I.B. Tauris, 2012), 225–30.
36   Sport, 'Below the Belt and Bleeding Fingertips'; Nick Henderson, 'Feminist Rockers You've Never Heard About', NFSA, accessed 9 July 2018, www.nfsa.gov.au/latest/feminist-rockers-youve-never-heard-about.
37   Michael Hurley, 'Gay and Lesbian Writing and Publishing in Australia, 1961–2001', *Australian Literary Studies* 25, no. 1 (2010): 42–70, doi.org/10.20314/als.c2b14e180e.
38   Larry Galbraith, 'Gay Theatre', in *Companion to Theatre in Australia*, ed. Philip Parsons (Sydney: Currency Press, 1995), 242; Bruce Parr, 'Peter Kenna's *Mates*: Camping It Up', in *Gay and Lesbian Perspectives III*, ed. Garry Wotherspoon (Sydney: Department of Economic History and the Australian Centre for Lesbian and Gay Research, University of Sydney, 1996), 71–89.

have been the focus of historiography.³⁹ Much more work remains to be done on tracing the ways that the gay and lesbian movements engaged in cultural production, and in particular the ways in which these movements were the crucible for a wide range of cultural activity that stretched well into the 1980s and beyond.

Magarey pointed out in 2004 that 'cultural disruption as a dimension of second-wave feminism [… had] gain[ed] little, if any attention in any of the histories written to date'.⁴⁰ Margaret Henderson contended too that 'the analysis of women's movement culture is left to the various realms of cultural criticism—literary studies, film studies, and so on … a broad ranging cultural history of the Australian women's movement remains to be written'.⁴¹ Indeed, most of the major histories of these movements have not investigated cultural aspects of this disruption in detail as they foreground the activism, campaigns and achievements of the women's and gay and lesbian movements. This volume builds on that important scholarship and makes a valuable contribution to the histories of women's liberation and the gay and lesbian movement in 1970s Australia by exploring the wide range of ways, from the quotidian to the cultural, that these movements transformed Australian society.

This book emerges at a time when we are paying renewed cultural attention to the social and cultural transformations wrought by the sexual and feminist revolutions of the 1970s. The 2017 postal survey on same-sex marriage and the successful passage of legislation to permit same-sex couples to marry in December that year prompted many to reflect on the significant changes to gay and lesbian life since the 1970s, but also to question the narratives of progress that were used to frame these changes. In 2018, there was a wave of public memorialisation of the gay and lesbian movement. The year marked the fortieth anniversary of the first Gay Mardi Gras (later known as the Sydney Gay and Lesbian Mardi Gras), a street march that ended in violence but which blossomed to become an internationally significant celebration of the LGBTIQ

---

39   Sally Gray, 'America and the Queer Diaspora: The Case of Artist David McDiarmid', in *Transnational Lives: Australian Lives in the World*, ed. Desley Deacon, Penny Russell and Angela Woollacott (Canberra: ANU E Press, 2008), doi.org/10.22459/TT.12.2008.16. On William Yang's work in the 1970s, see Russel Storer, 'William Yang: Diary of a Denizen', in *Up Close: Carol Jerrems with Larry Clark, Nan Goldin and William Yang*, ed. Natalie King (Melbourne: Schwartz Publishing, 2010): 213–31. On the artistic response to the HIV/AIDS crisis in Australia, see Ted Gott, *Don't Leave Me This Way: Art in the Age of AIDS* (Canberra: National Gallery of Australia, 1994).
40   Magarey, 'Feminism as Cultural Renaissance', 235.
41   Henderson, 'Wonders Taken for Signs', 107.

community. The anniversary was flagged as a significant national event, marked not just by exhibitions, but also by the ABC, which commissioned a feature film about the events of 1978, *Riot*. Somewhat astonishingly, *Riot* was the first feature film that directly depicted Australia's social movements of the 1970s. The film sketched a genealogy of the Mardi Gras by situating it in a longer history of gay and lesbian protest in Sydney.[42]

Yet, given the strength and enduring influence of women's liberation in Australia, it's remarkable that there has not yet been a feature film or documentary treatment of the Australian women's movement equivalent to the American series *Makers* (2013) or the film *She's Beautiful When She's Angry* (2014), although film-maker Catherine Dwyer is currently developing a feature documentary, *Brazen Hussies*, about women's liberation in Australia.[43] In Australia, the only historical treatment of the women's movement in the 1970s is the one offered somewhat tangentially by the ABC miniseries about the birth of popular feminist magazine *Cleo*, *Paper Giants*. Other historical depictions of the period have dramatised the lives of pre-feminist women, like the Network 10 series *Puberty Blues* or the Nine network series about a Kings Cross hospital for relinquishing mothers, *Love Child*.[44] Stephan Elliott's 2018 film about suburban 1970s life, *Swinging Safari*, presents an image of the 1970s that is at once nostalgic for the freedoms enjoyed by the gang of children who all live in the same beachside cul de sac, and also condemns the self-absorption of their sexually experimenting parents. These two perspectives on the 1970s—was it a decade of liberation or one of destruction?—continue to colour contemporary Australian cultural debate today. We still live with the legacies of these changes, and we will be debating their impact for many years to come.

---

42 Michelle Arrow, 'History-Making at the 2018 Sydney Gay and Lesbian Mardi Gras: *Witches, Faggots, Dykes and Poofters*, The Museum of Love and Protest, the 2018 Sydney Gay and Lesbian Mardi Gras Parade, and Riot', *Australian Historical Studies* 49, no. 4, (2018): 493–500.
43 *Makers: Women Who Make America* (2013) Ark Media; *She's Beautiful When She's Angry* (2014) dir. Mary Dore. Catherine Dwyer is working on *Brazen Hussies*, see Documentary Australia Foundation, accessed 25 January 2019, documentaryaustralia.com.au/project/brazen-hussies/.
44 *Paper Giants: The Birth of Cleo* (2011), Southern Star; *Love Child* (2014–17), Playmaker Media; *Puberty* Bues (2012–14), Southern Star. On the postfeminist politics of these series, see Margaret Henderson, 'A Celebratory Feminist Aesthetics in Postfeminist Times: Screening the Australian Women's Liberation in Paper Giants – The Birth of *Cleo*', *Australian Feminist Studies* 28, no. 77 (2013): 250–62, doi.org/10.1080/10304312.2016.1166559; and 'Retrovisioning Chicko Roles: Puberty Blues as Postfeminist Television Adaptation and the Feminization of the 1970s', *Continuum* 30, no. 3 (2016): 326–35.

Everyday Revolutions

Everyday Revolutions brings together new research on the cultural and social impact of the feminist and sexual revolutions of the 1970s in Australia. This book is unique in its focus not on the activist or legislative achievements of the women's and gay and lesbian movements, but on the pervasive cultural and social dimensions of these revolutions. The chapters in the book are concerned with a range of themes including education, popular culture, film, art and publishing, alternative lifestyles, and moves to transform gendered norms in work and language. It is a diverse and rich collection of essays that reminds us that women's and gay liberation were thoroughly revolutionary movements.

This book emerged from the successful and well-attended conference 'How the Personal Became Political: Re-Assessing Australia's 1970s Revolutions in Gender and Sexuality', held at The Australian National University, 6–7 March 2017, funded by the ANU Gender Institute. One of the most fascinating aspects of this conference was the ways it fostered interactions between several generations of scholars and activists. The event brought together many of the women and men who fought for change in the 1970s alongside a younger generation of researchers for whom these events are history. As early career researcher Chelsea Barnett commented on the Australian Women's History Network's VIDA blog after the conference, 'it was exciting to see so many Ph.D. students and ECRs have their work embraced by established academics and second-wave feminist activists, suggesting that this moment in Australian history remains rich with potential'.[45] This book is just one sign of this 'rich potential', as emerging scholars ask new questions about the decade and activists turned researchers reflect on their experiences in new ways.

It is worth noting that the collection reflects the papers offered for the conference: it is neither fully comprehensive nor exhaustive in its coverage of the period. Much more needs to be written on the ways the 'everyday revolutions' of the 1970s were, for the most part, enacted by white women. The notion that 'the personal is political' also assumed, to some extent, that the personal was universal, and it could work to conceal differences between women. Just as the men and women of the

---

45   Chelsea Barnett, 'How the Personal Became Political', VIDA Blog, accessed 2 December 2017, www.auswhn.org.au/blog/personal-became-political/.

1970s liberation movements struggled to come to terms with difference, so too we historians must continue to acknowledge the importance of intersectionality, and the very real effects of racial inequalities for example, when we write our histories of these movements. Nevertheless, this book offers a kaleidoscopic array of angles from which to view the profound social and cultural changes of the 1970s. And it demonstrates, yet again, the feminist theoretical insight that gender and sexuality are inextricably intertwined.

The chapters

Everyday Revolutions is divided into four sections, each investigating a different aspect of the ways that the mantra 'the personal is political' revolutionised all aspects of contemporary life in 1970s Australia. Our opening section, 'Everyday gender revolutions: Workplaces, schools and households' investigates attempts to transform dominant ideas about gender in three key sites: male-dominated trades, the education system and in alternative households.

In her chapter, 'Of girls and spanners: Feminist politics, women's bodies and the male trades', Georgine Clarsen notes that women's attempts in the 1970s to move into male-dominated trades have been largely forgotten and overlooked in histories of Australian feminism. These occupations have proven remarkably resistant to feminist campaigns for change: today, less than 2 per cent of women are working in construction, electrical and automotive trades. The ongoing marginalisation of women in such non-traditional jobs has significant financial consequences for women and gender pay equity, Clarsen observes: 'the average weekly earnings of a hairdresser, for example, are approximately half that of a carpenter, mechanic or electrician'. Yet she also suggests that this work was not only significant for its economic impact, but also for its transformative effects on women's embodiment—this was a politics of *doing*. Georgine herself was one of those women who 'picked up a spanner' in the 1970s, and she writes warmly and thoughtfully about her experiences of finding pleasure and empowerment in the bodily competency these trades offered. Women's aspirations to trade work, Clarsen notes, simultaneously constituted a politics of space and embodiment.

Julie McLeod's 'The discovery of sexism in schools: Everyday revolutions in the classroom' offers a fascinating account of the intersections of two social movements of the decade: the women's movement and the radical, de-schooling movement in education. In contrast to Clarsen's focus on male-dominated trades, education employed far more women and feminism gained considerable influence in education across the 1970s, through the development and implementation of formal policies on equal opportunity and non-sexist education. The Australian Schools Commission's landmark 1975 report *Girls, School and Society* was one high-profile manifestation of feminist activism in education, but McLeod points out that feminists also undertook considerable grassroot activity in schools. Meanwhile, movements to democratise schooling, to make it less hierarchical and more participatory, were also seeking to transform education. As McLeod notes, the stories of these two movements are typically told separately, but she brings them together in this chapter, reading them against and with each other to suggest new links and connections between them.

Carroll Pursell's chapter also investigates the intersections between social movements, examining the gender politics of the 'back-to-the-land' movement in the 1970s. Pursell draws on two key Australian alternative living publications, *Grass Roots* and *Earth Garden*, examining letters and articles written by both men and women to consider the implications of this lifestyle for both gender relations and gendered roles. The back-to-the-land movement had a complex relationship to women's liberation: on the one hand, lesbian separatist communities like Amazon Acres set out to create female-only feminist utopias through sustainable living; on the other hand, it is clear from Pursell's research that for many men and women, this lifestyle entrenched existing gender role differences. Pursell's fascinating chapter opens up an under-examined facet of alternative lifestyles in the 1970s for further research.

Section Two is 'Feminism in art and culture'. Ever since the publication of Linda Nochlin's groundbreaking 1971 essay 'Why have there been no great women artists?', the exclusion of women artists from galleries and museums, and the under-representation of women in art history has come under sustained attack from the women's movement. Women's and feminist art has flourished, and the lives and works of women artists have increasingly been restored to art history and museum collections, though as the ongoing work of the feminist collective Guerrilla Girls demonstrates, the project of promoting diverse female artists remains incomplete.[46] Catriona Moore and Catherine Speck's chapter 'How the personal became (and remains) political in the visual arts' offers a large-scale overview of the ways that this iconic phrase reshaped art history and practice from the 1970s onwards. Women's liberationists sought not only to create their own art and gain greater recognition for female artists, past and present, they wanted to trouble the ways that artistic canons were structured to exclude women in the first place. 'Feminist insistence upon the personal as political challenged the public/private divide and knitted together art and domestic spheres in new ways', Moore and Speck write, but they also note the ways that Indigenous artists and artists from non-English-speaking backgrounds challenged the notion that the 'personal' could offer a unifying female perspective. Their fascinating essay shows that the 'personal is political' remains a useful concept in feminist art today.

Elizabeth Emery's 'Subversive stitches' delves into one aspect of 1970s feminist art practice: the reclaiming and refashioning of needlework by Australian feminist artists. Historically, needlework had long been part of women's domestic craft, signifying at once 'the despised domestic feminine, while simultaneously representing women's resistance to and subversion of male dominance'. Feminist artists of the 1970s took up needlework, making 'the domestic visible in visual art', as Emery writes. Needlework drew on different traditions of women's creative work, and constructed an alternative feminist art heritage that celebrated the creativity of 'ordinary' women. Emery notes that there was resistance to reclaiming the kinds of creative works produced in the domestic sphere: did celebrating the making of doilys, for example, merely perpetuate women's subordinate social position? Yet she also argues convincingly that Frances Phoenix's 'disobedient doily' artwork, *Kunda*, for example, was both subversive and powerful, making a personal and domestic object political. Both Emery and Moore and Speck's chapters convey the tremendous energy and experimentation of the feminist art scene of the 1970s.

Feminist presses were crucial to the creation of a feminist literary culture in late twentieth-century Australia. Trish Luker's chapter, 'Women into print', situates the rise of women's presses from the 1970s onwards against the backdrop of the women's liberation movement's fostering of women's writing and feminist readers. In light of the move towards digital

---

46   Guerrilla Girls, www.guerrillagirls.com.

publishing, and a corresponding archival turn in feminist scholarship, Luker examines the role of feminist print and publishing cultures. Underscoring the importance of print media to the dissemination of feminist ideas, feminists took control of the means of book and periodical production when they established feminist presses such as Sybylla Co-operative Press, Sugar & Snails (which produced feminist children's books), Everywoman Press and Women's Redress Press. Luker's chapter is a valuable reminder of the importance of print culture to women's liberation, not just in Australia but transnationally.

Women's liberation sought not only to remake art, but also to create new kinds of writing and literature that reflected women's experiences. Zora Simic's chapter on Helen Garner's famous debut novel *Monkey Grip*, '"Unmistakably a book by a feminist"', deftly places this groundbreaking work in its feminist contexts. Using a wide range of textual records generated by the women's liberation movement, Simic carefully traces the ways that *Monkey Grip* has been read as a feminist book since its publication in 1977. *Monkey Grip* was released in the late 1970s, a time when feminism was widely regarded to be in crisis or retreat, but it also ushered in a wider interest in Australian women's writing and feminist publishing, which flourished in the decade following *Monkey Grip*'s release.

In Section Three, 'Redrawing boundaries between public and private', we have three chapters that trace the ways that the women's and gay liberation movements prompted new divisions between public and private worlds. Catherine Freyne's 'A phone called PAF' examines the history of pioneering gay organisation CAMP's 'Phone-A-Friend' service, which started in 1973. By investigating the ideology and practice of phone counselling, based in deep archival and oral history research, Freyne offers new insights into the history of gay and lesbian activism and its complex and changing relationship to the public/private divide within gay and lesbian politics. By the mid to late 1970s, PAF was impacted by larger conflicts within CAMP, which was increasingly riven by competing ideas about its primary purpose: was it to provide private counselling and support to lesbians and gay men, or was it to stage political actions? However, as Freyne notes, this was not a case of the personal 'gazumping' the political, because the 'very existence of a gay counselling service was politically productive'.

The gay liberation movement, as Leigh Boucher shows, developed over the course of the 1970s and comprised multiple currents. A central focus was the demand for decriminalisation of homosexuality on the basis of liberal democratic rights (and for it to go beyond consenting adults in private). But there was also the fraught issue of homosex in public. Focusing on the gay rights movement in Victoria, Boucher productively examines the spectacular 1979 'kiss-in' held to protest two men's arrest for 'offensive behaviour' for kissing in public. He puts this carefully managed media event in fruitful tension with the movement's ambivalence about beat sex. By its very nature, beat sex subverted distinctions between public and private, personal and political. Boucher convincingly argues that the 'kiss-in' was a neatly contained event that can be read as an instance of celebratory liberation, but seeing it in the context of the unsteady political discourse around beat sex makes the movement seem less certain.

Catherine Kevin's 'Creative work: Feminist representations of gendered and domestic violence in 1970s Australia' takes up Magarey's call to consider the cultural output of the women's liberation movement as intrinsic to its political activism. Her chapter makes a nuanced contribution to our understandings of the ways that the women's movement reshaped the meanings of domestic violence in the 1970s. Examining cultural representations of violence against women in film, poetry, fiction and visual culture, Kevin points to the power of artistic and cultural representations of domestic and family violence to help convey feminist interpretations of such violence. The chapter demonstrates that careful readings of feminist culture, especially visual culture such as cartoons and posters, can enlarge our understanding of the impact of the women's movement in transforming social attitudes towards women.

In her intriguingly titled '"Put on dark glasses and a blind man's head", Nicole Moore scrutinises Australia's first and only successful defamation case about poetry. Brought against the writer Dorothy Hewett by her first husband, Lloyd Davies, the case involved a number of offences and charges relating to Hewett's portrayal of Davies's family and their prior sexual history. It raised landmark questions about freedom of expression, but also about privacy. As Moore notes, the notion of privacy and the private sphere had been extensively critiqued by the women's movement; indeed, the notion that 'the personal is political' was a succinct statement of this critique. In her careful reconstruction of this complex case, Moore suggests that it can be read as a microcosm of larger cultural debates provoked by feminist cultural production in the 1970s, in particular the question of feminist art's access to the private sphere of intimacy and sexuality.

The final section of the book is titled 'Re-gendering language, authority and culture', and it contains three fascinating essays that together reveal some of the ways in which feminism and gay liberation challenged conventional understandings of masculinity in Australian cultural life. Amanda Laugesen's 'Challenging "man made language"' charts the ways in which language became a contested domain in 1970s culture. As she points out, the cultural nationalism of 1970s Australia saw a new celebration of 'Australian English' and ocker speech, but it was also a period in which language was newly scrutinised and contested for its deeply embedded sexism. Laugesen examines 'feminist linguistic activism' in the 1970s and 1980s: not only the ways in which women's liberationists sought to reclaim language previously deemed 'unladylike', but also the campaigns to remove sexist terms and phrases from Australian cultural and social life. As she notes, while much has changed, gender-neutral and non-sexist language can still provoke strong reactions today.

In 'A race of intelligent super-giants', Bethany Phillips-Peddlesden considers the ways that gendered bodies and ideas of masculinity worked to shape notions of power within mainstream electoral politics. Gough Whitlam captured the national mood when he was elected in December 1972, and Phillips-Peddlesden argues that part of his electoral appeal was his particular brand of embodied masculinity. Whitlam's height, voice and middle-class status were all crucial to shaping perceptions of his leadership, especially when juxtaposed with his political opponent, the Liberal Prime Minister William McMahon. Phillips-Peddlesden then considers the ways in which gender shaped the ALP's political messaging in 1972. The campaign deployed the charismatic and 'modern' Margaret Whitlam to woo progressive female voters. Phillips-Peddlesden suggests that, even as social and cultural expectations of women were changing in the 1970s, political authority was still gendered masculine, and to a significant extent it remains so.

Megan le Masurier presents a compelling account of *Cleo* magazine's contribution to Australia's sexuality revolution in the 1970s. Aimed at younger women, not or not yet political activists, this new magazine merged women's liberation with sexual liberation. *Cleo* encouraged women to become sexually active, informed about their bodies and assertive in their pursuit of erotic pleasure. In le Masurier's words, it pushed 'the sexual politics of the fair go'. *Cleo* made up for the absence of sex education in schools and elsewhere, helping women overcome shame, ignorance and guilt. And it actively supported the burgeoning feminist health advice literature, as well as emerging women's reproductive health centres. Featuring letters from women readers that were often very graphic about their bodies and experiences, the magazine was an influential forum for discussion of female orgasm.

In 'Male chauvinists and ranting libbers', Chelsea Barnett examines the popular men's magazine *Pix* (which became *Pix/People* in 1972) to investigate changing attitudes towards single men in the decade of women's and gay liberation. Barnett notes that, while the unmarried man has long been a figure of cultural and social significance in Australian history, the place of the bachelor in postwar Australian culture has been relatively unexamined. She suggests that the magazine encouraged single men to embody the label of 'male chauvinist' in response to the challenge of the women's liberation movement. In a decade in which an assertive new national identity was typically articulated through a brash, ocker masculinity, there was little place in *Pix* for a femininity shaped by feminism, Barnett argues. Her reading of letters and articles in the magazine helps shed light on 'ordinary' people's responses to the revolutions of the 1970s.

Everyday Revolutions brings together fresh, interdisciplinary approaches to the history of the transformative revolutions of the 1970s. Our contributors have foregrounded not the activist or legislative achievements of those revolutions, but their ubiquitous cultural and social dimensions. Collectively, they remind us that change happens in multiple sites, and that cultural production and fostering new modes of community were significant forms of social change. Several chapters in the book also remind us that gendered ways of viewing the world that entrenched the dominance of heterosexual masculinity have been stubborn, and difficult to change. We hope that this collection will stimulate more scholarship in this field, from a range of disciplines. Applying a diverse array of disciplinary lenses reminds us that women's and gay liberation were revolutionary movements with powerful effects and legacies, even as much more remains to be done.

EVERYDAY GENDER REVOLUTIONS: WORKPLACES, SCHOOLS AND HOUSEHOLDS

CHAPTER 2

Of girls and spanners: Feminist politics, women's bodies and the male trades

Georgine Clarsen

In mid-2017, a federal Senate Committee inquiring into gender segregation in the Australian workforce tabled its final report, after nine months of deliberation.[1] The committee was set up to investigate ongoing industrial and occupational gender segregation in Australia, its economic consequences for women and to recommend approaches for addressing it. The aims are wearyingly familiar. How many such inquiries have been held at state and federal level, I wonder, following feminists' renewed activism around women's employment since the 1970s? How many individuals, organisations and agencies have undertaken research, collated data, compiled reports and volunteered their time to table submissions? How many research papers and reports languish in archives and desk drawers around the nation? What, indeed, will be the fate of this latest Senate Committee report?

Certainly the need for feminist action on gender segregation in the workforce remains. For many categories of work, this latest inquiry concluded, the figures show that occupational segregation has remained substantially unchanged since systematic data on gender has been

---

1 Finance and Public Administration References Committee, *Gender Segregation in the Workplace and Its Impact on Women's Economic Equality* (Canberra: Australian Government Publishing Service, 2017), www.aph.gov.au/Parliamentary_Business/Committees/Senate/Finance_and_Public_Administration/Gendersegregation/Report.

compiled in this country. The significance of workplace segregation in women's daily lives, as all the reports across the last half-century and more emphasise, is evident in the pay disparities between men and women.

A sadly depleted Australian Bureau of Statistics publishes an annual report, Gender Indicators Australia, which makes for depressing reading.[2] The latest report shows that the gender wage gap for full-time workers sits at more than 23 per cent, which translates into an average income gap of some $27,000 per year. That gap is even larger than it was 20 years ago. It fell to its narrowest in 2005 and has been widening steadily ever since. Data collected from employers by the Workplace Gender Equity Agency, a legacy of Julia Gillard's prime ministership and published in their annual Gender Equity Scorecard, further confirms this conclusion.[3] So on this one key indicator at least, feminist gains have been lost over the last decade.

Dominating media debates on gender segregation in the workplace have been campaigns to increase women's access to positions of power, to 'smashing through the glass ceiling'. Marian Sawer's *Sisters in Suits* documents the rise of the femocrat, who worked in government agencies during the 1970s and 1980s to achieve progressive ends.[4] Women's desires to enter into the public service, politics, the professions and upper management; to be appointed to ASX listed boards and to prominent positions in the media; and to reach senior levels of higher education have received a great deal of attention and are now at least part way to being fulfilled. For example, women have made up 50 per cent of the professional workforce since 2000.[5] We are still, however, far from parity in other fields of employment. The most recent reports place women

---

2   Australian Bureau of Statistics, '4125.0—Gender Indicators, Australia, Sep 2018', accessed 21 January 2019, www.abs.gov.au/ausstats/abs@.nsf/mf/4125.0.
3   Workplace Gender Equity Agency, 'Australia's Gender Equity Scorecard, 2015–16', accessed 21 January 2019, www.wgea.gov.au/sites/default/files/80653_2015-16-gender-equality-scorecard.pdf.
4   Marian Sawer, *Sisters in Suits: Women and Public Policy in Australia* (Sydney: Allen & Unwin, 1990). See also Hester Eisenstein, *Inside Agitators: Australian Femocrats and the State* (Sydney: Allen & Unwin, 1996); Suzanne Franzway, Dianne Court and R. W. Connell, *Staking a Claim: Feminism, Bureaucracy and the State* (Sydney: Allen & Unwin, 1989). For a recent analysis, see Susan Harris Rimme and Marian Sawer, 'Neoliberalism and Gender Equality Policy in Australia', *Australian Journal of Political Science* 51, no. 4 (2016): 742–58, doi.org/10.1080/10361146.2016.1222602.
5   Department of Family and Community Services: Women NSW, 'Women in the Trades: The Missing 48 Percent', *Women NSW Occasional Paper* (Sydney: the Department, 2013), 4, www.women.nsw.gov.au/__data/assets/pdf_file/0017/268010/3000_WNSW-OccasionalPaper_document_ART.pdf.

at just 16 per cent of chief executive officers and only 37 per cent of managers are women. The salary gap at the highest levels of management is more than $90,000 per year.[6]

Much less prominent in debates about gender segregation at work, however, are the even more intractable figures at the other end of the occupational scale. Extreme gender segregation continues to characterise the working-class trades. Identifying the precise patterns of change over time is not a simple matter, however, as occupational reclassifications and changes to the ways that data is recorded have made rigorous comparisons difficult. But the broad picture is clear. As the 2013 report 'Women in the Trades: The Missing 48 Percent', asserts:

> It is clear that women's representation in non-traditional trade and especially in the core trades of construction, electrical and automotive has been consistently tiny for three decades at least.[7]

This most recent Senate Committee report, four years later, confirms the continuing inequities. The numbers of women working in the core male trades, which account for almost half of the skilled trade workforce in Australia, remain minuscule, with women representing under 2 per cent in these areas of work or in training courses that lead to trade qualifications in these fields.[8] That figure has not changed since at least the 1980s and arguably since the end of World War Two. In terms of women's earnings, the consequences of these disparities are stark. The average weekly earnings of a hairdresser, for example, are approximately half that of a carpenter, mechanic or electrician.[9] So, unlike in elite levels of employment, in the area of women's engagement in working-class male trades, there have not ever been any feminist gains that we can now lament are under threat.

In this chapter, I will examine the fortunes of Australian feminist campaigns to encourage women to enter into 'non-traditional' trade employment, focusing particularly on efforts to advocate for women in the motor trades. In the first instance, I aim to simply place on record the history of a neglected aspect of feminist politics as it emerged during and in the decades after the upsurge of activism in the 1970s, and to reread

---

6   Finance and Public Administration References Committee, *Gender Segregation in the Workplace*.
7   Department of Family and Community Services: Women NSW, 'Women in the Trades', 12.
8   Construction, electrical and automotive trades accounted for 47 per cent of the skilled trades in 1986; 50 per cent in 1995; 58 per cent in 2006; and 56 per cent in 2012. 'Women in the Trades', 12.
9   Karen Struthers, 'Paving the Way for Girls into Male-Dominated Trades: Reducing Gender Segregation in the Trades' (PhD thesis, School of Human Services and Social Work, Griffith University, 2016), 36.

some of the key literature that emerged from it. Efforts to desegregate working-class employment have largely been forgotten in histories of feminism and rarely have been recognised in the historiographical literature.[10] These campaigns have fallen outside the purview of feminist collective memory, partly because few tradeswomen move in the circles that formally document, archive and theorise feminist histories.

Second, in this chapter I make a start at considering why change in this area of women's lives has been so minimal. It seems there has been an implicit assumption in public debates and perhaps even in some feminist advocacy that placing women in positions of power and leadership would carry over to benefit women in less powerful positions, in a 'trickle-down effect'. However, when feminist debates and practices have been so influential in other areas of national life, we need to ask questions of ourselves: Why has progress been so intractable in this area of employment? What have been the limits of feminist thinking and action in this field of national life? Where are the gaps in our interest, energy or capacity to campaign around these issues? Do these 'blind spots' share anything in common with other omissions in feminist thinking and activism in Australia? Might there be more effective ways to engage in these campaigns? These questions, I might add, are not easily answered. They demand a great deal of attention and collective thought, and I offer this chapter as just one contribution to that larger debate.

Before I do so, however, I want to briefly recognise and honour the work that is still going on in this area of feminist advocacy by a new generation of activists. Supporting and Linking Tradeswomen (SALT), is one of the most active grassroot organisations. SALT was established in Wollongong by NSW TAFE teacher Fiona Shewring, and the group works under the slogan 'jobs don't have a gender'.[11] Groups like SALT continue to encourage women to attend 'taste a trade' and 'tradie-ladies' days at depleted TAFE colleges. Dedicated tradeswomen still visit high schools and community centres, towing trailers filled with tools. They have established women's sheds to share their skills and enthusiasm for trade work. Women scattered

---

10   Georgine Clarsen, 'Women's Leadership in the Trades: A Historical and Theoretical Overview', in *The Encyclopedia of Women and Leadership in Twentieth-Century Australia*, ed. Shurlee Swain and Judith Smart, Australian Women's Archives Project 2014, www.womenaustralia.info/leaders/biogs/WLE0626b.htm.

11   SALT, saltaustralia.org.au/; Fiona Shewring, 'One Step Forward Two Steps Back: Advocating for a New Generation of Women in Male-Dominated Trades', in *Encyclopedia of Women and Leadership in Twentieth-Century Australia*, ed. Shurlee Swain and Judith Smart, Australian Women's Archives Project 2014, www.womenaustralia.info/leaders/biogs/WLE0632b.htm.

in small workplaces around Australia, and indeed around the world, have formed support groups through social media and face-to-face meetings. They organise conferences to bring tradeswomen together to discuss issues of importance to them. Some feminists continue to analyse data and write research reports. It is notable, however, that this contemporary advocacy, unlike in the heady days of the femocrat and agencies like the Affirmative Action Agency and Women's Group Training Companies, largely remains volunteer work, unsupported by adequate public funding or institutional support.[12] Activists report that in the current climate it is private companies who are most likely to offer support for their work. After decades, much effort in this area remains ad hoc, sporadic and undervalued—and not always eager to claim the fraught f-word.

On the record: (Some) women were there (of course)

'Give a Girl a Spanner' and 'Girls Can Do Anything' were slogans of 1970s feminism, and I was one of the 'girls' who picked up a spanner to become a motor mechanic in those years. It was hard work and it was fun. Though data is not available, it seems likely that for the most part tradeswomen worked (as I did) as the sole female in otherwise male workplaces.

Some public utilities, however, such as bus depots and water boards aspired to hire more than one female 'tradie' as part of a strategy to build a critical mass of apprentices. For the women I knew, even if we worked as the only female apprentice or tradeswoman in a worksite, that work was done with a sense of collectivity secured by broad feminist interest and support. Tradeswomen garnered considerable symbolic cachet in the women's movement of the 1970s and 1980s. Feminists brought their cars to be repaired at our garages and hired female carpenters, plumbers and electricians. The iconography of second-wave feminism, too, reflected a valorisation of women's skilled manual labour; for example, in the cartoons that illustrated feminist reports and in the routine use of the language of 'workshops' and 'toolboxes' in even the most non-manual of feminist organisations.

---

12   Jo Pyke, 'Affirmative Action in Training 1987–2008', in *Encyclopedia of Women and Leadership in Twentieth-Century Australia*, ed. Shurlee Swain and Judith Smart, Australian Women's Archives Project 2014, www.womenaustralia.info/leaders/biogs/WLE0627b.htm.

Figure 2.1: 'Mabel the Mechanic' and her workmates, c. 1977, photograph.
Source: Courtesy of Carol Ruff, Gallery East, Clovelly.

Women's deliberate intrusion into spaces where men and masculinity was the norm meant that we were not just making individual choices about our own lives. For us, picking up spanners or hammers or wrenches was also a politics of representation and a performance of female 'empowerment'. The pleasure we took in the work was a form of resistance through which we were self-consciously out to challenge ideas about masculinity and femininity and expand the range of places where women could legitimately be.[13] Our bodies—in overalls appropriately colour-coded to our trades, sporting steel-capped boots, our hands dirty and our waists slung with tool belts—became a poster for our acts. A cohort of activists, who were largely not themselves tradeswomen, simultaneously devised political campaigns and structures to enable more women to take up trade apprenticeships.

Throughout the 1980s and into the 1990s—particularly in the Hawke/Keating years and during Joan Kirner's premiership in Victoria—there were concerted efforts by feminists in government agencies, TAFE and unions to encourage women to enter the male trades. Those women

---

13   Louisa E. Smith, 'Trading in Gender for Women in Trades: Embodying Hegemonic Masculinity, Femininity and Being a Gender Hotrod', *Construction Management and Economics* 31, no. 8 (2013): 861–73, doi.org/10.1080/01446193.2013.833339.

established a number of programs—Women's Group Training companies, Affirmative Action in Training schemes, pre-apprenticeship courses at TAFE, school outreach programs like Tradeswomen on the Move, as well as research and policy agencies like the National Centre for Vocational Education Research (NCVER), which continues to be active. At the end of the 1990s, however, the Howard Government defunded or 'mainstreamed' those agencies, and the social justice remit of the vocational training system was severely curtailed by neoliberal 'reforms' that saw its rapid privatisation.[14] There is an extensive literature into the 1990s, however, which records feminist efforts to influence government policy, educational programs and business practices, as well as the career choices of potential tradeswomen.[15]

---

14 Jo Pyke, 'Affirmative Action in Training 1987–2008'.
15 For just some of that literature, see: National Working Group on Women in Apprenticeship, *Report of the Working Group on Women and Apprenticeship* (Canberra: Department of Employment, Education and Training, 1987); Lucy Callaghan, *Girls Can Do It* (Ballarat: Ballarat Community Education Centre, 1986); Lois Welch, 'Strategies for Employers for Supporting Female Apprentices in Non-traditional Trades', *Affirmative Action Issues Papers*, no. 1 (Canberra: Affirmative Action Resource Unit, Office of the Status of Women, Department of the Prime Minister and Cabinet, 1985); Women's Bureau, *Occupational Segregation: Women's Work, Women's Pay. Action for Women* (Canberra: Department of Employment, Education and Training, 1990); Jo Pyke, *Women in Building: The Missing 51%* (Canberra: Department of Employment, Education and Training, 1993); Annie Cowling, *Breaking New Ground: A Manual for Survival for Women Entering Non-Traditional Trades* (Melbourne: Building Workers' Industrial Union, 1991); Noeline Kyle and Jan Wright, *Breaking Down Traditional Barriers: The Attitude of Small Industry to Non-traditional Schooling and Work* (Canberra: Women's Bureau Department of Employment, Education and Training, 1993); Elaine Butler and Mike Brown, eds, *A-Gendering Skill: Conversations around Women, Work and Skill: An Australian Perspective* (Geelong, Vic.: Deakin University, 1993); Claire Burton, *The Promise and the Price: The Struggle for Equal Opportunity in Women's Employment* (Sydney: Allen & Unwin, 1991); Sue Morley, *Women's Participation in Non-Traditional Vocational Training: Strategies to Increase Women's Participation in Australian Vocational Certificate Projects in Industries and Occupations Where They Have Been Underrepresented in the Past* (Canberra: Department of Employment, Education and Training, 1994); Barbara Pocock, *Demanding Skill: Women and Technical Education in Australia* (Sydney: Allen & Unwin, 1988); Linda Tivendale, *Women in Building* (Melbourne: Victorian Building and Construction Training Council, 1987); Kim Windsor, *Shortcircuiting: Women in Electronics, Skills, Training and Working Practices* (Canberra: Department of Employment, Education and Training, 1991); Mally Jane, 'Equal Access to Learning and Employment through TAFE: The Barriers to Teenage Girls', *Victorian TAFE Papers*, no. 2 (Hawthorn: Hawthorn Institute of Education, 1985); Heather Holcombe and Anthera Rutter, *Girls Who Want to be Chippies: A Negotiated Targets Project Evaluation Project* (Melbourne: Western Metropolitan College of TAFE, 1992); Laurel Black, 'Commonwealth Initiatives to Promote Women in Non-Traditional Training and Employment', *Victorian TAFE Papers*, no. 4 (April 1986): 36–40, hdl.voced.edu.au/10707/102168; Peter D. Earley, 'Girls, School, and Work: Technological Change and Female Entry into Non-Traditional Work Areas', *Australian Journal of Education* 25, no. 3 (1981): 269–87, doi.org/10.1177/000494418102500305; Australian Human Rights Commission, *Women in Male-Dominated Industries: A Toolkit of Strategies* (Canberra: the Commission, 2013), www.humanrights.gov.au/sites/default/files/document/publication/WIMDI_Toolkit_2013.pdf; Australian Department of Employment, Education and Training, *Women in Entry Level Training: Policy Review of the 1987 Report Women in Apprenticeship* [WELT report] (Canberra: Australian Government Publishing Service, 1991); Elaine Butler, Kira Clarke and Linda Simon,

In one of the earliest studies, in 1978, Ann Calvert noted that of about 36,800 apprentices in Victoria, some 2,200 were estimated to be female. However, when the trade of ladies hairdressing was excluded, there were only 340 female apprentices, less than 1 per cent of the total.[16] Her research was based on Victorian Apprenticeship Commission reports, in-depth interviews with a small number of female apprentices as well as employers. Calvert's groundbreaking study presented a wide-ranging discussion of the factors that limited women's entry into the trades—factors that would soon become familiar: parental attitudes and those of girls themselves; careers advice at schools; employers' prejudices; and industrial regulations such as lifting restrictions. Calvert employed the then relatively new feminist terms to consider broader social factors such as 'sex role stereotyping' and the structural impediments of the 'dual labour market'.

Ten years later, a 1987 Department of Employment, Education and Training (DEET) report similarly lamented that statistics on female apprenticeships remained ad hoc and difficult to obtain.[17] They concluded that 'the current low level of female participation in the [male] trades is the result of a wide range of social and institutional factors, both on the supply and the demand side'.[18] Key factors included 'negative attitudes' of women jobseekers, the general community and employers; lack of information about opportunities; employer concern about 'adequate facilities for women'; fear of 'adverse reaction' by male staff; biased recruitment methods and the lack of coordination between the several agencies responsible for this area. Their comprehensive list of recommendations included raising women's awareness of trade employment through effective marketing; systematic evaluation of affirmative action programs; Group Apprenticeship schemes; more preparatory and pre-employment courses for women; securing the cooperation of industry; compiling registers

---

Women and Girls into Non-Traditional Occupations and Industries: Broadening Career Options for Secondary School Students, report from economic Security4Women (North Sydney: Security4Women Inc., 2014), www.security4women.org.au/wp-content/uploads/eS4W-Career-Exploration-Project-Report-20140615.pdf; Judy McNamara, *A Fair Go for Women in Apprenticeship* (Melbourne: Outer Eastern Municipalities Association, 1986); and Georgine Clarsen, 'Auto-Erotics: The Sexing of a Skill' (MA thesis, Department of Women's Studies, University of Melbourne, 1993).
16   Ann Calvert, *Girls and Apprenticeships* (Melbourne: TAFE Services, 1979).
17   Australian Department of Employment, Education and Training, Australia Working Group on Women in Apprenticeship and Australia Commonwealth–State Training Advisory Committee, *Report of the Working Group on Women in Apprenticeship* (Canberra: Australian Government Publishing Service, 1987).
18   Ibid., 6.

of women in the trades; subsidising pilot projects; establishing targets; better coordination across agencies and monitoring the effectiveness of programs.

By 1992, the Victorian Affirmative Action in Training (AAIT) organisation was cautiously hopeful about progress in this area, noting there had been an increase of 18 per cent in the number of women who had entered motor mechanic trade training between 1983 and 1991, with a dramatic jump of 30 per cent in the 1990/91 financial year. The numbers, however, remained small. There were only 95 women in motor trade training in Victoria, which represented less than 2 per cent of apprentices in the industry. The study surveyed those apprentices in the hope of discovering strategies that might lead to similar increases in other male-dominated trades. They concluded that women who had entered that trade could be described as a cohort who 'dared to be different'.[19] They had higher than usual exposure to the trades at school or at home and had taken advantage of policies and strategies designed to encourage women to enter the trades. In order to 'dismantle the gender divide', however, 'strategies to tap into the larger recruitment pool needed to be developed', which could attract women who have the ability to enter those fields of work but currently 'simply don't consider it'.[20] Kimmel's recommendations were familiar: comprehensive trades promotion that emphasised the people-centred aspects of trade work; school information programs; the development of a comprehensive database; the funding of preparatory courses to build a critical mass of tradeswomen; the establishment of support networks; affirmative action programs for all Group Training Companies; and careful ongoing research to investigate high attrition rates and develop the best strategies to foster social change.[21]

There was little room for sustained optimism, however. In the same year, the parliamentary report *Half Way to Equal* noted that programs to boost employment opportunities in the vocational trades had appeared to benefit boys rather than girls.[22] Just a few years later, advocacy programs

---

19   Georgie Kimmel, *Why Motor Mechanics? A Report on the Reasons Given by Victorian Women for Choosing Motor Mechanics Trade Training as a Career Option* (Melbourne: Affirmative Action in Training Inc. July 1992), 1.
20   Ibid.
21   Group training companies were established to foster apprenticeships among disadvantaged groups and also to assist small employers to take on apprentices.
22   House of Representatives Standing Committee on Legal and Constitutional Affairs, *Half Way to Equal: Report of the Inquiry into Equal Opportunity and Equal Status for Women in Australia* (Canberra: Australian Government Publishing Service, April 1992), 49.

were defunded, though some agencies and academics continued to publish studies.[23] Most recent is a report by a consulting firm for the NSW State Training Services, *Ducks on the Pond: Women in Trade Apprenticeships*, and Karen Struthers's PhD thesis, 'Paving the Way for Girls into Male-Dominated Trades: Reducing Gender Segregation in the Trades'.[24] Both of these detailed studies lament the lack of change in women's take-up of apprenticeships in terms that echo much of the earlier research.

My survey of the literature across the 40 years suggests that most feminist studies analyse the lack of progress in terms of broad factors such as 'ingrained negative attitudes', 'limited perceptions', 'outmoded beliefs', 'prejudices', 'stereotypes' or 'lack of role models'. Tellingly, since the 1990s, an air of exasperation has crept into some of the literature at the apparent irrationality of the career choices made by working-class girls. In spite of all of the best efforts to make places available to them, the implication is that young women are not 'taking up opportunities' to move into jobs that were the domain of men. Programs are needed to educate girls so that they do not make the 'wrong' subject choices at school. They, their teachers and their parents should be 'persuaded' that their image of the trades is not correct, and be 'enticed' or 'convinced' that it is in their best interests to move into them.[25]

Why is there so little change in this area?

The dismal failure to bring about a significant shift in the proportion of women in the male-dominated trades over four decades suggests that new forms of analysis and action are well overdue. Most effort to date has been based on the strategic fiction that men and women stand in much the same relationship to the job market and that men's and women's bodies are potentially interchangeable, if only women are given the chance to

---

23 Pyke, *Women in Building: The Missing 51%*.
24 Quay Connection, *Ducks on the Pond: Women in Trade Apprenticeships* (Sydney: NSW Board of Vocational Education and Training (BEVT), 2014); Karen Struthers, 'Paving the Way for Girls into Male-Dominated Trades: Reducing Gender Segregation in the Trades' (PhD thesis, School of Human Services and Social Work, Griffith University, 2016).
25 National Board of Employment, Education and Training, *The Australian Vocational Certificate Training System: Report of the Employment Skills Formation Council* (Carmichael Report) (Canberra: AGPS, March 1992), 99; Shirley Sampson, 'Increasing Women's Participation in the Male-Dominated Trades', in Department of Employment, Education and Training, *Dismantling the Divide: Conference on Women in Male-Dominated Occupations* (Canberra; Australian Government Printing Service, 1991), 34–36.

'catch up' with men by developing the appropriate knowledge, confidence and skills. Such a strategic fiction could be justified if it were delivering intended results, as it has been in upper sectors of the employment market. In the case of the male trades, however, clearly it is not. While what Joan Eveline in 1992 called the 'pragmatics of equality politics' suggests that we should accept uneven changes in the improvement of women's position in the workforce, it is important not to lose sight of how advances for some women may be taken to be gains for all women, or even mask losses for others.[26]

To a large extent, affirmative action initiatives to introduce women into the male trades have sought to rectify or compensate for a perceived disadvantage. They have been based on presumptions of young women's lack and this takes feminists onto dangerous territory. The patent absence of success might be taken to support a conservative conclusion that women 'don't want to be equal' in spite of all the 'opportunities' placed before them, and so are complicit in their own oppression. Similarly, the focus on women's lack can serve to perpetuate the belief that young women do not enter the trades because those areas of work are, indeed, no place for a woman. While the feminist research and programs since the 1970s certainly have some value in opening out debates and opportunities, it is more than time to acknowledge that those campaigns have failed to address the larger and more complex issues at the heart of women's absence. To that extent, they do not and cannot ring true to the depth of the difficulties women in those areas of work encounter. Rather than focusing on the ways that that young women may be misguided, lacking in confidence or limited in some other way, it is more than time to broaden the terms of the debate and view their actions in a more positive light.

The liberal feminist strategy of presuming that it is only 'irrational stereotypes' that prevent equality best serves women who seek to move into the professional and managerial job market. There, bodily differences between men and women are considered to be of marginal importance to the job, though recent scandals highlight the continued harassment and discrimination that women face daily in those areas of work.[27] Feminisms of equality are even less adequate, however, in areas of employment where

---

26   Joan Eveline, 'The Police of Advantage', *Australian Feminist Studies* 9, no. 19 (1994): 130, doi.org/10.1080/08164649.1994.9994729.

27   For example, Women in Media, 'Mates Over Merit: Women in Media Report', Media, Entertainment and Arts Alliance, 2016, last updated 11 February 2019, www.meaa.org/resource-package/mates-over-merit-full-report/.

sexed, bodily difference is perceived as central to the performance of a job. In primarily 'manual' jobs, presumptions of equality barely touch the issues that legitimise their assignment to male or female bodies. The definition of women's bodies as unsuited to certain kinds of work, and the structuring of work in such ways that women's bodies are anomalous to its performance, are complex processes, central to an understanding of the position of working-class women and the skilled trades. Yet, in spite of calls to the contrary—for example, in the theoretically nuanced work of Joan Eveline and Elaine Butler—feminist employment policies have largely perpetuated the strategic fiction that working-class women stand in much the same relation to issues of bodily difference as middle-class women.[28] In Butler and Ferrier's terms, it is time to stop being so polite about the entrenched masculinist cultures that actively work to repel women from the male trades and eject those few brave women who venture into them.[29]

To understate or discount the complexity of the issues, and to avoid openly naming the role of men and masculinist practices in making those workplaces unwelcoming to women, is to fail to do justice to the strength of the forces that place working-class women on the outer when it comes to that job market. It is more than time to acknowledge that it has proven counterproductive to place the primary focus on young women who are choosing not to enter the trades. Indeed, an obsessive focus on data, with its calculus of women's absence, serves to reinforce rather than challenge the message that the trades are not for women. More importantly, it misses the point that women's absence should not be read as a failure but as instead a knowing act of recognition that those workplaces are not accidentally or coincidentally male dominated.

What is to be done?

A feminist politics true to the complexities of this area of activism needs to shift the focus from women's purported lack to an analysis of the interested operation of male power. Women's reluctance to enter those workplaces should be understood as a considered response to the knowledge that

---

28   J. Eveline and M. Booth, 'Gender and Sexuality in Discourses of Managerial Control: The Case of Women Miners', *Gender, Work and Organization* 9, no. 5 (2002): 556–78, doi.org/10.1111/1468-0432.00175.
29   Elaine Butler and Fran Ferrier, *'Don't Be Too Polite, Girls': Women, Work and Vocational Education at Training, a Critical Review of the Literature* (South Australia: NCVER, Australian National Training Authority, 2000).

they have been constructed through the particular historical practices of specific male actors. That is, that they are environments that have been designed to repel women, for the benefit of men. This new starting point makes better sense of the conclusion made in many research studies, often called the 'consistency gap', that girls generally express strong approval of females in non-traditional occupations, but express little interest in entering it themselves.[30] Young women overwhelmingly and wisely judge that those workplaces are not structured around their interests, their fantasies, their bodies or their imagined life narratives, and that any who choose to participate must enter on terms that are set by men.

Feminist activists have, of course, always been aware of the extreme harassment of all kinds that female apprentices have routinely faced in their workplaces and at TAFE colleges. A 1986 Hunter Valley study, for example, noted that the incidence of female apprentices reporting harassment was extremely high. Some 80 per cent of women experienced harassment and most were reluctant to report it. The study also found that many male apprentices were 'extremely hostile' to women's entry into that work and to the 'special attention' they perceived females to have received.[31] Given that feminist programs have relied on the goodwill of male gatekeepers, it is not surprising that the normative masculinism of the workplaces that women were being encouraged to enter was played down in almost all of the literature. However, with this strategy having proven to be so ineffective over 40 years, there seems little to lose in feminists taking a more direct approach to the key structural impediment that women in these areas of work face.

My argument is that we need to name the situation more directly, as is routine in the higher end of the employment market, as a situation of male domination, of systemic gendered injustice. Instead of looking at women, we might focus on the impact of male behaviours that self-interestedly structure the practices and cultures to make these workplaces unwelcoming to women. We might better analyse the trades as places where men produce and reproduce a kind of masculinity that is yoked to a particular male body and a particular kind of masculine culture, which is used to justify the exclusion of women. Certainly, as young tradeswomen

---

30 Suzanne S. Dillon, *Jobs for the Girls: Why Not Technical?* (Melbourne: Knowledge Systems Research, 1986).
31 Patricia Moran, 'Trading Tradition: Evaluation of the Issues Arising from the Experiences of Female and Male Apprentices in Male-Dominated Trades in the Hunter Region', *Australian Journal of TAFE Research and Development* 2 (1986): 119–25.

in the 1970s and 1980s, we acutely felt those processes in action and tried to find words for them. But at that time there was not the language to think about it clearly, or articulate it in terms that might have helped us to better navigate the contradictions.

A conceptual framework that foregrounded sexed embodiment also leaves us better able to think about the pleasures we found in that work and how it was central to our investments in it. In spite of the difficulties, we were able to find enjoyment where apparently women were not supposed to—in the pleasures of being completely absorbed in physical actions; in our growing strength; of sensing a new relationship to technologies; of knowing how to use our bodies to get things done; of finding a knack for using tools well; of developing a capacity to listen differently and hear what had previously not been meaningful to us and even to smell what might be wrong with a car. Articulating the joy we experienced in the work, even more so when it was shared, brings 'give a girl a spanner' campaigns closer to their feminist potential. As Louisa Smith similarly concluded, finding pleasure in the skilled trades embodies a different reality where the purported givenness of masculine cultures (or rather one version of them) is experienced as porous.[32] At that moment the gendered order, in the form of the disciplinary regime of the trades, is revealed as constructed, unstable and potentially open to feminist reinscription.

I take heart in knowing that the situation I have described here—struggles over embodied workplace practices—is paralleled by the similarly long battles by sportswomen for recognition. I note the astonishing elevation in the profile of women's sports we have seen in just this last year. These too are quintessentially bodily practices, though differently played out and in a much more public, performative forum. Sometimes the change you have been working toward so long is unexpected and sudden. It can take you by surprise and you need to be ready.

---

32 Louisa E. Smith, 'The Embodiment and Gender Contradictions of Women in the Male-Dominated Industries of Skilled Manual Trades and Information Technology (IT)' (PhD thesis, Faculty of Education and Social Work, University of Sydney, 2012).

CHAPTER 3

The discovery of sexism in schools: Everyday revolutions in the classroom

Julie McLeod

> Sexism is a process through which females and males not only progressively learn that different things are required and expected of them because of their sex, but learn these things in an unexamined way. Good education is incompatible with such a process; central to it is the examination of assumptions and the rational consideration of alternatives.[1]

Feminism was an influential movement in education in the 1970s, with formal state-based policies developed on equal opportunity and non-sexist education as well as substantial school-based and grassroots activity in Australia and elsewhere. Within teacher unions and curriculum associations, there was an explosion of publications, dedicated committees and high-profile activism. The impact of this work was felt across school programs, in classroom teaching and in heightened attention to 'sexism in education' as a category of policy, pedagogical and scholarly attention. This encompassed sustained attention to the sex role, sexuality education and new approaches to the explicit role of curriculum in teaching for and about 'human relations'. Educational reform was a key theme in the recommendations arising from the 1975 Royal Commission on Human Relationships. The report's first recommendation on education loftily directed that:

---

1   Commonwealth Schools Commission, *Girls, School and Society* (Canberra: Australian Government Publishing Service, 1975), 17 [2.30].

> The government should require the Department of Education to make a major effort to change the policies of all concerned with education so that these policies will be designed and directed to ensure the fullest possible development of the whole person, physically, emotionally, intellectually and socially.[2]

This chapter examines the ways in which new constructions of the personal were mediated in and by non-sexist and equal opportunity reforms in schooling and argues the personal was not only political but also pedagogical.

Importantly, the 1970s was also the era of de-schooling schools, a time when a raft of radical ideas and alternatives to regular schooling were in the air.[3] The language was of 'de-institutionalisation', democratic schooling, social transformation. This was also a time when new educational ideas were gaining ground about the child, pedagogy, freedom and the role of schools as places to foster self-discovery. By the early 1970s, a small but influential number of government schools with alternative forms of curriculum, school design and organisational structures were established in Victoria, offering new ways of imagining schooling, of being students and teachers.[4] New expressions of progressivism began to flourish, alongside radical critiques of conventional schooling and an evident optimism in the critical potential of schooling to disrupt entrenched power inequalities. Student-led curriculum, participatory learning and less hierarchical relations between teachers and students were advocated, along with broader calls for schooling to become more democratic, with the socially transformative potential of education at the forefront.[5]

---

2   Royal Commission on Human Relationships, *Final Report of the Royal Commission on Human Relationships*, vol. 1, *Introduction, Summary, and Recommendations* (Canberra: Australian Government Publishing Service, 1977), 17 [2.1].
3   Henry Schoenheimer, *Good Australian Schools and Their Communities*, (Melbourne: Victorian Technical Teachers Association, 1973); Anthony Potts, 'New Education, Progressive Education and the Counter Culture', *Journal of Educational Administration and History* 39, no. 2 (2007): 145–59, doi.org/10.1080/00220620701342304; Ronald J. Miller, *Free Schools, Free People: Education and Democracy after the 1960s* (Albany: SUNY Press, 2002).
4   *The Educational Magazine*, Special Issue on Free Schools, 30, no. 4 (1973): 1–20; *The Educational Magazine*, Special Feature on Open Education, 31, no. 5 (1974): 38–48; Schoenheimer, *Good Australian Schools and Their Communities*; G. Maslen, 'Huntingdale Technical School', *The Educational Magazine* 30, no. 4 (1973): 14–15.
5   Ivan Illich, *Alternatives to Education* (North Melbourne, Vic.: Australian Union of Students, 1972); David Pettit, *Opening Up Schools: School and Community in Australia* (Harmondsworth, UK: Penguin, 1980); Julie McLeod, 'Experimenting with Education: Spaces of Freedom and Alternative Schooling in the 1970s', *History of Education Review* 43, no. 2 (2014): 172–89, doi.org/10.1108/HER-03-2014-0019.

The mood of this era, and of education having a crucial role to play in driving social changes, was captured in and by the election of a Labor federal government in 1972, led by Prime Minister Gough Whitlam. Whitlam's government inaugurated a wave of educational reforms designed to redress educational disadvantage, which included establishing in its first year the Australian Schools Commission, with a remit to 'provide policy advice, carry out research and allocate Federal funding to schools'.[6] The commission's 1973 interim report, *Schools in Australia* (known as the Karmel Report after committee chair Peter Karmel), mapped out an ambitious program of reform to promote greater equality of education, with programs to tackle the effects of poverty and models for the distribution of school funding and the abolition of tertiary education fees.[7] Importantly, the Karmel Report found that to be a girl was an educational disadvantage, and that the degree of disadvantage was linked to socioeconomic status.[8]

In her early 1970s study of sex differences in educational qualifications, the Australian sociologist Jean Martin found that, despite little available data on sex differences, it was clear:

> girls remain at a disadvantage because they leave school earlier and because such qualifications as they acquire are less likely to equip them to move into those areas of tertiary education, particularly science and medicine, which fully utilize their talents and lead eventually to the higher-status and more lucrative occupations.[9]

Martin further argued that the well-established focus in Australia on:

> inequalities between government and independent, and metropolitan and urban schools, and between children from different socio-economic backgrounds, has over-shadowed interest in sex differences, and much excellent material on school populations is not broken down by sex.[10]

---

6 Craig Campbell and Helen Proctor, *A History of Australian Schooling* (Sydney: Allen & Unwin, 2014), 182.
7 Peter Karmel and Interim Committee, *Schools in Australia: Report of the Interim Committee for the Schools Commission* (Canberra: Australian Government Publishing Service, 1973); John McLaren, 'Karmel Report: Schools in Australia', DEHANZ, 1 February 2014, dehanz.net.au/entries/karmel-report-schools-australia/; Campbell and Proctor, *A History of Australian Schooling*, 182 and 191–95.
8 Karmel et al., *Schools in Australia*.
9 Jean Martin, 'Sex Differences in Educational Qualifications', *Melbourne Studies in Education*, ed. R. J. W. Selleck (Melbourne: Melbourne University Press, 1972), 96–123, 107.
10 Ibid., 104.

From the early 1970s, there was, then, considerable scholarly and policy momentum, infused by the women's movement, to address the systematic inequalities faced by girls in schools, with a clear linking of sex-based differences to the persistent effects of class-based advantage and disadvantage—a matter that continued to shape gender reform discussions well into the following decades.[11]

The influential 1975 report *Girls, School and Society*, auspiced by the Schools Commission and principally authored by educationalist Jean Blackburn, documented the details of this systematic disadvantage, providing evidence of participation and retention rates, patterns of curriculum choice and career aspirations.[12] The report argued unequivocally that schools and state education departments were responsible for implementing practices and policies that were non-sexist and that sought to improve girls' educational outcomes. Teachers and other commentators observed how pervasive sex-role stereotyping was and identified school practices—the hidden and the overt curriculum, teachers' expectations—as crucial socialising factors.

Feminist reforms in education were thus part of a wider questioning of the social purposes of schooling and associated concerns with schooling's potential to realise democratic and equality agendas. In turn, these were underpinned by a view of schools as predominantly socialisation agents that had the capacity both to reproduce and to challenge sexist views and practices. Schools were thus identified as key sites for feminist interventions—everyday places for the realisation and enactment of new ways of being girls and boys, women and men, and for countering sexism. As such, schools played a crucial role in mediating the social and political hopes of feminism.

Histories of feminism and schooling are a vital if often muted voice in histories of feminism more generally, and this is particularly pressing in relation to reassessments of the character and legacy of second-wave feminism. In her *Getting Equal: The History of Australian Feminism* (1999), Marilyn Lake argued that one of the defining characteristics of post-1960s feminism (compared to interwar feminism, for example) was its attention to the personal and to re-education of the self.[13] In such

---

11 Cherry Collins, Jane Kenway and Julie McLeod, *Factors Influencing the Educational Performance of Males and Females at School and Their Initial Destinations after Leaving School* (Canberra: Department of Education, Training and Youth Affairs, 2000).
12 Commonwealth Schools Commission, *Girls, School and Society*.
13 Marilyn Lake, *Getting Equal: The History of Australian Feminism* (St Leonards, NSW: Allen & Unwin, 1999).

formulations, education in its broadest sense is ever-present, often as part of the background, with schools implicitly the source of problems (sexist attitudes) and of possible solutions (resocialisation), with little elaboration of the level of work involved in schools to achieve such feminist goals. Moreover, education and specifically schools have less often been examined as themselves complex and dynamic sites of feminist activism, politics and theory, and are more likely to be treated as a sideline or niche thread within the history of feminism.[14] Equally, histories of progressive and alternative education often tell a somewhat introspective account of their own genesis and legacies, with limited acknowledgement of contemporaneous feminist activists or of the parallel critiques of social relations, inequalities and the project of schooling as freedom that, at some levels, their respective projects implicitly shared.

The larger project on which this chapter is based seeks to entangle these histories, proposing a reappraisal of feminist education that gives proper recognition to its central role in both histories of feminism and histories of progressive and alternative education. The personalisation of education and the political played out visibly in the alternative school movement, evident, for example, in the creation of purpose-built or found environments that reflected the promise of open plan, student-centred and deinstitutionalised schooling in which student voice, choice and preference were given elevated attention.[15] Feminist interventions were integral to a related process of personalisation, such that the interrogation of identity—who am I? what are my values?—was a prominent pedagogic strategy, oriented to reforming

---

14   Gisela Kaplan, *The Meagre Harvest* (St Leonards, NSW: Allen & Unwin, 1996); Lake, *Getting Equal*; Chilla Bulbeck, *Living Feminism: The Impact of the Women's Movement on Three Generations of Australian Women* (Cambridge: Cambridge University Press, 1997); Megan Jones, 'Historicising Feminist Knowledge: Notes Towards a Genealogy of Academic Feminism', *Australian Feminist Studies* 13, no. 27 (1998): 117–28, doi.org/10.1080/08164649.1998.9994895; Jean Curthoys, *Feminist Amnesia: The Wake of Women's Liberation* (London: Routledge, 1997); Ann Curthoys, 'Doing It for Themselves: The Women's Movement since 1970', in *Gender Relations in Australia: Domination and Negotiation*, ed. Kay Saunders and Raymond Evans (Sydney: Harcourt Brace Jovanovich, 1992): 425–29; Joyce Goodman, 'The Gendered Politics of Historical Writing in History of Education', *History of Education* 41, no. 1 (January 2012): 9–24; Michelle Arrow and Mary Spongberg, 'Editorial', *Australian Feminist Studies* 22, no. 53 (1 July 2007): 159–61, doi.org/10.1080/08164640701378570. See also 'Second Wave Feminism', 13 October 2013, Radio National, ABC, www.abc.net.au/radionational/programs/rearvision/second-wave-feminism/4983136; and Chen Yan and Karen Offen, 'Women's History at the Cutting Edge: A Joint Paper in Two Voices', *Women's History Review* 27, no. 1 (2018): 6–28, doi.org/10.1080/09612025.2016.1250531.
15   'The Swinburne Community School', *Farrago*, 5 May 1972; Julie McLeod, Philip Goad, Julie Willis and Kate Darian-Smith, 'Reading Images of School Buildings and Spaces: An Interdisciplinary Dialogue on Visual Research in Histories of Progressive Education', in *Visual Research Methods in Educational Research*, ed. Julianne Moss and Barbara Pini (London: Palgrave Macmillan, 2016), 15–35, doi.org/10.1057/9781137447357_2.

teacher and student sensibilities and habits of conduct. For the purposes of this chapter, I map key feminist reforms in schooling that sought to reconfigure the personal and analyse the pedagogic interventions that troubled conceptions of the sex role and subjectivity, linking these to broader aspirations for democratic education and the paradoxes at the heart of the governmental administration of freedom. The chapter concludes with reflections on the rise and fall narratives that characterise cultural and policy memories of second-wave feminism and education. I begin by considering the significant pedagogical and conceptual claims of the sex-role construct in second-wave feminist educational reforms.

Feminism and the sex role

A strong motif in feminist writing in the 1970s was the process of 'sex role socialisation', which placed itself against any form of identity determinism. As Kate Millett argued, '[s]exual politics obtains consent through the "socialization" of both sexes to basic patriarchal politics with regard to temperament, role and status'.[16] The operation and effects of sex-role stereotyping were identified by feminist educators in the 1970s as major causes of inequality between the sexes. Changing the values, attitudes and practices that constituted identity was judged to be the most effective way to eliminate sexism. Schools were thus positioned as prime socialising agents and accorded major roles in making possible—giving form, effect and setting—the remaking of persons and the enculturation of feminist, anti-sexist principles.

During the 1960s and 1970s, accounts of sex-role socialisation were widespread in the social sciences as well as in popular discourse.[17] They were drawn upon by social psychologists, sociologists and educationalists to explain the perceived and measurable differences between males and females in occupations, educational qualifications, aspirations, behaviours, life patterns and so on.[18] Silcock, for example, undertook a study of the 'sex role of Brisbane youth' in order to compare it with the

---

16   Kate Millett, *Sexual Politics* (London: Abacus, published by Sphere Books, 1972).
17   The publication of the journal the *Sex Role* began in 1975. Sociology journals from this time (such as the *Australian and New Zealand Journal of Sociology*) show an increasing mention of the sex role concept, e.g. Anne Edwards, 'Sex Roles: A Problem for Sociology and for Women', *Australian and New Zealand Journal of Sociology* 19, no. 3 (1983): 385–412, doi.org/10.1177/144078338301900302.
18   For example, Donald Edgar, 'Competence for Girls?', *Secondary Teacher* (July 1972): 9–12; Shirley Sampson, 'Sex Stereotypes: Some Evidence from Australian Schools', *Australian Journal of Education* 23, no. 2 (1979): 132–40, doi.org/10.1177/000494417902300204.

different models of sex role advanced by US sociologist Talcott Parsons and psychologist Daniel Brown.[19] Other educators and teachers might have taken a less scholarly approach but nevertheless insisted that the acquisition, operation and effects of the sex role were vital factors and these matters increasingly became the object of educational attention. It was for a time the dominant way in which subjectivity was conceptualised in educational discussions in Australia and provided the basis for much pedagogical activity and curriculum reform. Australian feminist reforms in education from the 1960s through to at least the late 1980s were strongly influenced by these ideas.

When, in the decades preceding the 1960s, sex-based differences in young people's education, their curriculum and career choices, or their futures and values, were acknowledged, it was as matters to be noted and accommodated rather than challenged or seen as signalling educational or social problems. The shift in the 1960s and 1970s to regard such matters as worthy of investigation was in large part a result of feminist intervention, and its recasting of differentiation as inequality. Schools were identified as social institutions with special responsibilities for preparing young people for futures that were not constrained by the traditional ideas of sex-appropriate conduct.

The sex-role concept articulated with, and gave expression to, the task of shaping autonomous, rational, unconstrained (by sex, by tradition, by nature) future citizens. Its influence was felt in pedagogy and curriculum design, as well as in common parlance. Sex-role theory has met with sustained critique and is now seen to be an explanation that feminism has left behind. There are valid and well-rehearsed reasons for repudiating both cognitive-developmental and behaviourist models of role theory: for example, they presuppose a prior organising agent to sort out roles, they are unable to explain why some behaviours are sanctioned and others not, or to explain socially anomalous behaviour, and they have a normative vision of gender identity development, one which offers an inadequate account of the formation of identity and sexual difference, establishes a simplistic relationship between the social and the self, and fosters a reductive opposition between mind and body and so forth.[20]

---

19   Anne Silcock, 'The Social Sex Roles of Brisbane Youth', *Australian Journal of Education* 10, no. 2 (1966): 170–85, doi.org/10.1177/000494416601000212.
20   Julian Henriques, Wendy Hollway, Cathy Urwin, Couze Venn and Valerie Walkerdine, *Changing the Subject: Psychology, Social Regulation and Subjectivity* (London: Routledge, 1998 [1984]).

While criticisms of role theory's conceptual shortcomings are thus well-founded, they have tended to obscure its (historical) effects as a set of influential ideas about subjectivity and gender and education. Defining and then examining the sex role, and even conceiving of identity as composed of multiple roles, opened a space for simultaneously freeing oneself from tradition and establishing practices for scrutinising habit and inclination—these can be examined as powerful practices of self-government and crucial in remaking the self in non-traditional ways. The concept of role also had a more conventional normative aspect, in that assimilation to certain roles was regarded as not only socially functional but as a measure of psychological and emotional adjustment. Even so, the reasoning of role theory can be understood as part of a systematic undoing of natural gender and inscription of gender as social, as portable, as contingent, as an independent variable of identity.[21]

Role theory underlined the work and responsibility of the individual in making their own identity and futures. In discussions about schooling and sexism, self-making is represented as an explicit activity, an ethical practice, both an artefact of and requirement for equality and the elimination of sexism. In this way, concepts such as the sex role and socialisation can be examined as not only flawed but also as productive. This gives rise to a number of questions that are important for understanding the form and legacy of second-wave feminism in schools: What kind of effects did these constructs have on educational practices? What was the impact of educational policies and pedagogies informed by these concepts? And, what gender norms did they help affirm as part of emergent cultural common sense?

---

21 The emphasis upon the radically social form of the 'sex role' chimes in some respects with ideas concerning the 'performance' of gender—noting that these emerge from different theoretical-political traditions. Judith Butler writes that 'if gender is a kind of a doing, an incessant activity performed, in part, without one's knowing and without one's willing, it is not for that reason automatic or mechanical. On the contrary it is a practice of improvisation within a scene of constraint ... the terms that make up one's own gender are, from the start, outside oneself, beyond oneself in a sociality that has no single author'. Judith Butler, *Giving an Account of Oneself* (New York: Fordham University Press, 2004), 1.

3. THE DISCOVERY OF SEXISM IN SCHOOLS

Utopian moments and bureaucratic reforms

Desires to transform student subjectivities as well as the work of schooling, to make it variously more democratic, less sexist, more student-centred and less hierarchical or factory-like, were manifested and put into practice in ways that were at once technical, organisational and aspirational. The larger purposes of formal education are usually allied to questions of prevailing social values and notions of social progress, even if it is in terms of how schooling might be hindering or complicating such ambitions. In this sense, formal education can be understood as having utopian elements, with high hopes projected onto its mission as well as onto its more mundane and everyday functions. While this can be expressed quite instrumentally in terms of schooling's role in preparing young people for future work, more expansive, normative and hopeful questions also arise. Ruth Levitas's work on 'utopia as a method' is helpful here, as it gives nuance to the different temporalities and purposes of such endeavours as expressed in social and political programs—in this case, formal schooling and systems of education. She proposes that 'utopia has three modes':

> The first is an archaeological mode: piecing together the images of the good society that are embedded in political programmes and social and economic policies. The second is an ontological mode which addresses the question of what kind of *people* particular societies develop and encourage … The third is an architectural mode—that is, the imagination of potential alternative scenarios for the future, acknowledging the assumptions about and consequences for the people who might inhabit them.[22]

Feminist reforms in schooling traversed these three intersecting modes. However, identifying the different registers helps to give not only greater analytic clarity but also a sharper account of the ambitions of their pedagogical and political projects. The following discussion attends primarily to the ontological mode, with some underlying reference to the architectural mode, the imagination of other possible worlds. In characterising the ontological mode, Levitas further describes this as entailing a focus on:

---

22   Ruth Levitas, *Utopia as Method: The Imaginary Reconstitution of Society* (New York: Palgrave Macmillan, 2013), doi.org/10.1057/9781137314253.

what is understood as human flourishing, what capabilities are valued, encouraged and genuinely enabled, or blocked and suppressed, by specific existing or potential social arrangements: we are concerned here with the historical and social determination of human nature.[23]

Second-wave feminism in education was directly concerned with how gendered—or, in the language of the day, sex-typed—capabilities were either enabled or constrained by 'specific existing or potential social arrangements'. A central plank was identifying the opportunities for, and indeed obligations of, schools to consider these matters as part of their social and cultural remit and as fundamental to their future-oriented educational mission to prepare young people for worlds beyond the school walls.

Feminist teaching required a commitment to challenging entrenched sexist beliefs and to a range of pedagogical techniques that enabled one to bring students to an awareness of the debilitating effects—for them personally and society generally—of sex-role stereotyping. The goal of feminist pedagogy, then, was to uncover the impediments to an idealised state of gender freedom and to institute a rational program of personal and educational reform whereby sexism would be eliminated and sex roles remade. These feminist educational reforms had clear utopian elements in the sense characterised by Levitas as the 'ontological mode'; they promised gender freedom, and also worked towards their own persuasive norms of feminist conduct and gendered identity.

As with the alternative school movements of the same period, an important aspect of feminist reforms is that they were undertaken within and supported by state departments of education, often resting on bureaucratic endorsement and infrastructure to implement what could be characterised as oppositional ideas, or at least ideas and practices that challenged the social and educational status quo. Feminism thus had a double-edged role in the administration of education. Across a wide range of public sector activism, and with education no exception, feminist politics became part of bureaucratic and policy structures as a result of deliberate initiatives from feminists to work from within the state, not only to critique it. This phenomenon was captured by the Australian neologism 'femocrats' to describe feminists working in the heart of government and state bureaucracies to achieve reformist ends.[24]

---

23 Ibid.
24 Anna Yeatman, *Bureaucrats, Technocrats, Femocrats: Essays on the Contemporary Australian State* (Sydney: Allen & Unwin, 1990).

Femocrats were certainly important in achieving feminist aims in schools, from Elizabeth Reid as Women's Advisor to the Prime Minister (1973) to leading figures in state departments of education such as Deborah Towns, first co-ordinator of the Equal Opportunity in Education Unit in Victoria (1977), or Denise Bradley, women's advisor to the Education Department of South Australia (1977); women leaders in teacher unions were also prominent in advocating against sexism in schools and initiating curriculum change, such as Helen Clarke from the Technical Teachers Union of Victoria and Claire Henderson from the Victorian Secondary Teachers Association.[25] There were indeed many influential and relatively well-known feminist actors during this period, undertaking vital work in governmental bureaucracies. The point I want to make here, though, is a slightly different one from that afforded by focusing on feminist leadership and the phenomenon of femocrats.

My interest here is in the everyday, but far from ordinary, work of classroom teachers in bringing feminist aims to life and in many respects making possible the changes in gender relations and identity envisaged by feminism. Of course, the two realms of activity were often interconnected, with, for example, teachers understanding themselves as part of the grassroots feminist movement, or classroom teachers moving to roles in the departments of education, and femocrats not necessarily seen as remote from the 'chalkface'. However, the regular labour of teaching—managing classrooms, designing lessons, inventing pedagogies, revising curriculums that might support feminist agendas—is too often overlooked or undervalued. Yet it is precisely this work that carried feminist dreams, and which commonly looked towards education—vaguely, expansively—to solve problems of sexism, socialisation and sex-role stereotyping. In the following sections, I offer a close-up look at the intended labour of teachers and the responsibilities they bore in helping to materialise the ambitions of second-wave feminism.

---

25 Deborah Towns, 'Government Schools', *The Encyclopedia of Women and Leadership in Twentieth-Century Australia*, www.womenaustralia.info/leaders/biogs/WLE0638b.htm; *Equal Opportunity Newsletter* (Victorian Equal Opportunity Resource Centre, 1982–92); Julie McLeod, 'A Decade of Changes: The Equal Opportunity Unit and Resource Centre', *Equal Opportunity Newsletter* 7, no. 1 (1988): 3–6; Julie McLeod, 'Regulating Gender: Feminist Truths and Educational Reform in Victoria since 1975' (PhD thesis, La Trobe University, 1996).

Importantly, in the decades preceding the 1970s, the teaching service had grown dramatically to match the expansion of secondary schooling from the late 1950s onwards.[26] One consequence of this significant growth was the influx of a new generation of teachers entering the teaching profession,[27] with many younger women and men, influenced by the social movements of the 1960s and 1970s, embracing a new sense of the possibilities of schooling and its wider social functions. Questions of equality and the role of teachers in striving for social change was at the forefront in numerous school-based reforms, such as the alternative schools noted above, as well as the anti-sexism work examined here.[28] For the new generation of women teachers, the feminist educational messages had a more personal resonance as well, with many coming of age at the burgeoning of second-wave feminism and with the social mobility afforded by more equitable access to higher education represented by the Whitlam era.

The history of feminism in education is approached here in terms of how it was administered in formal education and through bureaucratic and comparatively mundane and technical ways. This is not to deny the liberatory, at times utopian or even grandly romantic aspirations and rhetoric accompanying these practices. Rather, it is also to bring a close and critical focus to acts of translating such feminist ideals into administrative and educational strategies and techniques that could be put to work in everyday ways in schools and classrooms.

'Removing the last vestiges of sexism'

During the 1970s, numerous state and national reports on schooling found that schools discriminated against girls, that 'to be a girl was an educational disadvantage'.[29] Absence, lack, limitation, disadvantage were the terms commonly employed to characterise girls' formal engagement with schooling. Considerable evidence was found of, for example, girls' under-representation in the science and mathematics areas, their relative

---

26   L. J. Blake (general editor), *Vision and Realisation: A Centenary History of State Education in Victoria*, vol. 1, (Melbourne: Education Department of Victoria, Government Printer, 1973), 547.
27   Campbell and Proctor, *A History of Australian Schooling*, 191–92.
28   Julie McLeod, 'Experimenting with Education', 172–89.
29   Karmel et al., *Schools in Australia*; see also Commonwealth Schools Commission, *Girls, School and Society*.

poor retention rates and their narrow range of career options.[30] Schooling practices, including the hidden curriculum, teachers' attitudes and textbooks, were identified as reproducing dominant social beliefs and expectations.[31] Schools were presented as almost irredeemable institutions, inevitably reproducing dominant values and power relations.[32] Yet, at the same time, these critiques provided a rationale for attempting to do something new with schools, to offer different pedagogies and curricula.

Discovering, or rather uncovering, and eliminating sexism was a central preoccupation of feminist educators in the 1970s. This task was tackled with remarkable optimism and clarity of purpose. Upon exposure, sexism was to be rationally debunked and eliminated from the daily practices of both teachers and pupils. Such was the confident mood of the times that the then Victorian Minister for Education Lindsay Thompson could declare that the appointment in 1977 of an Equal Opportunity Co-ordinator would lead to 'the removal of the last vestiges of sexism' within state schooling.[33] So confident was he that this goal would be met, and in response to some 'complaints of the male sex', he predicted that 'it may be necessary to establish an organization to protect the interests of the male sex because they feel they are being victimized in certain areas'.[34] In the early stages of their development, the bureaucracies established by the Victorian (and other states) Department of Education and teachers' unions to 'eliminate sexism' emphasised the importance of 'raising awareness' about sexism and the roles people, often unwittingly, played in endorsing sex-stereotyped behaviour and attitudes. Despite the documentation of girls' entrenched educational disadvantage, there was enormous official optimism that schools could and should do something to ameliorate these inequalities. Departments of education, schools and teachers' organisations responded to calls for such ambitious changes through a range of officially sanctioned strategies and recommendations for implementing non-sexist schooling within a state education bureaucracy.

---

30   For example, ibid.
31   For example, Victorian Committee on Equal Opportunity in Victorian Schools, *Victorian Committee on Equal Opportunity in Victorian Schools: Report to the Premier* (Melbourne: the Committee, July 1977).
32   For an example of how practising teachers took up and interpreted these critiques, see Bill Cleland, 'Deficient, Disadvantaged or Different', *Secondary Teacher*, no. 3 (1975): 9–10; Bill Cleland, 'Ivan Illich in Melbourne', *Secondary Teacher*, no. 15 (1978): 12.
33   Victoria, Legislative Assembly, *Parliamentary Debates*, vol. 334, 20 October 1977, 10598.
34   Ibid.

Through professional magazines, such as teachers' union journals or curriculum association newsletters, and memoranda from departments of education, teachers were regularly alerted to the dangers of sex-role stereotyping and reminded that qualities and ambitions once thought of as sex-specific were now to be understood as potentially common to both sexes. The 1975 Commonwealth Schools Commission report, *Girls, School and Society*, advised that:

> The Committee believes that, to the extent that schools operate on unexamined assumptions about differences between the sexes or fail to confront with analysis sex stereotypes through the media, they limit the options of both boys and girls and assist the processes through which messages of dependence are passed to girls because they are female.[35]

The *Girls, School and Society* report recommended that states establish their own committees to investigate the status of girls' education and to develop appropriate policies.[36] The Victorian Committee on the Status of Women (1975) also urged the Victorian Government to establish such a committee and a Victorian Committee on Equal Opportunity in Schools was established in November 1975, meeting regularly and receiving submissions from the public throughout 1976.[37]

'We recognise that schools alone cannot bring about a state of perfect social equality, where only genetic differences exist between the sexes', observed the authors of the report on equal opportunity in Victorian schools (1977). But, they believed, 'the experience of schooling should not be such that it directly contributes to a lowered self-esteem, motivation or achievement for either sex, as has been reported to us from evidence gathered in this State'.[38] Like the earlier Commonwealth report

---

35   Commonwealth Schools Commission, *Girls, School and Society*, 157 [14.4].
36   Ibid., 159–60 [14.8–14.10].
37   The terms of reference for the Victorian Committee included investigations of sex-typed language and images in textbooks; sex-based differences in school rules, punishments and rewards, dress codes and behavioural expectations; absence of female role models in senior positions; 'time tabling arrangements and psychological pressures which effectively deny or inhibit participation in areas in which members of a particular sex have not traditionally participated'. The committee was asked to make recommendations on: 'i) What positive measures could be implemented to encourage girls to study a wider range of subjects and aspire to a wider range of occupations, to higher education, and to positions of authority; ii) Whether vocational guidance is biased, and how such guidance can be given so that the whole range of opportunities is presented to members of both sexes without assumptions as to what is suitable for either sex; iii) What alterations could be made to the structure of education to keep career options open for as long as possible'.
38   Victorian Committee on Equal Opportunity in Victorian Schools, *Report to the Premier*, v.

Girls, School and Society, the authors of the Victorian report emphasised the need for pupils to recognise the importance of making informed choices, and that their education, career and personal happiness were not to be constrained by any sex-specific characteristics:

> It is important for children to understand that the full range of human characteristics and abilities is present in each sex and that it is the aptitudes or feelings of each individual which are important.[39]

The opposition between 'human' and sex-specific qualities was a common theme in the equal opportunity literature, with the final promise one of escape from the impediments afforded by sexual difference. The reference to 'human' invokes an ideal of androgynous, class-free, culturally anonymous personhood, constituted by the full complement of human potentialities. And 'human' also denotes the sum of masculine and feminine attributes and roles—as if they too could be distributed equally and fairly across the population. '[E]ducation should be about human rather than sex-specific development', argued the authors of *Girls, School and Society*. 'There should be no distinction made between girls and boys in school curriculum or organisation, nor any sex-related expectations about behaviour, interests, capacities, personality traits or life patterns.'[40] Erasing the evidence and expectations of difference was, then, a central feature of these reforms. Pupils, and especially girls, were to be freed from the burdens of their confining sex roles and transported to a realm where they could simply blossom and emerge as asexually 'human'.[41] Traditional sex roles were, in this somewhat confusing ontological hierarchy, inferior to the abstract ideal of 'humanness'. The dreams of feminist reformers in education were to create gender freedom and an androgynous subject whose identity was social and therefore not indelibly fixed by tradition or by nature.

---

39   Ibid., vi.
40   Commonwealth Schools Commission, *Girls, School and Society*, 158 [14.7(a)].
41   Lesley Johnson argued that much work at that time on the education of girls located gender as a burden for women but not for men, and that one of the aims of reforms was to free girls from their gender in order for their individuality to emerge. Lesley Johnson, 'On Becoming an Individual: A Reassessement of the Issue of Gender and Schooling', *Discourse* 8, no. 2 (1988): 97–109.

Practical politics in the classroom

'I would encourage you to examine seriously your own teaching and the operation of your school for sexist implications', advised the Victorian Director-General of Education in 1980. He reminded teachers that '[b]ecoming aware of the subtle ways in which ... prejudice [based on a person's sex] is perpetrated requires individual commitment':

> As educationists, we are concerned that girls and boys develop their potential to the full. We must take some care that we are not blinkered by sex-role stereotypes or expectations, so that we direct boys and girls differently, irrespective of the talents they have. We all know about self-fulfilling prophesies![42]

The exhortations to perpetual vigilance are somewhat tempered by the avuncular tone, hailing everyone as potentially susceptible to a kind of ethical carelessness. The responsibility, nevertheless, lay with teachers and their willingness to reform their own attitudes and habitual practices. This required the development of techniques for interrogating personal beliefs, and this was a central part of feminist strategies. Values, attitudes and hidden, secret and unconscious desires—of both teachers and students—all became the object of scrutiny and target of reform. Non-sexist curriculum programs, teachers' in-service and professional development texts and policies invoked the ideal of a self-governing student and teacher, one able to be freed from prior personal and social identities and remade into a non-sexist self, unimpeded by sexual difference and sexist attitudes. This remaking of the self, however, could only happen through an endless and vigilant process of self-regulation. Consequently, teachers were to interrupt the socialisation process and no longer to base their actions 'on unexamined assumptions about sex differences'. To continue to do so, advised a national report and two Victorian Directors-General of Education, would be to 'limit the freedom of both boys and girls' and to be 'acting against sex equality'.[43]

---

42 L. W. Shears to School Principals, memorandum, 9 May 1980, Office of the Director-General of Education, 'Towards Non-Sexist Education'.
43 Commonwealth Schools Commission, *Girls, School and Society*, 17 [2.29]; reprinted in L. W. Shears to School Principals, memorandum; reprinted in N. G. Curry to School Principals, memorandum, 14 February 1983, Office of the Victorian Director-General of Education.

The ideal feminist teacher was to become an exemplar, in terms of both the ethical beliefs she held and in the way in which she exposed herself to self-examination. Numerous checklists were circulated during this time with advice on establishing a non-sexist classroom or questions to give teachers a sexist or non-sexist rating. Committed teachers were to ask themselves such questions as: 'Have you told a boy "Big boys don't cry"'?, 'Do you expect girls to do as well in spelling, reading, language arts and boys to excel in science, mechanical skills and mathematics?' 'Do you usually analyze material to see if female characters are represented in a non-stereotyped manner?'[44] The correct answers were, of course, well-known. Boys do have feelings and girls can be tough and mechanically minded. Like confessional exercises, the purpose lay not in the discovery of new answers, but in the attendant processes of self-reflection and the ritualistic knowing of the right answers. The difficulty was in translating this knowledge into everyday teaching practices. In this task, 'The most important "teaching method" is the teacher's attitude', exhorted one guide for non-sexist teaching. 'The support, encouragement and education of teachers who are prepared to question their own conditioning and classroom practice must be the first priority of the programme.'[45] Such weighty responsibilities called for the exercising of considerable self-regulation, adding to an already extensive catalogue of appropriate professional protocols.

- Yourself as a role model: as a person not bound by stereotypes, and with no guilt about this; as a person who cares for people, is assertive, supportive, respectful, strong, considerate, sharing and listening …

- Be aware of the behaviours you are reinforcing by your attitudes, actions and words …

- As teachers we must be seen by children as performing a wide variety of roles …

---

44   From a 'Checklist for Teachers' distributed in the late 1970s and early 1980s by the Equal Opportunity Resource Centre to interested teachers and to schools on in-service days. Checklist reproduced from the work of Dr M. Sadker, College of Science and Society, University of Wisconsin. For other examples of such checklists, see 'How sexist are you?', extract from 'Sexism in the Primary School', produced by the Three Union Elimination of Sexism Project, *Ms. Muffet*, no. 15 (June 1982): 3; 'Non-Sexist Teaching: Some Practical Hints', originally produced by the Women's Adviser to the South Australian Institute of Teachers, 1979, reproduced and amended by the New South Wales Teachers Federation [n.d. 1980?] and circulated by the Equal Opportunity Unit and Resource Centre in Victoria.
45   Anne Jones, Transition Education Girls' Project (Vic.) and Victoria Education Department Equal Opportunity Unit, *A Lucky Dip of Resources and Ideas for Non-Sexist Education* (Melbourne: The Project, 1982), 4.

- Send up sexism: point out how absurd it is. Laughter with a serious intent …
- Value everyone's ideas equally …
- Don't introduce counter sexism in a contrived, artificial way. Make it as natural and as close to the child's experience as possible …
- [C]onstantly monitor yourself for impartiality and the unconscious reactions which are the result of your own conditioning. (e.g. the feeling that 'girls are good at reading, boys are good at maths') …
- Encourage children to reflect on and analyse their own behaviour; to ask 'what's happening?' 'why?' 'what worked?' 'what alternative ways are there of doing/saying things?'[46]

This is a revealing list of professional demands, making clear the extent to which teachers had to scrutinise themselves, and to position themselves as non-sexist, moral exemplars. In many ways, they were impossible demands, asking teachers to have a self-awareness and reflexivity that transcended cultural norms. They were also contradictory: sexism was seen as everywhere, but somehow teachers were to make counter-sexism 'as natural and as close to the child's experience as possible'. Teaching thus explicitly required teachers to make endless ethical decisions about what was or was not appropriate conduct, and to display an ability to bring pupils also to see the need for such judgements. In this way, the teacher was to regard herself as a prototypical new person, at all times conscious of the gaze of others, and scrupulously embodying the desired attributes of non-sexist, non-stereotypical people. Teaching in a non-sexist manner was about instituting equal and fairer educational practices leading to improved outcomes for girls. It also involved a journey of self-discovery and empowerment for the female teacher.

'Be reasonable, be rational', advised feminist educators:

- Operate a non-sexist classroom; this will generate support for non-sexist ideas.
- Explain the concept of sexism. Have students question the relevance of the concept to their own lives and those of people they know.

---

46   Helen Menzies, *Non-Sexist Teaching: Some Practical Hints* (Adelaide: South Australian Institute of Teachers, 1979), 6–8.

- Have a child-centred approach to learning: group work, and the teacher as a non-authoritarian figure.
- Help break down rigid thinking by techniques like brainstorming and lateral thinking.[47]

In contradicting pupils' everyday (sexist) perceptions, the teacher was to call into question the validity of these perceptions and, at the same time, to affirm the pupils—and especially girl pupils—as 'real learners'. Most of this reforming work was directed at changing girls' attitudes and aspirations: the problem was girls' reluctance to be, for example, assertive or leaders or to follow non-traditional paths. There was, though, at this stage, little acknowledgement that such an orientation devalued and exposed as irrational the existing beliefs and behaviours of girls and young women. It was not, however, that girls were being expected simply to become like boys, but that femininity, being a girl, continued to be positioned as problematic, and as at odds with rationality. There was little regard here of the deep emotional investment children (and teachers) might have had in the personal identities and social relations formed by 'sexist values'. Having identified the systematic operation of sexism, there was little consideration of the reasons for any reluctance and difficulty involved in relinquishing these formative beliefs. Pupils were to be led to adopt the same kind of processes of self-reflection and monitoring that the ideal teacher practised. The teacher thus became a role model from whom students learnt not only certain non-sexist curriculum content, but also appropriate habits and dispositions.

The assessment of sex-role stereotypes held by students, especially in relation to career choice, often provided a focus for feminist work in the classroom. Testing before and after counter-sexist interventions demonstrated the pervasiveness of sexism as well as the possibilities for making some personal changes within the classroom.[48] Many of these assessments focused on students identifying occupations, styles of activity, attitudes and so on, according to whether they believed them to be sex-specific. Commonly, pupils would be asked to classify a list of occupations as male or female or as able to be performed by both sexes. There were few surprises in the results. From the following list of occupations, 'hairdresser, doctor, dentist, teacher, T.V. repair, watchmaker, truck driver,

---

47 Ibid., 15, 7.
48 Education Department of South Australia, *Careers and Girls Project Report: Intervention in Sex Role Stereotyping* (Adelaide: Education Department of South Australia, 1978), 1–22.

building houses, nurse, typist, prep teacher, cook, butcher, factory worker, judge', it is not difficult to imagine the occupations likely to be identified as male or female.[49] Yet the purpose of the lesson was to encourage pupils to reveal their true beliefs and observations, and then, through a process of rational examination, point out their folly and the unacknowledged sexism of their understandings.

There were numerous variations on this type of lesson—identifying characteristics that embody and reproduced gender binarisms, emotion/ reason, caring/detachment, etc.—but the common theme was to encourage students to question their taken-for-granted assumptions about sex roles and to revise these values in the light of new, non-sexist information. Their perceptions of sex roles and of their own sexed identity were expected to be transformed by the acquisition of this new knowledge. Unfettered by irrational beliefs and expectations, boys and girls were to discover that:

> [A] successful *person* probably lies between the two stereotypes— for example a person who is independent and supportive, and a person who is brave and kind will probably be more successful in any job and in life than either the tough dominant aggressive male or the passive dependent emotional female.[50]

We have here the ideal of the person constituted by the full complement of human characteristics, a person able to transcend sexual difference by embodying all the qualities once differentially allocated to the sexes. This was the ideal identity to which all students were intended to aspire and to which good non-sexist teaching would lead. In seeking to question the validity of sex stereotypes, however, such curriculum programs (paradoxically) can be seen now to entrench impoverished possibilities for expressions of femininity and masculinity. The female sex role becomes equated with a pathological inadequacy and the male is characterised by a surfeit of energy, repeating those familiar themes of lack and virility. The alternative to this dichotomy was to disavow sexual specificity and to embrace an ideal of equality in which such debilitating differences were erased. This resolution can be seen as representing a kind of fantasy of harmonious completeness, of a balance between male and female.

---

49   Ibid., Appendix 4, 1.
50   Curriculum Development Centre, *SENSE: Studies to Encourage Non-Sexist Education* (Canberra: Curriculum Development Centre, 1981), 20.

This fantasy represented not only a desire to overcome women's lack. It also represented a desire to have a more complete (because less repressed and one-dimensional) masculinity.

Pedagogical practices, such as these aptly named values-clarification exercises, or role playing, focused on techniques that privileged processes of self-reflection and self-monitoring. As a pedagogical technique, role-playing was said to encourage pupils to 'be other than they are—both positively and negatively',[51] but it also, perhaps paradoxically, encouraged them to perform roles in tightly sanctioned and normative ways. That is, while the emphasis was on the freedom to engage and learn through 'experimental behaviour', the range of acceptable behaviours and responses was quite circumscribed.[52] One was either explicitly sexist or non-sexist. In one set of lesson guidelines, for instance, the personnel manager is to be presented as an old-fashioned adherent to silly old stereotypes, and in the next game he is to be played out as the new, rational, open-minded, non-sexist manager (the personnel manager remains a man!).[53] After these sorts of exercises, students are to reflect on the issues raised and the 'participants [are to] tell the class about their feelings in the two roles'.[54] Through the experience of 'being' someone else, students were expected to have gained a keener insight into the complexity of an imagined issue, and to have developed a more reflexive attitude about their own sex-role behaviour. From acting out being 'other than they are', students are to learn new ways of becoming in their everyday lives. And, of course, these new ways are intended to involve giving up the familiar sexist ways and embracing a fantasised new self. Here girls would be empowered to be non-traditional, would have a greater sense of their options in life, and boys would be able to experience a wider range of emotional responses and realise that they too had, say, domestic responsibilities.

The securing of this fantasy and of new forms of gender identity, however, required vigilance by self-governing individuals, pupils and teachers alike, who, through the effects of the sorts of pedagogical techniques I have been discussing, learnt new ways of knowing and reforming themselves.

---

51 Ibid., 12.
52 Ibid.
53 Ibid., 52–55.
54 Ibid., 51.

The ungendered self and freedom

I have been discussing some of the ways in which feminism entered the classroom and was constituted as a pedagogical imperative. Carolyn Steedman and others have pointed to the ways in which women teachers, and especially primary school teachers, have been persuaded to occupy the position of mother, so that the classroom replicated a kind of maternal and nurturant space.[55] The feminist classroom of the 1970s was still to provide a therapeutic space for students to realise their inner potential and to be guided in their discoveries. But it was also to become more like a social laboratory in which emotions were tested, responses assessed and behaviours modified. Careful self-reflection, it seemed, was the only way to counter the possible eruption of deeply, if reluctantly, held beliefs and the only way to limit the risk of unconscious desires, unreconstructed sexist values, entering the field of the rationally ordered classroom. Non-sexist behaviour was equated with clear-headedness and counterposed to the irrationality of traditional and everyday beliefs.

The classroom became a kind of antidote to social wrongs as well as a microcosm of those practices, a small world where pupils could rebuild identities and attitudes in a controlled and safe environment. It was not, despite the progressive and child-centred rhetoric of the day, simply a space where pupils could freely express their attitudes in a relaxed atmosphere. These non-sexist reforms had definite and precise strategies that suggested a quasi-scientific resolution to the problem of undesirable thoughts.[56] This resolution also revealed the psychosocial heritage of feminism's then foundational ideas—the sex role, socialisation—about personal formation and transformation.

Feminist reformers dreamt of creating new persons, and I have documented here some of the ways in which these ideals and norms were produced by and in pedagogical techniques. On the one hand, these can be usefully understood in Foucauldian terms as 'technologies of the self' and, following Nikolas Rose, seen as techniques that were engaged in practical,

---

55   Carolyn Steedman, '"The Mother Made Conscious": The Historical Development of a Primary School Pedagogy', *History Workshop Journal* 20, no. 1 (1985): 149–63, doi.org/10.1093/hwj/20.1.149; Jennifer Laurence, 'Re-membering that Special Someone: On the Question of Articulating a Genuine Feminine Presence in the Classroom', *History of Education Review* 20, no. 2 (1991): 53–65.
56   Valerie Walkerdine, 'Progressive Pedagogy and Political Struggle', in *Feminisms and Critical Pedagogy*, ed. C. Luke and J. Gore (New York: Routledge, 1992), 15–24.

pedagogical and everyday ways to organise and govern the self.[57] On the other hand, however useful this approach might be, it nevertheless tends to eviscerate the animating optimism of the time and to step back from the urgent sense of a new political project, regardless of how mistaken or overblown that might now appear.

Levitas's framework for understanding practices infused by utopian aspirations offers an alternative angle, but one that I regard as generating crucial and complementary insights into grasping the contradictory and pragmatic imbrication of transformative agendas within technical and bureaucratic apparatuses. Feminist agendas were also in keeping with wider calls for democratic education and de-schooling in which freedom similarly figured as an organising trope for policymakers and activist educators alike. Openness was the catch-cry of the day but it always referred to more than a type of classroom space. It was a gesture to open-mindedness, to freeing the mind of old habits and ways of being a teacher and student, and it was a metaphor for more open, egalitarian social relations. There was a growing sense of schools breaking with tradition, and of instituting new practices that would allow the flourishing of new types of (non-sexist) children and young people that also heralded transformations in social relations.

Conclusion

In this chapter, I have examined some of the ways in which the daily work of teachers contributed to realising the hopes and strategies of second-wave feminism. In doing so, I have argued that the work of schooling was crucial to feminist cultural and political projects, even if it has had a minor place in subsequent historical accounts of the reach of 1970s feminism. This speaks to a broader question regarding how the history of second-wave feminism and education is remembered within and across different fields of activism, practice and scholarship. Among educational researchers and practitioners there are arguably three common representations of second-wave feminism and schooling. The first is that it serves as a kind of anchor or beginning point in a progressive narrative about policy movements to reform the education of girls. The second is that the 1970s was a time of important and relatively successful reform but one based

---

57 Nikolas Rose, *Governing the Soul: The Shaping of the Private Self* (London: Routledge, 1990), 218.

upon theories and concepts—the sex role, socialisation—which we now understand to be 'superficial', 'problematic', 'mistaken' and so forth. The third is that feminist reforms have waxed and waned, sometimes reflecting generational dynamics and sometimes changing preoccupations in feminist theory; from the radical social constructionism of the sex role, to a celebration of sexual difference and girls' (women's) ways of knowing in the 1980s, then to poststructural attention to the discursive construction of gender succeeded by a 'backlash' encapsulated in the 'what about the boys?' questions matched with declining policy urgency for gender equity, to a more recent resurgence of feminist activism and reforms galvanized by issues of sexual harassment and gender-based violence, sexuality and the experiences of LGBTIQ lives.[58]

Clare Hemmings's analysis of the 'political grammar feminist theory' seeks to 'identify the techniques through which dominant stories are secured, through which their status as "common sense" is reproduced' and in doing so to 'offer a rigorous point of intervention through which Western feminist stories might be transformed'.[59] She characterises the repeating tropes in histories of feminist theory as structured according to narratives of progress, loss and return.[60] The 'progress' narrative tells a story of the move from essentialism to difference, of a shift away from thinking of the unified subject of feminism to a celebration of difference and diversity, evident in the rise of identity politics and epistemologies and methodologies framed as postmodern. The 'loss' narrative depicts the end of the feminist political project, fragmented by the postmodern proliferation of difference, uncertainty and abstraction. It signals the loss of the radical political promise of feminism and a turning away from naming and reforming inequalities. The 'return' narrative represents an acknowledgement that feminism might have lost its way, but a new

---

58 Julie McLeod, 'The Administration of Feminism in Education: Revisiting and Remembering Narratives of Gender Equity and Identity', *Journal of Educational Administration and History* 49, no. 4 (2017): 283–300, doi.org/10.1080/00220620.2017.1343289; Susanne Gannon, 'Kairos and the Time of Gender Equity Policy in Australian Schooling', *Gender and Education* 28, no. 3 (15 April 2016): 330–42; Debbie Ollis and Lyn Harrison, 'Lessons in Building Capacity in Sexuality Education Using the Health Promoting School Framework: From Planning to Implementation', *Health Education* 116, no. 2 (2016): 138–53, doi.org/10.1108/HE-08-2014-0084; Vanita Sundaram and Helen Sauntson, eds, *Global Perspectives and Key Debates in Sex and Relationships Education: Addressing Issues of Gender, Sexuality, Plurality and Power* (London: Palgrave Macmillan UK, 2016).
59 Clare Hemmings, *Why Stories Matter: The Political Grammar of Feminist Theory* (Durham, NC: Duke University Press, 2011), 20.
60 Ibid., 132.

path forward is identified that offers of kind of resolution, a compromise that sees elements combined from the 'difference' turn and a return to questions about the body and social-structural relations.

In many respects, Hemmings's account is a remarkably introspective one—feminist theorist examining the tics and nuances of high feminist theory, plotting tropes and typologies in a very particular meaning system. Yet, it nevertheless alerts us to the rhetorical patterns and emotional investments of (generational) memory that can structure how feminism is told and why that matters in the present. As such, it offers a route into understanding the rise and fall narratives that can beset histories of radical reform, including feminism, in education. In part the generational dynamics that structure histories of feminist theory also resonate with the movement of feminism in education.[61] This is not to suggest, however, that second-wave feminism in schools simply mirrored a kind of 'real' or 'mainstream' feminism happening elsewhere. The experience and practices of feminism in schools also speak back to broader histories of feminism— be they social, cultural, intellectual—and to histories of radical and alternative education, not simply as niche activities, but as fundamental to the embodied work of feminist and progressive movements. I have shown some of the ways in which the politics of the personal was also pedagogical, and how second-wave ambitions in education traversed the utopian and the bureaucratic, the practical, the technical and the aspirational. In doing so, the work of feminism in schools did not simply reflect the mood of the times, but was instrumental in creating and sustaining that time of reform through everyday practices in classrooms that were materially forming the next generation and helping to make possible the very changes and legacies to which feminism lays claim.

---

61 McLeod, 'The Administration of Feminism in Education', 283–300.

CHAPTER 4

Making the political personal: Gender and sustainable lifestyles in 1970s Australia

Carroll Pursell

By 1973 two periodicals, *Earth Garden* and *Grass Roots*, were addressing an imagined community of Australians who were seeking to establish 'sustainable' lifestyles, in what seemed to many to be an increasingly commodified world, by moving 'back to the land'. These two journals offered their readers encouragement and practical advice on ways to adopt systems of food and energy production, shelter and entertainment that were small scale, locally made and simple to understand and use. The gender implications that went with these systems were seldom articulated but were nonetheless ubiquitous and powerful.

The urge to go 'back to the land' was not limited to Australia nor to the decade of the 1970s; rather it was a transnational movement with roots deep into the Romantic movement and resistance to the Industrial Revolution. Industrialisation overwhelmingly drove people off the land and into rapidly growing urban areas, but the ideal of rural virtue continued and by the mid-twentieth century had shaped the back-to-the-land movement that flourished in the post–World War Two era.

In the United States, Helen and Scott Nearing left New York City in 1932 and took up an abandoned farm in Vermont seeking, as they wrote, 'a simple, satisfying life on the land, to be devoted to mutual aid and harmlessness, with an ample margin of leisure in which to do personally constructive and creative work'. Years later, they described their objectives as economic, hygienic and both social and ethical.[1] Their 1954 book *Living the Good Life: How to Live Sanely and Simply in a Troubled World* was republished in 1970 and became something of a Bible to Americans seeking to follow their example.

In the United Kingdom, Sally and John Seymour played a somewhat similar role, setting up a farm on rented land in Suffolk and famously driving a horse cart rather than a car. Their 1973 book titled *Farming and Self-Sufficiency: Independence on a 5-acre Farm* sold strongly and their farm, like that of the Nearings, attracted numerous casual visitors seeking guidance and encouragement. One of the Seymour's children later recalled that 'one woman turned up who had left her husband and children after reading the book. She wanted to help out and live in our stable. My parents let her but later my mother persuaded her to go back and sort herself out'.[2]

There does not appear to have been any such dominant figures, or defining books, in Australia during this period, but two new magazines appeared to champion both back-to-the-land and self-sufficiency. Both followed the lead of the American journal *Mother Earth News*, started by John and Jane Shuttleworth in 1970 with a budget of $1,500 and published from their home. It has been described as embracing 'the revived interest in the back-to-the-land movement at the beginning of the 1970s', concentrating on 'do-it-yourself and how-to articles'.[3] When the magazine accepted an article by the Australian Keith Vincent Smith, he reported that the success gave him and his wife Irene 'the ambition to produce EARTH GARDEN', a journal 'concerned with the back-to-the-land movement, surviving in the city, living in the country, organic gardening, food and diet, living more with less, and the inner changes which follow when you are in tune with Nature'.

Keith had been a journalist and Irene a schoolteacher living in Sydney. They had thought about living in the country and finally decided, as they said, to leave their jobs, get married, buy a Morris van and take a trip 'right around Australia'. It was when they reached Melbourne that they

---

1   Helen and Scott Nearing, *Living the Good Life: How to Live Sanely and Simply in a Troubled World* (New York: Schockten, 1970 [1954]), vii.
2   Clare Bates, 'What Happened to the Self-Sufficient People of the 1970s?', *BBC Magazine*, 12 April 2016, accessed January 2019, www.bbc.com/news/magazine-35945417.
3   '*Mother Earth News*', Wikipedia, accessed January 2019, en.wikipedia.org/wiki/Mother_Earth_News.

learned that *Mother Earth News* had accepted Keith's manuscript, and it was there that their trip ended and they learned 'the intricacies of putting together a Web offset publication'. They got out their first issue of *Earth Garden* in 1972 with articles on a kibbutz, on a Chinese commune, one on encouraging earthworms, and one on Chinese cooking, among other topics.[4] They travelled widely across the country interviewing people who had made the move to the land, but according to one critic they tended to 'hide the harsh, unpleasant, drudgery side of rural life'.[5]

The following year David and Meg Miller introduced their new magazine *Grass Roots*, which they called 'the only complete subsistence course in Australia'. The editors wrote that 'today everyone is looking for an alternative to the life that big business forces on us' but, they added, 'when we first moved out of the city there was no-one to show the way and help us through our many mistakes'.[6] Over the next few issues, articles, many of them unsigned, covered 'Ropes and Stuff', 'It's Fun to Dye', 'You Don't Buy a Flute', 'Homespun Slippers', 'How to Shoe a Horse', 'Mud and Mud Bricks' and various aspects of solar power. The same analyst who criticised *Earth Garden* maintained that *Grass Roots* was more practical and realistic, perhaps because the editors were themselves trying to create 'a community in the bush'.[7]

Both magazines sought their audiences among the estimated 60,000 Australians who were 'alternative lifestyle participants' and 95,000 others who intended to become such. The differences in content and readership of the two magazines, however, was striking. Comparisons made in the 1980s found that while *Earth Garden* had a readership that was 68 per cent male, the comparable figure for *Grass Roots* was only 51 per cent. At the same time, 42 per cent of the content of *Grass Roots* was written by women and only 28 per cent by men (the other 30 per cent were not identified). The letters to the editor, a critical part of the content, were twice as often sent in by women as by men. While in all alternative lifestyle magazines 'nuclear family values are generally assumed and rarely are more radical family structures discussed', this was particularly true of *Grass Roots*. It was noted that the magazine did not 'devote much attention to feminist issues'

---

4   *Earth Garden*, no. 1 (1972): 42, 3.
5   Peter H. Cock, 'Australia's Alternative Media', *Media Information Australia*, no. 6 (1977): 7.
6   'Reading Between the Lines', *Grass Roots*, no. 1 (April–June 1973): 2.
7   Cock, 'Australia's Alternative Media': 8.

because 'it has developed a section of the market in Australia that is not feminist'. Feminism was 'not a typical theme of alternative lifestyles and is [a] subject rarely discussed by any journal'.[8]

While the gender implications of changing lifestyles were seldom referred to, and even less often analysed, both *Grass Roots* and *Earth Garden* published articles in which back-to-the-landers described their experiences and both carried letters to the editors. Many of these are suggestive of the kinds of people to make the move to the country, their reasons for the move, and what they encountered there. It is also from these that attitudes toward gender relations, and by implication feminism in general, can be discovered.

Eleanor, who lived 'as self-sufficiently as possible on ten acres of land in a pretty bush setting' with her husband and five children, described a fairly traditional division of labour. She reported that they rose at 6.30am and 'while my husband is milking the cow, I cut him a substantial lunch, fill a thermos with tea and prepare his breakfast'. He had a job off the farm because, as Eleanor explained, 'money being a necessary evil, we must have an outside income, and whereas I enjoy being on my own, my husband needs company so his work has a three-fold purpose'. For the gardening, she wrote, 'my husband and I have a system, which works well ... He does all the digging and preparing of beds and I take over from there'. Finally, she admits that 'my husband proves most helpful in our efficiency program as he is handy with most jobs'.[9]

A similar story was told by Walter Abetz, who was a radio technician for the Tasmanian Hydro Electric Commission. He and his family had migrated from Stuttgart, Germany, in 1961, and had been most recently living in a new subdivision close to Hobart. It was his dream, however, to have 100 or 200 acres of bush upon which he could not only live but roam. When he proposed such a move, 'Mum started grinning. She asked "who would take the children to school and Uni and so on. I mumbled something like Won't have time, that's Mum's business, better get your driving license"'. One of the children mentioned the need to also get to 'our youth activities at church', and Mum 'said loud and clearly: "I've told you already I'm too old to get a licence. Forget about that"'.

---

8   Frank Vanclay and Bill Metcalf, 'Alternative Lifestyle Magazines: An Analysis of Readers', *Media Information Australia*, no. 36 (1985): 49, 50; Bill Metcalf and Frank Vanclay, 'Alternative Lifestyle Magazines: What's in Them', *Media Information Australia*, no. 33 (August 1984): 51, 52.
9   Eleanor Hatswell, 'Living Self Sufficiently—Country Style', *Grass Roots*, no. 16 (Spring–Summer 1978): 48–49.

They moved instead to a 9-acre property closer to the city, bought a cow and began to farm on a small scale. Each had their special chores, with the youngest child, 15-year-old Eric (in 2017 a federal senator from Tasmania), looking after a dozen geese, two dozen ducks and the care of an Anglo-Nubian billy buck as well as his apparent favourite, 'a neutered buck called Amos'. And then, Walter wrote, 'there is the most important person—Mum … who runs the whole show. I mean it … She is flat out during the week, and only Sunday, which we observe, is her rest day'.[10]

Letters to the editors were numerous, briefer and more varied. A few were from single men, such as Neal who described himself as:

> … a 19-year-old nature conscious city dweller wishing to seek board on a farm in the New England district. I am poor and cannot afford to buy land, so am asking around about work in return for rent. I know quite a bit about farming as I went to Agriculture School, but I have not been able to put this knowledge into practice. I have my own goats and a hive of bees. I am desperate to get out of Sydney.[11]

Mike, who already had a farm, wrote that he was '29 years old and seeking a lady interested in farming and self-sufficiency and also another couple to share the land on a profit sharing basis'.[12]

Women comprised a larger group of letter writers. Jennie, who was a member of Truth and Liberation Concern (a Christian community in Victoria), wrote that 'with three small children under four I do very little apart from necessities but hope some time to be producing more than children'.[13] Gudrun wrote:

> I am a deserted wife with a 16-month-old boy and have lived in Cairns and the Sri Aurobindo Ashram and Auroville at Pondicherry in India. I am prepared to go into the country again if there is the possibility of either joining a group with similar interests or otherwise forming a new group.[14]

---

10 Walter Abetz, 'Just Nine Acres', *Earth Garden*, no. 5 (1973): 10–11.
11 *Earth Garden*, no. 20 (October–December 1977): 54.
12 *Grass Roots*, no. 16 (Spring–Summer 1978): 5.
13 *Grass Roots*, no. 16 (Spring–Summer 1978): 4.
14 *Earth Garden*, no. 7 (December 1973): 4.

Leslie and Debbie wrote that 'we are two "fresh out of school" chickees, and were wondering if you knew of any places where fruit-pickers-farmhands are needed (we will work at anything so long as it is out of the city). We are in dire need of money so we can keep our dream of getting our own farm alive'.[15] Donna explained, 'I am a reader of *Earth Garden* and would love to know anybody in the Geelong–Ballarat area willing to take me on to help on the farm. I would work for a very small wage, or food and shelter. Please write soon, I'm dying to get away'.[16]

Margo explained that 'I'm looking for a community, living naturally, I don't care where, who would let me learn in return for whatever I can do for them. Can anyone help me out of the unhappy city? I'm 18 and know nearly nothing about living self-sufficiently, but I really want to know, because if it's natural, it's got to be right'.[17] Linda said:

> I am a vegetarian girl, 21, and I left my home in the U.S.A. three years ago to find a simpler way of existence. I've been travelling through New Zealand and Australia; working, learning from people, experiencing their lifestyles and growing. Now I am looking for a place to live in the way I love most … I can milk cows, weed gardens and, on a good day, even hammer a nail straight.[18]

Jane said she was 'a mother with two small children (was brought up on organically run small-holdings in England) and I'm looking for other people (with children?) to join me in buying land'.[19] Wendy announced, 'I am an honest, clean, happy female, with three school-aged children. I have savings and a weekly income from a pension and would very much like to share a co-op, preferably in WA'.[20]

Heterosexual couples were numerous among the writers of letters to the editors. Muriel and Malcom explained that 'after a six month working holiday in UK with our four children, we came back to Australia even more determined to realise our long cherished ambition to live more naturally and to try to be as self-sufficient as possible'.[21] Paul and Janet

---

15   *Earth Garden*, no. 3 (1972): 57.
16   *Earth Garden*, no. 22/23 (June–August 1978): 139.
17   *Earth Garden*, no. 21 (January–March 1978): 26.
18   *Earth Garden*, no 25 (Summer 1978/79): 276.
19   *Earth Garden*, no. 13 (November 1975): 51.
20   *Earth Garden*, no. 18 (April–June 1977): 29.
21   *Earth Garden*, no. 9 (June 1974): 55.

declared themselves 'a young Christian couple with two boys ... [who] desire to join a community who praise Our Lord Jesus Christ anywhere near the coast of Australia'.[22] Bill and Vanessa were 'two teachers from East Gippsland, Victoria, who want to start a self-sufficient farming community'. Also they were 'vegetarians and study Yoga and meditation under the guidance of Self Realization Fellowship'.[23] John and Ailene wrote that they were 'an American couple with a two year old girl who are interested in emigration to Australia and also in the idea of a back-to-the-land community. We have no farming skills, but would be willing to learn. My husband is an ex-international ping-pong star, and is presently writing a book'.[24]

A fourth category of writers was composed of groups already formed or planning to do so. Brian and Jan announced that they were 'buying 200–300 acres on the north west of N.S.W. and wish to contact children whose parents are interested in self-sufficiency and progressive education. The aim would be to have our own dwelling in a community and form our own school and craft workshop'.[25] Jack and Shirley announced that their 'vegetarian land co-op [was] urgently seeking new members, particularly people with young kids, with a real interest in alternative forms of education. We've got 100 acres in southern NSW'.[26]

In 1975, *Earth Garden* carried a notice:

> Amazon Acres is a Women's farm, 280 miles north of Sydney ... It is a place where women can realize their full potential and grow ... We haven't finished paying the farm off yet and we would like new women to join the collective. We'd love to hear from women with skills—especially technical and building—but any skill at all will be useful.

---

22 *Earth Garden*, no. 25 (Summer 1978/79): 276.
23 *Earth Garden*, no. 7 (December 1973): 4.
24 *Grass Roots*, no. 16 (Spring–Summer 1978): 5.
25 *Grass Roots*, no 16 (Spring–Summer 1978): 4.
26 *Earth Garden*, no. 22/23 (June–August 1978): 139.

Amazon Acres was, from its establishment, a major lesbian gathering place.[27] Three years later a notice appeared:

> three or four of us wish to form a collective to set up a Resource Centre for Women to gain survival skills, herbs, massage etc. Living on Supporting Mother Pension means we are able to move out if we can set up a network to do so autonomously. Also we're interested in alternative schooling. The land needs to be within reasonable access to a station, three or four hours from Sydney or a large town. If you welcome new energies on your land, please contact us. Interested in buying a share of communal land and hearing from other interested women.[28]

The personal situations and aspirations described by most of these letters to the editors are powerfully redolent of gender structures at work, but drew no comment until 1976 when the ninth issue of *Grass Roots* carried a call for a combined conference/festival titled Alternative Australia, to be convened by Gough Whitlam's Deputy Prime Minister, Dr Jim Cairns. Citing the need for 'radical change in contemporary, industrial society', he called for 'presentations by alternative groups interested in community living, organic foods, herbs, personal growth and other alternative activities', as well as 'the needs of workers, students, ethnic communities, feminists and sexual reformers'.[29] The Confest, held during December along the banks of the Cotter River just outside Canberra, was considered a great success with perhaps as many as 15,000 people attending. Workshops were held on a wide range of subjects, and *Grass Roots* reported that there were people sitting 'quietly under pyramids and people dancing in concentric circles and people making children's toys out of grass and people learning to juggle three oranges without dropping more than two and people being massaged' and people 'discussing alternative rural communities'.[30] The event was also covered by the *Canberra Times*, but no mention was made of any discussions of feminism or other women's issues.

---

27   *Earth Garden*, no. 12 (July 1975): 19. See also Sand Hall, ed., *Amazon Acres, You Beauty: Stories of Women's Lands, Australia* (Wollongong: Shell Publishing, 2016); and Rebecca Jennings, 'Creating Feminist Culture: Australian Rural Lesbian-Separatist Communities in the 1970s and 1980s', *Journal of Women's History* 30, no. 2 (2018): 88–111, doi.org/10.1353/jowh.2018.0015. See also Judith Ion, 'Degrees of Separation: Lesbian Separitists Communities in Northern New South Wales, 1974–95', *Sex in Public: Australian Sexual Cultures*, ed. Jill Julius Matthews (St Leonards: Allen & Unwin, 1997), 97–113.
28   *Earth Garden*, no. 24 (September–November 1978): 56.
29   *Grass Roots*, no. 9 (1977): 40.
30   Bob Willis, 'Down to Earth at Cotter', *Grass Roots*, no. 10 (1977): 12.

The next year the second Confest was held at Bredbo, not far from the Cotter. Friends of the Earth erected a large marquee, which was the site for workshops, 'many of which were on alternative technology'. There was also a 'mud brick baking machine and an attempt to build a mudbrick house'.[31] This time the *Canberra Times* reporter, besides being impressed with the 'beautiful women with no clothes on', discovered a 'feminist tent, and outside it was a sign that assured us that "Lesbians are everywhere"'.[32]

Earth Garden first explicitly took notice of gender issues that same year. No. 20 carried a request from a male student from Tasmania:

> I do hope you can help me. In doing a major in psychology I have become interest in the stress factor in marriage (and any other permanent relationship) and also in the family unit itself. In particular, I am attempting to evaluate the effects of alternative lifestyles (those which are supposedly set aside from the stress of 'ordinary' society) on the marriage relationship and the family as a unit.[33]

Response to this request was not recorded, but contrary to any expectations based on readership and content, it was *Grass Roots* that first produced what the editor called a 'woman-powered' issue. Previous issues had been the joint effort of both Irene and Keith Smith, with Keith doing the editing and some of the writing and Irene the design, layout and paste-up. For this issue, however, Irene, as she proudly wrote, 'ended up doing the lot'. She spent three months as she searched for material:

> I rang, interviewed and talked to many people. Stories began to arrive, which then needed reading, sorting and editing. Then came filling in the gaps and reading and writing more letters … The response from women has been fantastic … [There is,] most important of all, the feminist/women's view told through interviews, shared experiences and a listing of groups and contacts.[34]

---

31   Peter White, 'The Bredbo Confest', *Grass Roots*, no. 14 (Autumn 1978): 10.
32   *Canberra Times*, 27 December 1977.
33   *Earth Garden*, no. 20 (October–December 1977): 20.
34   *Earth Garden*, no. 21 (January–March 1978): 2.

Figure 4.1: Changing Roles.
Source: *Earth Garden*, no. 21 (January–March 1978): 34.

The responses covered a range of advice and admonition. One reader described what she called 'The Group', a circle of her friends who met once a week to offer each other support and do some 'consciousness raising'. The author expressed delight that another group had also started up and that 'a number of our husbands have joined together to form a "men's group"' as well. All the women in the group were professionals, such as teachers and social workers, but any relation they may have had to the back-to-the-land movement was not made clear.[35]

---

35 Sue Brown, 'The Group', *Earth Garden*, no. 21 (January–March 1978): 48–49.

Another author addressed back-to-the-land women more specifically. Describing 'Changing Roles', she warned that 'this is a little tirade about self-sufficiency-and-equality-and male/female-roles-and-facing-adventure-head-on'. She continued:

> unless she's careful, a woman can find herself living a sort of extension of city life, while her man has to change his lifestyle far more drastically, learning new skills, taking on responsibilities and possibly undertaking all those extra jobs that aren't even considered in a nice settled urban existence ... The typical mistakes of the beginner include an automatic job-division. Because she had most concern with cooking, cleaning and provisioning in the city, then these mostly became her province. In the changed circumstances, the jobs extend to include an interest in gardening, bottling, preserving, animal-tending, spinning and weaving, needlework, perhaps leatherwork, pursuits agricultural and, indeed, any others that can be seen as an extension of 'womanly pursuits'.

On the other hand:

> regardless of his previous experience, a man is expected and expects to be able to understand the intricacies of pumping and lighting systems. Nobody is surprised if he decides to become his own mechanic, or teach himself how to grade or plough with his brand-new tractor. Nobody raises their hands in amazement if he can handle a hammer, saw or axe—people expect it of him ... If **he** can start from scratch at new and unfamiliar things, why not **she**? Quite often it's because she shares the world-in-general's attitude that such things are outside the female province.[36]

Another author asserted that 'the question: *Who is responsible for filling the wood box?* has caused more domestic strife in country homes than any other single point of domestic contention ... The answer to the question,' she continued, 'should be *the cook*. Personally, I'd as soon let some sulky man brush my teeth for me as expect him to chop the wood that makes his meals. Only the person who is going to *use* the fire knows what sort of heat is required.' She then followed with a detailed description of what she called 'Axewomanship', laying out the types of wood and tools required to do an informed and effective job of cooking.[37] For her, chopping wood was an example of what the author of 'Changing Roles' called 'an extension of womanly pursuits'.

---

36   Lesley Zolin, 'Changing Roles', *Earth Garden*, no. 21 (January–March 1978): 34–35. Emphasis in original.
37   Di Mercer, 'Axewomanship: The Gentle Art of Woodchopping', *Earth Garden*, no. 21 (January–March 1978): 12–13.

Figure 4.2: The Gentle Art of Woodchopping.
Source: *Earth Garden*, no. 21 (January–March 1978): 12.

A more comprehensive critique was offered in a letter drawing attention to the fact that 'even amongst a group of people who have embraced some radical ideas, the human potential of women is being neglected ... again'. She winced, she wrote, 'at some of the articles and interviews in *EG* and at an attitude that seems to be between the lines' that 'what men do is more highly valued, by both men and women, just because the men are doing it'. She warned that 'we must not think that earth gardeners have escaped the all-pervasive sex role conditioning and subtle assumptions, for example, that women have to be kept ignorant about mechanical things'. She concluded, 'I strongly suggest to readers who have not done so, that they read some women's liberation books on sexism. Getting together in groups to talk about it should be valuable too'.[38] Two years later, Robin Duke, the writer of the letter, was one of the founders of Plum Farm Women's Land, a lesbian rural retreat near Adelaide.[39]

---

38   *Earth Garden*, no. 21 (January–March 1978): 45.
39   'Robin, Eagle (1951-)', Trove, National Library of Australia, trove.nla.gov.au/people/551695?c=people; *The Rough Guide to Gay & Lesbian Australia*, ed. Neal Drinnan (London: Rough Guides, 2001), 213.

The writer of a second long letter in that number of *Earth Garden* identified herself as:

> a gardener who uses compost and TLC instead of superphosphate and DDT. I am a spinner, a cook, a vegetarian, a herb grower, a bit of a carpenter and a lesbian. OK, be honest now—how many of you inwardly cringed at that last word? Is sexuality, and women's sexuality in particular, a taboo topic in the back-to-the-land movement …?

In her opinion:

> the 'straight' ideal of a quiet, gentle, sweet, beautiful, young, long-haired, floral-smelling 'lady', who must combine being a far-out cook with being a far-out lay, is far more prevalent in the counter-culture (or whatever you want to call it) than the rest of society, where there is some evidence it may be just starting to break down.

'Well, let me inform you', she insisted, 'that women are over half the world's population (and probably over half of the back-to-the-landers) and women who love women are everywhere!'[40]

In light of the few studies of the back-to-the-landers of the 1970s in Australia, it is helpful to look at other sites of this transnational movement to try to gain some more general insight into what gender rules applied. Technology appears to have been one important area where gendered assumptions from the larger culture were carried over into countercultural situations. During the 1970s what was often called 'appropriate' or sometimes 'alternative' technology was urged as an option for both urban and rural locations. Hand tools, bicycles, wind mills and solar installations were all available for study and recommended for use by both men and women, but anecdotal evidence suggests 'appropriate' technologies were largely the preserve of the 'appropriate' (male) gender. A 1980 cartoon from Great Britain titled 'Alice's Alternative Adventures with AT Man' described Alice's hope that AT Man would liberate her from her dominating husband and three demanding children. Fleeing to a communal home, she asks AT Man whether they are headed for 'some kind of place in the country'. He replies 'nothing as bourgeois as that … it's a squat on the Edgware Road'. At the squat, it seems, all the men are writing books and giving lectures on political alternatives—

---

40 *Earth Garden*, no. 21 (January–March 1978): 45.

one man is too busy writing a book on 'Alternative Parenthood—The Male Role in Childcare' to actually do any and another believes that 'this housework thing just isn't my trip—it's all a bourgeois fetish anyway'. In the last panel, Alice is shown doing the dishes for all the five men and 14 children of the commune, as she muses that 'what we need are some alternative Alternatives'.[41]

In 1978, a group of women associated with the National Center for Appropriate Technology, located in the American farming state of Montana, published a manifesto titled *Something Old, Something New, Something Borrowed, Something Due: Women and Appropriate Technology*. One of the authors, Judy Smith, explained that 'women can and must take some control over the technology confronting them in their daily lives'. In turning to the movement for appropriate technology, she and her colleagues found 'a great deal of discussion of voluntary simplicity'. 'We also found', she continued, 'that the people who espoused those ideas and who led the movement were men, making decisions based on the same old values.' She concluded:

> Thus one of the basic problems we face in the appropriate technology and alternative energy movements is that adherents still reflect the value system we live in: men have the technical skills and make the technical decisions, their interests are self-assessed as more important.[42]

Smith singled out one bright spot: 'a new element has appeared within the women's movement: a growing number of small groups interested in country living … In these group settings women are learning self-reliance and skills from other women, in an environment far different in focus and tone than that of other back-to-the-land groups'. A cluster of such groups around the small coastal town of Albion, in northern California, even produced a journal called *Country Women*, and in 1976 published a book—*Country Women: A Handbook for the New Farmer*. That the feminists of Albion were not typical is suggested by the Berkeley journalist Kate Coleman who, in 1978, visited some of the groups and found the women there quite unlike those in the back-to-the-land movement that she had previously observed. While 'the women I knew [before]', she wrote,

---

41 Jo Nesbitt, 'Alice's Alternative Adventures with Atman', in Jo Nesbitt, Lesley Ruda, Liz Mackie and Christine Roche, *Sourcream* (London: Sheba Feminist Press, 1980), 20–23.
42 Judy Smith, 'Women and Appropriate Technology: A Feminist Assessment', *The Technological Woman: Interfacing with Tomorrow*, ed. Jan Zimmerman (New York: Praeger, 1983), 65, 66.

'were reverting to the Stone Age', some of the Albion women were forming a carpentry collective, an act that she found 'politically significant as well as practical: it is the working manifestation of these women's feminism'.[43] Many of the Albion groups were lesbian separatist, and women in these, not surprisingly, seemed to have the best luck learning and sharing new 'technological' skills. Historian Rebecca Jennings has found that attitudes toward some 'patriarchal' technologies seem to have varied from country to country, but that 'the idea of self-sufficiency from the patriarchy was fundamental to all the women's lands so they aimed to acquire skills to carry out all necessary tasks themselves'.[44]

Beginning in the early 1980s, two Canadian sociologists interviewed over 2,000 'back-to-the-landers' attempting to 'explore female independence and sense of fulfilment within a movement that attempts to recapture part of an idyllic past while still captive to modern notions of gender equity and deference'. Their conclusion was that although there was 'a clear division of labor along gender lines', this did not 'effect satisfaction with partner or other quality of life factors … particularly [among] females'. The women, they report:

> seek their own liberation from the constraints of the modern family by going back to pre-modern family forms. Working in partnership with their husbands and children to produce a substantial part of what their families consume, back-to-the-land women believe they can have a greater sense of freedom and find more fulfilment than if they were to pursue their own professional careers.

They admitted, however, that 'women were twice as likely as men to report dissatisfaction with the way particular farmstead tasks were divided up, and close to a third of women survey respondents were dissatisfied with having to do most of the house cleaning'.[45] However, writing specifically about Australia, Amanda McLeod has asserted flatly that domestic

---

43 Kate Coleman, 'Country Women: The Feminists of Albion Ridge', *Mother Jones* 3, no. 3 (1978): 23, 32. See also Desmond A. Jolly, ed., *Outstanding in Their Fields: California's Women Farmers* (Davis: UC Small Farm Center, 2005).
44 Correspondence to the author, quoted by permission.
45 Jeffrey C. Jacob and Merlin B. Brinkerhoff, 'Planetary Sustainability and Sustaining Family Relationships: Family Division of Labor and the Possibility of Female Liberation in the Back-to-the-Land Movement of the Late Twentieth [Century]', Paper presented to the Annual Meeting of the Rural Sociological Society, 12–18 August 1997, pp. 1, 6, 8. See also Dona Brown, *Back to the Land: The Enduring Dream of Self-Sufficiency in Modern America* (Madison: University of Wisconsin Press, 2011), 212.

'gendered divisions were not applicable to self-sufficiency in the 1970s'. In her opinion, 'there was simply too much to do on a self-sufficient smallholding'.[46]

For some proponents, the apparent regressive nature of the back-to-the-land movement was what was attractive about it. By 1961 there was in the United States a Christian Homesteading Movement that, though small, characterised the tendency. 'Women wearing anything but knee-length skirts and dresses are not allowed to visit [their community]. Women in shorts or pants' were advised 'to go home and get dressed properly'.[47] In 2015 an essay in *The Catholic Gentleman* titled 'In Praise of Catholic Homesteading', began:

> When the Papacy is vacant the whole Church looks longingly for a puff of smoke from a little chimney—the household of the Church feels lonely without Papa. When it comes we rejoice, because our father has come home. When I see puffs of smoke from little homesteads in the countryside I feel the same—a father has come home to be with his family by living together on the land.[48]

If the movement was predominantly masculine in the United States and Australia, it was also overwhelmingly white. There were rare exceptions, however. In the United States, historian Russell Rickford has shown that 'the "land question" was a major concern for African American theorists and activists in the late 1960s and early 1970s'. One attempt to establish 'a territorial base for the construction of an autonomous black community' was the work of The Republic of New Africa which advertised:

> COME TO THE LAND. Can you teach [/] man a saw [/] build a generator [/] tend an infirmary [/] drive a tractor [/] finish concrete [/] lay pipe [/] run a press [/] tailor a dashiki [/] shoot a gun? You can help make Black people's most important dream—our most important necessity—a reality by serving in Mississippi as we build a model community.[49]

---

46 Amanda McLeod, 'Self-Sufficiency in a "Time of Plenty": Mass Consumerism and Freedom in 1970s Australia', *History Australia* 14, no. 3 (September 2017): 411, doi.org/10.1080/14490854.2017.1358096.
47 Hal Smith, 'The Christian Homesteading Movement', *Mother Earth News* (March/April 1971).
48 Jason Craig, 'In Praise of Catholic Homesteading', *The Catholic Gentlemen*, 30 January 2015.
49 Russell Rickford, '"We Can't Grow Food on All This Concrete": The Land Question, Agrarianism, and Black Nationalist Thought in the Late 1960s and 1970s', *Journal of American History* 103, no. 4 (2017): 956 and journal cover.

In Australia, an Aboriginal homelands movement began in the late 1960s when outstations were established on traditional lands. In the 1970s the Whitlam Labor Government established the Woodward Royal Commission whose work led to the *Aboriginal Land Rights (Northern Territory) Act 1976*. By 2014, outstations (with fewer than 50 inhabitants) contained some 22,000 people and homeland communities with fewer than 100 inhabitants contained another 100,000. The need of these scattered communities for water, sanitation, energy and other infrastructures led, in 1980, to the establishment in Alice Springs of the Centre for Appropriate Technology, the leading Australian manifestation of what was itself a transnational movement.[50]

Given the transnational nature, at least in Anglophone countries, of both gender expectations and the back-to-the-land movement itself, it would be surprising if there were not parallels between their interactions in Australia, Great Britain and the United States. In Australia, the periodicals *Earth Garden* and *Grass Roots*, founded respectively in 1972 and 1973, gave moral and practical support to the imagined community of back-to-the-landers. In the United States, *Mother Earth News*, first published in 1970, later claimed that the 'tens of thousands of young adults and other adventurous souls' who made up the American back-to-the-landers 'were the core readers of Mother Earth News and the impetus for its creation'.[51] In the United States and Great Britain the philosophies and experience of Helen and Scott Nearing and John and Sally Seymour were emulated by thousands who sought self-sufficiency. In America the *Whole Earth Catalog* (1968) reached a broad and enthusiastic audience, while the *Country Women: A Handbook for New Farmers* (1976) addressed and appealed to a specific female audience. In Australia, Irene Smith, coeditor of *Earth Garden*, expressed the hope in 1978 that her special issue on women would lead to the creation of 'a useful book'.[52]

In all three countries, men were seen as dominating the self-sufficiency movement and the closely related movements to go back-to-the-land and for the adoption of alternative technologies. Among Australian alternative lifestyle magazines, it is not surprising that the hyper-masculine *Australasian Survivor*, with an 85 per cent male readership, had by far

---

50 Alan Mayne, *Alternative Interventions: Aboriginal Homelands, Outback Australia and the Centre for Appropriate Technology* (Adelaide: Wakefield Press, 2014), 11.
51 Heidi Hunt, 'What is Homesteading?', www.motherearthnews.com/homesteading-and-livestock/what-is-homesteading? (page discontinued; accessed 15 November 2016).
52 *Earth Garden*, no. 21 (January–March 1978): 2.

the greatest interest in alternative technologies.[53] And in all three, it was control of the relevant technologies that was seen as the mechanism for this dominance. At the same time, it was the role of women that appeared most concerning and the most commented upon. Besides being seen as not interested in or capable with technology, women were also expected to fulfil traditional gender roles even in their new circumstances. Tracey Deutsch has surveyed the contemporary convergence of local foods, history and women's work. 'Gender and gendered histories,' she writes, 'are at the center of these local food movements. Calls for a return to eating foods from within one's region are premised on histories of women and their cooking.'[54]

The contemporary resonance of the dilemmas faced by Australian women in the back-to-the-land movement is striking. Writing in 2015, three American scholars asserted that '[i]n an era of climate change linked to industrialized foods and disease epidemics caused by the modern Western diet, kitchen work has acquired political importance. Daily cooking must be understood as public, as well as private'. Four decades after many women moved back to the land in part to improve their health through growing and eating organic foods that they had raised themselves, the authors of this study found that 'feminists who cook with local foods are only beginning to ideologically integrate feminism and sustainable food cooking'.[55]

In 2009 Morgan Wills, who operated a studio/shop in Ballarat, used her blog to celebrate *Grass Roots* magazine. She first read it when she was about 15, she wrote; and when she was 19:

> I took myself off with my dreadlocked surfer dude boyfriend to live down near Warrnambool for a year. Thirty km from the nearest shop—we lived very simply in a small house on 5 acres of bush land with no electricity or running water … We ate eggs from the chooks and veggies from the garden and made all our own bread.

---

53 Vanclay and Metcalf, 'Alternative Lifestyle Magazines', 50, 52.
54 Tracey Deutsch, 'Memories of Mothers in the Kitchen: Local Foods, History, and Women's Work', *Radical History Review*, no. 110 (Spring 2011): 167, doi.org/10.1215/01636545-2010-032.
55 Holly A. Stovall, Lori Baker-Sperry and Judith M. Dallinger, 'A New Discourse on the Kitchen: Feminism and Environmental Education', *Australian Journal of Environmental Education* 31, no. 1 (2015): 110, doi.org/10.1017/aee.2015.11.

She expressed 'fond memories' of her experience, but also revealed that she had 'lived in the city ever since and have often thought of a move back to a lovely country town. I don't think [however] I would choose to live without running water and electricity again (especially not with children)'.[56]

Along with growing and preparing food, parenting was another of the major expectations faced by women who sought the advantages of self-sufficiency back on the land. For one thing, as Alice discovered when she joined a commune with AT Man, her own three children could suddenly expand to 14. For another, as Wills realised, raising children in isolation and without the modern technologies of electricity and running water was particularly challenging. Isobelle Barrett Meyering addressed the issues in a 2013 article, '"There Must Be a Better Way": Motherhood and the Dilemmas of Feminist Lifestyle Change'. The subject, she wrote, 'is necessarily transnational reflecting the influence of British and North American feminism in Australia, as well as the fact that feminist motherhood presented similar dilemmas in each context'. She pointed out that in the mid-1970s the search for 'new and positive lifestyles' controversially could lead to the prioritising of 'personal' over 'structural' solutions. Moving back to the land was certainly 'personal', but its connection to 'structural' was neither inevitable nor always even recognised.[57] As Beryl Donaldson observed at the time, 'the counter culture is essentially a male creation, in which the sexual inequalities of the dominant culture are maintained— albeit in hip form'. Finally, she warned, 'unless a more equitable division of labour is worked out, the women in these communes are likely to spend more time doing "housework" than the average suburban housewife'.[58]

For a large number of Australians in the 1970s, political commitment to issues of apparently out of control technology, of urbanisation, of commodification and of general erosion of the quality of life led to an attempt to find personal escape in an imagined self-sufficiency back on the land. While such a move represented a dramatic break with the material circumstances of their previous lives, it was not always so obvious

---

56 Morgan Wills, 'Grass Roots Magazine', 21 September 2009, accessed 30 October 2016, morganwills.blogspot.com/2009/09/grass-roots-magzine.html (page discontinued).
57 Isobelle Barratt Meyering, '"There Must Be a Better Way": Motherhood and the Dilemmas of Feminist Lifestyle Change', *Outskirts* 28 (May 2013): 1, www.outskirts.arts.uwa.edu.au/volumes/volume-28/isobelle-barrett-meyering.
58 Beryl Donaldson, 'Women's Place in the Counter Culture', in *The Other Half: Women in Australian Society*, ed. Jan Mercer (Penguin Books: Ringwood, 1975), 427, 433.

that the opportunity presented itself for an equally dramatic discarding of conventional gender expectations. While a feminist critique of the experience was slow in coming, and to some extent muted by a nostalgic aura of primitive masculine authority, the stark reality of life on the land, often cut off from modern amenities, could hardly escape the notice of female participants. Having made the political personal, they were confronted with the need to then make the personal political.

FEMINISM IN ART AND CULTURE

CHAPTER 5

How the personal became (and remains) political in the visual arts

Catriona Moore and Catherine Speck

Second-wave feminism ushered in major changes in the visual arts around the idea that the personal is political. It introduced radically new content, materials and forms of art practice that are now characterised as central to postmodern and contemporary art. Moreover, longstanding feminist exercises in 'personal-political' consciousness-raising spearheaded the current use of art as a testing ground for various social interventions and participatory collaborations known as 'social practice' both in and outside of the art gallery.[1]

Times change, however, and contemporary feminism understands the 'personal' and the 'political' a little differently today. The fragmentation of women's liberation, debates around essentialism within feminist art and academic circles, and institutional changes within the art world have prompted different processes and expressions of personal-political consciousness-raising than those that were so central to the early elaboration of feminist aesthetics. Moreover, the exploration and analysis of women's shared personal experiences now also identify differences among women—cultural, racial, ethnic and class differences—in order to

---

1 On-Curating.org journal editor Michael Birchall cites examples such as EVA International (2012), the 7th Berlin Biennial and Documenta 13 that reflect overt and covert political ideas. Birchall outlined this feminist connection at the Curating Feminism symposium, A Contemporary Art and Feminism event co-hosted by Sydney College of the Arts, School of Letters, Arts and Media, and The Power Institute, University of Sydney, 23–26 October 2014.

serve more inclusive, intersectional cultural and political alliances. These shifts continue to challenge and open up opportunities for more diffused 'personal-political' art projects and forms of united feminist action. This paper articulates these shifts and challenges for feminism through a discussion of key Australian artworks, exhibitions and organised actions since the mid-1970s.

Arts as a vehicle for feminist consciousness-raising

We start by exploring the rise of these events that were a part of a transnational, feminist movement in the visual arts from the later 1960s.[2] In 1969, the New York group, Women Artists in Revolution (WAR) split off from the Art Workers' Coalition (AWC) because the AWC was male dominated and would not protest on behalf of women artists. In 1971, female artists picketed the Corcoran Biennial in Washington DC for excluding women artists, and New York Women in the Arts organised a protest against gallery owners for not exhibiting women's art. Then Linda Nochlin set the ball rolling by challenging the status quo of the Euroamerican art academy with her provocative essay 'Why Have There Been No Great Women Artists?', first published in the American publication *ARTnews* in 1971.[3] It rapidly found a receptive audience with Australian artists, art historians and junior curators, and by 1973 the title of her provocative article was the subject of student essays in visual arts and fine arts courses at universities and art schools. Toni Robertson, then a Sydney University art history student (and artist), produced one of the first Australian elaborations of feminist art history and aesthetic theory.[4]

---

2   In Australia, the Sydney Women's Liberation group first met in Balmain and Sydney University in 1969. Two years later, Sue Bellamy and others organised the Art Workers for Liberation group in Sydney. See Barbara Hall, 'The Women's Liberation Movement and the Visual Arts: A Selected Chronology, 1969–90', in *Dissonance: Feminism and the Arts 1970–90*, ed. Catriona Moore (St Leonards, NSW: Allen & Unwin, 1994), 277–78.
3   Linda Nochlin, 'Why Have There Been No Great Women Artists', *ARTNews* 69, no. 1 (1971): 23–39, 67–71.
4   Toni Robertson, 'From Dabbler to Artists: Towards a Feminist Art', *Arena* 7, no. 3 (1974): 12–15. The essay was reprinted in Catriona Moore, ed., *Dissonance: Feminism and the Arts 1970–90* (Sydney: Allen & Unwin, 1994), 12–21.

5. HOW THE PERSONAL BECAME (AND REMAINS) POLITICAL IN THE VISUAL ARTS

The women's liberation movement of the late 1960s was changing the face of art history and art exhibitions, and importantly the status of women artists and the sense of worth in living women artists. Some key international milestones that reflect these changes are the publication in 1973 of Thomas Hess and Elizabeth Baker's book, a follow-up to Nochlin's foray, entitled *Art and Sexual Politics: Why Have There Been No Great Women Artists?*.[5] This was followed by Ann Sutherland Harris and Linda Nochlin's important exhibition first seen at the Los Angeles County Museum of Art in 1976, *Women Artists 1550–1950*, which turned the tables on the masculinist canon by showing 'the greats' such as Angelica Kauffmann and Judith Leyster whose work had been kept in museum stores.[6] But one year earlier, the Ewing and Paton Galleries in Melbourne under Kiffy Rubbo's direction had already hosted an exhibition, *Australian Women Artists: One Hundred Years, 1840–1940*, which reclaimed the history of women's art for International Women Year (IWY) in 1975. It was opened by Prime Minister Gough Whitlam's Advisor on Women's Affairs, Elizabeth Reid. The idea to 'examine more closely the contribution which women have made to Australian art' and to 'redistribute the art historical balance' evolved from a 1974 Ewing and Paton exhibition, *A Room of One's Own*, which featured the work of three contemporary artists, Lesley Dumbrell, Ann Newmarch and Julie Irving, and heralded an explosion of feminist exhibitions across the country through IWY.[7]

The feminist return to the archives began a trend that brought to light new histories, what has been called 'Part Two' in the history of Western culture.[8] Early counter-canonical texts included Karen Peterson and J.J. Wilson's *Women Artists: Recognition and Reappraisal from the Early Middle Ages to the Twentieth Century* in 1976 and the British-based Germaine Greer's *The Obstacle Race* published in 1979. The archival recovery and reappraisal of women's arts and crafts fuelled the development of academic and studio-based feminist historiography, which gained real pace in the 1980s and 1990s, although it took on differing complexions

---

5   Thomas Hess and Elizabeth Baker, eds, *Art and Sexual Politics: Why Have There Been No Great Women Artists?* (New York: Collier Books, 1973).
6   Ann Sutherland Harris and Linda Nochlin, *Women Artists 1550–1950* (Los Angeles: Los Angeles County Museum of Art, 1976).
7   Kiffy Carter, 'Foreword' and Janine Burke in Janine Burke, *Australian Women Artists: One Hundred Years, 1840–1940* (Melbourne: Ewing and Paton Galleries, University of Melbourne Union, 1975), 9. The 1974 exhibition *A Room of One's Own* (curated Kiffy Rubbo and Meredith Rogers) included work by women artists, filmmakers and video artists.
8   Norma Broude and Mary Garrard, eds, *The Power of Feminist Art: The American Movement of the 1970s, History and Impact* (New York: Abrams, 1994), 10.

across nations. In Australia for instance, and especially under the guidance of Joan Kerr, it was not a matter of finding more 'Old Mistresses' or great woman artists, as a corrective to the existing art history canon, instead she pointed out that 'we have to paint a new canvas and carve a new frame to fit [it] in'.[9] For Kerr then, you could not 'add in' women's arts to the history of Australian art without broadening the very conception of art upon which the national canon rests.[10] A liberal-feminist, 'add women', equal-opportunity strategy was not sufficient for the much-needed structural change to the art historical canon and its academic, market and museum supports. Women's work in its myriad forms challenged the canon's masculinist, institutional structures and biased assumptions concerning artistic subjectivity, media hierarchies and aesthetic value.

The idea that 'the personal is political' was an important strategy driving these ventures: it was one strand of a larger feminist project, and it grounded a speculative, studio-based feminist aesthetics that challenged the narrowly conceived formalist canon of late modernism. It set in motion an approach to art and art making that was radically different from what had come before by male artists, and to a certain extent by women artists. It drew on, explored and critiqued female experience through innovatory processes, media and forms. We sensed that these experimental modalities constituted a new, open-ended aesthetic category that allowed for the expression of non-canonical cultural perspectives: we called it 'feminist aesthetics'. Lucy Lippard called this approach to art and cultural politics 'a revolutionary strategy' because the traditional divide of what belonged in the public and private realms was discarded.[11] That divide had largely ignored domestic female experience, for instance, although there are some notable art historical exceptions, such as Vida Lahey's *Monday morning*, 1912, and Mary Cassatt's *The child's bath*, 1893.

As women artists turned to their own lives and the self as the source of art, they became the subject rather than the object of representation. The personal as political was both an aesthetic move and a political step that saw a melding of art and politics, as in the 'washing machine' street

---

9   Joan Kerr, 'Introduction', in *Heritage the National Women's Art Book*, ed. Joan Kerr (Roseville East, NSW: G & B Arts International, 1995), viii.
10   Joan Kerr, 'Art and Life', in *The Humanities and a Creative Nation: Jubilee Essays*, ed. Deryck M. Schreuder (Canberra: Australian Academy of Humanities, 1994), republished in Joan Kerr, *A Singular Voice: Essays on Australian Art and Architecture*, ed. Candice Bruce, Dinah Dysart and Jo Holder (Sydney: Power Publications, University of Sydney, 2009), 51–66.
11   Lucy Lippard, 'Sweeping Exchanges: The Contribution of Feminism to Art of the 1970s', *Art Journal* 39, no. 2/3 (1980): 362–65, doi.org/10.1080/00043249.1980.10793628.

performance by South Australian Women's Art Movement (WAM) members, organised by Jude Adams and others in 1981. It was an art performance that simultaneously aimed to 'cross through' the art institution and engaged with broader public audiences in order 'to get across some other social reality'.[12]

'The personal is political' challenged the mythic opposition between public and private realms, including art world divisions between the domestic spaces of home and studio (often the same space), the 'politics of the street' and the art institution. As today, in the 1970s feminist artists working in domestic and community settings drew connections between their own studio work and what they did in other fields—parenting, curating, teaching and community activism.[13] The phrase 'the personal is political' was understood 'to imply that the reality of women's lives was larger than their traditional circumscription in the realm of the private and the personal and that, indeed, the very categories of private and public, were themselves, political fictions'.[14] Norma Broude and Mary Garrard argued that the aligning of the political with the personal had two components: that it self-consciously articulated 'female experience from an informed social and political position', and that it had a universalising tendency of 'defining one's experience as applicable to the experience of other women'.[15]

North American artist and writer Judy Chicago integrated these ideas into an institutionally based, feminist art teaching program in 1970 at Fresno in California, which she expanded with Miriam Schapiro in 1971 at the California Institute of Art (CalArts) north of Los Angeles. The radically new 'personal is political' approach of working intensively with women students in spaces away from the campus, reading feminist material, sharing experiences and focusing studio classes on the subject of the body, often in collaborative performative work in the Feminist Art Program, led to an outburst of new work, especially that produced at *Womanhouse* in 1971. Their site, a condemned 17-room house in Los Angeles, was cleaned up and made into a feminist environment. Each room became a living breathing space, such as Vicki Hodgett's *Nurturant kitchen*—the walls

---

12   Angela Dimitrakaki, *Gender, artWork and the Global Imperative: A Materialist Feminist Critique* (Manchester: Manchester University Press, 2013), 210.
13   See Catriona Moore and Jacqueline Millner, 'Introduction', in *Feminist Perspectives on Art: Contemporary Outtakes*, ed. Catriona Moore and Jacqueline Millner (London: Routledge, 2018).
14   Broude and Garrard, *The Power of Feminist Art*, 29.
15   Ibid., 12.

and ceiling covered with breasts (that loosely resembled fried eggs)—or Judy Chicago's *Menstruation bathroom*. Chicago and Schapiro theorised and publicised their experimental and immersive art environment, *Womanhouse* in California, particularly how the ideas, forms and content for this immersive, environmental artwork had been created through collective feminist consciousness-raising techniques to assert a combined 'personal-political' art practice.[16]

Australian women artists, abreast of this, were mobilising to set up Women's Art Movements in Melbourne (1974), Sydney (1975) and in Adelaide in 1977[17] (initially in 1976 as a WAG, Women's Art Group, with the aim of setting up a slide register similar to that already underway in Melbourne). Slide registers were set up to create an archive of work by women artists in order to counter their absence in the art museums; the impetus for their establishment was the 1975 visit by US feminist art critic and curator Lucy Lippard. She had delivered the annual Power lecture on contemporary art, and she spoke to a women-only group in Melbourne and Adelaide about how women in the United States had set up such a slide register, the West-East Bag (WEB).

The Women's Art Movements were run as collectives, facilitating studio and exhibition-based consciousness-raising as a means to analyse the political implications of women's personal experiences through the forms, materials and processes of visual art. In a similar way to feminist art groups and programs overseas, the WAMs and their associated all-women events fostered safe and non-judgemental consciousness-raising (CR) methods derived from women's liberation—such as 'doing the circle'. This entailed taking turns to speak of one's own personal experience, sometimes around an agreed issue or theme, in order to individually and collectively articulate how the most intimate or personal areas of our lives are embedded within patriarchal relations of power and knowledge. These exchanges also took place within art studios and workshops, exhibitions, and in the fledgling Women and Art courses in Australian art schools, so that CR became a shorthand for creative methods of 'using one's own experience as the most

---

16   Judy Chicago and Miriam Schapiro, 'The Education of Women as Artists: Project Womanhouse', *Art Journal* 31, no. 3 (1972): 269. See also in this context Lucy Lippard, 'Household Images in Art', *Ms.* 1, no. 9 (1973): 22.
17   In South Australia, for instance, WAM was originally housed in the Jam Factory at St Peters, Adelaide, along with the Experimental Art Foundation.

valid way of formulating political analysis'.[18] The 'personal-political' basis for CR also became a platform for institutional intervention, as when Bonita Ely called for equity in art school staffing and the teaching methods be more sensitive to the experiences of the female art student majority back in 1977:

> [The student] may want to express something very personal in their work. If they've had a baby, if they've had a miscarriage they may want to make a statement about that. If they've become involved in the cycles of nature and would like to express a very personal affinity through their menstrual cycle, they could very well be made to feel embarrassed about such work and find that experience has to be sublimated or sidestepped.[19]

In contrast to the male-dominated art institution, the autonomous feminist studio, workshop and exhibition spaces were generative hothouses for queer, radical and socialist-feminist personal-political explorations of gender and sexual difference. More often than not, an idealist, universalising idea of a 'global sisterhood' sought the commonality of women's experiences, and affirmed affinities between women. Also worth noting is that the affirmation of women's shared experiences was often also shaped through the recognition in differences of class, sexuality, religion, geography, language, culture and race.[20]

'The personal is political' introduced radically new content, materials and forms of art practice, such as Ann Newmarch's screenprint *Women hold up half the sky* of 1978. This image (taken from the family album of her aunt Peggy and her husband) was cheekily titled with the oft-quoted Maoist slogan from the period, radicalising the social and political change under way by humorously showing women as literally fundamental to familial and social order. Moreover the medium of screen-printed images and photography producing multiple prints was seen as democratic and affordable, in contrast to the exclusive medium of oil paint or acrylic on canvas, and was adopted by many feminist artists and radical collectives at the time.

---

18 Judith Papachristou, *Women Together: A History in Documents of the Women's Movement in the United States* (New York: Knopf, 1976), 23.
19 Bonita Ely, 'Sexism in Art Education', in *The Women's Show 1977* (Adelaide: South Australian Women's Art Movement/Experimental Art Foundation, 1978), 48, cited in Catriona Moore, *Indecent Exposures: Twenty Years of Australian Feminist Photography* (Sydney: Allen & Unwin, 1994), 9.
20 The political emphasis and academic theorisation of intersectional feminism accelerated with the emergence of neoliberalism, as attested through early feminist slogans from the late 1970s such as (ex-British Tory PM) 'Margaret Thatcher: not my oppressed sister'.

Figure 5.1: *Women hold up half the sky*, Ann Newmarch, 1978, Prospect, Adelaide, colour screenprint on paper.
Source: Courtesy of Art Gallery of South Australia, Adelaide.

5. HOW THE PERSONAL BECAME (AND REMAINS) POLITICAL IN THE VISUAL ARTS

In August 1977, the Women's Art Movement in Adelaide hosted *The Women's Show* for the entire month. This was much more than a conventional visual arts exhibition. It was organised through an ambitious, multicollective structure of between 50 and 60 women, and was national in scope and participation, with subcollectives organising women-oriented elements for theatre, music, film, photography, poetry and literature, media, a conference and a visual art exhibition. Another collective arranged childminding. Funding was minimal for the entire event, which was realised through a $1,000 grant from the South Australian Government and $500 from the host institution, the Experimental Art Foundation.

The exhibition component of *The Women's Show* was of work submitted by women artists irrespective of profile or experience, with the aim of showing every work submitted, which amounted to over 350 works on view. The collective opted for a 'mixed show', which meant it was not ordered by an artworld-imposed theme, subject or genre—rather the universality of the women's experiences was the key factor. Unsurprisingly, in the lead-up to this decision, there was much discussion as to whether the event should be an unselected and inclusive women's show, or a more tightly curated feminist show. The politically acute decision for inclusion resulted in creative tensions, evidenced in the broad exhibition call-out and its unforeseen, overwhelming response; in the show's loose installation process; and in its eclectic exhibition design, where work of 'very different sorts of artists of entirely different backgrounds and experience were hung side by side'.[21] For instance, Margaret Dodds's *Made to serve*, c. 1977, a non-functional bright pink ceramic teapot bearing a woman's face whose head was covered with hair rollers and bex tablets, and Frances Budden's (later Phoenix) *Relic*, 1977, featuring the embroidered text, 'Mary's blood never failed me' along with her *Period*, 1977, shared the cavernous viewing space of the Jam Factory with the work of lesser-known women. This inclusive approach to process and display, while grounded in the feminist politics of the time, prompted one mainstream art critic (Peter Ward) to ask whether it was 'incorrigibly bourgeois' of him to complain that the exhibition areas weren't adequately swept, while much discussion at the accompanying conference theorised the feminist value of inclusivity.[22]

---

21 On that tension, see Anne Marsh, *Difference: A Radical Approach to Women and Art* (Adelaide: Women's Art Movement, 1985), 2; and J. Ewington, 'Hanging the Exhibition', in Women's Art Movement, *The Women's Show, Adelaide, 1977* (St Peters, SA: Experimental Art Foundation, 1978), 10–11.
22 See P. Ward, 'Of Women, by Women for Women', in Women's Art Movement, *The Women's Show, Adelaide, 1977*, 37; and 'Julie Ewington Answers Peter Ward', and Ewington, 'Hanging the Exhibition', in Women's Art Movement, *The Women's Show, Adelaide, 1977*, 10–11.

Figure 5.2: *Kitchen Bench C*, Ann Newmarch, 1977, colour screenprint on paper.
Source: Courtesy of Art Gallery of South Australia, Adelaide.

Picturing life experiences

Ann Newmarch probed her own life experiences in two exhibits in *The Women's Show*. In *Three months of interrupted work*, 1977, she focused on the difficulty of combining her work as an artist with motherhood in which she suggested her world *is* her kitchen with its tidy, ordered objects tastefully arranged on the bench and the shelf above, rather like a Morandi sculpture. Then her photograph *5 years and 5 days*, 1977, of her boys Jake and Bruno, documented and validated the intimate moments of motherhood. By 1980, Newmarch was working with a group from the Women's Art Movement and the Prospect Mural Group on an anti-rape mural, *Reclaim the night*, 1980. Newmarch has had a longstanding commitment that 'art should be made out of personal experience not out of "art" concerns', but, she added, 'personal experience is only a useful source of art when it is accompanied by an understanding of the social conditions in which it arises. An artist has a responsibility as an image maker to concerns wider than herself or her art'.[23] This focus has continued in later decades in work that continued to take in the personal—such as *Tear*, 1992, in which a high chair she made for her middle son was modified to have 'a very unstable base—almost like a crutches high chair',[24] becoming a metaphor for life itself.

In 1975, founding Sydney WAM member Marie McMahon similarly reread her family photo album to investigate the social construction of femininity through institutions of the family, school, church and community. Her critical, autobiographical focus also followed the feminist tenet of 'the personal is political', giving the (then unfashionable) category of 'personal experience' a sharp, analytic purchase. McMahon scaled up her family photographs on vitreous enamel panels to challenge the related ideological and social apparatuses that contour women's lives. Intimate photographic moments are cast as turning points in the formation of feminine identity. McMahon questioned the material traces of a woman's life—the family album, the confirmation dress, the wedding ring, the baby's layette. Like Newmarch, she proposed a different sense of time (what the psychoanalyst and cultural writer Julia Kristeva would later call

---

23 Ann Newmarch quoted in Julie Robinson, *Ann Newmarch: The Personal is Political* (Adelaide: Art Gallery of South Australia, 1997), 27.
24 Julie Robinson interviewed by Catherine Speck, 21 April 2015; Janine Burke, 'Taken at Face Value: Self Portraits and Self Images', catalogue essay, *Self Portrait/Self Image*, Victorian College of the Arts Gallery, July–August 1980, 8.

'women's time').²⁵ McMahon's herstory measured a life of (re)productive labour as punctuated by birthdays, the onset of menstruation, the loss of virginity, weddings, child-rearing, home maintenance and menopause, rather than the time of productive labour (measured by the shareholder's report, Budget night or the financial year).

Feminist artists emphasised women's shared experiences of migration and cultural heritage, traditional craft skills, domestic and (low) paid labour, often within community arts and trades union–hosted art projects of the 1980s. These activist projects visualised what gender-sensitive multiculturalism might look like, and spearheaded a form of social art practice that emphasised dialogue over proselytising or directive artistic authorship. In this way, the predominantly middle-class, Anglo-Celtic feminist artists working on these projects were challenged by the diversity of women's socioeconomic, racial, religious, political and cultural agency.

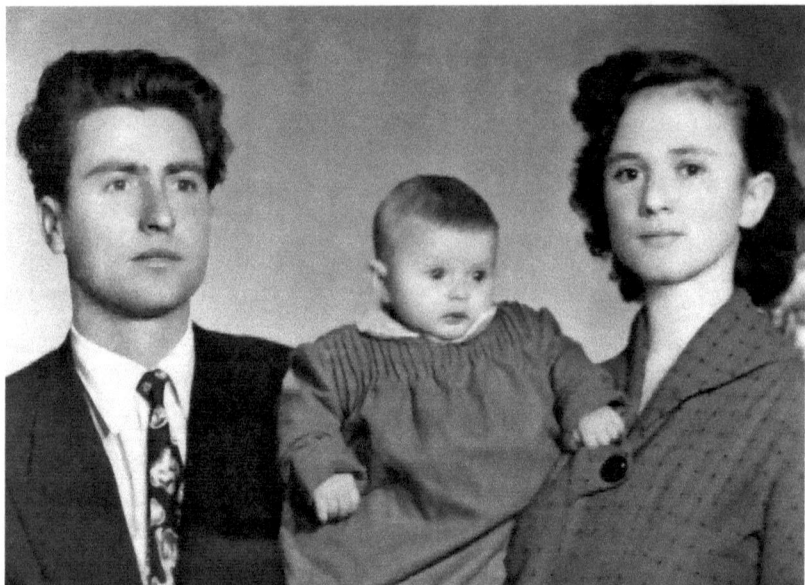

Figure 5.3: *Innocent reading for origin*, Elizabeth Gertsakis, 1988, gelatin silver prints.
Source: Courtesy of Monash Gallery of Art, City of Monash Collection.

---

25   Julia Kristeva, Alice Jardine and Harry Blake, 'Women's Time', *Signs* 7, no. 1 (1981): 13–35, doi.org/10.1086/493855.

Through the 1980s, the Macedonian-born, Melbourne-based artist Elizabeth Gertsakis and others (like Dina Tourvis and Jacky Redgate) also pulled images from personal albums to dislodge related stereotypes of Australian immigrant experience.

Gertsakis's *Innocent reading for origin* (1988) resisted any simple recourse to her family album as a purveyor of naive or unmediated personal experience, however. She played up the family photograph's 'untutored' informality as a visual equivalent for broken English, adopting a pseudo-innocent, interrogative voice in captioning each of her family photographs. This enabled the artist and spectator to ask disarmingly humorous questions that dislodged the stereotyped migrant narrative of the 'voyage out' and arrival in 'the new country', with its well-worn tropes of emotional authenticity and nostalgia. Gertsakis instead wanted to complicate the push and pull of the migrant story, with its driving theme of homesickness/sickness of home. She wanted to test the personal experiences showcased in her family album up against the commonly understood character of white Australian identity, to argue against any essential or a priori quality to either migrant or host cultural identity. This work challenged any self-evident understanding of 'the personal' as an authentic, essential or originary locus for identity politics. Increasingly through the 1980s, feminist art reinvented 'the politics of the personal' as a more nuanced, differentiated social field. The Sydney-based, Turkish-Australian artist Cigdem Ademir's performance work continues this tendency—a longstanding strength of Australian arts feminism—of dislodging stereotyped or essentialist images of 'the personal'. Through clever clowning she enacts a spectrum of mass-produced nightmares: veiled, feminised Islamism; the subjugated and suppressed woman; the sexualised Orientalist beauty; the veiled woman as exotic cultural commodity; the unknown terrorist threat.

Indigenous artists' use of the family album as counter-narrative also challenged essentialist notions of 'the personal' as the well-spring of a politically reductive, unitary female perspective. Brenda L. Croft's group portraits from 1993, collectively titled *The big deal is Black,* bounced off the huge colonial archive of ethnographic studio portraits of Aboriginal people, group portraits and 'typical Aboriginal scenes' that formed a staple of the colonial view trade, tourism glossies, instrumental welfare imagery and human interest documentary photography. While most of this massive image-bank is characterised by unbalanced power relations between the (white, colonial) photographer and his dispossessed, powerless and scrutinised subjects, Croft says her series 'is about letting you see something of us on our own terms'.[26]

Her large-scale yet emotionally intimate family portraits were shot in the context of Prime Minister Paul Keating's 'Redfern speech' (1992), Mabo (*Native Title Act 1994*; amended in 1998), the Stolen Generations ('Bringing Them Home' inquiry 1995–97) along with other Indigenous art projects charged with reconciliation politics. These renditions typically combined oral histories, film, photography, maps, paintings and other archival citations to stress family and community connectivity. Croft stresses these qualities in her portraits of local Aboriginal families in easy relationship with the photographer. These crisp, informally shot colour portraits are scaled up, larger than life: this is a 'big deal', and we sense these women are big personalities. Together, they command our attention and play the room. They were first exhibited at the Australian Centre for Photography in Sydney, accompanied by audiotapes discreetly placed in the corner of the gallery, which played a soft soundscape weaving snatches of domestic conversation, laughter and shared memories, and grounding both portraits and spectators in a living, communal setting. As Brenda L. Croft explained:

> The Big Deal—is a card game, is the Mabo issue, is a land deal, is no big deal, but it all comes down to being BLACK and living in the city, and all the roads that lead you here … All this BIG DEAL is about letting you see something of us on our terms. This is about being a Black woman—you might be mother, sister, aunt, cousin, daughter, friend—no difference, the DEAL is the same.[27]

Feminist insistence upon the personal as political challenged the public/private divide and knitted together art and domestic spheres in new ways. Australian feminism derives extra benefit from the strategic links that Indigenous artists and curators make between art practice, personal experience, community wellbeing, customary law and

---

26 Brenda L. Croft statement regarding *The Big Deal is Black*, Art Gallery of New South Wales, n.d., accessed June 2016, www.artgallery.nsw.gov.au/collection/works/392.1993/. Also cited, Lisa Bellear, 'The Big Deal is Black: Brenda L. Croft', 100% mabo, *Photofile*, no. 40 (November 1993): 19–22. See also Wayne Tunnicliffe in Hetti Perkins and Cara Pinchbeck, *Tradition Today: Indigenous Art in Australia* (Sydney: Art Gallery of New South Wales, 2014).
27 Brenda L. Croft, *The Big Deal is Black*, catalogue, Boomalli Aboriginal Artists Cooperative at the ACP, Sydney, 1993, cited in Bellear, 'The Big Deal Is Black', 19.

environmental justice. As we have argued elsewhere,[28] feminists now acknowledge how Indigenous communal spaces of art production, reception and exchange push the radical possibilities of personal-political 'domestic critique' still further. Today we see the indigenous bush camp, ceremonial ground or community art centre as related sites of art and education, landownership and custodianship, law and kinship. In this sense, 'the domestic', as a privileged location of personal experience, does not denote specific home or studio spaces in the Western-colonial sense.[29] For instance, in the remote Eastern Kimberley region of Western Australia, young Gija people may first know a particular *Ngarranggarni* (creation) story through looking at a painting by their father, aunty or grandmother. They might then be taken to the country where the story took place and that it shaped: knowledge central to Gija identity.[30] Indigenous artists and curators relay personal, community, cultural, environmental and political issues in a way that resonates with, and subtly reformulates, the longstanding feminist slogan, 'the personal is political'. Importantly, Indigenous artworkers stress the need to recalibrate art and teaching institutions to ensure that cross-cultural ethics and protocols are practised—a necessary part of forging intersectional alliances.

We have described a broadening, at times fragmented, yet generally aligned cultural field of identity politics shaped through the feminist idea: 'the personal is political'. We now also acknowledge how the force of our feminist critique has evolved through the genius of radical drag. A feminist, queer politics continues to question the gendered and embodied nature of personal experience, and how this may link to a broader cultural and social politics. For instance, in an early work, Sydney-based artist Liam Benson simply and elegantly interrogated the neat fit between masculine heteronormativity and the national story of egalitarian mateship and common prosperity, as sung to the Oz-country twang of John Williams's iconic song 'True Blue' (*True Blue*, 2010).

---

28 Jo Holder and Catriona Moore, 'A Feminist Curator Walks into a Gallery…', in *Feminist Perspectives on Art: Contemporary Outtakes*, ed. Catriona Moore and Jacqueline Millner (London: Routledge, 2018), doi.org/10.4324/9781315162072-2.
29 Ralph Juli, 'Story Is Good for Me', in *Garnkiny: Constellations in Meaning* (Western Australia: Warmun Art Centre, 2014), 81.
30 Anna Crane, 'Introduction', in *Garnkiny: Constellations in Meaning* (Western Australia: Warmun Art Centre, 2014), 3; Shirlie Purdie, 'Ngali-Ngalim-Boorroo (For the Women)', in *Curating Feminism: A Contemporary Art and Feminism Event*, ed. Alana Hunt and Anna Crane (Sydney: University of Sydney, 2014), 28.

Figure 5.4: Liam Benson, *True Blue*, 2010, video still from single channel video.
Source: Courtesy of the artist and Artereal Gallery. vimeo.com/69784371.

In closing, we note that, in the absence of an organised feminist art movement, today the personal is political remains a vital form of arts activism. In a variety of social spaces, personal-political analysis drives a 'pop-up' arts pedagogy and political networking that are elaborated as performance, feminist 'teach-in', curatorial laboratory and as a form of contemporary art known as social practice. For instance, the Brisbane feminist collective LEVEL invokes the communal, domestic power of the personal is political through their ongoing project *We need to talk*, a series of picnics, salons and dinners from 2012.[31] Their 'convivium' format emphasises collectivity and inclusion, in contrast to art market traits of individualism, careerism and opportunism.[32] They pay homage to longstanding consciousness-raising strategies, but in a contemporary context, following bell hooks' advice that 'consciousness raising groups, gatherings and public meetings need to become a central aspect of feminist practice again. Women need spaces where we can

---

31 LEVEL at the time included Courtney Coombs, Caitlin Franzmann, Rachael Haynes, Anita Holtsclaw and Courtney Pedersen.
32 An early outline of the critical possibility of communally based artwork is conceptual artist Mel Ramsden's 'On Practice' (1975), cited in Alexander Alberro and Blake Stimson, *Institutional Critique: An Anthology of Artists' Writings* (Cambridge, MA: MIT Press, 2009), 8. Another LEVEL-associated project is *Conversation Pieces* (Curator: Rachael Haynes), Boxcopy Contemporary Art Space. Artists included Catherine or Kate, Agatha Gothe-Snape, Alex Martinis Roe, Hannah Raisin, Scott Ferguson, Courtney Coombs and Caitlin Franzmann. International Women's Day, 8–29 March 2014, www.boxcopy.org.

explore intimately and deeply all aspects of female experience'.[33] In June 2014, for instance, a themed picnic (*Talking feminism and food*) on the Queensland Art Gallery's GoMA (Gallery of Modern Art) forecourt at the opening of the *Harvest* exhibition provided a critical focus for the exhibition: 'how we can use the idea of the "recipe"—a shared set of ingredients and methods—as a way forward to a better world. Together we will develop a recipe for a revolution'.[34]

'The personal' now mixes diverse sexual, gendered, cultural, racial and class-based experiences as active political ingredients. It continues to generate diverse intersectional action, without recourse to its more universalising companion slogan from the 1970s, 'global sisterhood'. The personal is political remains a cornerstone of today's more fluid identity politics, not simply invoked to safeguard difference but, as Angela Dimitrakaki proposes in the UK context, 'to justify the social demand of acting with others … Identity, including self-identity, is mobilized to enable alliances rather than question their desirability of viability'.[35] We have demonstrated that the personal is still political. This directs the consciousness of addressing and fighting for the rights of *all women* and it has been a prevalent feature of feminism in the arts since the early 1970s. Intersectional alliances require more than ethical-behavioural choices, of course, although we would argue that white feminists need to follow protocols of permission and acknowledgement when collaborating with Indigenous artists and their communities. More than this, however, we suggest that non-Indigenous feminists engaging in the struggle for environmental justice and against racism need to couple pragmatic, ethical-behavioural issues with an understanding of structurally embedded

---

33 bell hooks, *Teaching to Transgress: Education as the Practice of Freedom* (New York: Routledge, 1994), 639.
34 'We Need to Talk Feminism and Food', 23 June 2014, artists' statement, blog.qagoma.qld.gov.au/we-need-to-talk-feminism-and-food/, in the 'We Need To Talk' gallery installation (SEXES, Performance Space, Carriageworks, Sydney; Curators: Bec Dean, Deborah Kelly and Jeff Khan; 25 October – 1 December 2012 www.performancespace.com.au). Note earlier in 2012 LEVEL organised a series of dinner party and banner-making workshops, including 'Food for Thought', a collective project by LEVEL, 2012 Next Wave Festival, Melbourne, Footscray Community Arts Centre, Melbourne.
35 Dimitrakaki, *Gender, artWork and the Global Imperative*, 231. She also cites, in the context of organising a common transnational platform for feminist curating in Europe, papers presented at the Common Differences symposium (Tallinn, May 2010), especially Katja Kobolt's paper 'Feminist Curatorial Practices and Feminist Canon-Building Strategies as Political Actions'. See common-differences.artun.ee (accessed 1 February 2017). Dimitrakaki, *Gender, artWork and the Global Imperative*, 239.

inequities of race, class and gender privilege.[36] This is what 'the personal is political' has taught us, after all. Forged in the hothouse of postmodern feminism, it still provides a useful conceptual bridge for contemporary political alliances. Of all the old feminist slogans, 'the personal is political' possibly remains the most useful in respecting difference and strategic, identity-based separatism, while continually probing the meaning of inclusivity and democracy.

36 Ibid.

CHAPTER 6

Subversive stitches: Needlework as activism in Australian feminist art of the 1970s

Elizabeth Emery

Needlework is herstory.[1]

The 1970s saw a flourishing of interest in needlework as an activist material within feminist visual arts practice. Ridiculed and undervalued within the discourse of male-centred visual arts, needlework was reimagined for its limitless possibilities by feminist artists, ushering in an era of experimentation with formerly neglected materials. For feminist artists, needlework signified the despised domestic feminine, while simultaneously representing women's resistance to and subversion of male dominance. Needlework was a reminder of women's oppression under patriarchy but, concurrently, needlework carried with it its own culture, specific to women's her-story. In an era when women's liberation critiqued the domestic as oppressive to women's lives, feminist artists working with needlework saw a radical possibility in bringing attention to the domestic as not simply a site of oppression, but of creativity. This chapter discusses the emergence of feminist needlework in the 1970s and its relationship to the burgeoning politics of second-wave feminism, using the Sydney-based Women's Domestic Needlework Group (1976–80) as a case study. Particular attention is given to artwork produced by feminist artist

---

1 Slogan from screenprinted poster, *Needlework is Herstory*, Marie McMahon, Earthworks Poster Collective, screenprint, 1976.

Frances Phoenix (nee Budden),[2] a founding member of the Women's Domestic Needlework Group, whose contribution to the development and archiving of feminist needlework in Australia has been immense.[3]

While the Women's Domestic Needlework Group was first and foremost a collective, this chapter primarily refers to the work and writing of Phoenix and Marie McMahon as two of the most active members of the group. Their writing on the topic of feminist needlework, published in various feminist publications during the 1970s and 1980s, has been extremely valuable to the building of a history of Australian feminist needlework.

No great women artists

In her 1971 essay, the feminist art historian Linda Nochlin posed the question, 'Why have there been no great women artists?'[4] Nochlin's question became one of the key motivations for feminist analysis of the gendered hierarchies within visual arts discourse. In her essay, Nochlin argues that the historical idea of 'great art' and 'artistic genius' were thoroughly gendered male through institutions that enforced patriarchal ideology. Nochlin argued that it is not that women, as feminine subjects, are naturally lacking in the ability to produce great art, as for centuries patriarchal culture had claimed. Rather, ideologies of femininity confined women to the private domestic sphere, thereby segregating women from participating in the arts by their marginalisation from male-defined spaces of art production.[5] The ideology of 'great art' was based almost exclusively on a male-centred, Western, grand narrative of history, a history that was exclusionary to women and other marginalised groups. As Nochlin argued, it was women's lack of access to education, knowledge and certain institutions that prohibited them from creating art in the same sphere as male artists, rather than an essentialist notion of women's 'nature' being somehow deficient in creativity:

---

2   In this chapter, I use Frances's chosen name of Phoenix. Her name also appears in various documents of her art and writing under her birth name Frances Budden.
3   The legacy of Frances Phoenix's contribution to the devlopment and archiving of feminist needlework, and Australian feminist art more broadly, was immense. Phoenix's death in 2017 has been a profound loss to this history, and I here pay acknowledgement to her profound contribution to the discourse of Australian feminist needlework, and beyond.
4   Linda Nochlin, 'Why Have There Been No Great Women Artists', in *Women, Art and Power*, ed. Linda Nochlin (New York: Harper and Row, 1988).
5   Ibid., 150.

> The fault, dear brothers, lies not in our stars, our hormones, our menstrual cycles or our empty internal spaces, but in our institutions and our education—education understood to include everything that happens to us from the moment we enter this world of meaningful symbols, signs and signals.[6]

Feminist analysis of the visual arts encouraged women to understand women's absence from the history of art, not as a failure of women, but as a sign of sexist culture itself. In addressing the inherent sexism of women's exclusion from the grand narrative of Western art, the objective of a feminist art was to challenge the male-dominated fields of painting and sculpture, and to reclaim forgotten female artists from the periphery of arts history.[7] Feminist art criticism aimed to make women visible within the historical canon of art and, by extension, to further generate a new feminist culture of art-making beyond the discourse of male-centred art production.

The category of the domestic was seen as one such avenue of exploration that could be used in the building of a new culture of feminist art, which referred to the history of women's lives, while also signifying women's resistance to male domination. Importantly, the category of the domestic was largely divorced from a male presence, thereby making it an ideal subject matter for feminist inquiry into women's history and lived experience.[8] The exploration of the domestic in feminist art gave representational form to the feminist ethos of 'the personal is political', by making visible the connection between the personal, lived experience and the political sphere. Through making the domestic visible in visual art, feminist art of the 1970s transformed the abject domestic space into a wholly political space; it politicised the domestic sphere as a signifier of women's lived experience.

In her influential text *The Subversive Stitch*, Rozsika Parker argues that needlework has been one of the most compelling signifiers of the historical relationship between women and the domestic sphere. Parker chronicled how needlework was used as a means of indoctrinating women and girls into the European feminine ideal, to uphold the ideology of femininity and domesticity.[9] The gendering of European needlework as a feminine craft

---

6 Ibid.
7 Griselda Pollock, *Differencing the Canon: Feminist Desire and the Writing of Art's Histories* (London: Routledge, 1999), 5.
8 Janis Jeffries, 'Crocheted Strategies: Women Crafting Their Own Communities', *Textile: Cloth and Culture* 14, no. 1 (2016): 17, doi.org/10.1080/14759756.2016.1142788.
9 Rozsika Parker, *The Subversive Stitch* (London: Women's Press Ltd, 1984).

has its origins as far back as the 1500s, when embroidery and other textile crafts began to be equated with the work of women. By the beginning of the eighteenth century, needlework became thoroughly gendered feminine, and it was subsequently defined in relationship to the domestic, in contrast with the public sphere of masculine arts.[10] Needlework was used to enforce the ideology of femininity by equating needlework crafts with 'natural' feminine qualities. However, while needlework was used to enforce the ideology of femininity, it also had the capacity to be used by women for their own subversive purposes. While needlework was used to contain women within the ideology of femininity, women in turn used needlework to communicate covertly in ways undetectable by patriarchal culture.[11]

It was this tension, between patriarchal domination and women's resistance to it, that made needlework an appropriate material to feminist artists seeking new ways to represent the politics of second-wave feminism, with particular reference to women's relationship to the domestic. Needlework, with its historical associations with women's passivity under patriarchy, was laden with reference to the lived experiences of women in the domestic.[12] Feminist needlework drew upon the abject associations of women's needlework crafts and its culturally maligned status within grand narratives of art, to create a critical discourse surrounding the domestic feminine.

Feminist needlework was a reflection of second-wave feminism's larger critique of the oppressiveness of the domestic. However, feminist artists using needlework did not perceive needlework as only a source of female subordination. Rather, needlework was positioned as a source of women's creativity and knowledge produced within the oppressive conditions of the domestic.[13] Historically associated with submissiveness, repetition and unoriginality, needlework signified the denigration of women's work by male-centred culture. Utilising needlework as a feminist material was thus fraught with contradiction, seemingly a symbol of oppression, while also claiming to resist patriarchal domination. In addressing these contradictions, feminist textiles historian Janis Jeffries says of the liberating potential of using women's domestic needlework crafts:

---

10   Ibid., 11.
11   Ibid.
12   Rachel Maines, 'Fancywork: The Archaeology of Lives', *Women's Art Forum* 3, no. 4 (Winter 1974–75).
13   Jeffries, 'Crocheted Strategies', 17.

[T]he potentially radical yet problematic promotion of women's 'traditional' arts in textiles and other craft related processes enabled not only a distancing from an aesthetics of the 'purely' visual, but also provided a strategy for mobilising textiles as a weapon of resistance against an inculcated 'feminine' ideal.[14]

As Jeffries argues, needlework provided a radical departure from the dominant visual aesthetics of media such as painting, as it drew upon an entirely different tradition of women's creative work. For feminist artists, needlework seemed to transcend the boundaries of existing dominant forms of visual art, allowing for experimentation with materials that had long been disparaged.[15] The emergence of feminist needlework in the 1970s was thus not only a material practice of art making, but also an expression of activism that signified creative strategies of resistance.

The Women's Domestic Needlework Group

Emerging from within the activist and artistic circles of Sydney University in 1976, the Women's Domestic Needlework Group (c. 1976–80) was established by a collective of feminist artists with the aim to promote needlework as a legitimate form of artistic production. The activities of this group brought together the history of women's domestic needlework, with feminist politics, to critically explore the meaning of women's creative labour. Founding members of the group include Joan Grounds, Frances Phoenix, Marie McMahon, Bernadette Krone, Kathy Letray, Patricia McDonald, Noela Taylor and Loretta Vieceli.[16] Between 1976 and the early 1980s, the Women's Domestic Needlework Group facilitated a range of activities that brought women together to explore the history and materiality of needlework as an expression of feminist activism. The strength of feminist needlework, as an activist practice used for political resistance, can be located within the media associated with collective organisation.[17] The Women's Domestic Needlework Group identified needlework as a material practice that carries collectivist meanings and associations, separate from modernist ideas of individual

---

14   Ibid., 17.
15   Ibid.
16   The Women's Domestic Needlework Group, *The D'oyley Show: An Exhibition of Women's Domestic Fancywork* (Sydney: D'oyley Publications, 1979), 2.
17   Jeffries, 'Crocheted Strategies', 26.

creative genius. This separateness from a dominant, male-defined field of individual art production enabled the group to utilise needlework as a material to build collective-focused feminist politics.[18]

Needlework has long been practised among groups of women in such forms as quilting bees, knitting circles, mothers' groups and in the creation of ritual textiles for specific cultural events. The formation of such groups has historically been a space where needlework knowledge is exchanged among women, creating and building a discourse of shared textiles knowledge and traditions.[19] The needlework group is a collective space where knowledge is not owned by one, it is shared among all who contribute. Additionally, the needlework group has throughout history been a space for women to share personal stories, support one another and build consciousness around issues affecting communities. The Women's Domestic Needlework Group can be seen to continue in this historical lineage of women's craft circles by facilitating a space for women to share needlework knowledge, while simultaneously creating a platform for feminist consciousness-raising.

Central to the objectives of the Women's Domestic Needlework Group was the promotion of women's needlework crafts as a vital site of female knowledge and women's culture.[20] Needlework, as separate from a male arts culture, provided a discourse for women's work and a history to draw upon in the construction of new feminist histories of art. Asserting the existence of this history was an entirely political act for the Women's Domestic Needlework Group, as it made visible the work of women made invisible by male domination. In a 1977 issue of *Lip*, writing on their aims of exploring the history of needlework, Phoenix and McMahon state:

> With the belief that needlework is the women's art, we have begun a study which includes talking to needlewomen and collecting 'textile evidence for the lives of women'; doilies patterns, tools and books about the story of needlework. We have mainly worked with domestic needlework as it reflects the aesthetic and cultural lives of mainstream women.[21]

---

18   The Women's Domestic Needlework Group, *The D'oyley Show*, 4.
19   Jeffries, 'Crocheted Strategies', 26.
20   Frances Budden and Marie McMahon, 'The Fancywork of the Great Goddess, and other Mainstream Women', *Lip*, no. 2 (1977): 63.
21   Ibid.

Phoenix and McMahon identified needlework as an important signifier for, and historical evidence of, 'an expression of women's creativity'.[22] For Phoenix and McMahon, a focus on the creative work of 'mainstream' women, 'ordinary' women or 'non-artists' was critical in their investigation as part of a feminist reappraisal of history and the absence of women's creativity from historical records. Phoenix and McMahon were both influenced by the writing of Rachel Maines who, in her 1974 essay 'Fancywork: The Archaeology of Lives', presented one of the first feminist evaluations of needlework.[23] In 'The Archaeology of Lives', Maines examines needlework as historical evidence of a women's culture distinctly separate from men, which could therefore provide a substantial material culture for feminism to draw upon. Maines identified that a subversiveness was intrinsically linked to women's domestic needlework due to its historical position within this separate women's culture. For Maines, needlework signified its own language, knowledge and discourse, which had existed throughout history separate from a dominant patriarchal culture. Needlework was therefore a symbol of women's resistance:

> Since men are not now and seldom have been educated in the complex language of needlework symbology, any message transmitted in a textile medium was almost completely safe from falling into the wrong hands. We therefore find stunningly honest and forthright statements in needlework, delivered to us across space and cultural barriers on every subject from politics to sex.[24]

In a 1976 issue of *Lip*, Phoenix writes of her development of a feminist consciousness surrounding the history of women's domestic needlework, which would become the basis for some of the working methods used by the Women's Domestic Needlework Group. This method of feminist work combined the politics of second-wave feminism with the rich history of women's needlework. For Phoenix, using a domestic material such as needlework to articulate feminist politics was not contradictory to the politics of feminism. Phoenix argues that the feminist use of needlework is an entirely feminist action, as it politicises the denigrated work, and worth, of women.[25] In the *Lip* article, Phoenix's feminist exploration into the history of needlework is articulated in a vivid and subversively

---

22 Ibid.
23 Maines, 'Fancywork: The Archaeology of Lives'.
24 Ibid., 2.
25 Frances Budden, 'A Note on Australian Embroidery', *Lip*, no. 1 (1976): 23.

humorous description of some of her earliest experiments with lace and embroidery: 'The first doily was embroidered "Fuck Patriarchy" and the second, "Women's Work = Slave Labour"'.[26]

The doily archive

Transforming the denigrated status of women's work was fundamental to the aims of the Women's Domestic Needlework Group, resulting in the creation of an extensive archive of Australian women's doilies. The archive was part history project, part feminist consciousness-raising, with the core objective of bringing public attention to the creative domestic work of women. The doily archive project involved the collection of hundreds of examples of lace doilies from the late nineteenth century to the late 1970s. The archive was a celebration of the domestic needlework of women who did not necessarily come from a visual arts context, women who wouldn't be considered professional artists. The doilies made by women who had worked as domestic servants and housewives, and the gift-giving acts of mothers and grandmothers, were shown as equal in status to the work produced by artists in the Women's Domestic Needlework Group. In constructing this archive of Australian women's doilies, the group critiqued the arbitrary distinctions of 'high art', 'low art', 'hobby art' and 'craft' in their declaration that all women's creative work was worthy of examination alongside grand narratives of art.

It is important here to note that the archive focused on collecting artefacts that were created within the specific European traditions of needlework, the type of domestic needlework steeped in an ideology of Eurocentric femininity. The Women's Domestic Needlework Group also actively acknowledged the rich culture of textiles produced by Aboriginal women, both prior to and after colonial invasion, and further acknowledged themselves as colonial subjects in Australian history. For members in the group acknowledging the specific history and meaning of Aboriginal women's textiles was crucial to their feminist aims as a non-hierarchical, antiracist collective. Acknowledging these issues as white women living on Aboriginal land, the group stated in the doily archive catalogue:

26 Ibid.

> The D'oyley Show deals primarily with the work of women of European origin; however Aboriginal women were making baskets, woven mats, bead and shell work, netting and string games long before Captain Cook arrived … Like all aspects of Aboriginal identity, this work has been subjected to systematic assault and destruction by white society. Aboriginal handiwork and Aboriginal life have always been interdependent. For Aboriginal people the loss of their land has meant the breakdown of their traditional skills. The practice of these skills is part of the struggle to maintain Aboriginal identity.[27]

Beginning with its first showing in Sydney at Watters Gallery in October of 1979, the archive travelled as *The D'oyley Show: An Exhibition of Women's Domestic Fancywork*. *The D'oyley Show* toured through parts of Australia from 1979 to 1980, being exhibited in a range of galleries and feminist spaces. Accompanying the exhibition was a catalogue book that featured images of examples from the doily archive, along with doily patterns, and articles written by group members on the history of needlework. The doilies in the archive had never been exhibited publicly as 'art' and, as such, this was a groundbreaking achievement of the Women's Domestic Needlework Group; they transformed the doilies from objects of domestic ubiquity to the status of art objects. An excerpt from the D'oyley Show exhibition book reinforces the group's focus on elevating women's domestic needlework to the status of art, while also highlighting some of the contradictions of needlework as art:

> The work in this exhibition is not revolutionary. It contains the contradictions of work under capitalism. However, the contradictions under which this fancywork has been produced, the functions it has served and the beauty of the designs provide a valuable record of women's work for us today.[28]

The D'oyley Show was a document of women's creative domestic work produced under the conditions of capitalist patriarchy. For the Women's Domestic Needlework Group, the construction of the archive was a form of feminist activism that highlighted the denigration of women's domestic work, and its relationship to ideologies of European femininity. However, it is important to acknowledge that there was resistance to the celebration of the domestic in visual art during the period of second-wave feminism,

---

27 The Women's Domestic Needlework Group, *The D'oyley Show*, 6.
28 Ibid., 4.

as it was viewed by those who critiqued its use as merely perpetuating women's subordinate position in society.[29] A doily, with its historical and ideological associations with women's oppression, was viewed by some as counterproductive to the objectives of women's liberation. With the politics of second-wave feminism in mind, a politics that sought to free women from male domination, it would be reasonable to suggest that the celebration of the material culture of domestic needlework was still deeply tied to sexist ideology.

The intention of the Women's Domestic Needlework Group was to position the archive as a political document of the domestic work of women who had been otherwise made invisible within dominant narratives of culture.[30] The feminist methodology of the group aimed to assert that this form of women's work was valuable to the building of feminist consciousness, regardless of whether its production was tied to the conditions of patriarchy. The group acknowledged the complexities of this issue; that on the one hand needlework signified the very conditions second-wave feminism sought to resist, but that acknowledging this history was in itself a feminist act, as it gave validity to the largely invisible work of women.[31] The radical claim of the group was that this form of material culture was an important document of the creative work of women who endured under oppressive circumstances. Addressing the invisibility of needlework in historical records, the group state in *The D'oyley Show* book:

> There are histories available on 'Art Embroidery' and other styles of needlework produced for the use of consumption by the church and the ruling classes. However, there has been virtually no documentation until recently on the history of needlework produced by middle and working class women for use in the Australian home.[32]

Alison Bartlett and Margaret Henderson argue that feminist objects, feminism's material culture, are of great significance to how feminist politics are read, understood and, ultimately, how they are remembered.[33] Feminist objects articulate feminist politics through their materiality,

---

29 Jeffries, 'Crocheted Strategies', 17.
30 The Women's Domestic Needlework Group, *The D'oyley Show*, 4.
31 Ibid.
32 Ibid., 5.
33 Alison Bartlett and Margaret Henderson, eds, *Things that Liberate: The Feminist Wunderkammer* (Newcastle: Cambridge Scholars Publishing, 2013).

across space and time. Just as all objects do, the meaning of feminist objects transform through their historical location, 'their meanings are neither fixed nor stable'.[34] The majority of the doilies collected and archived by the Women's Domestic Needlework Group were not made by women with feminist intentions. They were largely made as objects for the home, as decorations, keepsakes and as tender gifts of love exchanged within families. However, when held together in the form of an archive, as an articulation of feminist activist work, these decorative doilies were given new meanings as feminist material culture.

In reflecting upon the activism of the Women's Domestic Needlework Group, it can be argued that their activities, and the archive they produced, were far more revolutionary than they credited themselves for at the time. In an era when needlework was still perceived by heavily stereotyped ideas of unoriginality, repetition and domestic submissiveness, a collective of women elevated the domestic needlework of women to a status equal to art being made in the contemporary moment of the 1970s. They were not simply championing needlework as art, but arguing that it signified an important example of women's lived experience and unique culture. An archival record of the lace doilies of Australian women at that time was unprecedented. The Women's Domestic Needlework Group were the first to survey with seriousness this material culture. Given the group's efforts to archive the history of Australian women's needlework, it is the greatest tragedy that the entire doily archive was destroyed by fire in a Sydney storage facility in 1985.

No goddesses, no mistresses

The abject and undervalued status of needlework was not only appealing to feminist art for articulating the lived experience of women in relation to the domestic, but also for challenging the very structures of hierarchy that had excluded women from narratives of history. Needlework was revolutionary for feminist art as it was thoroughly separate from the arts establishment, the commercial art marketplace, the concept of male 'genius' and the canon of Western art. Among feminist textile artists, needlework was considered a form of countercultural production that was free from the associations of the commercial, male-dominated art world.[35]

---

34 Ibid., 3.
35 Jeffries, 'Crocheted Strategies', 17.

The real revolutionary potential of needlework as art/activism was in the medium's very separateness from male-centred cultural production. Feminist needlework was radical in that it transcended these hierarchies, and searched for less hierarchical methods of organisation.

The Women's Domestic Needlework Group used needlework to foster collaboration, and create networks for knowledge sharing, and rejected hierarchical organisation to instead embrace shared participation. The focus on collaboration enabled the dynamic of the group to avoid following the hierarchical tendencies that were still heavily entrenched within male-dominated visual arts in the 1970s.

The Women's Domestic Needlework Group's non-hierarchical methods were, of course, not reflective of all feminist methodology during the era of second-wave feminism. While hierarchy was entrenched within the traditions of male-dominated art, hierarchical organisation was still practised by feminist artists and within second-wave feminism more broadly. Phoenix and McMahon's involvement with the production of Judy Chicago's feminist art installation *The Dinner Party* (1979) is a revealing example of the type of hierarchical organisation that was practised, in contrast with how the Women's Domestic Needlework Group operated. When Phoenix and McMahon volunteered to assist with the creation of Chicago's seminal feminist artwork, the two artists became disillusioned with what they saw as Chicago's authoritarian approach to art making.[36]

Chicago's *The Dinner Party* was initially premised as a collaborative project that would bring women together in an environment of collectivism to create an artwork celebrating the artistic achievements of women throughout history. *The Dinner Party* consisted of a triangular dinner table setting, with placemats made for 39 women of cultural significance; Chicago's reimagining of forgotten women of history. To construct the large-scale installation, which comprised embroidered table-runners as well as handmade ceramics, Chicago was assisted by a team of volunteer women who donated their time and labour to the monumental project. For many of the volunteers, their involvement with *The Dinner Party* was initially seen as an opportunity to work collaboratively with other feminist women, in an environment that broke away from the hierarchical organisation of male-dominated art.[37]

---

36   Isabel Davies, "'The Coming Out Show' Discusses 'The Dinner Party'", *Lip* (1980): 48.
37   Ibid.

In contrast with the initial collective premise of *The Dinner Party*, Phoenix and McMahon found that the project was structured hierarchically by Chicago, with volunteers treated not as equals but as workers used simply to bring the artwork to completion. Chicago's authoritative approach to collaborative art making was at ideological odds with the anarchic, non-hierarchical politics of the Women's Domestic Needlework Group that Phoenix and McMahon had been fostering. The use of needlework in *The Dinner Party* was further critiqued for replicating more of a sweat shop–style production than feminist creative work.[38] Those that produced the embroidered table-runners for *The Dinner Party* did not always have their physical bodies considered during the painstaking and physically demanding work involved in its creation.

In a subversive act of defiance against Chicago's dominant/subordinate structure of labour, Phoenix created a small embroidery of her own. The embroidery read, 'No Goddesses, No Mistresses', a play on the anarchist slogan, 'No God, No Master'. Phoenix's small, subversive embroidery critiqued what was seen by many as Chicago's extreme use of hierarchy, rather than employing more egalitarian methods of collaborative work. Phoenix's embroidery was sewn into the underside of one of *The Dinner Party*'s cloth panels, a small, defiant act of rebellion within the monumental installation. The embroidery itself was signed, not with Phoenix's name but instead with an emblem—an 'A' in a circle—a symbol of anarchist-feminism. By using the anarchist-feminist symbol, rather than her name, Phoenix distanced herself from association with individual artistry. In transforming the anarchist slogan 'No God, No Master' into the feminine 'goddesses' and 'mistresses', Phoenix critiqued the role of women in creating hierarchical power structures over other women. Her embroidered statement is a reminder that feminism is not immune from carrying out dominance over women. Phoenix's hidden embroidery was eventually discovered by Chicago, removed and discarded.

The small non-hierarchical group model was seen by those who critiqued hierarchical feminist organisation as a revolutionary alternative to large-scale leader/follower structures. It was believed that small groups allowed individuals to contribute to a collective aim, while also gaining personal development, rather than performing as a single body within a larger system. The small group format was felt to enable all feminists to contribute to the development of feminist culture and politics by celebrating all women's

---

38   Ibid., 49.

contributions, rather than focusing on leaders. In the essay 'The Tyranny of Tyranny', Cathy Levine argues against hierarchical organisation in the women's movement, in favour of women working in small groups where leadership was disbursed amongst all:

> By working collectively in small numbers, the small group utilises the various contributions of each person to their fullest, nurturing and developing individual input, instead of dissipating it in the competitive survival-of-the-fittest/smartest/wittiest spirit of the large scale organisation.[39]

Levine's description of the small, non-hierarchical collective is reflected in the working methods of the Women's Domestic Needlework Group, based on an anarchist principle of shared collective responsibility and a rejection of leaders.[40] Here is a distinct example of contrasting approaches to methodologies of collaborative work in feminist art during the 1970s, with the Women's Domestic Needlework Group representing an embrace of shared participation, in contrast with Chicago's reliance on the leader/follower format. In a 1980 interview for 'The Coming Out Show' on ABC radio, Phoenix and McMahon retold their experiences working with Chicago on *The Dinner Party*, with Phoenix stating:

> I was pleased to leave after six weeks. I was exhausted and most of the time pretty unhappy in that environment. I didn't find it the supportive environment it was made out to be.[41]

A disobedient doily

This chapter has concentrated on an examination of the collective work of the Women's Domestic Needlework Group. In this final section, I turn attention to analysis of an artwork created by Frances Phoenix in 1976, to further illustrate the blending of feminist politics with the history of domestic needlework. As much as Phoenix was a member in a collective, and collective work deeply informed her feminist politics, she was also an artist in her own right, with her artwork representing some of the most compelling examples of feminist needlework produced during the 1970s.

---

39 Cathy Levine, 'The Tyranny of Tyranny', in *Quiet Rumours, An Anarcha-Feminist Reader*, ed. Dark Star Collective (Oakland: AK Press, 2012): 77.
40 Ibid.
41 Davies, '"The Coming Out Show" Discusses "The Dinner Party"', 49.

Figure 6.1: *Kunda*, Frances Phoenix (Budden), 1976, crochet doily and zip.
Source: Image reproduced with the permission of the estate of the artist. Courtesy of Sally Cantrill.

The abject status of domestic needlework was used by Phoenix to critique the denigrated position of women as subordinate bodies under patriarchy, and her 1976 artwork *Kunda* (Figure 6.1) is a powerful articulation of this.[42] *Kunda* is a crochet representation of a vulva, made using a scallop stitch method of crochet in soft pink hues of thread. A zip has been sewn into the centre of the artwork, representing the entrance of a vagina. In *Kunda* Phoenix refers to the ubiquity of the doily as a common domestic object, but she also refers to the history of doily making as an expression of women's knowledge and discourse. As Maines argues, doilies were not simply made to be decorative objects for the home, they carried symbolic meaning often only detectable to women who understood the

---

42 *Kunda* has been exhibited with the alternate title and date *Queen of Spades*, 1975, in the exhibition *Unfinished Business: Perspectives on Art and Feminism*, Australian Centre for Contemporary Art, Melbourne, December 2017 – March 2018.

language of needlework.[43] Phoenix's appropriation of the traditional doily aesthetic pays homage to the history of women's doily making, as a discourse of knowledge, not mere decoration.

Kunda refers to the subversive history of women's domestic needlework, but as much as it subverts it can also be seen to *pervert* this history, through its explicit and unapologetic use of the vulva as central motif. The doily as an object of ubiquitous domesticity, functional and frilly, is made perverse in Phoenix's gesture toward the intimacy of the sexual body. The scalloped frilly edging along the outside of the artwork references traditional decorative lace, while also alluding to pubic hair and the physical shape of the vulva. In her use of vaginal iconography, Phoenix refers to women's relationship to the domestic space as one that has been oppressive toward women's identities and sexualities. However, Phoenix's artwork also suggests liberation from these conditions in the subversive humour and tactility of her creation; she presents a subversive interpretation of so-called 'domestic bliss'.

Kunda can be described as a most feminist uncanny object, as Phoenix uses the familiarity of feminine domesticity to unsettle and disorient the category of the domestic feminine. In Phoenix's *Kunda* the uncanny, as a de-familiarising of the familiar, is met with a feminist revision of the denigration of the category of feminine. Alexandra Kokoli articulates that in the feminist uncanny:

> The return of the feminine bears the mark of its imposed exile, from which it broke free; its scars are what is uncanny and its return against the odds is terrible. The feminist uncanny is thus perpetually suspended between revision and revenge.[44]

That revision and revenge form a central theme in feminist uncanny artwork is evident in *Kunda*, as an object that revises women's subordinate position within patriarchal culture, then taking revenge upon this subordination by reasserting the domestic feminine in a perverse and rebellious manifestation.

---

43   Maines, 'Fancywork: The Archaeology of Lives', 2.
44   Alexandra Kokoli, *The Feminist Uncanny in Theory and Art Practice* (London: Bloomsbury, 2016), 39.

Kunda is a disobedient doily, one that escapes its traditional place as docile, passive object, to instead possess an unnerving and menacing aura, as though it were in fact possessed. The unsettling appearance of *Kunda* centres on Phoenix's use of the inserted zip with its reference to vagina, reproduction and the despised feminine. The reference to the vulva and vagina reflects the interest of 1970s feminist art in central core imagery. Central core imagery refers to the representation of the vulva and vagina in art as a way to reinsert women's experience into a phallocentric culture where women's bodies have been at the mercy of the male gaze.[45] The dominance of the masculine phallus was challenged by the feminist positioning of central core as a source of feminine power. The use of central core imagery enabled a visual means for centring women's experience, by giving particular focus to reproduction, menstruation, motherhood and sexuality. Jude Adams states that the power of using central core within feminist art was that, 'It reasserted the despised feminine'.[46]

However, the use of central core imagery also came under critique within feminist debates for focusing too heavily on an essentialist view of womanhood as linked to biological embodiment. Central core imagery was eventually viewed by some feminist artists as problematic in what it appeared to assume about the experience of women's embodiment.[47] This critique of central core raised important questions about feminist claims of womanhood as a universal experience, bringing to the centre critical debate around essentialist ideas of womanhood. Despite its limitations, central core imagery was still a powerful activist strategy in its time, which made visible the despised feminine, when such subject matter was almost entirely taboo within art.

Kunda is an artwork that potently reflects the climate of feminist politics at the time of its production. It is very much an object of its historical context and the politics that influenced its production. Phoenix's use of central core imagery makes a political subject out of the feminine body by putting on display all of its taboo corporeality, making visible the lived experience of the abject body. *Kunda* is alive with its bodily references, as it simultaneously refers to the history of women's subordination as well

---

45   Jude Adams, 'Looking from with/in: Feminist Art Projects of the 70s', *Outskirts* 29 (November 2013), www.outskirts.arts.uwa.edu.au/volumes/volume-29/adams-jude-looking-with-in.
46   Ibid.
47   Ibid.

as to women's resistance to domination. Phoenix's artwork is at once an object of activism as much as it is an object of art; a wholly politicised tribute to the work, bodies and histories of women.

Conclusion

Feminist needlework of the 1970s was revolutionary in its claim that the creative work of all women was worthy of serious examination. In elevating women's domestic needlework to the status of art, feminist needlework was as much an expression of activism as it was a creative material. In its separateness from a male-centred art culture, needlework was experienced as liberating for those feminist artists who engaged with its history and materiality. Needlework transcended the hierarchical boundaries of an elite art world, providing limitless possibility in its application as a material. Needlework, like women, was an outsider. It was its status as abject outsider that was in fact what gave needlework its freeing quality for feminist art; like the status of women, needlework was neglected, denigrated and treated with derision. While European ideals of femininity had been constructed in connection with the ideology of needlework, women in turn used the tools of this ideology to create their own culture, subversively separate from a male-centred culture. Feminist needlework artists continued the legacy of women's work before them, and located this past within the subversive stitches made in their present.

CHAPTER 7
Women into print: Feminist presses in Australia

Trish Luker

'The freedom of the press belongs to those who control the press' was one of the enduring slogans of the second-wave women's movement. Reflecting the belief that the printed word could incite social change, feminists asserted their position in the public sphere of publishing, as authors, in print production and through the establishment of feminist presses. Reclaiming and celebrating women's writing was a defining characteristic of second-wave feminism, and feminist literary and cultural historians took up the literature of Australian women writers from the nineteenth and early to mid-twentieth century.[1] The Australian second-wave women's movement emphasised cultural forms; it was a catalyst for feminist writing, in the form of journalism, autobiography, short fiction, novels, poetry and plays, as well as feminist history, political theory, gender and sexuality studies. These texts, in turn, form a body of cultural memory that informs how feminism marks its own past, providing a narrative for individual and collective remembering.[2]

While there has been attention to the impact of second-wave feminism on Australian literature and the literary form, as well as the contested terrain of what is meant by feminist writing, there has been less attention to the significance of feminist engagement with the material production

---
1   Drusilla Modjeska, *Exiles at Home: Australian Women Writers, 1925–1945* (Sydney: Angus & Robertson, 1981); Susan Sheridan, *Along the Faultlines: Sex, Race and Nation in Australian Women's Writing* (St Leonards, NSW: Allen & Unwin, 1995); Dale Spender, ed., *The Penguin Anthology of Australian Women's Writing* (Ringwood, Vic: Penguin, 1988).
2   Margaret Henderson, *Marking Feminist Times* (Bern, New York: Peter Lang, 2006).

of print. As Kathryn Flannery argues, many of the historical accounts of second-wave feminism emphasise women interacting with each other, sharing experiences through discussion, rather than women engaged in the production of 'writing, reading, creating artwork or illustrating copy, running printing presses, or distributing print materials'.[3] During the 1970s in Australia, feminists produced newsletters, newspapers, magazines, posters, pamphlets, flyers and postcards to disseminate political ideas, promote activism, advertise cultural events and act as a medium for personal connections. They also established presses, providing independent printing facilities for the women's liberation movement, left-wing and community groups, and direct mail-order distribution for feminist literature and feminist book publishing.

Print, and particularly the printed form of the book, has been understood in the West as a knowledge-making practice. This principle was adopted by second-wave feminists in Western countries such as Australia where the majority of political ideas were disseminated through publications. Stacey Young argues that feminist presses exemplify a theory of power and an approach to activism in which discursive struggle is central.[4] She suggests that feminist publishing, as well as feminist writing and other discursive aspects of activism, 'represent the most direct attempts by the women's movement to change fundamentally the way people think'.[5] The printed word was central to the women's liberation movement. From the 1970s onwards, published women's writing grew exponentially, inspired by second-wave feminist theory and activism and fostered by access to higher education. New feminist writing explored areas of women's lived experience with attention to sexuality, family and new forms of community.

The twenty-first century has seen a dramatic shift to a digital age, profoundly changing the materiality of all forms of publishing. At the same time, it has prompted an archival turn in feminist attention, concerned with the documentary and cultural products of feminist activism.[6] This chapter is concerned with the role of feminist presses established in the 1970s in Australia. Feminist print and publishing cultures of this period

---

3 Kathryn Flannery, *Feminist Literacies, 1968–75* (Urbana: University of Illinois Press, 2005), 2.
4 Stacey Young, *Changing the Wor(l)d: Discourse, Politics, and the Feminist Movement* (New York: Routledge, 1997), 26.
5 Ibid., 3.
6 Kate Eichhorn, *The Archival Turn in Feminism: Outrage in Order* (Philadelphia: Temple University Press, 2013).

were characteristically both personal and political activities. It is valuable to examine feminist interventions into printing and publishing, the materialist processes of feminist print production, as a way of interpreting the archive of published work of the time. As Jaime Harker and Cecilia Konchar Farr argue: 'Feminist print culture is an essential context for understanding literary artifacts that arose from second-wave feminism'.[7]

Feminism as writing

Key texts are identified as making and defining the women's liberation movement. Indeed, some have characterised it as a 'writers' movement'.[8] 'This book is an action', claimed Robin Morgan in the first line of the radical feminist anthology of writing by women *Sisterhood is Powerful*, indicating a belief that writing is a form of activism. Published in 1970, this anthology of over 50 contributors from the women's liberation movement included many who had never published previously. Feminist texts were seen to connect the movement together, transnationally, through the activities of writing and reading. Recent attention to the importance of writing and reading to the second-wave women's movement, particularly in the United States, has highlighted the way it served to link 'art and activism' and has produced a distinctive 'feminist canon':

> Early feminists wrote in a wide variety of genres—poetry, manifestos, plays and performances, personal and scholarly essays, science fiction and detective novels, avant-garde experimental texts, and coming-of-age novels—and they purposefully explored a range of alternative aesthetics. What united them was a firm belief that books could be revolutionary, that language could remake the world, and that writing mattered in a profound way.[9]

Reading, as Harker and Farr argue, 'was essential in early conceptions of second-wave feminism, as books became a provocation to conversation about readers' own lives and experiences'.[10] In Australia, Germaine Greer's *The Female Eunuch* (1970), Anne Summers's *Damned Whores and God's*

---

7   Jaime Harker and Cecilia Konchar Farr, eds, *This Book is an Action: Feminist Print Culture and Activist Aesthetics* (Urbana: University of Illinois Press, 2016), 7.
8   Diane Brown, 'Feminist Publishing: 1970 – 2006', in *Making Books: Contemporary Australian publishing,* ed. David Carter and Anne Galligan (St Lucia: University of Queensland Press, 2007), 268–78, 269.
9   Harker and Farr, *This Book is an Action*, 1.
10 Ibid., 4.

Police (1975), Miriam Dixson's *The Real Matilda* (1976), *The Other Half,* edited by Jan Mercer (1975), as well as the work of Simone de Beauvoir, Kate Millett, Shulamith Firestone, Betty Friedan, Gloria Steinem, Juliet Mitchell and Ann Oakley were required reading for second-wave feminists. Fiction was also seen as a way of 'transforming readers' politics'.[11] Writers such as Margaret Atwood, Alice Walker, Adrienne Rich, Marge Piercy and Rita Mae Brown used fiction as a way of exploring new forms of feminist subjectivity. In Australia, short fiction, semi-autobiographical writings and poetry were key forms, leading to the publication of books such as *Mother I'm Rooted*, an anthology of poetry edited by Kate Jennings (1975), Elizabeth Riley's *All That False Instruction: A Novel of Lesbian Love* (1975), Glen Tomasetti's *Thoroughly Decent People* (1976) and Helen Garner's *Monkey Grip* (1977). For many who first encountered feminist ideas at the time, experiences of reading these books are etched in memory as key moments, often a vehicle for 'consciousness-raising' and providing frameworks and vocabularies for new politicised understanding and knowledge.

Some feminists embraced opportunities to explore their writing and publishing skills as journalists, photographers, cartoonists and graphic designers in left-wing and progressive print media newspapers and magazines, such as the Communist Party of Australia's *Tribune* (1939–91), *Nation Review* (1970–81), *The National Times* (1971–86), Friends of the Earth's magazine *Chain Reaction Magazine* (1975–), as well as the emerging alternative and community radio media at 2JJ (1975–), 3CR (1976–), 3RRR (1976–) and 2SER (1979–). Feminists were also contributors to political, academic and literary journals, such as *Meanjin* (1940–) and *Arena* (1963–), as well as student newspapers such as *Honi Soit* (University of Sydney). However, women who took up feminist themes in their writing for alternative and left-wing publications often experienced sexism and condescending attitudes and had difficulty getting their work published because feminist's issues were not seen as central to the political struggle.

In higher education, student activism led to the introduction of women's studies in Australian universities, notably following a strike by staff, students and unions in the Department of Philosophy at Sydney University in 1973; as well as at Flinders University and The Australian

---

11 Ibid.

National University.[12] The new cohort of enthusiastic students created a demand for feminist academic texts. Feminist academics working in these disciplines began to write theoretical articles and books to reflect their areas of research and support their teaching.

Feminism as print production

It was not only as writers that feminists engaged with print culture. Second-wave feminism was actually a print media movement.[13] According to Kathryn Adams, 'between March, 1968, and August, 1973, over 560 new publications produced by feminists appeared in the United States, each one serving as a mailing address for the movement'.[14] There were also over 200 feminist bookstores across the United States.[15] As Jaime Harker and Cecilia Farr point out:

> These presses operated on a shoestring budget, dependent on donated labor and often marked by inexperienced printing and editing, but they produced some of the most remarkable artifacts of Women's Liberation and launched many writers and texts that have become essential to Women's Liberation and to the U.S. women's literary tradition.[16]

Of course, this was not the first time feminists had employed print media to disseminate radical political ideas. First-wave feminists in late nineteenth- and early twentieth-century Britain also entered the public sphere by creating a feminist press to organise and mobilise for suffrage and other campaigns, as a vehicle for debate and to influence public opinion.[17] In Australia also, in 1888, Louisa Lawson established a printery and published the radical women's paper *The Dawn*. She employed all-women staff to produce and print the paper, leading to a boycott by the printers' union.[18]

---

12 See contributions to *Australian Feminist Studies* 13, no. 2 (1988), edited by Alison Bashford.
13 Barbara Grier, Publisher, Naiad Press, quoted in Young, *Changing the Wor(l)d*, 25.
14 Kathryn Adams, 'Paper Lesbians: Alternative Publishing and the Politics of Lesbian Representation in the United States, 1950–1990' (PhD thesis, University of Texas at Austin, 1994), 193, cited in Harker and Farr, *This Book is an Action*, 6.
15 Junko Onosaka, quoted in Harker and Farr, *This Book is an Action*, 6.
16 Harker and Farr, *This Book is an Action*, 6.
17 Maria DiCenzo, Leila Ryan and Lucy Delap, *Feminist Media History: Suffrage, Periodicals and the Public Sphere* (Bassingstoke; New York: Palgrave Macmillan, 2011).
18 Louise Poland, 'Setting the Agenda: Feminist Presses and Publishing Politics in Australia, 1974–2003' (PhD thesis, Monash University, 2007), 78.

However, by the second wave of the women's movement, in Britain, United States, Australia and other Western countries, feminists had begun to understand language and popular media as instruments for subordination of women. This led women to establish an alternative feminist press, by creating magazines and newspapers that allowed them to disseminate and control the circulation of feminist political ideas. Feminist periodicals were widely divergent, ranging from small-scale newsletters to mass market magazines. In the United Kingdom, *Spare Rib* (1972–93) was an iconic magazine that was instrumental in shaping feminist debates. Founded with a manifesto that set out to correct misunderstandings about women's liberation, challenge stereotyping and exploitation of women and 'reach out to all women, cutting across material, economic and class barriers',[19] it sought to provide an antidote to existing women's magazines that treated women as 'passive, dependent, conformist, incapable of critical thought'. *Spare Rib* soon moved to a non-hierarchical structure with an editorial collective; it sold around 20,000 copies per month.[20] In the United States, *Ms* magazine (1972–89) was established as a commercial mass media publication that became a central vehicle for disseminating popular feminist ideas to a wide readership. Co-founded by Gloria Steinem and Dorothy Pitman Hughes, it acquired a circulation up to 500,000 and an estimated readership of 3 million.[21]

In an account of the cultural production of the second-wave women's movement in Australia, Margaret Henderson claims that in terms of genre, 'journalism marks the 1970s, while the novel is central to the 1980s'.[22] This is reflected in the proliferation of feminist periodicals that emerged during the 1970s. During this time, many women became involved in the production of magazines, newsletters, newspapers and pamphlets through feminism. Feminist magazines including *Shrew* (Brisbane, 1971), *MeJane* (Sydney, 1971), *Mabel* (Sydney, 1975), *Hecate* (Brisbane, 1975), *Sibyl* (Perth, 1974), *Refractory Girl* (Sydney, 1972), *Vashti's Voice* (Melbourne, 1973), *Apron Strings* (Darwin, 1973), *Scarlet Woman* (Sydney and Melbourne, 1975), *Womanspeak* (1975), *Bluestocking* (1975), the Women's Electoral Lobby's newsletters, the *Anarcho Surrealist*

---

19   'Facsimile of Spare Rib manifesto', 1972, Facsimile format, held by British Library as part of Spare Rib collection items: www.bl.uk/spare-rib/collection-items.
20   *Spare Rib*, British Library, www.bl.uk/spare-rib.
21   Amy Erdman Farrell, *Yours in Sisterhood: Ms Magazine and the Promise of Popular Feminism* (Chapel Hill: University of North Carolina Press, 1998), 1.
22   Henderson, *Marking Feminist Times*, 25.

Insurrectionary Feminists journal (Melbourne, 1973) and *Koore Bina* 'A Black Australian News Monthly' (1976) all began during this time and were essential for dissemination of radical ideas, political analysis and debates that were otherwise not available in the public domain.[23]

These publications were vehicles for feminist ideas, as well as news about political and social events, fundraising and meetings. Reflecting on the first issue of *MeJane*, Suzanne Bellamy describes it as:

> a new territory of language and definitions. There is a mix of news (abortion fight updates with vivid disclosures and information, anti-war issues, conference reports, group meeting times), book reviews (Greer), a focus on child care, working women, women in gaol, and redefining housework as work.[24]

Contribution to the print production of these magazines involved women taking on roles as writers, editors, proofreaders, designers, illustrators, cartoonists and photographers. As Laurel Forster argues:

> 'the experience of production' was highly valued as a feminist activity. If print was the means of spreading the word, then engagement with the publishing industry or print cultures demonstrated participation in the cause of women's liberation.[25]

However, unlike the United States, where the Women in Print movement emerged with women who already worked in the publishing industry, in Australia, most women did not have previous experience, particularly in print production. You learnt on the job:

> Looking back on the production process now is more significant than we thought it at the time. What really now can be considered early print technology was what we had to use: Letrasett, graph paper, scissors, typed galleys and the long thread of silver tape streaming out of the varitype machine all over the floor as Gale worked through the nights typing up columns and teaching us how to do it too.[26]

---

23 Mary Spongberg, 'Australian Women's History in Australian Feminist Periodical 1971–1988', *History Australia* 5, no. 3 (2008): 73.1, 73.2.
24 Suzanne Bellamy, 'Newspaper: MeJane', in *Things That Liberate: An Australian Feminist Wunderkammer*, ed. Alison Bartlett and Margaret Henderson, 105–12, (Newcastle upon Tyne, UK: Cambridge Scholars Publishing, 2013), 107.
25 Laurel Forster, 'Spreading the Word: Feminist Print Cultures and the Women's Liberation Movement', *Women's History Review* 25, no. 5 (2016): 813.
26 Bellamy 'Newspaper', 106.

The first *Melbourne Women's Liberation Newsletter* (1972–84) (MWLN) was published by a collective and printed on a Gestetner printing machine. While relatively easy to operate without printing skills, it was labour-intensive and often unreliable. Nevertheless, use of the Gestetner allowed full control over content and all aspects of production. Later, during the 1980s, photocopiers became an alternative, but not necessarily more reliable, printing option. As the editorial of the MWLN in August 1983 comically put it:

> Because when you're freezing your proverbial off at 3 o'clock in the morning doing battle with the recalcitrant photocopier because the gestetner broke down for the fourth time and paper is too damp to put through the machine and you've tried drying it in front of the one-bar radiator for hours and now it's dry but the edges are curled and the other gestetner machine eats it but doesn't digest it and so the drum revolts and regurgitates gross insults against the professionalism of women's libbers, and so does the Maintenance Man …[27]

Mabel: Australian Feminist Newspaper was published about four times per year from Sydney. The second issue explained that:

> … an important aspect of the paper is that it is anonymous—we do not sign contributions. MABEL is not a vehicle for stars but a collective attempt to communicate some of the ways feminists see the past, present and future—we have no paid workers.[28]

The rationale for establishing *Mabel* was directly linked to the political crisis of 1975, when the progressive Whitlam Labor Government was dismissed by the Attorney-General:

> Mabel was born two weeks before the December 13 [1975] election. She was going to be a broadsheet from an ad hoc collective of Sydney women in the Women's Movement giving our views on the political crisis and its effects on women. The response of ideas and article and money is so great that in only eight days she blossomed into a 24 page newspaper 30,000 copies of which were distributed prior to the elections.[29]

---

27 Cited in Jean Taylor, 'Gestener', in *Things That Liberate: An Australian Feminist Wunderkammer*, ed. Alison Bartlett and Margaret Henderson (Newcastle upon Tyne, UK: Cambridge Scholars Publishing 2013), 93.
28 Cited in Paula Byrne, 'Mabelled', *Hecate* 22, no. 2 (1996): 87–100, 88.
29 *Mabel* 2 (March 1976), cited in Byrne, 'Mabelled', 89.

Hecate was founded in 1975, International Women's Year, in Brisbane by Carole Ferrier, as an 'interdisciplinary journal of women's liberation'. The journal's editorial policy was made clear in the first issue: 'As feminists and socialists, we view this journal as a means of providing a forum for discussing, at a fairly theoretical level, issues relating to the liberation of women'.[30]

Mary Spongberg points to the contribution of feminist periodicals, particularly those identified as vehicles for the emerging field of women's studies, to Australian feminist historiography. She argues that *Refractory Girl*, one of the longest standing Australian feminist periodicals, produced a 'distinctly Australian feminist historiography, to overtly insert women into the narratives that had framed Australian history, and to alter the parameters of Australian history in order to make women's experience central'.[31] On the other hand, *Hecate*, based in Brisbane, 'situated itself within a socialist-feminist tradition' that was more concerned with class oppression under capitalism. It published labour history, focused on:

> women workers' resistance to capitalist oppression in the past; treated domestic and voluntary labour as labour; and put the spotlight on highly marginalised groups of women workers such as Aboriginal women and domestic servants. Many of these articles signalled the importance of thinking about race in relation to women's experience of work and capitalist oppression.[32]

These magazines were clearly distinguished from commercial and mass media, the majority run voluntarily by individual women who formed collectives, with editorial meetings, writing and production of galley proofs and artwork often occurring in their homes. This reflected commitment to the principle of the personal as political through alternative, non-patriarchal and anti-capitalist ways of working. In this way, it was a separatist activity, involving women working autonomously with control over the materialist processes of print production. However, the act of publishing itself is action in the public sphere and also required engagement with the male-dominated commercial publishing and printing industries.

---

30 *Hecate* 1 (1975).
31 Spongberg, *Australian Women's History*, 73.3.
32 Ibid., 73.10.

Some feminists, particularly lesbians and sexuality activists, encountered antagonism and censorship from commercial printers when they attempted to get posters, pamphlets, magazines and newspapers printed. This was an obstacle to the dissemination of radical ideas and images and the organisation of political activism. In April 1974, Maxwell General Printing refused to print an issue of *Refractory Girl* dedicated to lesbian content 'alleging it was offensive because of the reprinting of a poem by Penny Short that it deemed "filthy". Several other printers also declined to do the job after Maxwell's refusal'.[33]

Feminist, lesbian and gay fictional writers also experienced difficulty getting their work published with mainstream book publishers. While commercial publishing houses recognised the market for conventional women's fictional writing, they were, at least initially, often unprepared to take on new authors or innovative writing that departed from traditional representations of women, as well as writing that challenged established genres.[34]

Feminist presses

In the United States, feminist, lesbian and gay publishers proliferated during the 1970s and 1980s. The Women in Print movement drew together women working in the publishing industry, both mainstream and independent. Its first conference, held in 1976 in Nebraska, was attended by 200 feminist presses, publishers and booksellers. This 'feminist revolution in literacy'[35] provided the context for the publication and wide distribution of key works, as well as sparking the interest of mainstream publishers in feminist literature. However, debates around feminist publishing engagement in the commercial arena, particularly *Ms* magazine, were vehement.

---

33   Sue Wills, 'Seventies Chronology, Part II, 1973–1979', *Australian Feminist Studies* 23, no. 55 (2007): 136.
34   Michael Hurley, 'Gay and Lesbian Writing and Publishing in Australia, 1961–2001', *Australian Literary Studies* 25, no. 1 (2010): 42–70.
35   Onosaka, quoted in Harker and Farr, *This Book is an Action*, 6.

In the United Kingdom, a different culture emerged, largely focused around the success of Virago (1973) and The Women's Press (1978).[36] Virago aimed to be the first mass-market publisher of books for women. Founder Carmen Callil believed that establishing a successful commercial publishing house was an essential aspect of feminist activism. It published an extensive list of fiction and nonfiction, as well as a reprint series, branded with the publisher's logo and distinctive green book spines. Virago attracted 'a loyal readership and boasted some big-name authors, arguably generating greater publicity and profile than an enterprise of its size and scope could expect'.[37] All books published included the statement that Virago was a feminist publishing company together with a quote by Shiela Rowbotham from *Women, Resistance and Revolution*. There were a number of other, smaller feminist presses that emerged in the UK from the 1970s. Simone Murray argues that while these smaller presses were often more politically radical, all were:

> united in their perception that the act of publishing is, because of its role in determining the parameters of public debate, an inherently political act and that women, recognising this fact, must intervene in the processes of literary production to ensure that women's voices are made audible.[38]

In Australia, feminist interest in controlling the means of publication and taking on skills traditionally identified as masculine, such as printing, gave rise to a small number of feminist printing and publishing ventures. During the 1970s to 1980s, over a dozen feminist presses were established in Australia.[39] These presses did not position themselves clearly within the commercial arena. They were much fewer in number than in the United Kingdom or United States, operated on a smaller-scale financially and often embraced alternative forms, with a strong emphasis on non-hierarchical, collective structures, skill sharing and consensus decision-making. Most importantly, however, members and workers saw their involvement as feminist activism. As Louise Poland explains:

---

36 Virago was established by Carmen Callil, Rosie Boycott and Marsha Rowe in 1973, all of whom had been involved in the establishment of *Spare Rib* magazine. The Women's Press was established in 1977 by Stephanie Dowrick and entrepreneur Naim Attallah.
37 Catherine Riley, '"The Message is in the Book": What Virago's Sale in 1995 Means for Feminist Publishing', *Women: A Cultural Review* 25, no. 3 (2014): 235.
38 Simone Murray, *Mixed Media: Feminist Presses and Publishing Politics* (London: Sterline, VA: Pluto Press, 2004), 2.
39 Louise Poland, 'The Devil and the Angel? Australian's Feminist Presses and the Multinational Agenda', *Hecate* 29, no. 2 (2003): 123.

Australia's feminist presses were politically- or culturally-led rather than market-driven. Some provided the means for feminist and other left-wing publications to be produced without censorship, some sought to shape and reflect the political concerns of the Australian women's liberation movement, while others aimed to encourage women writers and present experimental and potentially transformative women's fiction to their readership.[40]

Australian feminist presses of this time attempted to negotiate the conflicted terrain between participation in the commercial—that is, in the parlance of the time, capitalist—patriarchal publishing industry and their commitment to progressive, radical feminist politics. These were 'ideological struggles about economic and political purity',[41] where survival was always tenuous. Each of the presses attempted to navigate this precarious terrain differently, sharing the key principle that women own and control the means of production. The presses were neither always separatist, nor necessarily always demonstrably in support of each other, and they interacted with, and reacted against, the mainstream publishing industry in different ways.[42] However, they all attempted to put into practice feminist principles in the belief that control over the production of print was a form of political power. As Diane Brown and Susan Hawthorne argue, 'feminism at work in publishing is a different kind of engagement with texts and the politics of cultural production, where the agency of feminism exposes and contests power relations through the development of risky publishing lists'.[43]

In Melbourne, concern about sexism in children's literature led a group of women from the Box Hill Women's Liberation Branch in May 1974 to form a book group called the Women's Movement Children's Literature Cooperative Ltd, with shares of $1.00 each sold to a wide group of women in the Melbourne women's movement. Later changing its name to Sugar & Snails Press, the cooperative began by packaging children's books for publication by other small publishers. Later, Sugar & Snails began its own publishing program, producing illustrated children's books. During the 1980s, the press produced a number of schoolbook series in cooperation

---

40   Poland, *The Devil and the Angel*, 123.
41   Jennifer Gilley, 'Feminist Publishing/Publishing Feminism: Experimentation in Second-Wave Book Publishing' in Harker and Farr, *This Book is an Action*, 24.
42   Forster, 'Spreading the Word', 814.
43   Diane Brown and Susan Hawthorne, 'Case-study: Feminist Publishing', in *Paper Empires: A History of the Book in Australia*, ed. Craig Munro and Robyn Sheahan-Bright (St Lucia: University of Queensland Press, 2006), 263.

with an educational publisher. Between 1974 and 1991, Sugar & Snails Press produced over 50 book and non-book items that contributed to the emergence of non-sexist children's literature in Australia and assisted in launching the careers of a number of now well-known authors, illustrators, editors and publishers.[44]

Two presses were established during this time to provide access to alternative feminist-run printing services. In Sydney, Everywoman Press was set up in 1976 by a collective of four women to provide printing facilities for the women's liberation movement and left-wing and community groups. Each contributed $1,000 to buy a printing press and other equipment,[45] and three members of the collective completed technical courses in offset printing and platemaking.[46] One of the founding members, Kath McLean, recalled that:

> We set it up in the belief that women could and should control their own printing—part of the feminist belief in knowledge and information being power, and printing being a major communications medium for knowledge and information, hence power … We were highly motivated by our ideology. We also believed that 'women can do anything!'[47]

Everywoman Press printed feminist publications, including *Scarlet Woman* and *Refractory Girl*, posters and other resources for feminist organisations including the Leichhardt Women's Health Centre and the Sydney Rape Crisis Collective, as well as occasionally taking on jobs considered 'commercial' such as for the University of Sydney. They offered 'good prices to political groups, especially women's groups', and maintained low profit margins, with minimal capacity to pay their workers. 'As a result of exhaustion, the press was sold in 1980 and the partnership was dissolved, but not before the full-time press workers passed on their skills to other women in the movement.'[48]

In Melbourne, Sybylla Co-operative Press (later Sybylla Feminist Press) was established in 1976 by eight women, all of whom were active in the women's movement. It was intended to provide access to printing facilities, without risk of obstruction or censorship, to support the growth

---

44 Sugar & Snails Papers in the University of Melbourne Archives.
45 Poland, 'Setting the Agenda', 93.
46 Ibid., 96.
47 Email to Louise Poland, 5 September 2000, reproduced in Poland, 'Setting the Agenda', 96.
48 Poland, 'Setting the Agenda', 96–97.

in periodicals, flyers, posters and cards created for women's movement activities. The decision to set up the press was a response to the broad political climate at the time, sparked by the 1975 dismissal of Prime Minister Gough Whitlam. This event sent a cold shiver through feminist and left-wing political communities and there was concern about the potential backlash against progressive and radical politics.

The collective purchased a second-hand printing press with donated funds—a single-colour Multilith 1250 WLD. It had a printing policy that established that it would not print the work of projects that were sexist, racist or anti-working class. It also specified that:

> No commercial advertising of commodities. Restaurants accepted. No real estate agents. No church groups with some exceptions. Brotherhood of St Laurence and left wing groups. No Spartacists. Anarchists accepted. La Trobe Maoists out.[49]

Eventually operating out of a shopfront in Collingwood, Sybylla provided commercial printing services, pre-press layout and bromides, collating, stapling and guillotining to a wide range of political, community and educational organisations in the women's movement and on the Left generally.

Sybylla was established as a workers' cooperative but operated on collective decision-making principles. While initially run entirely on voluntary labour, by the early 1980s it had secured seed financial assistance under the Victorian Co-operative Development Program to establish a financially viable cooperative business. By 1985, it employed six full-time workers who performed the roles of printers, publishing editor, graphic designer, shopfront staff and administrator, all of whom were paid wage parity at printing industry award levels. There was a commitment to the integration of manual and intellectual labour, skill sharing and training. Sybylla contributed to the creation of a network of feminist writers, editors, designers, illustrators, cartoonists and bookshops in Melbourne.

During this time, Sybylla began a small publishing program with a commitment to publishing innovative, radical and alternative literature by women that reflected personal and political lives, including fiction and nonfiction.[50] In 1982, Sybylla published its first title, *Frictions*:

---

49   Sybylla Press Archive: Margaret McCormack, p. 18, cited in Poland, 'Setting the Agenda', 99.
50   I was a collective member and paid worker at Sybylla Feminist Press between 1985 and 1991.

An Anthology of Fiction by Women, edited by Anna Gibbs and Alison Tilson. It was one of the first anthologies of fictional writing by women published in Australia. The published collection, launched at the Women and Labour Conference in 1982, included contributions from 23 writers, many of whom went on to become established authors. Over the subsequent years, 10 books of fiction and nonfiction were published by the press.

Louise Poland claims that the 'story of Sybylla Press, the longest surviving feminist press in Australia, is an extraordinary one of feminist activism, dedication and commitment, and of five collectives of women over 26 years'.[51] It put into practice a belief that providing an independent feminist alternative to the male-dominated mainstream commercial printing and publishing industries was a form of activism where power was vested in control over the published word. As Poland argues, feminist presses were 'as interested in how the books were produced as they were in the output. Arguably, a refusal to separate the publishing process from the output is central to most feminist publishing'.[52] There are a number of ways that feminist presses demonstrated this discursive activism, including what they published, the relationship established between the publisher and the authors, and how the press operated and was organised. Being committed to encouraging previously unpublished writers and new forms of writing that challenged conventional genres was key to their identity.

At Sybylla Press, there was a clear commitment to new and emerging authors and to close and supportive relationships with authors in the editing and production of books. The press's subsequent title, *A Gap in the Records* by Jan McKemmish, was a groundbreaking feminist spy thriller that subverted the genre in form and content. *Working Hot*, by Kathleen Mary Fallon, was an experimental novel of lesbian love written in prose, verse and libretto.[53] It won the Victorian Premier's Literary Award for new writing in 1989 and continues to be read in tertiary Australian literary studies. None of these books would have been taken up by mainstream publishers at the time. Each of them involved lengthy and painstaking collaboration between the author and the publisher in relation to editing, design and print production.

---

51 Poland, 'Setting the Agenda', 97.
52 Poland, 'The Devil and the Angel', 125.
53 For an account of the importance of this book, see Fiona McGregor, 'The Hot Desk: *Working Hot* by Mary Fallon' *Sydney Review of Books* (25 February 2019), sydneyreviewofbooks.com/the-hot-desk-working-hot-by-mary-fallon/.

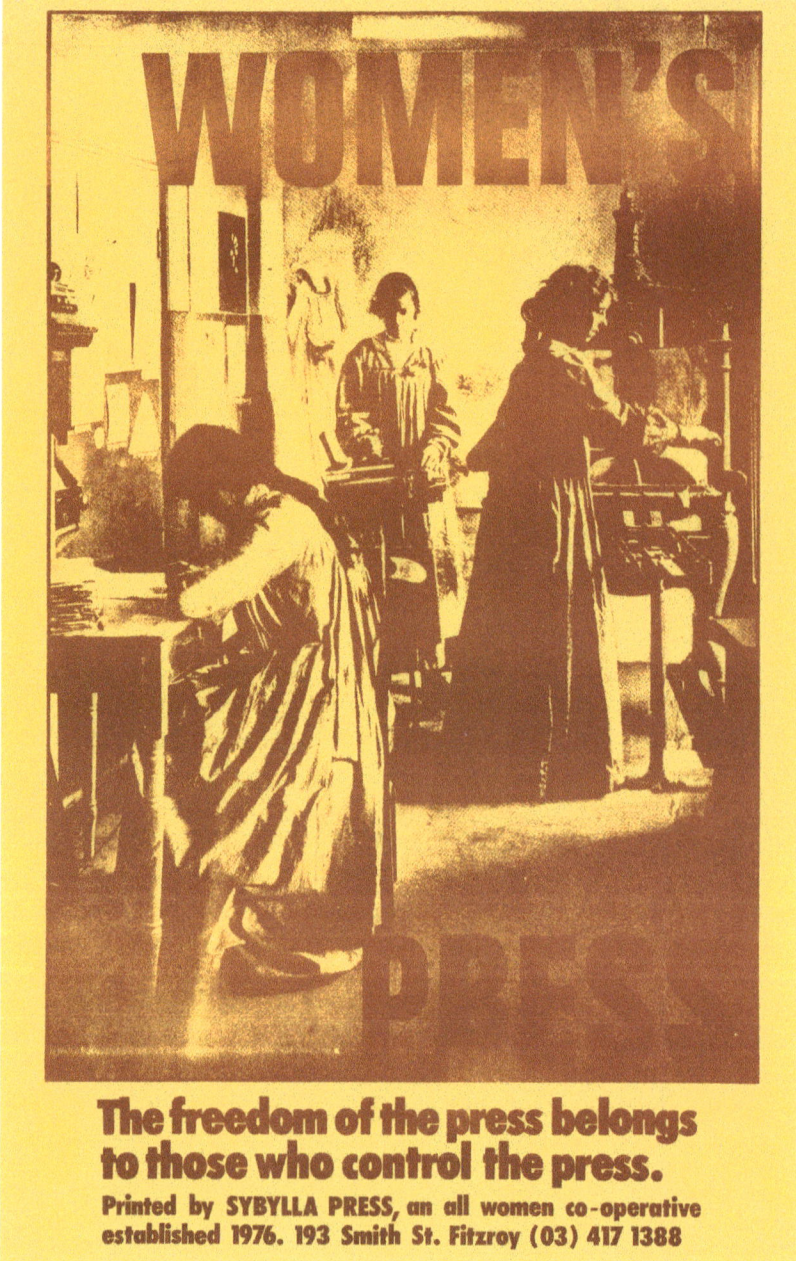

Figure 7.1: 'Women's Press', A3 poster, printed and published by Sybylla Press, Fitzroy, Victoria [between 1976 and 1979].
Source: Held by State Library of Victoria, Riley and Ephemera Collection, posters. Reproduced with kind permission of Spinifex Press.

In 1979, Sisters Publishing was established in Melbourne by five women publishers, including Hilary McPhee and Diana Gribble, each of whom was a director and shareholder. The group was set up in recognition of the belief that serious women writers were largely overlooked by mainstream publishers. They had an innovative response to the perennial distribution problem facing small publishers in Australia, by setting up as a mail-order book club providing both their own and other publishers' books, including Virago and Women's Press, to subscribers at a discount, through a newsletter. 'Its bookclub was instrumental in influencing the reading tastes of a generation of Australian feminists.'[54] They operated as a business, with the aim of becoming solvent, producing books on a low budget. Sisters published writing by women across all genres, but focused on forms that were not well represented in mainstream publishing: poetry, short stories, literary fiction and radical ideas.[55] The company launched the careers of a number of significant women writers, as well as distributing to readers in metropolitan, outer suburban and remote areas of Australia.

In Sydney, Women's Redress Press was established in 1983, financially floated by offering shares of $100 to over 200 women. Redress was a nonprofit publisher run by women to publish and promote progressive and first-time women writers. It also provided access for women to acquire experience in editing and book production. Initially it was a feminist book-packaging cooperative that provided constructive feedback and training in editing and publishing skills to women whose manuscripts had been rejected by mainstream publishers. However, it had difficulty finding publishers that were willing to purchase packaged books. Wild & Woolley, owned by Pat Woolley, one of the contributors to Redress Press, sponsored its first four titles. Within a couple of years, it had become a publisher run by volunteer staff and went on to publish a diverse list of approximately 20 books. One of its first books was Faith Bandler's *Welou, My Brother* and over the next decade it went on to publish a diverse list of fiction and nonfiction, including a number of anthologies that included first-time authors. Other feminist publishers followed. In Adelaide, Tantrum Press was established in 1987, with a focus on readings and publishing local authors and locally written and produced women's plays.[56] Spinifex Press was established in Melbourne in 1991, and Artemis Publishing in 1992.

---

54 Poland, 'The Devil and the Angel', 124.
55 Sisters Archive, S0005, Baillieu Library, University of Melbourne.
56 Poland, 'The Devil and the Angel', 124.

By the mid-1980s, second-wave feminist politics and feminist presses were having a discernible impact on mainstream book publishing. Feminism had a transformative effect on the field of Australian book publishing and played an important role in producing the conditions for the growth in women's writing. Mainstream publishers, including large commercial, independent and university presses, had recognised the commercial viability of feminist writing, including the significant growth of women's studies texts. Many established imprints, employed feminist editors and took on the republication of key out-of-print texts. It appeared to some that the rationale for independent feminist presses no longer existed. Combined with commercial challenges and depleted energy, this led the majority of the presses, including Sybylla and Redress, to winding up. However, Spinifex Press continues. It has published over 200 titles, fiction and nonfiction, in print and ebook form, that the publishers maintain would not be published by mainstream presses.

Conclusion

In this chapter, I have argued that the second-wave women's movement in Australia can be characterised as a print media movement. Feminist engagement with the material production of print was based on the belief that dissemination of feminist ideas through publishing was a vehicle for social change. Recognition of the value of reading and writing as feminist activities led feminist activists into direct engagement with print production through the publication of magazines, newspapers, newsletters and pamphlets. It also led to the establishment of alternative, independently owned presses and publishing houses. These engagements by feminists in print and publishing ventures have resulted in a valuable archive of published work and unpublished records that reveal some of the personal and political imperatives, priorities, conflicts and achievements of women into print.

CHAPTER 8

'Unmistakably a book by a feminist': Helen Garner's *Monkey Grip* and its feminist contexts

Zora Simic

> Helen Garner has written a book called 'Monkey Grip', about a woman called Nora who falls in love, passionately and most unwisely with a junkie. Hardly a 'liberated plot'. Yet this is unmistakably a book by a feminist.
>
> Sue King, *Vashti*, 1978

For Sue King, writing in *Vashti*, the journal of Melbourne Women's Liberation, Helen Garner's book *Monkey Grip* (1977)—like some other critics, she stopped short of calling it a novel—was clearly a feminist read. Nora, she observed, is 'not overtly "political" in the sense of working for political change on the macro level, or even consistently working out the politics of everything that happens to her'. Nor can she, as a denizen of a 'rather strange sub-culture' be properly described as an 'everywoman'. Yet for King, Nora was also 'clearly recognisable as a woman whose central identity is her own'. 'It's just so nice', she enthused, 'to read a story where no one is married or wants to be; where people may on occasion be jealous or dependent, yet feel no entitlement to do so'. King devoured the book in 24 hours, but while her review came with a strong personal recommendation, she did wonder whether anyone beyond 'an arty little sub group' would relate to it. She concluded on a note of uncertainty: 'is this something we have to pass through on the way to … ?'[1]

---

1   Sue King, 'Monkey Grip', *Vashti*, no. 21 (Summer/ Autumn 1978): 35.

To the uninitiated, the 'something' captured in *Monkey Grip* is the sexual politics and social mores of bohemian inner-city Melbourne in the mid-1970s and in particular the intimate world of Nora, closely resembling Garner herself, who is a single mother in her 30s caught in a stop-start relationship with Javo, a part-time actor and full-time heroin addict. By the standards of middle-class Australia, Nora and her friends do not live conventional lives, though they mostly all seem to be originally from the middle class. They live in communal share houses, take collective responsibility for child-rearing (or they try to), dabble in creative projects, regularly drink and take drugs and experiment with new types of sexual and romantic relationships. Nora is frank about the pleasures and the costs of all of this and the general naivete of their pursuit: 'we all thrashed about swapping and changing partners—like a very complicated dance to which the steps had not yet been choreographed, all of us trying to love gracefully despite our ignorance'.[2]

The final words of King's review also speak to an impasse evident in feminist circles and wider society in the aftermath of the first heady years of the sexual and feminist revolutions. If women's liberation had established that the personal was political, and if sex was supposed to be a source of liberation rather than oppression, what did this mean for everyday relationships? King's ellipsis cautiously suggested an as yet unknown future in which some of the dilemmas featured in *Monkey Grip* may have been resolved. The questions Nora returns to, and discusses with her female friends throughout the book, revolve around finding a balance between freedom and attachment, the self and other, or loving men and being a feminist, intimately though not sexually involved with other women. At a time when the women's movement in Australia and elsewhere was preoccupied with lesbianism within feminism, *Monkey Grip* was an emphatically heterosexual book that nevertheless resonated with committed feminist activists such as Sue King, one of the most energetic members of Melbourne Women's Liberation[3]—the same collective Garner herself was earlier involved with, in a more tangential fashion.

---

2 Helen Garner, *Monkey Grip* (Melbourne: McPhee Gribble, 1977).
3 Melbourne women's liberation began as a network of autonomous groups in 1970, then from 1972 there were monthly meetings held in the Women's Centre in Little Latrobe Street. The newspaper of the movement *Vashti's Voice* (later *Vashti*) ran from 1972 to 1981. In 1975, Sue King was employed as full-time coordinator, the first paid position in Melbourne Women's Liberation. Emma Graeme, 'Melbourne Women's Liberation', in *Australian Feminism: A Companion*, ed. Barbara Caine, Moira Gatens, Emma Grahame, Jan Larbalestier, Sophie Watson and Elizabeth Webby (Melbourne: Oxford University Press, 1999), 456–57.

Yet not all feminists, or as we shall see, literary reviewers, embraced *Monkey Grip*—a novel that was controversial on arrival and only grew more so after Garner won the National Book Council Award in 1978. The finer details of the mixed critical reception have been well covered elsewhere, and while I will necessarily revisit some of these responses, including as part of ongoing scholarly interest in the 'gendering' of Helen Garner as an author,[4] the main purpose of this chapter is to more closely consider the various ways *Monkey Grip* has been read, located and assessed as feminist. My most basic reason for doing so is because *Monkey Grip* has been oft-described as Australia's first feminist novel. While this status has been disputed, there is no doubt that it was the first novel by a writer associated with second-wave feminism to generate national attention and debate. The novel's 'adult themes', including casual sex and heroin addiction, made *Monkey Grip* an instant sensation. Further, its content, its publishers, the author's own feminist identity and the timing of its publication all ensured it was read in relation to feminism.

Relatedly, the novel is also a distinct product of the 1970s. Firstly, it was an 'everyday revolution' that enabled Garner to write the book in the first place. As she later told Jennifer Ellison:

> I was living on the Supporting Parents Benefit [introduced by the Whitlam Government in 1973] for four years and it was during that time that I wrote *Monkey Grip*. It was the first time in my life that I'd had a lot of time each day and a bit of money coming in.[5]

More broadly, Judith Brett's assertion that *Monkey Grip* 'would not have been published a decade earlier and probably would not have been written' has been reproduced and extended by later observers, with Kevin Brophy adding it's doubtful the book would have been published 10 years later either—that is, post-pill, but pre-HIV/AIDS. As Garner's first literary biographer Kerryn Goldsworthy noted, 'the stages reached in the sexual revolution, in feminism, and in the ethos of communal households … are mapped quite precisely in the *Monkey Grip* characters' conversation, behaviour and assumptions'.[6] Her most recent biographer Bernadette Brennan adds that *Monkey Grip* 'assumes a community of readers

---

4   Bronwen Levy, 'Women and the Literary Pages: Some Recent Examples', *Hecate* 11, no. 1 (1985): 5; Kerryn Goldsworthy, *Helen Garner* (Melbourne: Oxford University Press, 1996).
5   Jennifer Ellison, ed., *Rooms of Their Own* (Ringwood: Penguin, 1986), 134.
6   Judith Brett, cited in Kevin Brophy, 'Reviewing and Reputation: A Case Study in Public Perception: Images of *Monkey Grip*' (MA thesis, University of Melbourne, 1992), 8, cited in Goldsworthy, *Helen Garner*, 10–11.

versed in rock and literary culture', from Joni Mitchell and Jo Jo Zep through to the books and poems Nora reads, including Doris Lessing's *The Golden Notebook* (1962) and Diane Wakoski's *The Motorcycle Betrayal Poems* (1971),[7] by then already established as feminist exemplars of semi-autobiographical writing not dissimilar to how *Monkey Grip* would come to be interpreted.[8]

In the spirit of interdisciplinary feminist scholarship that has encouraged attention to women's liberation as a 'cultural renaissance',[9] to 'popular feminism' (that is, feminism circulating in the public sphere)[10] and to the emotional affect of feminism in public,[11] this chapter focuses on *Monkey Grip* and its various feminist contexts, including the ways in which its author, and the contents of the book, were interpreted as 'feminist' (or not). Of particular interest is how Garner's fellow women's liberationists made sense of a book that thinly fictionalised attempts to reconcile heterosexual relationships with feminist politics. This discussion will necessarily involve consideration of the wider context of feminism in Australia. By the time *Monkey Grip* was released, some of the earlier optimism about the potential for feminism to transform not only women's lives but society more generally had dissipated for reasons both external and internal to the women's movement. I will return to this context in the final section of the chapter. The first part elaborates on the book's claims to 'first feminist novel' status and its transformation into a modern Australian literary classic. I then pan out to consider more broadly the place of writing within women's liberation and Garner's dynamic role within what has been described as a 'female revolution' within Australian literature, post-*Monkey Grip*.

---

7   Bernadette Brennan, *A Writing Life: Helen Garner and Her Work* (Melbourne: Text Publishing, 2017), 45–46.
8   See, for example, Carole Ferrier's essay on Diane Wakoski's poetry in which she compared her 'intensely personal poetry' to Lessing's *The Golden Notebook*: 'it is hard to separate the persona of the central character from that of the author herself'. Carole Ferrier, 'Sexual Politics in Diane Wakoski's Poetry', *Hecate* 1, no. 2 (1975): 89.
9   Susan Magarey, 'Feminism as Cultural Renaissance', *Hecate* 30, no. 1 (2004): 231; Margaret Henderson, '*Wonders Taken for Signs*: The Cultural Activism of the Australian Women's Movement as Avant-Garde Reformation', *Lilith* 17/18 (2012): 107–20.
10 See special issue of Australian Feminist Studies, 'Living in the Seventies' for a series of articles on popular feminism in Australia. *Australian Feminist Studies* 22, no. 3 (2007).
11 Victoria Hesford, *Feeling Women's Liberation* (Durham and London: Duke University Press, 2013), doi.org/10.1215/9780822397519.

While there was growing unease around the time *Monkey Grip* was published that the women's movement had lost some of its momentum, or at least its political influence as the Fraser Government (1975–83) wound back some of the gains of the early 1970s, the broader cultural impact of second-wave feminism was becoming more apparent. This was perhaps especially obvious in the literary field, hitherto dominated by white male authors, or at least at first glance. Part of the cultural and historical project of second-wave feminism involved recovering and recalibrating a longer tradition of Australian female writers, while the success of *Monkey Grip* indicated a growing reading public eager for women's stories, including feminist ones. Published in 1977, the same year as the bestselling US 'feminist novel' *The Women's Room* by Marilyn French, *Monkey Grip* was inevitably compared to it in some reviews; however, beyond their healthy sales, evident feminism and clearly autobiographical elements, the two books did not share much in common. *The Women's Room*, for one thing, was a much more brazenly ambitious novel: it was marketed as 'life-changing' and through French's focus on the politicisation of her protagonist Mira, the book encouraged the 'click' to feminist consciousness and many female readers, including some Australian ones, responded accordingly.[12] In contrast, *Monkey Grip* tended to inspire— initially at least—a more uneasy or qualified sense of identification among its feminist readership. Nor did *Monkey Grip* come to share *The Women's Room*'s reputation as 'man-hating'—indeed, some readers, feminist and otherwise, thought that Garner or Nora let men too easily off the hook. What sort of book then was Australia's so-called 'first feminist novel' and how did Helen Garner come to write it?

'Pure pleasure and happiness'

Monkey Grip was released by independent publishers McPhee Gribble. The first edition appeared in hardcover and featured a striking photograph of a woman in a sunhat riding her bicycle. Literary scholar Brigid Rooney is not alone in her suggestion that the cycling woman on the cover of the first edition appears to be Garner herself, contributing to the early and

---

12   The reviewer of *The Women's Room* in *Vashti* praised the book as 'much more than a good read … it is part of that subversive activity … a growing feminist art'. Merrilee, 'The Women's Room by Marilyn French', *Vashti*, no. 22 (Autumn/Winter 1978): 14.

enduring impression that her work is at the least semi-autobiographical.[13] For some Garner fans, the bike is central not only to the contents of the book, but also to the story of its genesis—as the author herself has confirmed. Garner would later recount riding her bike from her share house in Fitzroy every day to the State Library of Victoria on Swanston Street in Melbourne where she would write until she had to pick her daughter Alice up from school.[14] She wrote the book over the course of a year and later recalled 'to me, this didn't seem like work, it seemed like pure pleasure and happiness'.[15] The vision of Helen Garner, or her fictionalised self, Nora, on her bike became part of the popular memory of the novel, aided by the 1982 film version that was replete with scenes of Noni Hazelhurst as Nora cycling between the share houses and music and theatre venues that made up her bohemian milieu. Historian Clare Wright describes the appeal of this image as capturing a moment in time when the 'foot-binding has come off, the corsets have come off ... it's about a freedom of access to society that is represented through her mobility on her bike'.[16] As Wright's reflection suggests, *Monkey Grip* has been consistently read as a *zeitgeist* text and this was at least partly due to Garner's candid evocation of female sexuality at a time when the social impact of second-wave feminism was being keenly felt or at least closely assessed. It was hardly surprising then that *Monkey Grip* was upon its release comprehended as a feminist book, though beyond this recognition there was less consensus about what this meant.

Certainly *Monkey Grip* arrived with some feminist cachet, and Garner was already a rather sensational figure in her own immediate orbit. As independent publishers in a publishing scene still largely tethered to Britain and dominated by men, and even more so as young photogenic women with feminist leanings, Hilary McPhee and Diana Gribble had already generated significant media interest by the time Helen Garner arrived at their Melbourne office in 1976, with the draft of the novel in two folders in her bike basket.[17] Garner herself, while never a consistently committed activist and not yet self-identifying as a writer, had some

---

13 Brigid Rooney, *Literary Activists: Writer-Intellectuals and Australian Public Life* (St Lucia: University of Queensland Press, 2009), 153.
14 Fiona Tuomy, dir., *Helen Garner's Monkey Grip*, documentary film, ABC TV, 30 September 2014.
15 Ellison, *Rooms of Their Own*, 135.
16 Tuomy, *Helen Garner's Monkey Grip*.
17 In her memoir, McPhee described how the media covered the novelty of two women setting up a business together with a series of 'Brains and Beauty in South Yarra' stories. Hilary McPhee, *Other People's Words* (Sydney: Picador, 2001), 154.

presence within Melbourne's counterculture, including among women's liberationists. She had appeared in the highly controversial 'junkie' film *Pure Shit* (1975)—the making of which she went on to fictionalise in *Monkey Grip*—and contributed nonfiction pieces for the alternative magazine *Digger*, including what would later become an infamous account of her sacking from the Victorian Education Department for giving an unscheduled sex education class to her 13-year-old students at Fitzroy High School. According to Garner, her anonymous article 'Why Does the Women Have All the Pain, Miss?'[18] led to her sacking once her identity was discovered. In protest, the Victorian Teachers' Association went out on a one-day strike in 1973. Garner was not reinstated and later fashioned the episode as both a bona fide feminist protest and the making of her career as a writer.[19] Garner was also active in the Women's Theatre Group as a writer and actor and contributed writing to *Melbourne Feminist Collection 1*, one of the earliest feminist publishing initiatives, and to *Vashti's Voice*,[20] as well as a poem in the trailblazing anthology of Australian women poets, edited by Kate Jennings, *Mother I'm Rooted* (1975).[21]

Garner's local infamy meant that when *Monkey Grip* was first released, it was in inner Melbourne that the first stirrings of disapproval were felt, as various acquaintances tried to decipher who was who among the barely concealed 'characters'. As noted in the *Australian Book Review* in 1978, when *Monkey Grip* first came out, 'it was actively campaigned against by some Melbourne people … Ms Garner arouses in some people the dislike that used to be reserved for Germaine Greer'.[22]

---

18   Helen Garner, 'Why Does the Women Have All the Pain, Miss?', *Digger* 6 (November 1972): 4–8, reprinted in Helen Garner, *True Stories* (Melbourne: Text Publishing, 1996).
19   For a discussion of the wider significance of this essay in Garner's career, see Cath Darcy, 'What's in a Name?: Helen Garner and the Power of the Author in the Public Domain', in *Australian Literature and the Public Sphere: Refereed Proceedings of the 1998 Conference Held at the Empire Theatre and the University of Southern Queensland, Toowoomba, 3–7 July 1998*, ed. Alison Bartlett, Robert Dixon and Christopher Lee ([Toowoomba, Qld]; Association for the Study of Australian Literature, 1998), 44–50.
20   Emma Graeme, 'Helen Garner', in Barbara Caine et al., *Australian Feminism: A Companion*, 425.
21   Helen Garner, untitled, *Mother I'm Rooted: An Anthology of Australian Women Poets*, ed. Kate Jennings (Fitzroy: Outback Press, 1975), 182. See also Ann Vickery, 'The Rise of "Women's Poetry" in the 1970s', *Australian Feminist Studies* 22, no. 53 (2007): 265–85. doi.org/10.1080/08164640701378596.
22   Elizabeth Riddell, 'A Year's Publishing', *Australian Book Review*, December 1978, 9.

Yet as with Germaine Greer's *The Female Eunuch*, *Monkey Grip*'s reach extended far beyond Garner's own town. While *Monkey Grip* never had the international impact of Greer's blockbuster polemic, Garner's novel became a major hit by Australian standards. Hardcover sales topped 4,000 within weeks, an astonishing figure for a debut novelist without the financial backing of a major publishing house,[23] and sales continued to increase after the novel won the 1978 National Book Council Award and after the release of the film in 1982. *Monkey Grip* is among a select group of Australian books that went on to become bestsellers and literary classics.[24]

Now over 40 years old, *Monkey Grip* is well established in the canon of Australian literature, including as a much beloved 'Melbourne' book.[25] It has never been out of print and its many editions include a Penguin Classic and British, US and French editions. The book has been the subject of a 2014 ABC documentary, numerous personal accounts of reading or rereading it and features prominently in surveys of Australian writing—most often, but not exclusively, as the paradigmatic novel of new women's writing from 1970 onwards, particularly in the domestic realist mode.[26] Within Australian literary history, *Monkey Grip* has been used to exemplify the bolder and more confident national culture that emerged in the post-Menzies Australia, the rise of 'sexy' fiction[27] and the turn towards the contemporary urban world as a rich source for storytelling. Not surprisingly, given its focus on alternative lifestyles, including drug use and addiction, communal housing and sexual experimentation, *Monkey Grip* has also been historicised as a 1970s 'time-capsule' and as a precursor to 1990s grunge fiction.[28] Furthermore, the autobiographical elements of *Monkey Grip* ensured Garner a permanent place on writers' festival

---

23   McPhee, *Other People's Words*, 144.
24   Lucy Sussex, *Blockbuster! Fergus Hume and the Mystery of the Hansom Cab* (Melbourne: Text Publishing, 2015), 135.
25   John Bailey, 'Melbourne by the Book', *Sydney Morning Herald*, 12 August 2012, www.smh.com.au/entertainment/books/melbourne-by-the-book-20120811-2412n.html; Nina Gibb, 'Radiant Badlands', *The Lifted Brow*, no. 19 (September 2013): 16, 18–19.
26   Delys Bird, 'New Narrations: Contemporary Fictions', in *The Cambridge Companion to Australian Literature*, ed. Elizabeth Webby (Melbourne: Cambridge University Press, 2000), 183–208, doi.org/10.1017/CCOL0521651220.008.
27   Kenneth Gelder, 'Sex in Australian Fiction 1970–1987', *Meanjin* 47, no. 1 (Autumn 1988): 125–34.
28   Margaret Henderson, 'Sex, Writing, and "The River Ophelia." (The River Ophelia: Four Views)', *Hecate* 21, no. 2 (1995): 65; Kirsty Leishman, 'Australian Grunge Literature and the Conflict Between Literary Generations', *Journal of Australian Studies* 23, no. 63 (1999): 94–102, doi.org/10.1080/14443059909387538.

panels about writing the self and others. Indeed, Garner's authorial 'I' has arguably been the most debated aspect of her writing career with numerous analyses dedicated to assessing her self-presentation as a writer and the influence that she yields but is sometimes reluctant to claim.[29]

Literary scholars Kevin Brophy and Kerryn Goldsworthy, among others, have given ample coverage to the early reviews, particularly the hostile ones, and for good reason—this corpus of commentary provides vivid evidence of the shock of the new, that is, the 'women's writing' that was emerging from feminism, as well as setting the tone for some of the later assessments of Garner's work. In making sense of it, some critics failed to comprehend *Monkey Grip*'s radical form and content. As Brophy noted, of the four broad categories of reviews—'the love story, the feminist-in-love story, the story of sex and drugs in the counter-culture, and finally, the story of Helen Garner's life'—the first wave of critiques overwhelmingly presented the novel as a love story, a feminising effect that has continued to plague Garner's career in various ways, even as this simplistic reading of *Monkey Grip* has faded and Garner's literary reputation has grown.[30]

Interestingly, some of those who advanced the 'love story' description of *Monkey Grip* did so in the context of challenging the book's extra-textual reputation. For example, the *Age* reviewer John Larkin countered that while some people are 'treating it as some sort of drug directory', it is, in fact, he argued, a 'distillation of the incredible eddying, the ebbs and flows, of human relationships'.[31] Barbara Giles, poet and publisher of the female-focused (but not explicitly 'feminist') literary journal *Luna*, made a similar point, while adding that Nora's dilemma is not unique to feminism, or even particularly feminist, but rather about 'the usual feminine bind of responsibility for bringing up a child, of love which makes demands on her, and her attitude is not so different from that of strong women always'.[32]

---

29 See, for example, Brennan, *A Writing Life*; Darcy, 'What's in a Name?'; Goldsworthy, *Helen Garner*; and Rooney, *Literary Activists*.
30 Kevin Brophy, 'Helen Garner's *Monkey Grip:* The Construction of an Author and Her Work', *Australian Literary Studies* 15, no. 4 (1992): 271, doi.org/10.20314/als.fca3ca5d39.
31 John Larkin, 'Different Style of Living and Surviving', *Age* (Melbourne), 22 October 1977, 24, cited in Brophy, 'Helen Garner's *Monkey Grip*', 271.
32 Barbara Giles, Reviews, *Luna* (1978), 42, cited in Brophy, 'Helen Garner's *Monkey Grip*', 272.

For Giles and others, *Monkey Grip* was also a failed love story about flawed people—as Brophy notes, adjectives used to describe it included perverse (by Irina Dunn, writer, activist and later a Senator, writing in the progressive publication *Nation Review*), tedious and hopeless (according to journalist Penelope Rowe, who took strong objection to the style of parenting in the book) and repellently egocentric (Peter Corris).[33] Negative or ambivalent critics tended to focus most on the sex and drugs depicted in the novel and, following from this, either concluded the lives of a minority countercultural group are unable to illuminate themes of universal interest or relevance (what Ronald Conway described as 'her musings amid a narrow sick drug sub culture' in conservative publication *Quadrant*[34]) or, relatedly, that the book's close attention to a particular social world closely resembling the author's own disqualified *Monkey Grip* as popular literature, even if Garner's talent was somewhat begrudgingly acknowledged. Conway concluded his review with 'Ms Garner has some future as a writer capable of deep insight … [i]f she can step outside the waning counter-culture … which this novel partly celebrates'.[35]

Another oft-cited mixed review of this kind was from crime writer Peter Corris, titled 'Misfits and Depressives in the Raw' and published in *The Weekend Australian* in November 1977. His claim that Garner essentially just published her diaries—in other words, she had not written a 'real' novel—was one she would both combat and clarify in subsequent interviews.[36] Like Conway, Corris somewhat condescendingly acknowledged Garner's talent ('Ms. Garner is a very good writer of English') while being generally dismissive of what he read as an unapologetic conflation of author and her subject: 'This is an audacious book for it assumes that the reader will share the author's absolute fascination with herself'. And to sign off: 'Can she [Garner] write about something other than herself?'[37]

For some of Garner's feminist readers, including those who would come later, Corris's criticisms were typical of male literary gatekeepers who did not value women's writing, take women's lives seriously as a literary

---

33   Irina Dunn, 'The Fringe and the Core', *Nation Review*, 3 November 1977, 17; Penelope Rowe, 'Friends in Need', *24 Hours*, January 1978, 64; Peter Corris, 'Misfits and Depressives in the Raw', *Weekend Australian*, 5–6 November 1977, 12, all cited in Brophy, 'Helen Garner's *Monkey Grip*', 272.
34   Roland Conway, 'Lost Generation', *Quadrant*, May 1978, 77.
35   Conway, 'Lost Generation', 77.
36   See, for example, Helen Garner, 'I', *Meanjin*, no. 1 (2002): 132–35.
37   Corris, as cited in Brophy, 'Helen Garner's *Monkey Grip*', 275.

theme, understand female literary traditions or recognise genuine literary innovation—including in relation to similar experiments by men. A decade later, speaking in the context of a still-raging debate in the Australian literature scene about women's writing,[38] Garner's friend and fellow writer Drusilla Modjeska speculated that perhaps one of the reasons that *Monkey Grip* was 'poorly reviewed but widely read' was not 'only because it was about communal houses and feminism and dope and sex and rock and roll but because it didn't follow the old-fashioned narrative shape of conflict and climax and resolution'. Rather, *Monkey Grip* 'sloped along following the rise and fall of tension and desire'; a new(ish) way of writing to be sure, but then again 'such narratives were hardly remarkable in the mid seventies, even in Australia'.[39]

For Brophy, critical preoccupation with Garner's subject matter and her autobiographical impulses has muted alternative readings of her work.[40] Brophy wanted to encourage 'vigorous, openly political and feminist' interpretations of *Monkey Grip* and advanced one of his own: rather than reiterate the oft-made parallel between drug addiction and addiction to romantic love, Brophy argued that Garner presented the 'patriarchal value system—the ideology that socialises us from childhood'—as 'the overwhelming addiction suffered by characters who are wanting to reinvent social relations'.[41] As for Garner, she would later suggest that it was precisely these sorts of qualities that endeared readers to the book. Feminism, and the 'whole ethos of collective households', she told one interviewer, had got her 'out of a big mess at a certain point in my life' and for people who did not 'live like that', the depiction of this world was part of *Monkey Grip*'s attraction—'the fact that there were these open households where people cared about each other and tried to create some sort of alternative to the family'.[42]

---

38 In 1986, writer and reviewer Gerard Windsor sparked a minor controversy with his contentious address at Writers' Week at the Adelaide Festival 'Writers and Reviewers', later published in the literary journal *Island* alongside a series of responses from some of Australia's better-known reviewers. Within a general critique of the 'factionalism' of Australia's reviewing culture, Windsor attributed the 'transparently enthusiastic encouragement' women writers were perceived to be receiving as having a 'sociological' rather than literary explanation. What Windsor called [Beverley] 'Farmer/ Garner territory—domestic pain' appealed, he said, primarily to women who were part of or had grown up with the women's movement. See Gerard Windsor, 'Writers and Reviewers', *Island* 27 (Winter 1986): 15–18.
39 Drusilla Modjeska, 'The Emergence of Women Writers since 1975', Sydney Writer's Festival January 1987, *Australian Feminist Studies* 2, no. 4 (1987): 120.
40 Brophy, 'Helen Garner's *Monkey Grip*', 280.
41 Ibid., 278.
42 Ellison, *Rooms of Their Own*, 140–41.

Monkey Grip made such an immediate and also lasting impact that literary critic Gillian Whitlock would describe the rising popularity and status of women writers in Australia in the 1980s as evidence of AMG—After *Monkey Grip*. Further, Garner's success and that of other women's writers who emerged or were rediscovered from the late 1970s—including Kate Grenville, Sara Dowse, Jessica Anderson, Thea Astley, Olga Masters and Elizabeth Jolley—was also 'related to a series of effects produced by the re-emergence of feminism'.[43]

First feminist novel…?

Women's liberation in Australia and elsewhere created feminist readers and writers. Reading and writing were integral to consciousness-raising and within the women's movement, journals, magazines and newspapers were launched, small presses inaugurated and writing and reading groups formed. Subscription lists charted the explosion in new titles by, for and about women, and feminist bookshops stocked them. Women's writers' festivals, poetry readings and book launches were opportunities to find and promote new work, and to meet other feminists. Some women writers from the past were rediscovered and many contemporary female writers were championed. A specifically (and increasingly sophisticated) feminist literary criticism began to develop. More generally, feminism also helped to expand the market for women's writing, so much so that by the 1980s major publishers were developing lists of women's fiction and/or subsuming feminist presses into their operations (Garner's publishers McPhee Gribble, for example, were bought by Penguin).[44]

The turning or tipping point from feminists championing women's writing, or more particularly women's fiction, in their own publications and within their own circles to established male authors and critics grumbling about the ascent of women writers came with the publication of *Monkey Grip*, which was marketed as having the power to 'change women's lives', just as Marilyn French's *The Women's Room* (1977) was in the United States.[45] As already noted, the book was published by McPhee Gribble, the Carlton-based publishing company that began in 1975. One

---

43   Gillian Whitlock, ed., *Eight Voices of the Eighties: Stories, Journalism and Criticism by Australian Women Writers* (St Lucia: University of Queensland Press, 1989), xiv–xv.
44   Zora Simic, '"Women's Writing" and "Feminism": A History of Intimacy and Estrangement', *Outskirts* 28 (May 2013), www.outskirts.arts.uwa.edu.au/volumes/volume-28/zora-simic.
45   Delys Bird, 'Women Writers, Gendered Readings, Literary Politic', *Southerly* 57, no. 3 (1997): 115.

of their first publications was by Melbourne folk singer and anti-war and women's rights activist Glen Tomasetti—*Thoroughly Decent People*, released to mostly positive acclaim in 1976, and another contender for the 'first feminist novel', though its focus on 'the stultifying gentility of daily life in Melbourne in 1934'[46] made it a less obvious selection, including among feminists.[47]

McPhee Gribble were not an exclusively feminist publishing company—they also published Tim Winton and Murray Bail, among others—but they were feminists and active in the burgeoning feminist publishing scene, for instance as part of Sisters Publishing, a wider collective of feminist identified publishers that launched in 1979 with a book club and subscription mailing list. For Garner having McPhee Gribble as publishers was crucial: 'If I'd had to take *Monkey Grip* to a male publishing company, … it would have been thrown out immediately as being too emotional'.[48] She also shared that she had shown an earlier draft to some male publisher friends who 'returned it to me some days later looking very embarrassed and said it was over emotional'.[49]

Garner would later claim she was genuinely shocked by the strong reactions to *Monkey Grip*, but McPhee Gribble certainly seemed well aware that *Monkey Grip* promised to be a sensation. They took great care with the publication and with publicity—at least insofar as the latter was in their control. They also took risks with new talent, while displaying a keen commercial sense for books that captured new audiences. In 1979, they published a book by two teenagers, Gabrielle Carey and Kathy Lette, called *Puberty Blues*. *Monkey Grip* and *Puberty Blues* can be read as 'success stories despite (but also paradoxically, in some senses, because of) the odds'. As Bronwen Levy elaborates, 'attempts to silence each book failed. The louder the cries of disapproval from the literary pages … the higher rose the sales'. Each novel posed a conundrum for some mainstream reviewers, namely could such 'seedy' and subcultural subject matter—whether share house living and loving in Carlton in the mid-1970s or teen sex and surfing in Cronulla in the same period—be worthy of genuine literary treatment.[50]

---

46 Hilary McPhee's description, *Other People's Words*, 139.
47 The reviewer in *Vashti* criticised aspects of the book as 'non-feminist' because the aggressive patriarch antagonist was explained away in Freudian terms. B.P., '"Prostitutes" and "Decent People": Two New Books', *Vashti*, no. 17 (Summer 1976/77): 26.
48 Ellison, *Rooms of Their Own*, 144.
49 Ibid.
50 Levy, 'Women and the Literary Pages', 5.

Monkey Grip has been popularly identified as the 'first feminist' novel to come out of Australia, or at least to break through to popular consciousness, particularly after it was awarded the National Book Council Award in 1978. Following this, Drusilla Modjeska would drily note later, 'that strange creature women's writing was suddenly visible and talked about as though it was a new event'.[51] As several feminist literary scholars have pointed out, the 'honour [of being the first feminist novel in Australia] probably goes to *All That False Instruction*',[52] published by Kerryn Higgs under the pseudonym Elizabeth Riley in 1975 by Angus and Robertson. It was a very different book to *Monkey Grip*. Garner's book demanded to be read in the wake of women's liberation, as the protagonist Nora struggled to reconcile her love for the 'bludger' Javo with the allegedly progressive sexual politics of her inner-city countercultural milieu. In contrast, *All That False Instruction*, subtitled in its first edition as 'A Novel of Lesbian Love', was set a decade earlier in the pre-feminist conformist 1960s. It does conclude, however, with the arrival of New York women's liberationist Jody, 'sprouting the radical feminist rhetoric of Melbourne in 1973'—a late-in-manuscript inclusion Higgs made after she workshopped her draft novel with the feminists she met in Melbourne after she returned from living in London for a few years.[53]

For various reasons—whether being published first or taking as its focus a lesbian life, to name two obvious ones—*All That False Instruction* was also assessed more favourably, less ambivalently and more often within women's liberation journals than *Monkey Grip*. Most women's movement publications featured substantial reviews of *All That False Instruction*, with the majority of these noting that however conventional formal aspects of the novel may at first appear, its focus on a lesbian woman elevated the novel to a more radical and thus feminist level. In *Scarlet Woman*, Deirdre O'Sullivan compared it favourably to French lesbian feminist Monique Witig's futuristic novel *Les guérillères*, published in French in 1969 and translated into English in 1971, due to a shared 'imaginative dimension'. Crucially, for O'Sullivan, the protagonist Maureen Craig's 'awareness that the male can never be an adequate alternative in her life to women' ensures 'the book plots its vision for the lesbian' and in doing

---

51 Modjeska, 'The Emergence of Women Writers since 1975', 118.
52 Bronwen Levy, 'Editorial', *Hecate* 21, no. 1 (1995): 4.
53 Kerryn Higgs, 'The Life of Riley', *Southerly* 61, no. 3 (2001–2): 93.

so 'deserves to be communicated and read'.[54] Meanwhile, in a three-and-a-half-page assessment in women's studies journal *Refractory Girl*, Suzanne Bellamy reflected on her own identification with Maureen as a contemporary who came of age before 'the new women's movement and lesbian consciousness had … really surfaced in Australia'. 'It would be good to know', wrote Bellamy, 'how a non-contemporary felt about the book',[55] thereby flagging a dilemma also acknowledged by other feminist reviewers of new feminist-related titles, including *Monkey Grip*.

Taking the attention paid in feminist publications as an index, *All That False Instruction* then was clearly recognised as a serious political and literary milestone. It was also published at what was arguably the peak of debate in the women's movement about the place of lesbians in Australian feminism, beginning with the Hobart Women's Action Group Paper 'Sexism in the Women's Movement Or—Why Do Our Straight Sisters Sometimes Cry When They Are Called Lesbians' presented at the Mt Beauty feminist theory conference in 1973 and reprinted in several movement publications over the next couple of years, commensurate with the increased focus on the 'lesbian' question.[56] Higgs's workshopped coda to the novel was also reflective of both her own intensifying commitment to women's liberation and of the new visibility of lesbian sexuality and politics in some parts of the Australian women's movement. From this perspective, *All That False Instruction*'s status as 'first feminist novel' is ensured, both chronologically and politically.

The debates the book generated within feminist circles and among feminists were another complicating factor for the 'first feminist novel' status of *Monkey Grip*. These sometimes questioned the sort of feminism evident in the book or whether *Monkey Grip* could be classified feminist at all given, for instance, Nora's relationship with Javo or, in the words

---

54 Deidre O'Sullivan, 'A review of Elizabeth Riley's *All That False Instruction*', *Scarlet Woman*, no. 3 (February 1976): 27.
55 Sue Bellamy, 'Fucking Men is for Saints', *Refractory Girl*, June 1976, 33.
56 For example, the Hobart Women's Action Group article was published in the 'lesbian issue' of *Refractory Girl* in the summer of 1974, published in tandem with Lesley Lynch's article 'Mythmaking in the Women's Movement' in which she argued that the lesbian/heterosexual/bisexual divide that she felt was undermining US feminism was threatening to do so in Australia. In a retrospective assessment, Susan Tiffin notes the 'issue of lesbianism' largely disappeared from *Refractory Girl* after the special issue but not from the Women's Movement, which 'continued to struggle to rethink feminism and feminist practice in the light of the challenge the lesbian issue posed'. Susan Tiffin, 'Lesbianism—an Early Controversy', *Refractory Girl*, nos 44/45 (1993): 76–84.

of feminist writer and academic Suzanne Edgar, writing in the *Canberra Times*, a 'male chauvinist bloody pig … conveniently concealed by the alternative conventions of total personal autonomy'.[57]

What the feminists thought

The three judges for the 1978 National Book Council Awards—*Monkey Grip* was awarded first prize followed by Aboriginal writer Kevin Gilbert's groundbreaking memoir *Living Black*—included two high-profile feminists: feminist author and publisher Joyce Nicholson, author of the recent bestselling sociological study *What Society Does to Girls* (1975); and writer Anne Summers (the third judge was *Australian Book Review* editor John McLaren). The judges' report read:

> This book was neither an easy nor an early choice. Its subject matter—heroin addiction, inner city communal living and obsessive love—has been criticised and even regarded as distasteful by some reviewers, and did arouse some resistance among the judges … Yet the book destroys these doubts. It is in fact beautifully constructed … The author is not disillusioned, but utterly honest in the facing the dilemmas of freedom, and particularly of social and sexual freedom for women trying to create for themselves a role which will recognise their full humanity.[58]

Anne Summers was of course herself a recent feminist publishing sensation at the time following the publication of *Damned Whores and God's Police* in 1975, and would go on to provide the blurb on the 1978 edition released to coincide with the win—'the best Australian novel this year'.

In general, feminist responses to the book were more receptive than those of the book critics of the mainstream press though not uniformly, and among those who endorsed the book there also tended to be two quite distinct tendencies: positive or over identification with Nora's story as resonant with personal experience, or praise for a new kind of women's writing (the latter view tended to come later). For example, for Pam Gilbert, writing in defence of the book following criticisms it was not worthy of a major literary prize on the basis of its 'diary-like' form, it was important to note the feminist innovation of the form:

---

57 'What Our Reviewers Said', *Canberra Times*, 14 October 1978, 17.
58 Judges Reports, 'National Book Council Awards for Australian Literature', *Australian Book Review*, October 1978, 30.

> [T]he text lies at the boundaries of two discursive forms: the discourse of literature and the discourse of the personal diary. It has to be pulled back into the framework of literature, if the personal, self-confessional diary form is to be read as universally significant.[59]

Gilbert's assessment was part of a larger suite of feminist literary critique that reclaimed *Monkey Grip* as a work of art.

In *Womanspeak*—a Sydney-based magazine launched in 1975 with the aim of reaching the 'everywoman' beyond 'the radical media belt'—Lesley Morgan, like Peter Corris and other mostly male reviewers, classified *Monkey Grip* as 'more a diary than a conventional novel' and easily conflated Garner/Nora. For Morgan, the book does not have 'any great message to impart' and nor 'is it self-consciously part of a growing genre of feminist novels'. Rather, where Garner succeeds is in holding up what to 'many of us' is a 'realistic social mirror'. Despite being set in a very specific scene—'Melbourne's urban, literary, Pram Factory hangers-on, drug culture set'—*Monkey Grip* also captured for Morgan a wider resonance for heterosexual feminist women:

> In part it's the old story of women repeating the same self-destructive patterns despite their conscious feminism … Many feminists face this dilemma on a very pragmatic level. There is a large gap between intellectual understanding of feminism and living as a feminist.[60]

If, for Morgan, *Monkey Grip* is an 'at times oddly non-intellectual, unreflective book', it also 'touches a nerve' she extrapolated out to other readers, 'a nerve to relate to our own experience'.[61] In a feminist publication that championed women's writing without being at the vanguard of feminist literary criticism, and that generally avoided lesbian issues, *Monkey Grip* was a highly relatable book for feminists, but also—by virtue of a perceived lack of intellectualism—not easily assimilated into the genre of self-consciously feminist books.

For some feminist critics writing in the mainstream or wider press, *Monkey Grip* was clearly a book *about* feminism and of primary interest to women trying to live a more authentic life in the aftermath of women's

---

59 Pam Gilbert, *Coming Out from Under: Contemporary Australian Women Writers* (Sydney: Pandora, 1988), 10.
60 Lesley Morgan, 'Monkey Grip by Helen Garner', *Womanspeak* 3, no. 5 (March–April 1978): 29.
61 Morgan, 'Monkey Grip by Helen Garner', 29.

liberation and the Sexual Revolution. According to Goldsworthy, among feminists *Monkey Grip* was widely read as a book about the gap between theory and practice prompted by feminist consciousness and new ways of living and loving such as the 'theoretical desirability of sexual freedom and the painful realities of jealousy, competition and rejection'.[62] Or as Rosemary Creswell, in an arrestingly titled review 'Survivors among the Primal Screamers', put it: 'The life of Nora in *Monkey Grip* is the battleground of a full scale-war between psycho-social conditioning and the ideologies of feminism and counter-cultural communal living … The result: a series of uneasy, mostly token truces'.[63] While Creswell saw Nora's ideological struggles played out in her love life to complicated and resonant effect, Veronica Schwarz in the *Australian Book Review* offered a more optimistic, perhaps even utopian reading of the feminism on offer in *Monkey Grip*: 'Nora is a feminist in a world of feminists … the posturing and pretences of the wider sex role culture are absent'.[64] As Brophy has noted, however, this was quite an idiosyncratic reading of *Monkey Grip*, a ringing endorsement of alternative ways of living, rather than the common sympathetic assessment of the book as focused on painful and human, rather than political, conflicts.[65]

These responses also implicitly suggest, to varying degrees, that the time was right for *Monkey Grip*—that it came out in the aftermath of the second wave, of the optimism of the early 1970s in Australia. While the origins of the book are sometimes described with reference to the social and cultural policies of the Whitlam Government—including the Supporting Mothers Benefit that allowed Garner to write the book in the first place—the book was published in a period of backlash and retreat in the wake of the Whitlam dismissal. By 1977, there was a new conservativism in Australian life as Fraser's Liberal Government won a second landslide victory. It was also in that year that the Royal Commission on Human Relationships, originally commissioned by the Whitlam Government in 1974, released its final report; its release on the one hand bringing into public conversation previously taboo topics such as abortion, incest

---

62 Goldsworthy, *Helen Garner*, 39.
63 Rosemary Creswell, 'Survivors among the Primal Screamers', *National Times*, 13 March 1978, 30, as cited in Brophy, 'Reviewing and Reputation', 273.
64 Veronica Schwarz, 'Multiplying and Dividing', *Australian Book Review*, June 1978, 17.
65 Brophy, 'Reviewing and Reputation', 273.

and teenage sex, and on the other offering all sorts of opportunities for conservative commentators to blame a purported decline in morality and an increase in family breakdown on divorce.[66]

What is particularly striking in reading through feminist periodicals and writings of the time and in the decade after—for *Monkey Grip* was continually referenced throughout the 1980s as the foundational text of what became known as the 'Woman's Decade' in Australian literary fiction—was how often the book was talked about or around rather than directly to. As Levy noted when later assessing the claim that *Monkey Grip* was the first feminist novel in Australia, 'most of the feminist debates at the time on this question were not published'.[67] Reappraisals or feminist defences of the book also took note of wider 'talk' about *Monkey Grip*'s feminist credentials, as in a 1979 survey article on feminist publishing by Susan Higgins and Jill Matthews in literary journal *Meanjin*. Their biographies note their academic and feminist credentials and the authors go on to make both political and artistic claims for *Monkey Grip* as justifiably 'feminist'. *Monkey Grip*, they shared, was perceived in some quarters to be 'not feminist enough, in that [it] excused the oppressive behaviour of their male characters and made the heroines too dependent on their men'. However, they argued, 'the intimate realism of the writing, the close and sympathetic observation of social behaviour bar [the author] from expressing polemically [her] awareness of the sexual politics involved in relationships between men and women'. Further, the critical examination of the way cultural norms such as domesticity and romantic love ensnare women or are deeply internalised 'makes it legitimately, even necessary to describe [*Monkey Grip*] as feminist'.[68]

The assessment from Higgins (later Sheridan) and Matthews reflects an assured confidence about the possibilities of feminist writing, as well as an intervention in what was by then an already somewhat exhausted question: what constitutes feminist writing? Given its success and eventual recognition as a classic and/or trailblazing novel, *Monkey Grip* played a pivotal role in the evolution of these questions—about form

---

66 For more detail on the royal commission, see Michelle Arrow, '"Everyone Needs a Holiday from Work, Why Not Mothers?" Motherhood, Feminism and Citizenship in the Australian Royal Commission on Human Relationships, 1974–1977', *Women's History Review*, 25, no. 2 (2015): 320–36, doi.org/10.1080/09612025.2015.1083225.
67 Levy, 'Editorial', 1, 4.
68 Susan Higgins and Jill Matthews, 'For the Record: Feminist Publications in Australia since 1975', *Meanjin* 38, no. 3 (September 1979): 328–29.

and content, in relation to both politics and art—within both Australian feminism and Australian literature. That some of her earliest feminist readers, such as Sue King in *Vashti* and Lesley Morgan in *Womanspeak*, each identified the book's 'realism' about heterosexual relationships under feminism as both the source of its appeal and its possible limits as a bona fide feminist book with the capacity to speak beyond inner Melbourne or the women's movement, or to consciousness-raise, is in retrospect not so much a case against *Monkey Grip* as 'feminist' as testimony to the novel— and Garner's capacity—to challenge and transform assumptions about both feminist writing and literature in general. Where each reviewer was unequivocal was in recognising that Garner was onto something, namely the difficulty of reconciling theory and practice, a theme the author traces back to her days at *Digger* magazine and that would recur in subsequent fiction and nonfiction,[69] including what would become possibly the most divisive book among Australian feminists of the late twentieth century, *The First Stone* (1995).

Conclusion

Kevin Brophy observed in 1992 that Garner's first novel had grown in stature beside her, which he described as 'curious' given the mixed critical reception the book initially received.[70] Brophy was writing before the publication of Garner's nonfiction book *The First Stone* (1995), a highly personal account of a sexual harassment case at the prestigious Ormond College at the University of Melbourne. The controversy that erupted over the book—one expression of which manifested as a purported generational war within Australian feminism that pitted the hardened warriors of women's liberation such as Garner against their younger, more easily wounded third-wave 'daughters'[71]—recast both *Monkey Grip* and Helen Garner within Australian feminism and feminist memory, while also enhancing her status as a public intellectual. For many feminists, Garner's empathy in *The First Stone* for the college master and her comparative

---

69 Goldsworthy, *Helen Garner*, 38–39.
70 Brophy, 'Helen Garner's *Monkey Grip*', 271.
71 For a full account of *The First Stone* as media event, see Anthea Taylor, *Mediating Australian Feminism: Re-reading the First Stone Media Event* (Oxford & Bern: Peter Lang, 2008). For an astute analysis of the faux-generationalism of *The First Stone* within Australian feminism, see Mary Spongberg, 'Mother Knows Best? Bridging Feminism's Generation Gap', *Australian Feminist Studies* 12, no. 26 (1997): 257–63, doi.org/10.1080/08164649.1997.9994865.

contempt for the two young women who pursued charges against him was tantamount to treachery. *Monkey Grip*'s cherished status as a feminist book was sometimes evoked in these condemnations, as this quotation from Katherine in an article marking the 10th anniversary of *The First Stone*'s publication illustrates. It also captures well the attachment a later group of feminists had to *Monkey Grip*:

> I remember the outrage and the feeling of betrayal. We were, after all, huge fans of Helen Garner—I was proud to live round the corner from the house featured in the *Last Days of Chez Nous* and my flatmate Katie even went and bought King Gee overalls to wear in order to emulate *Monkey Grip*'s heroine. It was absolutely shocking that someone we so admired could get it so wrong.[72]

Clearly then, *The First Stone* controversy is one of the feminist contexts in which *Monkey Grip* has been read (or reread) and I conclude with it here for that reason. However, the primary focus in this chapter has been on the earlier feminist contexts—such as the emergence of feminist publishing and the creation of feminist readers—that informed both the novel's creation and reception, including among other feminists, in the late 1970s. As Garner herself would acknowledge many times over the next 40 years, it was the advent of women's liberation that gave her the confidence to start writing in the first place. Sometimes this recognition comes with a caveat—'I don't write as a feminist: I think that's a killer' or 'I had never thought of myself as being a political person'[73]—but these are not contradictory claims, but rather consistent with the themes and feelings first captured in *Monkey Grip*. Lastly, her qualifications are also reflective of the wider everyday implications of the 1970s feminist mantra 'the personal is political', a notion that was enlarged by women writers of this period, perhaps none more so than Helen Garner.

---

72   Zora Simic, 'On Reading the First Stone Ten Years Later', *Lilith* 15 (2006): 18.
73   Sonya Voumard and Helen Garner, 'The Interviewer and the Subject', *Meanjin Papers*, June 2012, 3.

REDRAWING BOUNDARIES BETWEEN PUBLIC AND PRIVATE

CHAPTER 9

A phone called PAF: CAMP counselling in the 1970s

Catherine Freyne[1]

The 1970s were a watershed in the homosexual history of Australia. It was the decade when gay and lesbian people found and used their political voice; a decade of collective 'coming out' in public life that enabled myriad private comings-out. Activists banded together to challenge negative perceptions of homosexuality in Australian society through media campaigns and submissions to government inquiries. Law reform agitation resulted in the decriminalisation of homosexuality in two jurisdictions before the decade was out, and laid the groundwork for most other states to follow in the 1980s. There was the emergence and proliferation of gay publications, venues and organisations that made homosexual people visible and coherent as a community. The decade opened with the formation of the first openly homosexual political organisation CAMP (the Campaign Against Moral Persecution) and Dennis Altman's landmark treatise on homosexual oppression and liberation.[2] It ended with the defiant and consequential events of the first and second Mardi Gras demonstrations.

The activists of the 1970s recognised that the task at hand was not only to change the way the world thought about homosexuality. It was also to change the way homosexual people thought about themselves. This chapter explores the collapse during the 1970s of consensus within

---

1   This research is supported by an Australian Government Research Training Program Scholarship.
2   Dennis Altman, *Homosexual: Liberation and Oppression* (New York: Outerbridge & Dienstfrey, 1971).

the New South Wales branch of CAMP about the complementarity of these twin objectives, and a perception of opposition that developed around which to prioritise. In the mid to late 1970s, a deep faultline developed between CAMP NSW's 'welfare wing', made up largely of those involved in its telephone counselling operation, established in 1973, and its political actions group. A so-called 'bloodless coup' in 1978 left the welfare faction in charge.[3] In the new decade, Australia's first openly gay political organisation dispensed with its old name, the famous acronym with its playful yet militant edge. Instead of a Campaign Against Moral Persecution, the organisation was now to be known as the Gays Counselling Service.[4]

This volume documents the challenge the social movements of the 1970s presented to the long-established divide between public and private affairs in Australian life, and the new insight that emerged where the two spheres overlapped: 'the personal is political'. Equipped as we are today with this powerful inheritance, it is easy to recognise the political significance (as well as the pragmatic function) of social services established as adjuncts to emancipatory movements. It is clear that women's refuges and rape crisis centres, for example, were both produced by and productive of a feminist political consciousness in the period. Similarly, in the crucible of the gay and lesbian activist movement, the personal and the political were uniquely fused. This is not surprising, given the intimate matters of sexuality and kinship arrangements at the heart of the struggle. What is perhaps surprising to learn is the extent to which the personal and the political were prised apart in this early period. From the perspective of the present, however, it is possible to see that this fragmentation was ultimately productive, and contributed substantially to the movement's progress during the 1970s.

---

3   Bob Hay, 'CAMP Is Changing', piece drafted for publication in the *Sydney Star*, n.d., c. 1980, box 13, folder 79, 3, Gays Counselling Service of New South Wales records, 1970–1985, MLMSS 5836, State Library of NSW, Sydney.
4   The organisation is variously referred to as the 'Gays Counselling Service' and the 'Gay Counselling Service'. An explanation for this inconsistency is offered by Phone-A-Friend (PAF) counsellor Peter Trebilco: 'We were told by Telecom that we weren't allowed to be called the Gay Counselling Service but we could use the word "gays". And so we changed from Camp NSW to the Gays Counselling Service—because we were by that stage only providing telephone counselling services'. Peter Trebilco interviewed by John Witte (Pride History Group), Glebe NSW, 1 February 2010; audio and logs accessed at Pride History Group, Glebe NSW.

An archive of friends and factions

Most of the records of CAMP NSW are held in a collection comprising 19 boxes at the State Library of New South Wales, Sydney, labelled 'Gays Counselling Service of New South Wales records, 1970–1985'. The contents list includes many references to the 'Phone-A-Friend' (PAF) telephone counselling service, including 'logs of calls' and 'correspondence with counsellors'.[5] As part of my doctoral research, I acquired permission to access the restricted collection.[6] My project, 'The Family as Closet: Gay Married Men in Sydney 1970–2000', emerges from my own family experience: my late father came out at the age of 60 after 30 years of marriage and many secret relationships with men.[7] In the logs of calls and correspondence, I hoped to find stories about men like my father, and perhaps even their wives. And there were a few. There were also statistical breakdowns of calls, one of which suggested that 28 per cent of male callers between 1973 and 1978 were either married or had been married.[8] Another breakdown identified that in 1973, of the callers identifying as heterosexual (which were a small minority of 10 per cent), more than 60 per cent were female.[9] Might some of these women have been calling about homosexually active husbands?[10]

The disappointment was that the 'logs of calls', though eloquent in their own way, were very slight, with often just a single word for a description, for example, 'lonely', 'suicide', 'info', 'silent'.[11] Much more detailed were the contents of the correspondence with Phone-A-Friend's parent

---

5   Contents list for Gays Counselling Service of New South Wales records, 1970–1985, box 10, folder 63, MLMSS 5836, State Library of NSW, Sydney, online catalogue, accessed 2 November 2017, archival.sl.nsw.gov.au/Details/archive/110546966.
6   The Gays Counselling Service later became the Gay and Lesbian Counselling Service, which now operates the QLife phone and web hotline under the auspices the LGBTIQ youth organisation Twenty10. The Executive Director of Twenty10 authorised my access to the records, providing that the names and identities of clients remain confidential.
7   I borrow the term 'gay married men' from the Australian organisation established in the 1980s in NSW and Victoria to support heterosexually partnered men exploring homosexual inclinations—the Gay and Married Men's Association.
8   'Phone-A-Friend Statistics to 1976', box 13, folder 82, GCSNSW records, MLMSS 5836, SLNSW.
9   Brian Woodward and John Kennedy, 'Our Vital Statistics', *CAMP Ink* 4, nos 3/4 (April 1975), 17.
10   Also of value to my doctoral research were folders relating to CAMP NSW's 'married gays' group and clippings of articles about the 'the married homosexual'. These illuminate understandings of the phenomenon of the heterosexually partnered, homosexually active man before the advent of HIV/AIDS transformed that discussion.
11   Log of calls to Phone-A-Friend, no date, box 10, folder 63, GCSNSW records, MLMSS 5836, SLNSW.

organisation, CAMP NSW, and with subscribers to its magazine *CAMP Ink*. As I quickly discovered, the Gays Counselling Service was the later name of CAMP NSW, so this collection comprised the records of the venerable gay political organisation itself, and all of its projects, which included the counselling service. This explained why there was so much correspondence relating to CAMP and *CAMP Ink* in the boxes.[12] It was in these letters that I found detailed stories of individuals' circumstances. Even after the phone line was established, many lonely and distressed people made initial contact by letter.

It is clear from looking at the records that CAMP in the early years became a clearing house for all kinds of correspondence and requests for information and advice. This stands to reason, since CAMP was the first and for a long time the only visible gay organisation in the whole country. Nevertheless, I was struck by the sheer volume of correspondence received from individuals struggling with their own personal difficulties relating to sexual orientation, and by the consistent warmth and generosity of each individually crafted reply. For example, in 1974, one of the hundreds of letters CAMP NSW received came from interstate. 'I've obtained your address from that terrific women's magazine *Cleo*', the correspondent wrote:

> It has taken me some time to get around to writing to you. However I feel I must be honest with myself and admit that I would dearly like to have a close lesbian friend. I'm ... married, with a 12 mths old little boy.[13]

She said her husband's work would be bringing the family to Sydney for some weeks the following month. The letter finished, 'Could you please advise me what I should do now'. The secretary of CAMP NSW, Mike Clohesy responded:

> It was beaut to receive your letter on Friday: I'm glad you got around to writing.
>
> I'm afraid neither I nor anyone else can 'advise me what I should do now'. That's up to you, hard as that may sound. All I can say is that there are many women around who are or have been in

---

12   Correspondence is held in various folders within GCSNSW records, MLMSS 5836, SLNSW, e.g. 'Correspondence regarding membership CAMP Ink subs', box 5, folder 33; '1973 correspondence', box 7, folder 38; '1974 general correspondence', box 8, folder 39; 'Counselling correspondence local and overseas 1977–1980', box 13, folder 80; 'Correspondence with members', box 13, folder 81.
13   Letter to CAMP NSW, 14 August 1974, box 8, folder 39, GCSNSW records, MLMSS 5836, SLNSW.

a similar situation to yours. The solutions to the situations are many and varied. I think perhaps the best thing for you to do would be, when you get to Sydney, to come along to our clubrooms and coffee shop at 33a Glebe Point Road … Wednesday night is particularly devoted to women. I think you will meet some beaut people and have a good chance for a talk over things …

Please don't hesitate to get in touch at any time if you think we could be of further help.

Love and peace.[14]

Triangulating these primary sources with the historiography of Australian gay and lesbian activism in the 1970s, it emerges that the question of whether CAMP NSW had anything of value to offer women was already vexed by the time of this exchange.[15] Nevertheless, in the correspondence CAMP received from the time of its inception, from women as well as from men, the 'welfare' need amongst homosexuals was apparent. This clear need was the principal catalyst for Phone-A-Friend.

Judging from the collection, there were a couple of other galvanising factors. The first was the fact that one of the CAMP NSW organisers, Chris Stahl, had been involved in setting up a similar service in Sweden called Jourhavande Vän ('Friend On Duty').[16] The other was a letter published in the *Australian* newspaper in February 1973 from the secretary of the Humanist Society, commenting on the inadequacy of the Lifeline telephone counselling service.[17] She objected to the claims by Lifeline's founder, the Methodist minister Alan Walker, that 'only Christians are capable of helping people in need' and that therefore 'only Christians are allowed to work in Lifeline'. She wanted to know where that left callers who had 'no spiritual affinity' with Christianity:

---

14   Mike Clohesy letter, 19 August 1974, box 8, folder 39, GCSNSW records, MLMSS 5836, SLNSW.
15   Denise Thompson, *Flaws in the Social Fabric: Homosexuals and Society in Sydney* (North Sydney, NSW: Allen & Unwin, 1985), 2–3, 55–61; Sue Wills, 'Inside the CWA—The Other One', *Journal of Australian Lesbian Feminist Studies*, no. 4 (June 1994): 6–22; Rebecca Jennings, *Unnamed Desires: A Sydney Lesbian History* (Clayton, Vic.: Monash University Publishing, 2015), 75–80, 91–100.
16   Chris Stahl, 'Friend on duty', 7 November 1972, box 8, folder 39, GCSNSW records, MLMSS 5836, SLNSW.
17   Lifeline had been running since 1961.

> We need counselors with warmth and human understanding to provide moral support in times of crisis ... At present, people whose behaviour Mr Walker considers deviant (such as homosexuals) are not dealt with satisfactorily.[18]

CAMP contributed to the discussion that ensued in the letters pages of the *Australian* that coincided with the lead-up to the launch of Phone-A-Friend, winning much-needed publicity and even a $50 donation from a reader for its fledgling service.[19]

The internal newsletter circulated on 14 April 1973 described the launch of the service the day before:

> PHONE-A-FRIEND STARTED Friday, 13th April 1973. Our first telephone Counsellor was Ron A. and the Supervisor was Peter B.B. Chris S., Allan H., Michael S., Peter B-B and Ron A. celebrated the opening with a bottle of Kaiser Stuhl Pink Champagne. The telephone was baptised in the name of Jesus Christ Super Star, and named PaF![20]

What becomes clear from the oral histories of PAF's founders, recorded recently as part of the Pride History Group's 100 Voices project, is that the duly baptised phone was actually located in the Balmain loungeroom of CAMP founders Peter Bonsall-Boone and Peter de Waal. Co-founder Brian Woodward recalled in 2010:

> We started it off in Peter's lounge room, and then it moved to Chris' bedroom in Beattie St [Rozelle] ... Chris and I were living next door to each other in Beattie St. And then it ... moved between the 2 houses ... we had a very long telephone cord ... the houses had a common courtyard at the back.

He also described the early philosophy of the service:

> We didn't actually set it up as a counselling service. We really set it up as ... somewhere that people could ring and talk to other gay people ... there were say 10 or 12 of us who were ... reasonably comfortable with the way we are ... The word 'friend' was really the thing that we actually wanted it to be. We wanted people to feel like they could actually phone us as a friend ... it wasn't

---

18 Mrs W. G. Weeks, 'Lifeline', Letter to the Editor, *Australian*, 27 February 1973.
19 PAF newsletter, 25 March 1973, box 10, folder 63, GCSNSW records, MLMSS 5836, SLNSW.
20 PAF newsletter, 14 April 1973, box 10, folder 63, GCSNSW records, MLMSS 5836, SLNSW.

a problem line, it wasn't an advice line, it wasn't a pick up line, it was [for] whatever … people might want to talk about … We didn't have any formal training, or at least most of us didn't. We had, I guess, a listening ear and common sense.[21]

These records reveal the mix of improvisation, intuition, informality and empathy that animated the early spirit of Phone-A-Friend, and suggest an underlying principle of shared past experience as a basis for help and support.

Phone-A-Friend in context

As Graham Willett describes it, the 'first wave' of Australian gay and lesbian activism crested with the national celebration of Gay Pride Week in September 1973, then broke into a turbulent swirl for several years before the events of June 1978 revived solidarity.[22] But even as the movement fragmented during the middle years of the 1970s, its progress was sustained. Willett argues that the secret to the movement's success during this period was the 'action group model' that saw the formation of 'scores, if not hundreds' of special interest groups, most of them loosely affiliated with the broader movement, many operating autonomously within larger organisations such as CAMP NSW or Melbourne Gay Liberation. A group might be oriented:

> towards a particular occupation (such as gay teachers) or politics (such as lesbian feminists or socialist homosexuals); [it] might work on an ongoing task (such as the gay radio groups, counselling groups or law reform organisations) or a short campaign (such as running a candidate in an election).[23]

In this way a thriving ecosystem took root, and many fronts were tackled. Of all the species of action group that sprang up during this period, the 'archetypal' one, says Willett, was the counselling group.[24]

---

21 Brian Woodward, interviewed by John Witte (Pride History Group), NSW, 11 April 2010; audio and logs accessed at Pride History Group, Glebe NSW.
22 Graham Willett, *Living Out Loud: A History of Gay and Lesbian Activism in Australia* (St Leonards, NSW: Allen & Unwin, 2000), 110.
23 Ibid., 114.
24 Ibid., 118.

CAMP NSW's Phone-A-Friend was not the first. It was preceded by the Homosexual Guidance Service (HGS) established in April 1972 by Sue Wills, who had just joined CAMP NSW and would soon become its co-president, and CAMP founder John Ware. Wills and Ware, both psychology graduates, were focused on challenging psychiatric views on homosexuality, with the provision of counselling services to 'troubled homosexuals and their families' as an associated program. Unlike the PAF collective, the HGS group included several 'sympathetic straights' and people with qualifications in psychology and psychiatry.[25] Its traces are slight in the archives of its parent organisation by comparison with those of Phone-A-Friend, reflecting HGS's lower profile and shorter life.

During the early to mid-1970s, counselling services were established in most states, with local variations. At the first National Homosexual Conference in 1975, Jocelyn Clark, who had worked as a counsellor for the Melbourne Gay Liberation Front (GLF), outlined the philosophy of Gay Liberation counselling. She spoke of an attitude of 'libertarian anarchism', of 'the influence of the anti-psychiatry movement' and:

> the very natural suspicion which homosexuals have of mental health professionals, because we have been the victims of psychosurgery, aversion therapy, hormone therapy and all sorts of other harassment and torture.

But Clark noted that this philosophy hadn't served them ideally at all times:

> Such has been Gay Liberation's attitude to professional 'help' that when, in the early days of Melbourne GLF, a member who was completing a social work degree offered his services as a social worker to the centre, the idea was completely rejected because of its overtones of professional authority. Later we were faced with the sad possibility that this rejection had contributed to the man's suicide.[26]

When a Gay Counselling Service was established in Adelaide in 1976, a very different approach was taken. One of its founders, Peter Migalka, described the service in a 1977 letter that is held in the CAMP NSW collection. Its volunteer staff were described as 'fully qualified professionals with a range of experience in psychotherapy, counselling, clinical psychology,

---

25   Sue Wills, 'The Politics of Sexual Liberation' (PhD thesis, University of Sydney, 1982), 85.
26   Jocelyn Clark, 'On Counselling or Personal Problems: Mine and Other Peoples', *Papers and Proceedings of the First National Homosexual Conference, Melbourne 16–17 August 1975* (Melbourne, Vic.: Homosexual Conference Collective, 1975), 67.

group work' who were themselves serviced by 'medical practitioners, psychiatrists, and social workers'. They trained collaboratively to develop special expertise in 'the delicate and sensitive area of sexuality, particularly the field of homosexuality and sexual (dis)-orientation'. Migalka added:

> Personally I feel somewhat critical of gay phonelines which purport to offer counselling by unsuitable or untrained personnel. It is poor criteria because one is gay or a professional counsellor, or both, to validate assisting people who are homosexual or unsure of their own sexual proclivity. We have witnessed appalling and disastrous attempts of gays and professionals creating even more serious situations by their 'help'.[27]

At least one disastrous situation is documented in the NSW collection—a statement by a PAF staffer in 1980 details a complaint made by an 18-year-old client regarding a counsellor who allegedly exerted 'emotional pressure on him by threatening disclosure of personal information entrusted to him to the clients' parents in return for his company at his (the counsellor's) home'.[28]

There are references in the oral histories too, to a nickname PAF acquired in the early days: Phone-A-Fuck, because of the not-unheard-of phenomenon of sexual encounters developing between counsellors and callers.[29]

In Western Australia, the counselling service was led by clinical psychologist Vivienne Cass, who later went on to author an influential theory of homosexual identity formation.[30] With CAMP WA president Brian Lindberg in August 1975, Cass gave evidence before the Royal Commission on Human Relationships. Their testimony shows that the WA service ran along professional lines and entailed both telephone and face-to-face counselling.[31]

---

27 Peter Migalka, letter to Bob Hay, 25 January 1977, box 9, folder 49, GCSNSW records, MLMSS 5836, SLNSW.
28 Report to CAMP secretary from PAF administrative coordinator, 7 July 1980, box 13, folder 82, GCSNSW records, MLMSS 5836, SLNSW.
29 For example, John Greenway interviewed by John Witte (Pride History Group), Wentworth Falls NSW, 31 March 2008; Peter Trebilco interviewed by John Witte (Pride History Group), Glebe NSW, 1 February 2010; audio and logs accessed at Pride History Group, Glebe NSW.
30 Vivienne Cass, 'Homosexuality Identity Formation: A Theoretical Model', *Journal of Homosexuality* 4, no. 3 (1979): 219–35, doi.org/10.1300/J082v04n03_01.
31 Vivienne Cass and Brian Lindberg, testimony, 21 August 1975, *Royal Commission on Human Relationships: Official Transcript of Proceedings* (Sydney: Commonwealth Reporting Service, 1974–1976), vol. 6, 2112–123A.

At CAMP Queensland, counselling was handled by the Befriending Group, with a phoneline established in November 1974.[32] Statistics enabling a comparison of the volume of calls received by CAMP NSW's Phone-A-Friend and CAMP Queensland's telephone service were published in two consecutive editions of *CAMP Ink* in 1975.[33] Even though the population of Queensland was less than half that of New South Wales in this period, the Queensland service received a far higher volume of calls: an average of 110 per week, compared with PAF's weekly average of 37 calls. The writer attributed this to advertising. Whereas PAF in Sydney was apparently not permitted to advertise in the newspaper, the *Courier Mail* put up no objection, so the Queensland service advertised daily. Another difference (for which no theory was offered) was that only 7 per cent of callers to the Queensland service were female, whereas the NSW figure was 18.5 per cent. Among the records of CAMP NSW is a later handwritten tally titled 'Phone-A-Friend statistics to 1976' that shows the percentage of female callers to be just 13.4 per cent of total calls examined.[34] More interesting to consider than the difference between Queensland and NSW, in this regard, is the extreme gender disparity these statistics suggest in the take-up of such services.

Gender dynamics

We saw that CAMP NSW secretary Mike Clohesy's advice to the female correspondent cited earlier was to visit the CAMP coffee shop on a Wednesday night, which is 'particularly devoted to women'. He added 'If you're a little hesitant… give a call to our telephone listening service, Phone-A-Friend'. The following month the same correspondent wrote again, this time from Sydney:

> [W]e have only a couple of friends in Sydney and I find it impossible for me to visit the club and coffee shop on Wednesday nights as you had suggested. In other words I've no excuse for going out at night by myself.

---

32   Willett, *Living Out Loud*, 119; Roger Sawkins, 'The Brisbane Telephone Service', *CAMP Ink* 4, no. 4/5 (no date, c.1975), 22.
33   Woodward and Kennedy, 'Our Vital Statistics'; Sawkins, 'The Brisbane Telephone Service', 22.
34   'Phone-A-Friend Statistics to 1976'.

She said she had since learned that CAMP had branches in other cities too, including her own, and that she would follow up there.[35] Whether she availed herself of PAF as Clohesy suggested is not apparent. But this exchange of correspondence usefully introduces to the discussion the fact that men and women in 1970s Australia faced different challenges as they worked through questions to do with sexual orientation. In this case, the difference was to do with the gendered distribution of access to privacy and autonomy outside the domestic sphere.

Other gender-based differences existed too, for example, the experience and consequences of 'coming out'. Writing about North America, Canadian sociologist Roy Cain has traced the shift in normative views of disclosure of homosexuality from the 1950s to the 1980s. He shows how 'coming out' came to be viewed as desirable in this period by mental health professionals, gay political activists and sociologists alike, and emerged as the 'central political act' of gays in the collective sense.[36] This ideology was certainly borne out in the language of CAMP activists in the early to mid-1970s, as Robert Reynolds has summarised.[37] Consistent with this discourse, what PAF offered was often referred to in-house as 'coming out counselling'.[38] But as Rebecca Jennings discovered in oral history interviews with lesbians of the period, there was real ambivalence about the idea of openness as a form of liberation. She writes that for many women, 'the influence of feminist ideas and activism in opening up new opportunities and freedoms was often more significant in reshaping their experience than the ideology of "coming out"'.[39]

For this reason, and for the political critique of patriarchy offered by the feminist movement, many lesbians were attracted to women's liberation groups, where several lesbian groupings emerged as a result, and where 'consciousness-raising' rather than 'coming out counselling' was the preferred modality.

---

35 Letter to CAMP NSW, 27 September 1974, box 8, folder 39, GCSNSW records, MLMSS 5836, SLNSW.
36 Roy Cain, 'Disclosure and Secrecy Among Gay Men in the United States and Canada: A Shift in Views', *Journal of the History of Sexuality* 2, no. 1 (July 1991): 25–45.
37 Robert Reynolds, *From Camp to Queer: Remaking the Australian Homosexual* (Carlton South, Vic.: Melbourne University Press, 2002), 55.
38 Hay, 'CAMP Is Changing', 1.
39 Jennings, *Unnamed Desires*, 96.

The tensions within CAMP NSW about the place of women have been described vividly by Sue Wills who was co-president from 1972 to 1974. They emerged within months of the organisation's founding. A women's group was established in June 1971 and soon began meeting away from CAMP's premises because they 'had come to feel so unwelcome'. At a meeting in 1972, 15 to 20 women voiced their criticisms of the organisation, which included:

> that CAMP really wasn't concerned about lesbianism; that the men expected the women to clean up after them and little else besides; and that a lot of men did not really want women there at all. In short, their complaint was that the organisation was sexist. More particularly, that there was a group of male members who disliked women intensely.[40]

Around this time, a new constitution was drawn up requiring the election of two co-presidents: one male and one female. Nevertheless the tensions continued. Jennings sums it up: 'Although individual women continued to work within CAMP throughout the 1970s, the group's appeal to women declined and its female membership was extremely small.'[41]

We saw earlier that only men were present at the baptism of PAF. But in the early PAF newsletters written (by the Swedish-born Chris Stahl 'in a new language, Swenglish') in the lead-up to the launch of the service, there is evidence of a push to achieve equal gender representation. For example, in the newsletter dated 8 March 1973:

> <u>Male-Female situation</u>. At present moment we are 11 male and 7 females. This means that we need 3 girls more to be able to start rostering a male and a female on the same shifts. I hope that the girls will be arranging for this for us, in their own interests.[42]

The 'girls' seem to have heard the call because in the next newsletter it is reported: 'We have today in our group 14 males and 13 females'.[43] But parity does not appear to have been sustained. For example, in a typed list of PAF members in 1977, of 15 names, only two are those of women.[44] Meanwhile, a somewhat unsympathetic 'us and them' attitude

---

40   Wills, 'Inside the CWA', 8–9.
41   Jennings, *Unnamed Desires*, 79–80.
42   PAF newsletter, 8 March 1973, box 10, folder 63, GCSNSW records, MLMSS 5836, SLNSW.
43   PAF newsletter, 25 March 1973, box 10, folder 63, GCSNSW records, MLMSS 5836, SLNSW.
44   'Phone-A-Friend Telephone Numbers', 10 September 1976, box 13, folder 82, GCSNSW records, MLMSS 5836, SLNSW.

around gender can be detected in the following excerpt from an oral history interview with long-term CAMP activist and PAF counsellor Peter Trebilco:

> Interviewer: It would have been a bit strange with women ringing in and men answering the phone and vice versa, did you have any problems in those early days?
>
> PT: The men didn't. In fact the male counsellors always felt a little put down when a woman said 'No, I want to talk to a woman.' But we would always say 'That's fine, but if you'd like to talk to me my name is Peter, I am a gay man.' 'No I'd prefer to talk to a woman.' 'That's fine, Monday night' … no I think lesbian night was Friday night … Goodness, endless bloody problems [staffing] that. Because they want to be seen to be doing something rather more than listening to other women bitching, as one of them said to me.[45]

Jocelyn Clark cited misogyny as a key reason for her decision to stop working on the phones at Melbourne Gay Liberation. 'It is not very pleasant for a woman to be cossetting a man with a problem, and suddenly realize that the problem is that he hates women.'[46]

Welfare versus politics

In the mid to late '70s, people with professional experience in community health and welfare entered the ranks of PAF. Terry Goulden and Bob Hay were part of this new cohort. With mental health and psychology backgrounds, they came to hold key positions at PAF. Their perspective is clearly articulated in the CAMP NSW collection in the form of a conference paper, which they delivered at the First International Gay/Lesbian Health Conference in New York in 1984. In this paper, they looked back on the evolution of PAF, and acknowledged the challenge this new emphasis on professional standards represented to the anti-professional, anti-establishment orientation of the PAF collective. Yet according to Goulden and Hay, the influence of professional people and a synthesis of their experience helped lay down many of the fundamental principles on

---

45 Trebilco interviewed by Witte (PHG), timecode 84:03.
46 Clark, 'On Counselling', 67.

which the service could grow from 'a small, face-to-face group of friends aiming to befriend fellow gays "coming out"... to a service organisation which is funded by government and the gay community'.[47]

A clear picture emerges in the organisation's papers, that this evolution of PAF was accompanied by the emergence of bitter divisions within CAMP NSW in the mid to late 1970s. Two opposing factions developed, with those primarily interested in welfare service provision on the one hand, and those who understood PAF's and CAMP's most important function as being political action on the other. According to accounts in the collection written by Bob Hay, the political faction was taking the organisation into militant territory:

> They publicly aligned us with the alternative movement of the day, affiliating CAMP NSW with many non-gay organisations ... Those of us concerned primarily with counselling and welfare issues, saw party political alignment and the militant use of gay and feminist symbols as driving away the very people we wished to serve.[48]

In May 1978, CAMP NSW split along this faultline. Within the organisation, this watershed was apparently later referred to as the 'Palace Revolution'. The entire executive resigned and the vacuum was filled by the numerically stronger PAF personnel.[49]

Denise Thompson records that tension along these lines had emerged as early as 1974. In March of that year, Lex Watson and Sue Wills resigned as co-presidents, as did Gaby Antolovich as editor of *CAMP Ink*. In their letters of resignation, each criticised PAF as a depoliticising influence within the organisation. Sue Wills, for example:

> objected to the provision of 'help' and 'communion' for homosexuals being seen as the dominant function of CAMP, at the expense of the activities designed to remove the oppression which makes this 'help' and 'communion' necessary.

---

47   Terry Goulden and Bob Hay, 'The Changing Identity of a Gay Counselling Service: Paper Prepared for the 1st International Gay/Lesbian Health Conference, New York 16–19 June 1984', box 16, item 3, 3, GCSNSW records, MLMSS 5836, SLNSW.
48   Hay, 'CAMP Is Changing', 2.
49   Ibid., 3.

Thompson notes 'the prophetic aspects of [this] criticism' in 1974, but acknowledges it took some years to be borne out. In the meantime, 'CAMP's political activities not only continued undiminished, but actually increased in scope and intensity'.[50]

Peter de Waal, one of CAMP and PAF's original founders, had led many of CAMP NSW's political actions in the 1970s. In July 1978 he drafted 'A contribution to the political debate at CAMP NSW' for circulation in the CAMP newsletter. According to de Waal, the split within the organisation 'reflected the current trend towards a right-wing, conservative backlash in the community at large'. He lamented the splintering not of CAMP's energies, but of what he saw as the guiding philosophy that had previously integrated its welfare, social and political activities. He saw this particularly in the operations of the phone counselling service:

> PAF in the past was an instrument by which homosexuals were radicalised and encouraged to make a break with what society thinks is good for the homosexual. Now, referrals to steam baths and bars are on the top of the list. This of course means that homosexuals who go to these places financially support their own oppression.[51]

Disdain for saunas and bars and other profit-oriented operations catering to gay clientele was an attitude established in the early days of gay liberation. From the start, the premises of CAMP had included a coffee shop, run as an adjunct to the counselling program. The aim was to provide an alternative to gay bars and bathhouses, seen by early CAMP activists as commercially exploitative. But maintaining this position took some resolve as the commercial gay scene exploded in Sydney through the 1970s and became the site of a vibrant new gay male subculture. After the split, the new executive decided that the hostility that had grown up between the movement and the emerging gay male subculture had to be routed. In an article for the gay newspaper the *Sydney Star* in 1980, Bob Hay, who was then president, laid down CAMP NSW's guns on this issue. He wrote:

---

50   Thompson, *Flaws in the Social Fabric*, 18–19.
51   Peter de Waal, 'A contribution to the political debate at CAMP NSW', 31 July 1978, box 13, folder 81, GCSNSW records, MLMSS 5836, SLNSW.

> Perhaps we all need to realise that we no longer stand alone. Those of us who came to the gay eighties through the militant seventies often cannot really recognise the spirit of community even when it stares us in the face. At CAMP NSW we stand corrected and are prepared to join in that community as fully as we can.[52]

At the end of 1978, the membership voted in support of the new welfare-oriented executive. 'Since that time,' reported Hay in the *Sydney Star* piece in 1980:

> CAMP NSW has been identified by its members as a non-party political, non-religious, non-aligned kind of organisation concerned with gay welfare, community education and related issues.[53]

By the late 1970s, decriminalisation of male homosexual activity had been achieved in both South Australia and the ACT. An interesting question to consider in relation to the 'Palace Revolution' at CAMP NSW in 1978 is whether its outcome reflected a waning sense of political urgency as homosexual law reform in Australia got underway. There is little to suggest in the records of CAMP NSW that this rationale was consciously in play at the time of the split. One place where the broader trajectory of legal and political progress might have been referenced, had it been perceived as relevant by players at the time, was in the presentation by Bob Hay and Terry Goulden at the conference in New York. To this international audience, they made no reference to the political context in Australia, even though the conference took place just weeks after the passage of decriminalisation legislation in NSW. The political context that *does* seem to have been relevant to the tensions within CAMP was the conservative backlash in the post-Whitlam era against some of the broader left-wing causes that the 'political heavies' in CAMP NSW had aligned themselves with—for example, 'militant feminism', socialism and the anti-uranium movement.[54] The welfare faction saw an association with these movements as a deterrent to many people who would otherwise want to make contact with a gay organisation in the late 1970s.[55]

---

52 Hay, 'CAMP Is Changing', 4.
53 Ibid., 3.
54 Peter de Waal in 'A contribution to the political debate at CAMP NSW' noted that anti-uranium stickers and posters had been removed from the CAMP NSW coffee shop, 'apparently because political activity should not be seen to take place there'.
55 Bob Hay, 'CAMP Is Changing', 2.

Arriving in 'the gay eighties'

Australian gay and lesbian activism of the 1970s was riven with fascinating splits. Historians have devoted particular attention to the rift between the so-called 'reformers' who continued to align themselves with CAMP and the 'revolutionaries' who broke away to articulate a more radical agenda by way of a new group called Gay Liberation.[56] So too have historians charted feminist dissent within Australian gay activism and the emergence of a distinct lesbian politics during this period.[57] The contest explored in this chapter between the 'welfare' and 'political' factions of Australia's oldest and earliest gay political organisation is less well documented in the historiography. One notable exception is Denise Thompson who accorded the contest, and its outcome, a prominent place in her pioneering but not impartial history of 'homosexuals and society in Sydney' published in 1985. According to Thompson, CAMP NSW since the 'enforced withdrawal of the "political heavies"' at the end of 1978 had become 'just one more state-approved institution'. It had '[given] up any attempt to bring about social change'; its role had 'become that of looking after the welfare of the (male) gay community, while leaving "straight society" to its own devices'. In her reckoning, in a liberationist sense, CAMP NSW had failed.[58]

But an episode from the very end of the 1970s reminds us that the provision of sympathetic counselling, and support for people negotiating homosexual lives in a heteropatriarchal society, was itself a political challenge to the values of mainstream Australia at that time. Late in 1979, preparations were afoot for the 1980 Festival of Sydney and its Grand Parade through the city. In applying to enter a float, CAMP NSW enclosed a sample of leaflets for distribution that included pamphlets advertising its telephone counselling service. The application was refused. Festival director Stephen Hall explained in his letter that:

> The parade is largely a family affair watched by tens of thousands of young children; in our view it would be inappropriate to permit any group to use what we hope will be a happy, spectacular ending to the festival for the purposes of propaganda.

---

56 Willett, *Living Out Loud*, 60–62; Reynolds, *From Camp to Queer*, 69–75.
57 Thompson, *Flaws in the Social Fabric*, 55–61; Wills, 'Inside the CWA', 6–22; Jennings, *Unnamed Desires*, 75–100.
58 Thompson, *Flaws in the Social Fabric*, 11, 31–35.

Even when CAMP NSW suggested they drop the plan to distribute information, Hall confirmed the refusal. He wrote, 'there are certain aspects of life which parents of young children may not wish to be brought to the notice of their children'.[59]

It is possible that in 1979 Hall, himself a gay man, was under pressure from his patrons to keep the gays out of the parade.[60] The memories would then have been fresh, after all, of the violence and arrests into which that other Sydney street festival, the first Mardi Gras, had descended the previous year. But there is no suggestion of sympathy for CAMP's larger cause in Hall's letters of refusal. And if the views expressed in the letters were not his own, might he not have delegated the communications with CAMP to a festival colleague? This is the difficulty that gay and lesbian activists of the 1970s had been up against constantly. So real and entrenched was the marginalisation and stigma of homosexuality in Australian society, that many gay people were not prepared to disclose their homosexuality and join or even support the cause.

CAMP secretary Terry Goulden took up the argument with the festival:

> We wish to inform you that we do not accept your discriminatory exclusion of our entry from the 1980 Festival Parade … We are seriously angered with your imputation that being homosexual is something to be kept hidden and furtive. We are even more angered by the impact that this exclusion can have on the self-image of the many gay children who will be watching the parade and the effect on the many gay parents and their children.[61]

Despite an appeal to the Premier, Neville Wran, the Ombudsman and the Anti-Discrimination Board, they did not win entry into the parade in the 1980 festival.

---

59 Stephen Hall letters, quoted in Bob Hay, The Gay Walk, 'Scaring the Kiddies', last updated 16 February 1999, accessed 21 January 2019, pandora.nla.gov.au/nph-wb/19990228130000/http://www.ozemail.com.au/~vombatus/festive.html.
60 When Stephen Hall died in late 2014, various obituaries recorded that he was survived by his partner of 45 years, Vincent Dalgarno, e.g. Matthew Westwood, '"Festival" Stephen Hall was Sydney's master of ceremonies', *Australian*, 2 January 2015, 12.
61 Terry Goulden letter, quoted in Hay, 'Scaring the Kiddies'.

It was a different story the following year, however. The application was accepted and, along with the NSW Council of Gay Groups, CAMP NSW, now called the Gay Counselling Service, took part in the 1981 festival parade. Participant John Greenaway reflected afterwards on the experience in the CAMP NSW newsletter:

> After [a] rainy morning we were surprised that so many people were watching—an estimated 50,000 thronged the route. The reaction from the crowd was very interesting—bursts of applause, cheers, waving occurred all along the way. Some of course from gay people which we happily acknowledged, but a surprising amount from what looked like straight couples or groups. One elderly lady almost jumping up and down, clapping and cheering, called out: 'Good on you. Good for you' … the biggest benefit was to stand up proudly in front of 50,000 people and say 'we're here, we're proud of this great city.'[62]

At the dawn of the new decade, gay and lesbian people were taking their place in mainstream society and enjoying a profound shift in public attitudes. In this transformation, it is not possible to dismiss the contribution of any part of the activist work of the preceding decade: not the outward-facing work of the political activists whose concerns were systemic, nor the pastoral care of those whose orientation was individual welfare. Even though it had not felt like it to many activists at the time, the two agendas complemented one another very effectively. As Peter de Waal reflected in 2009:

> After the confrontation within CAMP about the PAF issue … that split became quite permanent. There [were those of us] who kept on working away on doing the submissions, the public appearances and all that and Phone-A-Friend went its separate way and there was a long period where we had very little to do with [that group] … We didn't fit in with what they were trying to do and vice versa. But … it didn't stop us from going ahead and doing lots of other things. So perhaps it was a good thing in some ways that there were two organisations formed.[63]

---

62   John Greenaway, quoted in Hay, 'Scaring the Kiddies'.
63   De Waal interviewed by Witte (PHG), timecode 119:10.

Impervious to the tensions within CAMP NSW and in the movement more broadly, the phone called PAF continued to ring. The steady stream of calls from individuals in states of crisis and uncertainty gave CAMP NSW and other activist organisations operating counselling services around the country a clear raison d'être during years when morale was fragile. Melbourne Gay Liberation Front was on the point of disbanding when at a meeting in early 1975 they decided to maintain the counselling service, prompting Jocelyn Clark to observe in 1975 that 'the counselling group is about the only part of GLF left'.[64] Even Denise Thompson acknowledged PAF's success in this regard:

> In comparison with the rest of CAMP's activities, PAF was more continuous, much in demand, and the first introduction for many people to the 'gay community.' It was obviously achieving something, and generated a sense of purpose among those who worked in it.[65]

By 1980, CAMP NSW had adopted a deliberate strategy to prioritise Phone-A-Friend as a community service and, in rebranding itself, to establish a break with the political past. It would be a mistake, however, to conclude that during the 1970s, the personal gazumped the political inside what had been Australia's first homosexual activist organisation. The very existence of a gay counselling service was politically productive. Nurturing the welfare and self-acceptance of individual homosexual people was an inherently political act. It represented a serious challenge to straight society, and an important point of entry for callers into a community of queers whose ranks and collective power were steadily increasing.

---

64 Willett, *Living Out Loud*, 119; Clark, 'On Counselling', 67.
65 Thompson, *Flaws in the Social Fabric*, 18.

CHAPTER 10

Discomforting politics: 1970s activism and the spectre of sex in public

Leigh Boucher[1]

In both scholarly histories and public memory, the 1970s are understood as the decade in which gays and lesbians 'came out' in Australian social, political and cultural life. After the stultifying heterosexism and homophobia of postwar Australia began to loosen their grip in the later 1960s, a visible and increasingly confident social movement directed towards the 'liberation' of some dissident sexualities and practices from legal prohibition and social and legal prejudice took shape.[2] The activists who propelled these transformations were not alone; the 1970s were a decade in which the forces of sexual, women's and gay liberation interacted to remake norms of intimate life, not least through public discussion of ideas and practices once seen as either private or shameful. These respective political vocabularies all shared an assumption that the uneven but potent privatisation of sexual and intimate life maintained

---

1   This research was produced as part of the ARC-funded project 'Gender and Sexual Politics: Changing Citizenship in Australia since 1969' with Barbara Baird, Michelle Arrow and Robert Reynolds. Thanks to all three for their continued engagement on this project and the latter for discussions about this particular case.
2   Featherstone describes how differing authorities (legal and medical) battled for control over the 'problem' of homosexuality in the late 1950s, and these were challenged in the late 1960s by liberal humanist ideas about tolerance. Lisa Featherstone, *Let's Talk about Sex: Histories of Sexuality in Australia from Federation to the Pill* (Newcastle Upon Tyne: Cambridge Scholars Publishing, 2011), 229–60.

sexual hypocrisy and gender inequality.³ Indeed, building on this political activism, queer and feminist theorists have since theorised the inherently political and almost impossibly freighted distinction between public and private in liberal democratic political cultures. Lauren Berlant and Michael Warner point out that 'hegemonic' political forms have been and are 'founded by a privatization of sex'. Moreover, heteronormative cultures position sexual desire and identity as both organic (rather than social or political) and stable (rather than politically contestable and historically dynamic).⁴ When liberationists claimed that the 'personal is political' they fundamentally ruptured this distinction, turning narratives, experiences and identities once seen as private and personal into political and public concerns. Bringing (homo)sex into public life represented a challenge to its coding as a criminal, moral or medical problem, and disrupted a foundational boundary of liberal democratic political culture.

At the end of the decade, and shaped by the confident politics of liberation movements, a 'kiss-in' protest occurred in Melbourne that would seem to confirm a set of remarkable transformations concerning the discussion and practice of homosex in Australian public life. The kiss-in featured couples of varying gender combinations; these gay liberation and feminist activists dramatised the uneven application of public indecency laws in the Garden State by asking which couples the police should arrest for the same act of intimacy. A few days before, two men had been convicted of public indecency for kissing at that very site. The *Age* newspaper published photographs of the kiss-in with supportive but amused captions.⁵ The arrest and kiss-in soon became the object of folkloric gay and lesbian collective memories, in part because they became the centrepiece of a national 'Summer Offensive' later that year to mobilise a national gay and lesbian constituency by activists.⁶

---

3   Feminists argued that ideas about private life protected violent husbands from appropriation; sexual liberationists argued that ideas about shame and privacy concealed the multiple and varied possibilities of sexual life; and gay liberationists argued that a nexus of shame and privacy was one of the mechanisms through which homosexual oppression was maintained. See Michael Warner, 'Public/Private', in *Critical Terms for the Study of Gender*, ed. Catharine R. Stimpson and Gilbert Herdt (Chicago: University of Chicago Press, 2014), 359–92.
4   Lauren Berlant and Michael Warner, 'Sex in Public', in *The Routledge Queer Studies Reader*, ed. Donald E. Hall, Annamarie Jagose and Andrea Bebell (London and New York: Routledge, 2013), 172–73.
5   *Age* (Melbourne), 9 October 1979, 6.
6   'The Kiss Out', *Gay Community News* 1, no. 1 (1980): 1.

Both the nature of this protest and its reportage reveal much about the changing attitudes concerning dissident sexualities and their public articulations in the 1970s. Only a decade before, newspaper readers were much more likely to read lurid accounts of homosexual depravity in the pages of *Truth* rather than encounter the *Age* providing editorial support for law reform.[7] Indeed, a gay man in Victoria in 1971 would have had difficulty believing that sex between men would be decriminalised in the Garden State within a decade; a wider campaign that was unfolding alongside the kiss-in achieved legal reform in 1980. It is probable that ideas about desire, identity, politics and public life shifted to such a degree that a man with dissident desires in 1971 would have had trouble recognising *himself* a decade later, let alone the changed social and legal context of his life. While the language of liberation implied that a stable homosexual self was hiding in the shadows, (im)patiently waiting to 'come out' into social and cultural life, we need to be careful about such satisfying teleologies. Following Ian Hacking, we might say that this person was being 'made up' from a set of shifting ideas and their histories in the same moment that claims were being made for social and legal change in his or her name.[8]

Bringing male homosex into public as a legitimate rather than criminal or pathological act did not occur in one moment of liberatory rupture. Rather, activists grappled with what Kane Race describes as the 'normative ideologies of healthy intimacy that have materially eviscerated queer lives'.[9] Ideas of healthy intimacy, then as indeed now, normalise sex between a heterosexual couple in private. The question of sex in public, in both discursive *and* practical terms, was a key element in the story of legal reform concerning male homosex in Australia because the categories of public and private were crucial to its policing. In Australian jurisdictions, most forms of male homosexual intimacy remained criminalised in the 1970s, but the state was much more likely to deploy public indecency

---

7 For a longer history of homosexual practice being rendered visible in the language of shame and disgust, see Wayne Murdoch, '"Disgusting Doings and Putrid Practices": Reporting Homosexual Men's Lives in the *Melbourne Truth*', in *Gay and Lesbian Perspectives IV*, ed. Robert Aldrich and Garry Wotherspoon (Sydney: Department of Economic History, University of Sydney, 1998), 116–31.
8 Hacking updates and revises some of his initial claims in a later discussion about the 'looping effects' by which specific modes of thought become the means by which people understand themselves, which, in turn, reshapes the categories themselves. We might think about the 1970s as an intensive period of these looping effects when the practices and actions of homosexual 'looped back' into medical, psychological and criminal definitions of homosexuality. Ian Hacking, 'Kinds of People: Moving Targets', *Proceedings of the British Academy* 151 (2006): 285–318.
9 Kane Race, *The Gay Science: Intimate Experiments with the Problem of HIV* (London: Routledge, 2017), 129, doi.org/10.1201/9781315544328.

rather than buggery as a mechanism to police homosex. It was much easier to find men 'procuring', 'loitering' or engaging in mild acts of intimacy that could be termed 'offensive' or 'indecent' than it was to discover two men engaged in 'buggery' in the bedroom.[10] In Victoria, this issue was pushed into public debate in 1976, when police entrapment of men at a beat in Black Rock led to a raft of arrests for various crimes relating to public order and morality. Activist networks had long discussed ways to achieve legal reform, but the arrests provoked them into a fulsome campaign for decriminalisation.

Bringing a discussion of sex into public *and* engaging with the behaviour of public sex itself was thus doubly disruptive. While forms of queer sociability and world-making took place at beats, these were nonetheless sites normatively freighted with shame and disgust.[11] *Talking* about abstract (homo)sexual rights in public remained a radical proposition through much of the 1970s; tarrying with the *practice* of sex at beats was an even more unsettling proposition. The campaign for law reform in Victoria was thus a politically, discursively and affectively volatile project and was textured with cultural legacies that were less easily shucked off than the idea of liberation might imply. In this chapter, then, I want to bring a sense of this unsteady and uncertain 'liberation' into focus. Taking Victoria as a case study, I start with a discussion of the kiss-in protest and situate this within the broader context of campaigns for decriminalisation of sex between men. Graham Willett has argued that the 'problem of sex in public seemed remarkably under-examined' by activists in the midst of the campaign given sex at beats was a crucial provocation for reform.[12] I want to suggest, however, that we read this apparent under-examination a little differently. Haunting the edges of this campaign was an uncertain and unsteady politics of sex in public that activists struggled to discursively manage. In the second half of this chapter, I bring this psychologically fraught uncertainty into sharper focus. The kiss-in, then, looks less like

---

10 To put it bluntly, police could more easily find men engaged in kissing and fondling in a public toilet than they would find them engaged in penetrative anal sex in public or private. This was, in part, I suspect because the kinds of intimate acts engaged in at beats did not always meet the requirements of an act of buggery (in legal terms).
11 On the history of Australian beats, see Clive Moore, 'Poofs in the Park: Documenting Gay "*Beats*" in Queensland, Australia', *GLQ* 2, no. 3 (1995): 319–39, doi.org/10.1215/10642684-2-3-319. On the queer world-making that took place at beats in an era of illegality, see Robert Reynolds and Shirleene Robinson, *Gay and Lesbian, Then and Now: Australian Stories from a Social Revolution* (Melbourne: Black Inc., 2017), 58.
12 Graham Willett, *Living Out Loud: A History of Gay and Lesbian Activism in Australia* (St Leonards, NSW: Allen & Unwin, 2000), 148.

a moment of confident liberation politics and more like a mechanism through which to manage the fraught politics of male homosex in public by activists seeking legal reform.

The 'kiss-in' and the campaign for law reform

In early September 1979, Terry Stokes and Darren Turner were arrested and charged with offensive behaviour, and a month later the Melbourne City Court would hear evidence that a constable saw them engage in what he called a 'very passionate kiss—a form a tongue kissing [that lasted] for approximately 15 seconds'.[13] Stokes, a PhD student at the University of Melbourne, was then expelled from his residence at Graduate House. A kiss-in protest—partly in response to the threat of eviction—was staged within days at the site of their arrest. Crucially, the protest was organised, not from within the networks of gay male activists, but by feminist students who supported Stokes. It then spread by word of mouth amongst activist groups. Challenging the notion that homosex was any different to heterosex, the participants offered a provocation to the police: would they arrest gay and lesbian couples while permitting the heterosexual couples to remain free? Kay Barry, the organiser, timed various re-enactments of the kiss for photographers from the *Age*, passers-by and reporters from Network Ten and 3AW. Here, then, would seem to be a politics of intimacy in public. The kiss-in dovetailed into a wider campaign of support for Stokes and Turner to appeal their conviction. Further public sparks flew when newspapers and broadcast radio in Melbourne reported on the possible eviction of Stokes and interviewed Graduate House staff for comment.[14] While Graduate House had initially claimed Stokes was expelled because he had overnight visitors (which was against their rules of residence), when the Graduate House manager framed homosex in a radio interview as something 'disgusting' to the general public it was clear this was discrimination in action.[15]

Activists saw this as a cause that could do much to mobilise interest in the campaign for law reform. The first issue of *Gay Community News*, a Melbourne-based monthly magazine with national ambitions, adorned

---

13 'The Terry Stokes Case', *Gay Community News* 1, no. 1 (1979): 3.
14 'No Title', *Farrago*, 18 October 1979, 5.
15 See 'Submission to the University Appeal Committee, including transcript of radio interviews', box 3, file 2 (Terry Stokes Case), Julian Phillips Collection, 1992.0165, University of Melbourne Archives.

their first cover with a photograph from the 'kiss out at the Woolshed'.[16] The editors declared that even those who did not see themselves as 'banner-waving political types' should be able to support the Stokes and Turner case. Support was about 'asserting our right to be visible, without fear'.[17] As one appeal for support for a defence fund later suggested, accompanied by a rather handsome sketch of Stokes, 'Is Terry Stokes Appealing? You bet he is—against a conviction for offensive behaviour'.[18] Indeed, the kiss-in occurred in the context of a wider campaign for law reform in Victoria and the social movement from which it grew.

Early activists, however, had been tentative in their ambitions for law reform. Society Five, an organisation that emerged as the Melbourne equivalent after CAMP NSW 'came out' in the *Australian*, was keen to assert that it was a 'reformist rather than revolutionary organisation'.[19] As Clive Moore notes, this first generation of 'activists' were 'fairly apolitical … quieter and even conservative'.[20] Soon, however, the ideas of gay liberation circulated in these networks and nourished a different political sensibility among some activists. Often centred around university campuses, but also deploying practices of consciousness-raising adopted from the feminist movement to incorporate non-students into the political project, these ideas and practices sought a more radical reconfiguration of the social and sexual order. Liberation was not a plea for acceptance, it was a forceful disruption. As Rebecca Jennings writes of the UK context:

> In contrast to earlier political groups, which had worked for social tolerance on the basis that homosexuals were 'normal' people, [the ideas of gay liberation] emphasized a gay identity as inherently positive through slogans such as 'Gay is Good' and argued that, rather than gay people attempting to adapt to hostile social values, it was the values and structures themselves that were responsible for the oppression of gay people and must therefore be changed.[21]

---

16 'The Kiss Out', *Gay Community News*, 1.
17 'Editorial', *Gay Community News* 1, no. 2 (1979): 4.
18 'Is Terry Stokes Appealing', *Gay Community News* 1, no. 2 (1979): 2.
19 Society Five Newsletter, March 1974, box 9, file 9, Records of Society Five, ALGA Society.
20 Clive Moore, 'Coming Out, Ready or Not: Gay Liberation Politics in Queensland, 1970s–1980s', in *Australia's Homosexual Histories,* ed. David L. Phillips and Graham Willett (Sydney: Australian Centre for Lesbian & Gay Research, 2001), 93.
21 Rebecca Jennings 'From "Woman-Loving Woman" to "Queer": Historiographical Perspectives on Twentieth-Century British Lesbian History', *History Compass* 5, no. 6 (2007): 1901, doi.org/10.1111/j.1478-0542.2007.00482.x. At the same time, however, we should be careful in assuming that these political differences produced two discrete networks of individuals. Members from both Society Five and Melbourne Gay Liberation would contribute to the political efforts of both, and a counselling and phone service for gays and lesbians would be staffed by activists of all political persuasions. Moreover, by the mid to late 1970s, the temperature of the initial animosity had somewhat cooled.

10. DISCOMFORTING POLITICS

In the early 1970s, activists from Society Five had often deployed the famous phrase from the 1957 Wolfenden Report in Britain that argued for the decriminalisation of homosexual acts that occurred between 'consenting adults in private'. Mobilising these ideas, Society Five members quietly worked hard to secure motions of support for law reform among church, civil and community groups usually relating to the protection of private sexual acts between adults.[22] Coverage in the *Age* soon began to look more sympathetic. In 1975 Phillip Adams wrote:

> the police [have] raided the home of a quiet, middle class homosexual couple … they were dragged into the bedroom and interrogated one at a time. In the mistaken belief that a relationship like theirs was perfectly legal behind closed doors [the couple] spoke frankly of their lives together … it was this information, freely given … that formed the basis of the subsequent prosecution … Believe it or not, the men were charged with the ancient crime of buggery … You may have heard Lindsay and John being interviewed [on radio]. They spoke of their deep love for each other and of their plans, now shattered, to buy a home together.[23]

Public opinion, that ever-slippery measure of social attitudes, seemed to be shifting in relation to sex between men in private. At the same time, however, members of Melbourne Gay Liberation were suspicious about what:

> law reform could achieve … [particularly if] law reform stops at the legalization of private homosexual acts … [L]aws that demand you hide your homosexual behavior from the public are a convenient means of preventing such homophobia being challenged … The only pay-off for law reform … might be respectability for the gay.[24]

In Victoria, activists were prompted into more forceful action in late 1976 when a police 'blitz' at a Melbourne beat produced a wave of prosecutions for public indecency and loitering for homosexual purposes. In response to the arrests at Black Rock, the Homosexual Electoral Lobby was formed. Soon renamed the Homosexual Law Reform Committee (HLRC), these activists were informed by the practices of the Women's Electoral Lobby, importing wholesale the practice of surveying candidates for their

---

22 For a discussion of these strategies, see Graham Willett, 'The Church of England and the Origins of Homosexual Law Reform', *Journal of Religious History* 33 (2009): 418–34, doi.org/10.1111/j.1467-9809.2009.00823.x.
23 Phillip Adams, 'Boys in Blue', *Age* (Melbourne), 9 April 1975, 8.
24 Melbourne Gay Liberation Newsletter, May 1975, box 3, file 1, Records of HLRC, ALGA.

attitudes on questions of sexuality and lobbying them for legal change. They faced some difficult questions about how to talk about homosex that did not occur in the bedroom; very early in its formation the members of the HLRC made the decision to argue for legal 'equality' to resolve this question. The principle of 'consenting adults in private', the HLRC now argued, did not offer enough protection from the ways in which the application of ideas about public and private could be deployed to criminalise homosex.[25] This would still make gay men 'second-class citizens' because they would still risk persecution for acts that would not be criminalised or policed in heterosexual couplings; activists frequently pointed out that amorous heterosexual couplings at the beach would rarely be policed like homosexual couplings, even if the acts were identical.[26] These arguments required not only a nuanced account of the ways in which homosex was criminalised in explicit and specific ways at law, but also through the uneven application of provisions to criminalise public indecency. The liberal principle of legal equality soon framed most of the materials the HLRC produced, its public engagement with the question and discussions with lawmakers; equality, rather than privacy, was the rhetorical and political solution here.[27]

At the same time, however, the HLRC ensured that the stories they told about homosexual life tended to resonate with conventional stories about public romantic coupling and private sexual intimacy in ways that mirrored the logic of Wolfenden. In a political context where sex at beats prompted the debate, the HLRC worked hard to sidestep any mention of sex outside the bedroom.[28] The president of the HLRC even assured the premier that 'our proposals for law reform do not mean that public sexual acts … would be decriminalised'.[29] Indeed, members of the HLRC clearly saw the Stokes and Turner case as something that illustrated the discriminatory and unjust operation of the law in relation to same-sex

---

25   Jamie Gardiner to R. J. Hamer, Premier of Victoria, 21 February 1977, overwritten with acknowledgement from secretary, Premier's Department, box 1, file 7, Records of HLRC, ALGA.
26   Second Class Citizens in Private, box 2, file 2, Records of the HLRC, ALGA.
27   'Equality for homosexuals, now', box 2, file 2, Records of HLRC, ALGA.
28   So too, the scandal of the Young Gay and Proud revealed the limits of liberal engagements with questions of sexuality. Daniel Marshall, 'Young, Gay and Proud in Retrospect: Sexual Politics, Community Activism and Pedagogical Intervention', *Traffic*, no. 6 (2005): 161–87; and Steven Angelides, '"The Continuing Homosexual Offensive": Sex Education, Gay Rights, and Homosexual Recruitment', in *Homophobia: An Australian History*, ed. Shirleene Robinson (Annandale, NSW: Federation Press, 2008).
29   Carl Reinganum to Vance Dickie, Chief Secretary (cc), 17 March 1977, box 2, file 2/3, Records of HLRC, ALGA.

desire in ways that could secure wider public support; here was a case that did not evoke problematic intimacy in public. Their political instincts were not mistaken. The Stokes and Turner case was picked up by Melbourne broadcasters and media personalities including Derryn Hinch, Peter Couchman and Mike Willessee. Drawing on recent polling data that supported the decriminalisation of sex between men, all three broadcasters evoked broadly liberal principles to suggest that the prosecution of Stokes and Turner represented an inequitable application of the law.[30]

The fears of activists regarding the discussion of public sex were animated, however, when they heard about the release of a US film *Cruising*. The film narrated the story of a policeman who was induced to go undercover in the leather and fetish scene in New York. In a world populated by sexual dissidents and the spectre of violence, he found himself lured into a subculture of semipublic sex textured by murderous intent. Activists were very nervous about what political impact this film might have—not only did it represent homosex in the very terms they worked hard to avoid through stories about Stokes and Turner and various other narratives, its release coincided with crucial stages of discussion and debate about law reform in parliament. The HLRC's efforts, and close engagement with the Attorney-General in particular, had produced draft legislation for far-reaching law reform.[31] Members of the HLRC proposed they 'prepare material to counter the effect of "Cruising" and educate people attending cinemas'. Members thought that the HLRC needed to respond to the film in order to 'get across a pro-gay image which will be of benefit to the gay community'.[32] It was, one reviewer noted in *Gay Community News*, 'the most oppressive, ugly, bigoted look at homosexuality ever presented on screen'.[33] Another reviewer noted that the film implicitly 'said that gay men are promiscuous, into violence … and degraded'. This reviewer also gently suggested that the real 'world of clones and leather and promiscuity needs more thought' because they may well be forms of self-oppression. Once more, the ambivalence around the question of public and possibly promiscuous sex made its presence felt.[34] Soon, a coalition of 'concerned activists' emerged to 'work against'

---

30 Gays Big Chance, with two drafts, box 1, file 7, Records of the HLRC, ALGA.
31 Graham Carbery, 'Interview with Haddon Storey', *Latrobe Journal*, no. 87 (May 2011), accessed 2 July 2018, latrobejournal.slv.vic.gov.au/latrobejournal/issue/latrobe-87/t1-g-t15.html.
32 Minutes of HLRC meeting, 13 May 1980, box 2, file 1, Records of the HLRC, ALGA.
33 'Cruising', *Gay Community News* 1, no. 1 (1979): 49.
34 'Cruising', *Gay Community News* 1, no. 2 (1979): 43.

the film by distributing leaflets around cinemas.[35] In Victoria, where the spectre of sex at beats both inaugurated and then haunted the campaign, activists who confidently spoke a language of legal equality revealed their uncertainties when confronted with representations of homosex in public that exceeded the scripts of recognisable monogamous coupledom. Perhaps, moreover, this was not simply a political calculation to avoid harm. A closer examination of activist practices and ideas reveal varying degrees of discomfort and uncertainty about the place of public sex in homosexual life. The kiss-in, then, looks less like a confident liberation of gay men from shame and more like a respectable claim to reform the relationship between the law and male homosex.

The disruptive politics of sex in public

While the 'kiss-in' could suggest a politics propelled by resistant pride, reading this moment in relation to the question of sex at beats suggests a different emotional dynamic. Activists could not simply amputate histories of shame and their legacies. Many scholars have noted how an interlocking dyad of disgust and shame had been a (if not the) principal emotional motor through which distinctions between heterosexuality and homosexuality were maintained in the twentieth century. Because heterosexuality (or to follow Sarah Ahmed's work, a heterosexual orientation) has positioned penetrative sex between men as disgusting, the spectre of this disgust has both policed the slide between homosociality and homosexuality in cultural and social life as well as justifying moral approbation and legal discrimination.[36] Moreover, whether we see emotional patterns as psychological universals or historically specific affective circuits, it is clear that in the late twentieth century human objects of disgust were (and probably still are) normatively positioned to feel deep shame about their apparently aberrant bodily and sexual practices.[37] It is little wonder that assertive forms of gay liberation claimed

---

35 'Cruising for a Bruising', *Gay Community News* 2, no. 5 (1980): 11. In NSW, where activists would soon take a much more aggressive and assertive approach to law reform, and more forcefully frame questions in relation to public sex, *Cruising* didn't represent such a problem. As CAMP NSW asserted in their newsletter, the film 'wasn't worth being troubled about'. *Camp Newsletter* 56 (June 1980): 1.
36 It is helpful, I think, to see heterosexuality as an orientation in the phenomological sense. Ahmed argues that particular 'orientations' normalise particular perspectives, obscure other possibilities from view and orient the subject towards objects in specific, and political, ways. Sara Ahmed, *Queer Phenomenology: Orientations, Objects, Others* (Durham: Duke University Press, 2006), 1–17.
37 Halperin and Traub's collection on gay shame brings together the key thinkers on this question. David M. Halperin and Valerie Traub, eds, *Gay Shame* (Chicago: University of Chicago Press, 2008).

public legitimacy in a language of pride; shame about the disgust of others had been central to the constitution of homosexuality. As early as 1971, mainstream press commentators could identify the emotional dynamics at play in liberation politics: unlike pleas for tolerance, these activists would bring 'the homosexual cause … out of the closet … without shame'.[38]

Activists in the 1970s were grappling with the potent legacies of this shame and disgust dyad. And, moreover, this disgust was often focused upon the spectre of public sex between men. Writing in support of law reform, one newspaper nonetheless opined that 'Australians regard homosexuality as something in which a full blooded Australian male does not indulge … A man who looks or acts like a fairy, a queen, or a poofter is a figure of fun and an object of derision and disgust', not least because 'public lavatories' were the location of their 'disgusting' acts.[39] Indeed, these 'Australians', when confronted with the possibility that two men who 'acted like friends' might in fact be homosexuals would 'shrink from this idea in disgust'.[40] The spectre of sex at beats was central to this imaginary. Homosexuals were, in this logic, 'wilful perverts whose disgusting graffiti disfigures our public lavatories'.[41] As Derek Dalton points out:

> [B]eat sex attracts intense legal, social and cultural hostility as 'dirty' sex that is out-of-place, repulsive, disgusting and offensive … Public conveniences are built and maintained for the purpose of enabling people to dispose of their bodily wastes. When these places become sites of sexual expression, this runs counter to their socially authorized use.[42]

Disgust, then, was and is constitutive of the beat—both for its users and its observers. Moreover, these 'disgusting' cultures were intensively shamed. In the 1950s and 1960s, homosexual subcultutres were routinely positioned as the 'shame' of the 'Australian city'.[43] So too, others claimed that it was a 'secret shame' that these cities were 'rotten' and 'decent citizens are cautious about entering public conveniences'. As cities like Melbourne and Sydney grew 'bigger and more cosmopolitan', this underbelly of 'shameful' sex in public would only proliferate.[44] Putting it bluntly,

38 'The Gay Revolution: An End to the Secret Life', *Canberra Times*, 4 September 1971, 2.
39 'Homosexuality and the Law: Part III', *Canberra Times*, 8 August 1969, 2.
40 'Primate Replies to Canon's Theories', *Canberra Times*, 29 July 1967, 6.
41 'Letters to the Editor', *Canberra Times*, 16 July 1969, 2.
42 Derek Dalton, 'Gay Male Resistance in "Beat" Spaces in Australia: A Study of Outlaw Desire', *Australian Feminist Law Journal* 28 (2008): 110.1.
43 'The Shame of Sydney', *Truth*, 2 May 1954.
44 'Sex Menace', *Herald*, 10 April 1952, 3.

homosexual men, a 'citizen' observed in 1972, do 'shameful things with each other'.[45] It's little wonder, then, that queer thinkers have analysed the political and social consequences of shame for dissident sexual identities and practices; as Sally Munt writes, it is difficult to imagine a modern 'homosexual subject *not* formed from shame'.[46]

In a political sense, a simple assertion of the right to privacy could be understood as both a response to these powerful dynamics and a solution that did not undo its emotional politics. Writing about the Wolfenden Report, Martha Nussbaum notes how even as the report argued for the legal protection of sexual acts between men in private, it also argued that the 'disgust' of the man on the 'Clapham omnibus' could not be ignored. In the logic of Wolfenden, intimacy between men required the protection of privacy, otherwise it might, in fact, disgust the public.[47] As Senthorun Raj argues, ideas about the 'right' to certain kinds of sex in private can easily become 'a legal container for public disgust' rather than a disruption of its heteronormative constitution.[48] Moreover, while an argument for the liberal idea of equality in Victoria might have side-stepped the question of shame and disgust, it could not make them disappear entirely because the beat was at the edge of this campaign. Indeed, elsewhere activists noted that 'even our straight supporters' are troubled by the fact that some have sex in 'those nasty little parks and public toilets'.[49]

However, this was not simply the attitude of 'straights' towards 'gays'. Later activists would complain that the respectability of campaigns for law reform tended to uphold:

> [A] gay hierarchy of glamour and acceptability which places dinner, dance and tupperware parties at the top; clubs and bars in the middle; saunas and other sex-on-premises venues down the lower end, and beats right at the bottom. The image of beats as the domain of marrieds, olds, desperates and poor dancers is often, unfortunately, held by beats users themselves.[50]

---

45 'Homosexual Liberation', *Canberra Times*, 13 September 1972, 2.
46 Sally Munt, *Queer Attachments: The Cultural Politics of Shame* (London: Ashgate, 2008), 95.
47 Martha Nussbaum, *Hiding from Humanity: Disgust, Shame, and the Law* (Princeton: Princeton University Press, 2004), 12.
48 Senthorun Raj, 'Disturbing Disgust: Gesturing to the Abject in Queer Cases', in *Queering Criminology*, ed. Matthew Ball, Thomas Crofts and Angela Dwyer, (London: Palgrave, 2016), 83–101, doi.org/10.1057/9781137513342_5.
49 'To Beat the Bashers', *Gay Community News* 2, no. 1 (1980): 4.
50 'The Problem of Respectability', *Brother Sister*, 2 November 1995, 13.

This is not to say that earlier activists from Society Five ignored the beat—indeed, from the early 1970s Society Five offices included a map of 'known' Melbourne beats and engaged extensively with men who used them.[51] The Gay Counselling Service often revealed to activists the locations where police were focusing their efforts (it was precisely this dynamic that would reveal the prosecutions at Black Rock), and Society Five members would 'attend' the beats in busy periods to hand out small printed cards, reminding men of 'your rights' and advising any man who was arrested to not 'sign anything you until you have spoken to a lawyer'. As an early Society Five newsletter acknowledged:

> [S]hort of blowing up all the most wanted public toilets in town … there appears to be no way of dissuading certain of us from doing the beat … if we are to persist with this … we should arm ourselves with a working knowledge of our rights.[52]

Here, then, early activists deployed the language of citizenship to frame encounters between public homosex and the law. Activists attempted to explain the limits of 'Police Powers and Citizen's Rights' while encouraging men to be polite if they were questioned by police.[53] By 1974, however, the secretary of Society Five was acknowledging the difficult line the organisation was treading in relation to sex and beats, recounting how a 'policeman' responded to a question about the rights of a man at a beat with 'poofters have no rights'. The secretary was 'coming to the conclusion that it is time we stood up for our rights'. Let's 'refuse to co-operate. SAY NOTHING. DO NOTHING. SIGN NOTHING … WE DO HAVE RIGHTS, DON'T GIVE THEM AWAY'.[54]

Activists' responses to sex in public in the later 1970s ranged from shame to excitement to confusion. An editorial in the newsletter for *Acceptance*, a social group for gay Catholics to work towards 'accepting their sexuality', conflated beat use with being 'hung up' and 'not quite at ease' with homosexual desire. Telling the story of a man who spent a tough year breaking up his heterosexual marriage in order to live as a gay man with 'acceptance for who I am', the spectre of the beat functioned as the point of absolute despair in this pedagogic narrative. The protagonist

---

51 Graham Willett, Wayne Murdoch and Daniel Marshall, eds, *Secret Histories of Queer Melbourne* (Parkville, Vic.: Australian Lesbian and Gay Archives, 2011), 109.
52 Society Five Newsletter, December 1973, box 9, file 9, Records of Society Five, ALGA.
53 Police Powers and Citizen's Rights, box 12, file 12, Records of Society Five, ALGA.
54 Society Five Newsletter, July 1974, box 9, file 9, Records of Society Five, ALGA.

could be found, 'sitting drunk on a public (beat) toilet seat ... at midnight ... a person in a state of emotional turmoil, suffering'.[55] Reviewing a book about beat use in the United States, a member of Society Five framed his own use of beats as 'an addiction' of which he would 'shyly confess'.[56] Others more forcefully suggested that 'cruising the beats is a function of centuries of repression and furtiveness, of concealment, self-hatred and fear'.[57] For these thinkers, the beat was produced by social, cultural and legal prohibitions—a symptom of a culture in which homosexual desires were closeted from public life. Some pushed this analysis further to suggest deeper insecurities were at play. Men meeting each other for sex in public was a 'furtive and guilt ridden' practice, one activist suggested, and represented a 'sad humiliating expression of our insecurity'. Beats encouraged homosexual men to understand themselves as shameful and represented 'one of gay culture's more sordid characteristics'.[58]

Some activists sought, however, to dispel this shame. In 1977, Garry Jaynes, whose political subjectivity was shaped by the tenets of gay liberation, wrote a letter to Ken Sinclair in Sydney. Reporting on a recent meeting about law reform, he noted:

> [The] most contentious part was beats—how we should talk to the straight world, especially the press, about sex in public toilets. Should we assert our right to have sex anywhere; be evasive and talk about the straight equivalent of beats and why gays are 'driven to them;' or be apologetic and say 'not all gays, etc.' I oscillate between the first and second.[59]

Others were even optimistic about the beat as a site of erotic and political possibility. Some thought beat sex revealed the hypocrisy of a social order hopelessly complicit with square life, 'a quick suck off in a bog [was] preferable to the weird games we play that pass off as social interactions at bars, parties and the like'.[60] In this rendering of public sex, the anonymity and danger of beats encouraged men to remake their assumptions about romance and monogamy. In an account of 'screwing around', a gay

---

55 *Acceptance Melbourne Newsletter*, no. 8, March 1977, box 3, file 4, Records of Society Five, ALGA.
56 *Society Five Newsletter*, December 1973, box 9, file 9, Records of Society Five, ALGA.
57 Mark Rowan, 'Polemic', *Gay Community News* 3, no, 4 (1981): 29.
58 Ronald Evans, 'Overcoming Homosexuality', *Campaign* 60 (December 1980): 39.
59 Gary Jaynes to Ken Sinclair, 29 September 1977, box 2, file 2/8, Records of HLRC, ALGA.
60 Brian Day 'Values Support Politics and Even Death', in *Papers and Proceedings from the First National Homosexual Conference* (Melbourne: Homosexual Conference Collective, 1975), 50.

liberationist reflected on his encounters with other bodies in the 'beats and bogs'. There 'seems to be a feeling these topics should be ignored because, we say, they represent sexual objectification … this ignores the fact that they do exist and form an important part of many homosexuals' lives'. For this activist, beat sex represented a moment when 'defences and barriers come tumbling down'. Beats were nothing less than a site where danger and illicity in public space created the conditions whereby neat divisions would be shattered—divisions between the 'mind and the body', the 'public and the private' and 'the casual and the meaningful'.[61]

Conclusion

Perhaps, then, it was this liminal potency that made talk of sex in public such a volatile political project. As Lee Edelman argues, because beat sex occurs in places that are neither fully private nor fully public, it inaugurates a kind of counterpublic that challenges spatial dimensions of liberal democratic political culture.[62] Thinking about the beat as a liminal or counterpublic space offers some explanation for the political potency it obtained. This was not simply a case of activists grappling with the shame of sexual identities and practices once coded as disgusting (although that was certainly at play). Rather, it is helpful to remember that beat sex— like liberation politics itself—destabilised the division between public and private. As Derek Dalton argues, beat sex 'takes a supposedly private act and places it in the public domain yet does this in a way that is still partially privatised (behind doors, bushes etcetera) … [Beat sex] moves continually in and out of public and private zones, and this disrupts the dichotomy itself'.[63] Indeed, in a psychoanalytic sense, because beats are liminal spaces they necessarily contain what Phil Hubbard described as a 'distinctive current of psychic charge'.[64] Placing sex in public, then, was a politics textured by these currents and activists struggled to manage them.

The 'kiss-in', then, was both informed by liberation politics and an attempt to manage the unruly and destabilising politics of sex in public this protest implied. The Stokes and Turner case offered activists

---

61 *Melbourne Gay Liberation Newsletter*, April 1972, box 3, file 2, Records of HLRC, ALGA.
62 Lee Edelman, 'Tearooms and Sympathy, or, the Epistemology of the Water Closet', in *The Lesbian and Gay Studies Reader,* ed. Henry Abelove, Michele Aina Barale and David M. Halperin (New York: Routledge, 1993).
63 Dalton, 'Gay Male Resistance in "Beat" Spaces in Australia', 1106.
64 Phil Hubbard, *Cities and Sexualities* (New York: Routledge, 2012), 115.

a discursively and politically manageable spectacle through which to bring homosex into public life (which isn't to say that Stokes and Turner did not feel the full force of the state in the moments of their arrest and conviction). Underneath this moment of assertive pride, then, was an uncertain and unsteady politics of sex in public. The sexual politics of the beat both reverberated with the politics of liberation and also exceeded the capacity of activist vocabularies to manage it. In a political field framed by what Janet Halley and Wendy Brown call 'left legalism', it is perhaps unsurprising that activists turned away from the sexual politics of the beat.[65] This was a sexual culture that, through its refusal to stabilise a distinction between the public and the private, disrupted the norms of 'identity, intelligibility, publics, culture and sex' that Berlant and Warner argue make heterosexual culture seem somehow foundational.[66] At the same time, however, we do these activists a historical disservice if we dismiss their efforts as hopelessly attached to the liberal democratic order—or, not queer enough. We need to remember that the liberation politics of the 1970s could be tremendously demanding in both discursive and psychological terms. Shucking off histories of shame and disgust in the space of a decade demands much of historical subjects in a context where they were trying to put themselves (back) together in ways that made a homosexual life liveable.

---

65   Wendy Brown and Janet Halley, 'Introduction', in *Left Legalism/Left Critique*, ed. Wendy Brown and Janet Halley (Durham: Duke University Press, 2002): 1–34.
66   Berlant and Warner, 'Sex in Public', 548.

CHAPTER 11

Creative work: Feminist representations of gendered and domestic violence in 1970s Australia

Catherine Kevin

The banner 'Justice for Violet and Bruce Roberts' is a portrait of a mother and son who were brutally victimised by their husband and father and then jailed for his murder (see Figure 11.1). In the face of this history, they are depicted here as dignified, ordinary and humane. They appear comfortably side by side, their faces smiling warmly. The text and native flower adornment (perhaps a gift) indicate support for their release. Their faces and torsos are embodied representations of the issue of domestic violence and the mistreatment of its victims within the criminal justice system, but there is no depiction of bodily injury. Instead the prison bars signal the injury of the state, suggesting the systemic failure to recognise suffering in domestic violence cases. The concentration of meaning in this image makes it a powerful representation of feminist responses to domestic violence in the 1970s, culminating in the campaign for the release of Violet and Bruce Roberts in 1980.

Figure 11.1: 'Justice for Violet and Bruce Roberts', banner, 1980, Toni Robertson (now held in National Museum of Australia).
Source: Photograph reproduced with permission of Toni Robertson, © the artist.

The artist Toni Robertson, a member of feminist activist group Women Behind Bars, was the campaign's resident artist. In an oral history with Ann Genovese in 1995, Robertson spoke of the need for protest to entail 'both visual consumption and spectacle'.[1] This was a crucial component of the creative representations that sought to solicit awareness of, and engagement with, feminist critiques of gendered oppression through a range of media including visual art, creative writing and film. This banner is part of Robertson's series of images for the campaign and is an important artefact of the history of feminist responses to, and representations of, domestic violence in this period.

Susan Magarey's account of women's liberation in *Dangerous Ideas*[2] is a reminder that activism is a form of cultural as well as political expression and that subversive creativity and collaboration are central to exposing the impediments to women's freedom, devising forms of resistance and imagining alternative futures. The painful process of identifying, naming

---

1 Ann L. Genovese, 'The Battered Body, A Feminist Legal History' (PhD thesis, University of Technology Sydney, 1999), 208.
2 Susan Magarey, *Danger Ideas: Women's Liberation—Women's Studies—around the World* (Adelaide: University of Adelaide Press, 2014).

and responding to gendered and domestic violence as a feminist issue is examined here through the lens of cultural history. There is now a considerable literature on Australian feminism in the 1970s, some of which addresses in detail the history of feminist responses to gendered violence. There has also been scholarly interest in what Magarey calls the 'cultural renaissance' born of 1970s feminism. These histories provide crucial context for a close examination of creative representations of gendered and domestic violence that I undertake here. The purpose of such an approach is to enrich existing historical analysis of the emerging feminist discourse of domestic violence by incorporating close readings of explicitly feminist cultural artefacts with an eye to traditions of visual signification and literary techniques while placing them in their immediate and broader historical context. I do this not so much to reveal the conditions of their production, which have been documented elsewhere, but to examine what it was their creators sought to communicate and the strategies of representation they deployed. By offering this account, I aim to increase the range of voices and the modes of expression that provide insight into feminism's documentation, analysis and response to gendered and domestic violence in this period. The phenomena that these artefacts addressed were confronting, for some they were threatening, and the nature of the creative representations was—in turns—immediate, graphic, challenging, subtle and sensitive. Here I showcase a sample of creative representations from four genres—still images, poetry, fiction and film—to demonstrate the rich range of registers and media through which feminists came to an understanding of, and responded to, the distinct issue of domestic violence.

In a 2013 article describing their project 'Cultures of Australian Feminist Activism 1970–1990', Alison Bartlett and Margaret Henderson note that histories of the Australian women's movement tended to be marked by (among other things) 'the neglect of cultural activism; an understatement of the "direct action" ethos of the movement; and an understatement of the role of humor, imagination and creativity in the movement's activism'.[3] While their project, and others begun since,[4] address this neglect by

---

3   A. Bartlett and M. Henderson, 'The Australian Women's Movement Goes to the Museum: The "Cultures of Australian Feminist Activism, 1970–1990" Project', *Women's Studies International Forum*, no. 37 (2013): 87, doi.org/10.1016/j.wsif.2012.10.013.
4   For example, Petra Mosmann, 'Encountering Feminist Things: Generations, Interpretations and Encountering Adelaide's "Scrap Heap"', *Journal of Australian Studies* 40, no. 2 (2016): 172–89, doi.org/10.1080/14443058.2016.1157700.

providing biographies of material objects originally held privately by participants in the movement, this chapter draws on creative artefacts that are available through public archives, libraries and art museums. My purpose is to contribute to a growing scholarship that reads a history of feminist activism through these vital forms of representation, in the hope of enriching existing histories of creative activism and the intersecting histories of feminism and domestic violence in this period.

While feminist analysis of gendered violence has consistently sought to locate domestic violence within larger social phenomena, during the 1970s a recognition and articulation of the urgency of the issue required a specific language to emerge that isolated this form of violence from other aspects of gendered oppression. Creative representations contributed to this process of identifying and describing domestic violence as a primary concern of feminists. In some cases, these representations foreshadowed more explicit prose discussion of domestic violence. The term itself would not become embedded in the feminist or wider lexicon until the late 1970s; when it did, it signalled the crystallisation of domestic violence as a policy issue and the impact of feminist work on wider discourses of gender, violence and family.

Women's liberation, women's refuges and domestic violence

In the development of an agenda for social revolution, women's liberation sought to fully understand, in order to expose and critique, the structures and effects of gendered oppression. The elimination of domestic violence must be understood as part of the wider revolution to which the movement aspired. At the same time, domestic violence—particularly its prevalence and severity—took some feminists by surprise. In Marilyn Lake's history of Australian feminism, she describes the commitment to a social revolution that was the defining feature of the women's liberation movement.[5] This meant calling for the overthrow of conventional roles within marriage, the family and the work force. It meant reimagining political aims outside of parliament and beyond equal citizenship status. Lake notes that from the early 1970s women set up informal temporary accommodation,

---

5   Marilyn Lake, *Getting Equal: The History of Australian Feminism* (St Leonards, NSW: Allen & Unwin, 1999), 231–52.

sometimes opening up their own houses to other women. Community action of this kind figured as a key strategy in this revolutionary politics, providing a first port of call for women abandoning marriages in pursuit of an alternative life.[6] Jacqueline Theobald's account of the Victorian women's refuge movement emphasises the critique of marriage at its heart, noting that women's changing attitudes to sexuality and their new-found access to work and decent wages were central to this. More than ever before, women could aspire to translate this into expectations of living free from the confines of marriage in financially autonomous households.[7] Rather than envisioning the provision of accommodation as having the single aim of an escape route from violence, women's liberationists sought to make available an alternative to the range of constraints in the marital home, not least unpaid labour and economic dependence, and to the increasingly recognised problem of women's homelessness.

The history of women's refuges, as historians of this period now understand it, began by a whisker in Sydney. The two Women's Commissions, held in March of 1973 and 1974 in that city, frame Janet Ramsay's story of the key turning points in a trajectory towards Elsie, Australia's first women's refuge, which was set up by squatter occupation on 16 March 1974, in Glebe.[8] The agenda of the 1973 Commission prioritised important themes such as 'women as workers' and 'women as mothers'. The issue of rape was raised as part of the theme of 'women as sex objects', but discussion of other aspects of gendered violence was not canvassed.[9] However, a year later, the 1974 Commission became a forum for concentrating on the violence suffered by women in their homes. Ramsay explains this in part by feminists' increasing focus on rape—inside and outside the domestic space—in the intervening year, noting the content of the *Sydney Women's Liberation Newsletter*. At the same time, the first 'public clues' about domestic violence began to appear, notably in the May 1973 issue of the newsletter, which published the correspondence between a woman who had fled a violent marriage and the Minister for Social Security, Bill Hayden. This correspondence explained the woman's circumstances and the terms of the new supporting mother's benefit, which was about

---

6   Ibid., 229.
7   Jacqueline Lee Theobald, 'A History of the Victorian Women's Domestic Violence Services Movement', (PhD thesis, RMIT University, 2011), 55.
8   Janet Ramsay, 'Policy Activism on a "Wicked Issue": The Building of Australian Feminist Policy on Domestic Violence in the 1970s', *Australian Feminist Studies* 22, no. 53 (2007): 247–48, doi.org/10.1080/08164640701364661.
9   Ibid., 247.

to be introduced.[10] By October that year both the *Women's Liberation* and *Sydney WEL* newsletters advertised a November meeting to discuss a women's night shelter. While the core issue this advertisement identified was homelessness, it also recognised that women were fleeing 'difficult domestic situations (like, their husband is beating them)'.[11] At the second commission in March 1974, woman after woman rose to speak of their suffering at the hands of the violent men they lived with. At one point, Anne Summers, one of the organisers of the November meeting, 'seized the microphone and invited the listening women to turn their shock into action the following weekend'.[12] This invitation was taken up and Elsie became the first of 12 women's refuges established across the country within a year.[13]

The fundamental role refuges played in responding to domestic violence became increasingly clear as more and more women's stories of enduring violence filled the discursive spaces that feminist activists created. Activists without direct experience of domestic violence came to their earliest understandings of the severity of this phenomenon through consciousness-raising forums such as the Women's Commissions and through their work supporting women who came to refuges in need of safety from harm. In the 1977 account of their work in the period 1974–76, the Melbourne-based Women's Liberation Halfway House Collective wrote that they had:

> uncovered, in the few months that [the Halfway House] has been operating, an <u>enormous</u> social problem that has always been there. Social workers have known it to be there because they have been dealing with these desperate women for years. The government departments have known about it. Every week they try to send dozens of women to us. Yet they never bothered to set up emergency accommodation for women. It took women, feminist women, to do that, and now that a Halfway House exists the enormity and the horror of it all is being revealed.[14]

---

10 *Sydney Women's Liberation Newsletter*, May 1973, cited in Ramsay, 'Policy Activism on a "Wicked Issue"', 248.
11 *Sydney WEL Newsletter*, 10 November 1973, cited in Ramsay, 'Policy Activism on a "Wicked Issue"', 248.
12 Ramsay, 'Policy Activism on a "Wicked Issue"', 248.
13 Suellen Murray, 'The Origins and Development of the Australian Women's Refuge Movement', *Parity* 19, no. 10 (2006): 11.
14 The Women's Liberation Halfway House Collection, *1974–76 Herstory of the Halfway House— Women's Liberation Halfway House Collective* (Melbourne: Women's Liberation Halfway House Collective, 1977).

Despite emerging work towards legal reforms seeking to criminalise violence within the home, the failure of government agencies to measure and expose the problem or make provisions for women persisted. While women's liberationists sought to respond to the immediate needs of victims and politicise the issue, the women who came to them for assistance provided the information that enabled them to better comprehend the problem, develop their vision for change and, in the longer term, secure government funding to support their work. The role of listening to victims in this process cannot be overestimated. Women's liberation refuges thus played a central role in gathering and publicising evidence of domestic violence in the process of responding directly to women's needs.

Unfortunately this was all too late and too far away for Violet Roberts and her son Bruce, who were charged with the murder of their sadistically violent husband and father in the New South Wales town of Pacific Palms in December 1975. Genovese's analysis of this case traces the production of the 'battered body' in law, thus offering another point of access to the history of the emerging discourse of domestic violence in this period.[15] Genovese illustrates that in the four years between the Roberts's imprisonment in 1976 and the successful culmination of the Women Behind Bars–led campaign for their release in 1980, public understandings and articulations of domestic violence became such that the campaign could garner considerable support in the media and the general public.

While Genovese's account is primarily focused on the legal category of the 'battered body' of a domestic violence victim such as Violet Roberts, a survey of the frequency of the term 'domestic violence' in the *Canberra Times* indicates that its use was on the increase during the late 1970s, but only really took hold in the 1980s.[16] The release of Violet Roberts and the established use of the term domestic violence both signalled the impact women's liberation had made on wider discourses of this form of gendered violence, including the creative renderings of artists such as Toni Robertson.

---

15   Anne Genovese, 'The Battered Body', *Australian Feminist Studies* 12, no. 25 (1997): 91–103, doi.org/10.1080/08164649.1997.9994843.
16   This is based on a word search survey of the digital *Canberra Times* archive undertaken in 2016.

Feminist creative representations of domestic violence

Interest in the feminist art movements of the 1970s has been illustrated by more than three decades of scholarship including Sandy Kirby and Louise Mayhew's work on feminist art collectives,[17] the collection of essays about women's film-making edited by Annette Blonski et al. and Mary Tomsic's historical work on this topic,[18] and Anne Vickery's and Zora Simic's histories of women's creative writing and publishing.[19] These accounts have focused on the innovations in approaches to production, ideas about authorship and ownership and narratives of women emerging from male-dominated creative practices into inclusive and politicised environments that facilitated the production and dissemination of their work. It provides important context for reading the artefacts I have chosen. These histories reflect the discussion of women's art that was occurring in the 1970s and generating the ideas that produced the innovative and radical work that is the legacy of this period.

More ephemeral, less recognised visual representations than those created by members of the feminist art and film movements include the illustrations contained in feminist periodicals. As well as publishing and thereby facilitating the new field of feminist inquiry, the many journals and newsletters of this period provided the opportunity for visual, poetic and fictional representations of feminist concerns. The varying life spans and preoccupations of these periodicals tell the story of feminist experimentation, diversity and debate in this period. They are also a rich vein of material for historicising the movement's agenda for change. Within their pages, illustrators and photographers, and poets and fiction writers, contributed to developing and debating this agenda.

---

17 Sandy Kirby, *Sight Lines: Women's Art and Feminist Perspectives in Australia* (Roseville, NSW: Craftsman House, 1992), 22; Louise Mayhew, *Girls at the Tin Sheds* (Sydney: Art Gallery of New South Wales, 2015).
18 Annette Blonski, Barbara Creed and Freda Freiberg, eds, *Don't Shoot Darling! Women's Independent Filmmaking in Australia* (Richmond: Greenhouse Publications, 1987); Mary Tomsic, 'We Will Invent Ourselves. The Age of the New Image is at Hand', *Australian Feminist Studies* 22, no. 53 (2007): 287–306, doi.org/10.1080/08164640701364679.
19 Ann Vickery, 'The Rise of "Women's Poetry" in the 1970s', *Australian Feminist Studies* 22, no. 53 (2007): 265–85, doi.org/10.1080/08164640701378596; Zora Simic, '"Women's Writing" and "Feminism": A History of Intimacy and Estrangement', *Outskirts* 28 (2013), www.outskirts.arts.uwa.edu.au/volumes/volume-28/zora-simic.

Illustrations from women's liberation movement periodicals

In this section, I examine three images from feminist periodicals that depict women in relation to violence. They reflect the generalised discourse of the enduring threat women face in a patriarchal society, one that restricts and demeans them with the spectre of violation and harm. The image 'Refractory Girl' was published on the second page of the first issue of *Refractory Girl*, the 1972/73 edition. It accompanied a poem of the same title about the women and girls imprisoned at the Parramatta Factory between 1821 and 1848. This poem located the origins of the journal's rebellious spirit in the convict women of the New South Wales penal colony, celebrating their deviance, defiance and survival. And yet the accompanying image spoke of something else. While a more recent reader with knowledge of the feminist historiography of the penal colony is unlikely to struggle to link the image to the subject of the poem, the poem itself made no explicit reference to convict women's subjection or physical injury. Indeed, it sought to emphasise the strength in their refusal to comply with expectations of feminine behaviour and their record of inflicting violence on others: 'The Assault-and-batter/ Parramatta/ Refractory/ FACTORY GIRLS!'. The addition of the drawing complicates the description of the Parramatta Factory inmates in the poem by indicating the physical harm and threat of violence that could also characterise the lives of the impoverished female criminal class that made up the majority of the earliest British migrant women in Australia. The woman at the centre of the image has a bandaged arm in a sling. Her posture, on her knees and attempting to defend herself with a raised arm against an assailant, signals a recent history of violence that continues. The threat to her safety is out of sight yet made present and, by the angle of her body, appears to come from her right. This approaching threat is the only counter to her isolation, and its invisibility suggests its source could be one man or every man. Her lack of class power, which compounds her vulnerability, is legible both in the accompanying poem and the rolled-up sleeve and apron she wears. The prominence of this poem and visual image in the first edition of *Refractory Girl* indicate that a distinctly Australian feminist historiography, sensitive to class and questions of agency, was central to the political project of the journal. As Mary Spongberg has noted: 'The early issues were largely concerned with generating a new Australian

Figure 11.2: 'Refractory Girl', *Refractory Girl*, no. 1, 1972/73, p. 2.
Source: Reproduced courtesy of Ann Curthoys on behalf of the *Refractory Girl* collective, © the artist.

history and an Australian identity that women could embrace'.[20] There is a suggestion of continuity, which is reasserted by the journal's analyses of the ongoing political implications of excluding accounts of women's experiences from Australian historiography.

The image in Figure 11.3 was published a couple of years after 'Refractory Girl' with a large, bold title: 'Avoid Rape: Dress Sensibly'. It takes up more than half a page of the first issue of the socialist feminist newspaper *Mabel*, published in December 1975. *Mabel* was based in Sydney and ran for just under two years.[21] This first issue contained four written references to what would now be described as domestic violence. For example, a testimonial from a resident of Elsie and a long announcement in full-capitals that an International Tribunal aimed at exposing crimes against women was to be held in Brussels. The announcement described a range of types of gendered violence including 'wife beating, rape and molestation of female children', and called on women to make submissions to their local women's liberation group. These items highlighted the issue, albeit without using the term domestic violence. The title of the image is a specific reference to sexual violence, a preoccupation that pre-dated but also assisted in generating a feminist focus on domestic violence. The photograph makes fun of the victim-blaming that characterised legal and public discourses around rape by juxtaposing the idea of safe dressing with an image of a woman on a bicycle whose extremely modest dress puts her in danger of accident and injury. There is an ironic tension in the image between the mobility of the bicycle, a century-old symbol of women's free movement in public space in Australia, and the garment covering all but her face that threatens to catch in the pedal or wheel and mocks the descriptor 'sensibly'. This makes the larger point that women's freedom of movement is compromised by the imperative that they take responsibility for their own safety in the face of an unpredictable threat.

---

20 Mary Spongberg, 'Australian Women's History in Australian Feminist Periodicals 1971–1988', *History Australia* 5, no. 3 (2008): 73.4.
21 Spongberg, 'Australian Women's History in Australian Feminist Periodicals', 73.3.

Figure 11.3: 'Avoid Rape Dress Sensibly', *Mabel*, no. 1, December 1975, p. 20.
Source: © the artist.

Figure 11.4: 'I Like to Put My Woman on a Pedestal', Barbara O'Brien, *Refractory Girl*, Winter 1975, p. 29.
Source: Reproduced with permission of Sally O'Brien, © Sally O'Brien.

In the same year, 'Woman on a Pedestal' was published in *Refractory Girl* (see Figure 11.4). The drawing accompanied a review by Mary MacLeod of Lee Comer's *Wedlocked Women* (1974). Already known for her feminist critique of Bowlby's maternal deprivation theory,[22] here Comer analysed the subjection of women in their roles as wives and mothers, crediting women's liberationists as her collaborators in the development of the ideas she presented. MacLeod makes no explicit reference to violence within marriages in her review, but here the metaphor of women's oppression in these roles is an enactment of violence. This confronting image of the trap

---

22 Lee Comer, 'The Motherhood Myth', *Refractory Girl*, no. 15/16 (1971).

of idealised femininity emphasises the woman's vulnerable sexualisation. Her naked body is tied with rope that prevents her physical resistance. She suffers the painful and frightening violation of having nails hammered through her feet into the pedestal she is standing on as her attacker speaks or thinks the words 'I like to put my woman on a pedestal'. The image powerfully conveys exposure, humiliation and entrapment. The words and the pedestal itself speak to a visual tradition of conveying raised status. This also invokes the metaphor placing women on a pedestal, which signals the inflation of women's virtue, narrowly defined. The precariousness of such an inflated position is worsened in this case because she is violently imprisoned on the pedestal by rope and nails. The image thus offers a feminist critique of the convention of courtly love as Kate Millett did in 1970 with explicit reference to elevating the love object to the level of a pedestal.[23] The entrapped woman's husband is not obviously clothed or nude. His sexless body dominates as he nails her to the paradoxical pedestal that robs her of all power and bodily integrity even as it raises her body above his.

It is difficult to identify the individual creators of these images. Indeed, where they have signed the work, artists have used only a first name. This practice suggests the feminist ethic of refusing individual ownership of creative work, thereby contesting the notion of 'the artist' and emphasising the collective nature of feminist journal production. These images are from the first half of the 1970s, when domestic violence had yet to be named as such, though gendered violence was clearly emerging as a key concern of the women's movement, both as lived experience and as emblematic of the female condition. Indeed, women's liberation journal collectives were closely linked with the work taking place in the women's refuges. By 1975 there were 12 women's refuges operating, and a growing awareness of the extent of brutality within marriages was evident in feminist periodicals in a number of ways.[24] These visual representations reinforced prose writing where it addressed gendered violence directly, but they also signalled to readers that lurking in the larger accounts prose writers offered of institutional marriage and women's history were untold intimate and domestic stories of violence.

---

23 Kate Millett, *Sexual Politics* (London: Abacus, 1970), 37.
24 For example, in July 1975, *Scarlet Woman* published a three-page analysis of the benefits and disadvantages for the Women's Liberation Halfway House Collective of seeking government funding, just one example of the ways in which the journals documented women's liberationists developing knowledge of and response to the issue of domestic violence. *Scarlet Woman*, no. 2 (1975): 12–15.

11. CREATIVE WORK

Posters from the Tin Sheds collective

The Sydney University Fine Art Workshop, better known as the Tin Sheds, became a community hub for students and artists from the late 1960s. It was a model of arts access and, while more clearly located within an artistic community than the illustrators working for the journals, also challenged the notion of 'the artist'.[25] Sandy Kirby explains that in 1976 Joan Grounds became the director, an appointment that 'confirmed the radical orientation of the Tin Sheds and growing impact of feminism there'.[26] Toni Robertson was a founding member of the Earthworks Poster Collective,[27] which was based at the Tin Sheds from 1972. She was also a core member of the Sydney Women's Art Movement, which began in 1974 and—among other activities—supported and promoted the work of women artists through the Women's Art Register. Robertson was a screen printer who applied her skills to poster- and banner-making, media that were ideal for political work. The relatively easy reproduction of posters in particular, and their cost-effectiveness, meant they could be widely distributed to disseminate political messages and information.

In 1977 Robertson made 'Walls Sometimes Speak', the title poster for an exhibition of posters that was the brainchild of Robertson and Chips Mackinolty (Figure 11.5). They invited other poster makers including feminist artists Jude Munro and Ann Newmarch and exhibited in Sydney, Melbourne and Adelaide. While, in literal terms, the title of Robertson's poster refers to the work of all artists who seek to communicate messages by plastering their posters on walls, this poster also evokes feminist representations. The two women, dressed in boiler suits and carrying the tools for their task, are framed at least twice within the poster. They are depicted representing themselves *in situ* and the words 'Walls Sometimes Speak' on a neglected public wall. The image and its text highlight interventions in public space as a feminist activist practice. The double meaning of the text signifies both the speaking walls on which posters, and possibly graffiti, appear and feminist work to expose what was once considered private and personal—located within four walls or 'behind closed doors'—as a political strategy towards describing and naming the oppressive nature of the patriarchal home, including the risk of gendered

---

25 Kirby, *Sight Lines*, 22.
26 Ibid., 22.
27 While this collective had a fluctuating membership, *Lip* published the following list of members in its 1978/79 edition: Jan Mackay Marie McMahon, Pam Ledden, Di Holdway, Loretta Vieceli, Toni Robertson, p. 66.

violence it posed. The visual echo in the image, which repeats itself in ever-diminishing size, poses a threat to those who would silence women who seek to expose abuses that have occurred in private.

Figure 11.5: '*Walls sometimes speak: An exhibition of political posters*, Toni Robertson and Chips Mackinolty', 1977, screenprint.
Source: Flinders University Art Museum Collection. Reproduced with permission of Robertson and Mackinolty, © the artists.

Women's poetry

In 1969, Australian poet John Tranter organised a poetry reading where—and I quote him—'a beautiful naked woman was featured as a "living poem"'.[28] Ann Vickery has used this anecdote to underline the struggle women poets faced to carve out a space for their work in the Australian poetry scene. It was the emergence of women's liberation newspapers and periodicals in the early 1970s that expanded the print-space for, and conceptual possibilities of, women's poetry. And then, in 1975, the recently established Outback Press published Kate Jennings's anthology *Mother I'm Rooted*. Of its 12 publications that year, this was the 'runaway success' for Outback.[29] It sold over 10,000 copies, attracting readers who would not usually buy poetry—a degree of success that rankled male poets at the time.[30]

Jennings's anthology was a collection by writers both known and unknown. She advertised for contributions in newspapers and drew over 500 responses. Ultimately the anthology included the work of 150 poets. Jennings wrote in the introduction that the anthology 'slowly metamorphosed into … a collective statement about the position of women in Australia' and described its central themes as 'childbirth, babies, menstruation, housework, female conditioning and feminine perceptions'.[31] Yet it also contains numerous evocations of male violence—in many cases suggested, in others explicitly described. For example, Judy Gemmel's 'Into the Sun' is a poem printed over four pages that describes a woman coming to the decision to leave her relationship. The poem deploys metaphors of light and dark, nightmares and dreams throughout, describing a feminist awakening that enables her to accept that she has suffered a life of gendered oppression. The male partner she addresses attempts to block the light offered by her 'sisters' with his imposing frame, but the poem is a refusal of his efforts. The final stanza reads:

---

28 John Tranter, 'Four Notes on the Practice of Revolution', *Australian Literary Studies* 8, no. 2 (1977): 127–35, quoted in Vickery, 'The Rise of "Women's Poetry" in the 1970s', 268.
29 Ann Vickery, 'The Rise of "Women's Poetry"', 273.
30 Ibid., 279.
31 Kate Jennings, 'Introduction', in *Mother I'm Rooted, An Anthology of Australian Women Poets*, ed. Kate Jennings (Fitzroy: Outbreak Press, 1975).

> For I am going anyway,
> Whatever you say or do—
> Although you try, so hard, to bind me
> With tears, fists, works, guilts
> And my still existing love for you –
> I am going anyway,
> Out of nightmares
> Into the sun.[32]

The stinging critique of the heterosexual relationship at the centre of 'Into the Sun' hints at violence without centralising it, reflecting the broader feminist activist framework within which domestic violence became increasingly apparent from 1974. Chris Sitka's 'Witch Poem' describes a woman's life as a mix of drudgery, boredom and violence. Here it is the endless work that is emphasised through repetition, but violence is clearly part of the picture of this woman's life:

> Day after day she returns to that machine
> and the murderous boredom of her job
> bearing the bruises of her husband's beatings.
> Night after night returns home to screaming children
> And yet more, and more, work.[33]

'Witch Poem' is a call to respond with outraged action to the relentlessness and ubiquity of women's oppression, which comes in many intertwined forms. Sitka describes the temptation to be paralysed by the enormity of the task, but the final stanza urges her reader to act purposefully to bring women's suffering to an end. Ann Newmarch's cover for the anthology, a photographic work entitled 'Queen of the Home', depicts the wall of a house with a picket fence and suggests violence to the woman's body in a number of ways (Figure 11.6). Confined between window frames, the crossbars not only evoke the woman's entrapment but also her exile from the interior. The barbed wire threatens any attempt to traverse the picket fence. The woman bends over, her hands protectively grasping the back of her own head, her nakedness an indication of exposure and vulnerability. So while the term domestic violence doesn't appear in the poetry or in Jennings's introduction, it is nevertheless a feature of the images of suffering that the anthology produces.

---

32 Judy Gemmel, 'Into the Sun', in Jennings, *Mother I'm Rooted*, 186.
33 Chris Sitka, 'Witch Poem', in Jennings, *Mother I'm Rooted*, 487.

11. CREATIVE WORK

Figure 11.6: 'Queen of the Home', Ann Newmarch. Cover art for Kate Jennings, ed., *Mother I'm Rooted, An Anthology of Australian Women Poets*, 1975.

Source: Reproduced with permission of Ann Newmarch, © the artist.

While *Mother I'm Rooted* reached a wide audience and became something of a classic, feminist periodicals also published poetry that evoked heart-rending scenes of violence in intimate relationships. A striking example by Kate Llewllyn called 'FINISHED' was published in *Refractory Girl* in September 1977. Each stanza begins 'there'll be no more', regularising the rhythm of the words, but the poem is divided in two. The first three stanzas describe scenes of domestic pleasure, both companionate and sexual. These descend in the second half of the poem to scenes of anger and violence; the deterioration of the relationship until love is extinguished.

> there'll be no more
> hits across my mouth love
> and crawling on the floor
>
> there'll be no more chainsmoking listening to you curse love
> or smiling drinking more
>
> there'll be no more crying because you rage love
> or dancing up your drive
>
> there's no more
> love love.[34]

The context throughout is the home: the verandah, the floor, the drive. While the man the poem addresses leaves and returns each day, the protagonist remains anticipating and then dreading his arrival. Domestic peace and pleasure are expunged by violence and pain.

The following year in *Vashti's Voice*, 'Where Have I Gone Wrong?' appeared. This was billed as 'a short story by Rose'. As well as describing a woman's husband arriving home late and drunk and his ensuing violence, the piece contains passages of inner dialogue in which victim/protagonist worries about the children, considers suicide and weighs up her options for escape. Finally it comes to this:

> To her surprise she stopped crying. *She is a bashed wife. She had to admit it to herself and she knew that she was not the only one.*
>
> There had been lots of talks on the radio about how women were leaving their husbands, and that there have been some houses established to accommodate women and children. *There seemed to be a new strength in her.*

---

34   Kate Llewellyn, 'FINISHED', *Refractory Girl*, no. 15 (1977): 45.

Without wasting any time she picked up the telephone book.
Maybe they could accommodate her?
That is what she needs.
Just for a short time.[35]

By the time this short story was published in 1978, there were women's refuges across the country for which government funding had become more or less assured and stable.[36] Reference to 'talks on the radio' suggests a broader conversation was taking place about domestic violence. Indeed, Australian feminists began penetrating the mass media from the mid-1970s. The Australian Women's Broadcasting Cooperative was established within the national broadcaster in 1975, the same year 'The Coming Out Show' began. This radio program, made by women and for women, brought feminist issues, including gendered violence, to a national audience.[37] 'Where Have I Gone Wrong?', a creative representation of consciousness-raising that made clear to readers of *Vashti's Voice* that help was available, served as a kind of community service notice, an encouragement to women to identify their situation knowing that there was somewhere they could flee to. Here women's liberation explicitly facilitated women's road to safety, responding to an increasingly recognised need in the community. This example, of course, is barely the tip of the iceberg of women's creative fiction and nonfiction writing in the 1970s. There is a wealth of women's liberation publications, including novels and anthologies of short stories and other work published and extracted in periodicals that were countercultural and experimental in their strategies for challenging representations of women and femininity and conveying experiences of domestic violence.

Two women's liberation movement films

The 1970s was a time of optimism among Australian film-makers generally. While growth in this industry and some government support increased the possibility of feminist film-makers finding a place within it, Mary Tomsic explains that women were critical of practices within this expanding industry and of some of the films that proved the most

---

35 'Where Have I Gone Wrong?', *Vashti's Voice* 22 (1978): 18.
36 See Eva Cox, 'Social Policy', in *Oxford Companion to Australian Feminism*, ed. Barbara Caine, Moira Gatens, Emma Grahame, Jan Larbalestier, Sophie Watson and Elizabeth Webby (Melbourne: Oxford University Press, 1998), 307–8; and Murray, 'The Origins and Development of the Australian Women's Refuge Movement'.
37 Katharine Lumby, 'Media', in Caine et al., *Oxford Companion to Australian Feminism*, 217.

commercially successful, such as the *Adventures of Barry McKenzie* (1972) and *Alvin Purple* (1973).[38] A number of women's and feminist film collectives emerged from 1971 promoting women's place in film-making and women's subject matter in films. Tomsic has documented their histories, exploring the distinctive aims of feminist film-makers and the ways in which they defined their success.[39] Debate about what constituted feminist techniques in film-making was part and parcel of involvement in the feminist film-making community and there was plenty of work to discuss.

Tomsic's analysis of Margot Nash and Robin Laurie's 1976 film *We Aim to Please* describes its exemplary feminist techniques and content.[40] I have included the film in my selection here for its depiction of gendered violence, but its representational strategies are pertinent. The film is neither narrative nor documentary but rather a pastiche of fragmented conversations, powerful images and improvised performances by Nash and Laurie. It contains in-jokes intended to make women laugh and to confront male viewers. In one scene, the two women write in lipstick on each other's bodies, an example of the film-makers taking control of the representations of their bodies and appropriating the tools of feminine adornment to political effect. Sounds and images evoke physical and sexual violence against women, standing in for the visual portrayal of the victim. Its mood shifts between humour and violence. At one point, a glass bottle is thrown and smashes against a cut watermelon lying in the bushes, a chilling soundscape eliminates any doubt that this moment is intended to evoke a violent, probably sexual, attack. This film both explores and challenges women's subjection and violation in a number of ways, suggesting violence that could be located both within and beyond intimacy and domesticity.

In 1980—the year of the Violet Roberts release campaign—Sarah Gibson, Susan Lambert, Martha Ansara and Pat Fiske made a film that directly addressed domestic violence. After years of experimentation with the form, this was widely regarded as having successfully conveyed the issue using techniques of representation that kept it firmly within a feminist frame. Using just one set, a fashionable and comfortable bedroom, the film privileges sound over image. In her analysis of this relationship, Jane Madsen

---

38 Tomsic, 'We Will Invent Ourselves', 289–90.
39 Ibid., 290.
40 Ibid., 292.

has identified five categories of sound: 'song, music, voice, sound effects and atmospheric sound'.[41] The main action is in the sound-collage including snippets of interviews with women staying in Sydney women's refuges. Songs are carefully selected to critique popular notions of romantic love, and the smashing of crockery signifies violent episodes. The audience hears the anonymous, invisible voices of these women. There is no voice-over, and no individual story is presented as coherent and complete, or as more or less important than the others. The film's single set reminds the viewer of the intimacy that at some point characterised the relationships that enter the film in spoken snapshots. While commentary has focused on sound, the set of white wicker furniture and colourful, floral bedding, cushions and carpet contributes to the shifting mood of the piece. To begin with, all is intact. The bed is made, cushions artfully arranged and magazines neatly stacked. The women's voices describe early expectations of their intimate relationships and the beginning of relationship breakdown. As the horror of the descriptions of violence intensifies, the camera moves more rapidly and the full colour spectrum is replaced with a blue and then a red filter. The red hues coincide with women speaking of weapons and injuries: an attempted stabbing, burning with cigarettes and boiling water, and internal injuries. The blue tones return for a discussion of sexual violence and the status of rape in relationships. Finally, as women describe their decisions to leave and life after the relationship, order is restored in the bedroom. The bed is now made again and a sense of visual calm is restored. *Behind Closed Doors* offers an explicit representation of domestic violence that is primarily aural but uses a domestic space that is empty of people to assist in conveying the meaning of the words and sounds heard.

The important place of this film in the history of domestic violence is explained in the story of its making and its use. At the 2017 Sydney Film Festival there was a screening and discussion of the film. Megan Nash interviewed the feminism and film section curator, Susan Charlton, who described the important connection between the film-makers and their audience, a connection that was established before the film was complete:

> Like Susan Lambert said … it was like an early form of crowdfunding. She and Sarah Gibson did a rough cut of *Behind Closed Doors* and screened it at women's centres and places like that, and people threw money in for it to be finished. So the films came out of this

---

41 Jane Madsen, 'Listening at Closed Doors: A consideration of the Use of Sound in *Behind Closed Doors*', in Blonski, Creed and Freiberg, *Don't Shoot Darling!*

community and they were for this community, and people used to hire them or buy them—schools, universities, health centres, women's refuges, hospitals. It was quite a successful business.[42]

Susan Sheridan has further attested to the political utility and effect of the film. She remembers how useful it was for teaching women's studies classes on the issue of gendered violence. It was the very absence of explicit imagery that rendered it a feminist representation that she could share with her students without risking a voyeuristic viewing of women's suffering.[43]

Conclusion

Creative representations including still and moving images and creative writing contributed to the process of identifying domestic violence as a specific aspect of gendered violence that should command the attention of the women's movement. The challenge of exposing, naming and analysing this issue was met in a range of media and registers that reflected the complexity of the task and the breadth of intellectual and creative talent that the movement boasted. The examples explored in this chapter assist in charting the increasing awareness of gendered and domestic violence within the women's movement itself, which, in turn, informed a larger public conversation that identified domestic violence as a public policy issue. They also provide clear evidence of the cultural renaissance that played a central role in 1970s feminist activism, the achievements of which cannot be disentangled from the intellectual developments that shifted ways of thinking about gender and power in this period. While I have sought to identify the role of creative activism in this particular history of 1970s feminism, there remains an opportunity to canvass a much larger sample of creative works, particularly writing, and to chart in more detail the emergence of particular representational strategies that spoke to the complexities of the experiences of domestic violence and the sophisticated feminist discussions about how these were best conveyed.

---

42   Susan Charlton (in conversation with Megan Nash), 'Feminism and Film—A Roundtable Discussion with Curator Susan Charlton', 1 July 2017, accessed 28 October 2017, fourthreefilm.com/2017/07/feminism-film-a-roundtable-discussion-with-curator-susan-charlton/.
43   Private correspondence with the author.

CHAPTER 12

'Put on dark glasses and a blind man's head': Poetic defamation and the question of feminist privacy in 1970s Australia

Nicole Moore

The only successful defamation case ever run against poetry in Australia has at its centre a contest more precisely about changing definitions of privacy than of public reputation. Launched against Australian writer Dorothy Hewett by her former husband Lloyd Davies, the charge was not restricted to a single poem or piece of writing, nor to a single Australian jurisdiction, and in the first instance was scheduled to be heard by the High Court before being settled on legal advice. The multiplying offences and charges are best outlined in a narrative, clarifying the detailed roles of the various agents and actors in what became a high-profile cause célèbre in the late 1970s that ramified across Australia's expanding culture industry. At stake was a highly gendered question about art's access to the private sphere—its ability to represent intimate life acutely, even savagely—and then, more than this, about poetry's ability to challenge legal measures of public truth. Stretching from 1969 into the early 1980s, notable dimensions of the case make it both exceptional and representative—a synecdoche for its times, in its conflicts and ambiguities, as well as a point of departure, in legal terms and in literary terms—in ways that illuminate transformative political and social change across the decade.

Second-wave feminist critiques of the legal concept of privacy can be seen to have arisen as part of attempts to break down gendered boundaries between the public and private spheres, which, in the long wake of first-wave feminism, targeted historical legal formations that subsumed women and children to a male political subject. Feminist efforts to make the personal political were directed against privacy's established social function to hide, shame and stigmatise intimacy, and to hold women, domesticity, family life and sexuality outside public life. Importantly, these efforts in many ways were shaped and informed by the kinds of cultural expression Hewett's poetry represented, as a new speaking out, a laying bare of intimate life. By the 1970s, this represented a dramatic shift from the mid-century Western liberal models of rights and freedoms that had informed the UK Wolfenden Report of 1957, for example, which had condemned criminalisation of adult homosexuality as an infringement of civil liberties. Its committee famously concluded: 'It is not, in our view, the function of the law to intervene in the private life of citizens, or to seek to enforce any particular pattern of behaviour.'[1] That model, sourced in British liberal philosophy, particularly the thinking of John Stuart Mill, rests on the assumption that intimacy depends on privacy, and in positing a sphere of relational security and familial dependency, distinct from government and political community, it replicates the Aristotelian model of a free male individual subject sustained to engage in public affairs by a wholly separate sphere of dependent women and slaves.

By 1976, when the writ against Hewett was formally brought, feminist critique of these separate spheres was fully fledged, as attested by the launch of the Australian Royal Commission on Human Relationships two years before, among other actions. Feminists understood a right to privacy, in so far as it was articulated as such only in the twentieth century, to protect the interests of upper and middle-class white men in particular, and to rest in unexamined moral values that perpetuated rather than guarded against shame and persecution.[2] Feminist activism and expression of many kinds contributed not just to deconstruction of the boundaries of the private sphere, as this volume explores, but a pointed recalibration of the role of government, through an insistence that it intervene against repressive actions in that sphere. In the contest between

---

1 *Report of the Committee on Homosexual Offenses and Prostitution*, CMD No. 247, 1957, p. 10.
2 No single author represents feminist thought on privacy from this period exactly and most work is only solidified in academic publications from the late 1970s onwards. Diverse work by Carole Pateman, Nancy Fraser, Drusilla Cornell, Catharine McKinnon and Anita Allen is indicative.

the Davieses' legal actions and the new ambits of confessional poetry, we see enacted some of the largest and most consequential social, political and legal shifts of the period.

My version of the defamative case narrative begins with a visit by the poet, playwright and then academic Dorothy Hewett, with her mother Rene Hewett, to the Perth home of her first ex-husband, the prominent left-wing barrister and writer Lloyd Davies, and his wife Jo Davies and their children, in 1969. As the Vietnam War ground on, Hewett was there on behalf of her son, Joe Flood, then 19, and one of his friends, to seek Davies's advice on legal recourse should either of their birth dates be drawn in the conscript lottery. Lloyd and Jo Davies were prominent in West Australian protests against the war, even more so than Hewett and her family, and Jo Davies had been the first West Australian to be arrested in the campaign—for throwing a shoe at Harold Holt, as a member of Save Our Sons.[3] Hewett and Davies had maintained an equable but distant friendship in literary circles in Perth, after marrying in 1945 and divorcing in 1951. Hewett left Davies for Sydney with her new partner Les Flood in 1949, and in 1950 her only child with Davies, Clancy, died of leukaemia when he was barely three years old. She returned to Western Australia in 1959.

Soon after this visit, Hewett wrote a poem with the encounter at its centre, titled 'Uninvited Guest'. It was published in *Poetry Australia* in October 1969.[4] Though still a young journal, housed in Sydney, *Poetry Australia* was a forum for some of the major and most recognised poets of the period, and through the late 1960s Hewett placed a number of her poems there. 'Uninvited Guest' is indicative of her poetic output from those years, which grew increasingly personal and confessional as Hewett detached it from the aesthetics of organised politics. By the time she left the Communist Party of Australia (CPA) after the Prague Spring in 1968, Hewett had moved her work determinedly towards newer literary trends in the West, towards intimate revelation and declarative interiority, and the kind of confessionalism demonstrated in the work of American poets Anne Sexton, Robert Lowell, John Berryman, Sylvia Plath and the more feminist Adrienne Rich.[5] Though her poetry had never been afraid of

---

3   Lloyd Davies, *In Defence of My Family* (Perth: Peppy Gully Press, 1987), 13; David Davies, interview by author, March 2015.
4   Dorothy Hewett, 'Uninvited Guest', *Poetry Australia*, no. 30 (1969): 14–15.
5   Cf. Kate Lilley, 'Introduction', in *Selected Poems of Dorothy Hewett* (Perth: University of Western Australia Press, 2010), 8.

the first person pronoun, her poems from the late 1960s and early 1970s meld Hewett's formal interest in poetic citation and mythic reference with workings-through of specific and clearly identifiable personal experiences. She wrote poems about the deaths of her father and mother, her activities in the CPA, her early suicide attempt, the retina of her right eye detaching, her work as a lecturer at the university (one poem directly satirises her former boss and mentor Professor Allan Edwards), her relationships with her husband the writer Merv Lilley and her former partner Les Flood, her love affairs of those years (including with the then well-known director of the Perth zoo, about whom she published one poem called 'Zoo-Keeper' and another called 'Zoo Story'), her desires, dreams, memories and disappointments, as well as different kinds of sex, writing itself, and politics.

Anne Sexton's poem 'For John, Who Begs Me Not to Enquire Further' from 1960 is Sexton's explicit riposte to criticism of the confessional impulse:

> I tapped my own head;
> it was a glass, an inverted bowl.
> It is a small thing
> to rage in your own bowl.
> At first it was private.
> Then it was more than myself;
> it was you, or your house
> or your kitchen.[6]

The concerns of 'Uninvited Guest' are exemplary in this mode, this turning inward to everyday agonies and the personal space of domestic life, to one's own life and the lives of those close—not least in that it is set largely in 'your kitchen', the Davieses' kitchen. This poem is only slightly distinguishable from others by Hewett of the period, principally in its tone (even more waspishly caustic) and in its detailed specificity (unambiguously about the Davieses). 'Re-Union', a companion poem published alongside in *Poetry Australia*, places Hewett in the same room as 'my husband, my ex-husband and my ex-lover' as well as the latter two's wives: 'The eyes of their women/ Deliberately pluck out my backbone'.[7] 'Uninvited Guest' extends such scarifying attention to the notably

---

6   Anne Sexton, 'For John, Who Begs Me Not to Enquire Further', *Selected Poems of Anne Sexton* (Boston: Houghton Mifflin, 2000), 26.
7   Dorothy Hewett, 'Re-Union', *Poetry Australia*, no. 30 (1969): 13.

misrepresented and unnamed children of 'my ex-husband's wife', subject to barbed and inaccurate description: 'her delinquent boys' (there is only one son in the family, if Clancy is not included); 'her autistic girl' with 'pale dopey eyes' (the Davieses' daughter suffered from significant hearing impairment in her childhood, not autism). The poem declares that Jo Davies talks too much, is abusing tranquilisers and has had her ovaries removed, and returns, brutally, cruelly, to the death of Clancy, Hewett's and Davies's lost young son, to charge Lloyd Davies with culpability: 'What poison did you carry in your genes? All the bright children of your body turned to death'.

The communist journalist and writer Joan Williams, a friend of both Hewett and Davies from the 1940s, drew Davies's attention to the poem in 1970.[8] As Davies reports, she saw it as a 'personal attack' on him, Jo and their children, and unarguably libellous.[9] According to him, Davies chose to ignore it then, characterising *Poetry Australia* as an 'insignificant' publication. After attending the premiere of Hewett's play *The Chapel Perilous* in January 1971, however, in which a character with a role parallel to his in Hewett's life is represented as impotent on his wedding night, he sought it out. Reading 'Uninvited Guest', he was 'shattered'. 'I did not think that anyone, let alone someone I had once loved, could be so venomous'.[10] Choosing to refrain from drawing further attention to the issue's contents, but with, it is understood, legal redress always possible, he reports telling Hewett herself of his hurt and offence in 1973, and warning her that only the small circulation of the journal had stopped further action.[11] Soon after this, Hewett and her family moved again to Sydney. In 1975, the poem was included in Hewett's new collection of poetry, *Rapunzel in Suburbia*, exactly as it had previously appeared. This collection was published by Prism—a venture of a different young poetry journal, *New Poetry*, run by Sydney poet Robert Adamson.

In response, Lloyd Davies and Jo Davies, with Lesley Davies and David Davies (then aged 20 and 18 years) launched a writ against Hewett—as Mrs Dorothy Lilley—in late 1975. The writ charged that Hewett had 'falsely and maliciously published of the plaintiffs a poem entitled "Uninvited Guest"' and that, by reason of its publication, the plaintiffs had 'been

---

8   Cf. Stephen Murray-Smith to Dorothy Hewett, 1 September 1976, bag 2, private collection held by Kate Lilley.
9   Davies, *In Defence of My Family*, 13.
10 Ibid., 21.
11 Ibid., 22.

seriously injured in their character and reputation and have been brought into odium and contempt and have suffered distress and humiliation'.[12] In what remained Perth's small world for legal matters, barrister Davies and his family were represented by a central Perth firm, while Hewett found a Sydney solicitor after advice from friends in New South Wales and Western Australia. Because the two parties were in separate states, the case had to be scheduled to be heard in the High Court, and was due before the Chief Justice in Perth on 16 September 1976. After advice to Hewett in August from Mr C. H. Smith QC that she stood 'little chance of success', which accorded with the views of most of her literary friends, the matter was settled out of court, in the weeks preceding the hearing.[13] Six thousand dollars settled on the Davieses represented injuries and costs, with the court arbitrating an injunction preventing Hewett from occasioning the poem to be published or distributed.[14]

In the months between writ and settlement, spilling afterwards into the next few years, public debate blew up about the case. This was not only because of Hewett's prominence as a writer and playwright, the role of the case as an effective precedent, or the climate of interest in questions of free speech and what was still then, during the Cold War, called cultural freedom. The case had impact as a gendered instance in which an ex-husband used the law to prohibit a woman writer from the expression of domestic and personal matters in her work. The mainstream newspapers covered the case, extrapolating from it, with plenty of space for Hewett and her defenders, on the question of a literary defence for libel and the threat to the ability of 'any writer or critic to work freely'.[15] The theatre critic Katharine Brisbane described the settlement as a decision taken to avoid a 'nasty legal precedent' for which every Australian writer should be grateful.[16] The *West Australian* was an exception in reporting descriptions of the 'shocking' poem's 'vitriolic tone' and Davies's insistence, '27 years after the end of their life together', on 'freedom from such attacks in print'.[17]

---

12   'DAVIES Lester Lloyd; DAVIES Joan Gladys; DAVIES Lesley Annette and DAVIES David Clancy versus LILLEY Dorothy Coade', Series A12920, Item Control 17/1975, National Archives of Australia (NAA), Canberra.
13   Letter from Keall, Brinsden & Co to Mrs Dorothy Lilley, 8 September 1976, private collection held by Kate Lilley.
14   'DAVIES Lester Lloyd; DAVIES Joan Gladys; DAVIES Lesley Annette and DAVIES David Clancy versus LILLEY Dorothy Coade', A12920, 17/1975, NAA, Canberra.
15   David Hummerston, 'Dorothy Hewett Slams Libel Laws', *Australian*, 16 September 1976.
16   Katharine Brisbane quoted in David Armstrong, 'Poet's Fight Starts Reform Bid', *Sydney Morning Herald*, 16 September 1976.
17   'A Poem with a Too-Clear Message', *West Australian*, 15 September 1976.

Stephen Murray-Smith, long-time editor of the Melbourne literary magazine *Overland*, tried to mediate between the two parties, explaining to Dorothy that he saw himself as 'one of the few people, perhaps the only one, with open lines to you both; and indeed, with sympathy with you both'.[18] Writing to Lloyd, he included his wife Nita in declaring:

> We were horrified when Dorothy's last book came out and revolted by references to personal friends of ours—not only you. We both made it clear to Dorothy … that we felt what she had done was morally indefensible … that the artist does not have licence to wound people and behave sadistically in the name of 'creative effort'.[19]

Murray-Smith nevertheless sought to dissuade the Davieses from taking legal action, visiting them with Nita after a Fellowship of Australian Writers meeting in Perth in August 1976. He reported to Hewett on 1 September: 'Great yellings and unpleasantness and some very harrowing scenes. No doubt at all that they are both worked up about the matter, Jo particularly'. He explained to Hewett that he and Nita had agreed 'that the poem was in bad taste, agreeing that it was wrong to draw Jo and the children into it, and so on, but insisting on your stature as an artist (which didn't help!) and insisting that two wrongs don't make a right, and that everyone stood to lose if this case got into court'. Davies subpoenaed Murray-Smith nevertheless, along with numbers of other mutual friends, wishing him to give evidence that the poem was 'published'. To Hewett, Murray-Smith declared himself 'open to give evidence for both sides … and the furthest I would go in condemning the poem would be to admit that it was in "bad taste"'. But he advised settling out of court, believing her 'almost certain to lose the case' and likely to be hit with costs.[20]

Support for Hewett afterwards concentrated on raising money for the settlement, as well as protest. This was despite what Davies perceived to be Hewett's then financial resources, having inherited from her parents' estate in 1971 and recently sold a holiday house at Yunderup, south of Perth, after the Lilleys' move to Sydney: Murray-Smith understood that this money had all gone to their Sydney mortgage. Soon after the first

---

18   Stephen Murray-Smith to Dorothy Hewett, 1 September 1976, private collection held by Kate Lilley.
19   Stephen Murray-Smith quoted in Davies, *In Defence of My Family*, 310.
20   Stephen Murray-Smith to Dorothy Hewett, 1 September 1976, private collection held by Kate Lilley.

writ was issued, a 'Literary Defence Committee' was formed by Hewett supporters in Victoria, with further members in New South Wales and South Australia. The theatre world was particularly supportive. With the injunction in place, a benefit variety night was held in the Adelaide Town Hall on 17 October 1976. Called *A Tatty Show* and over four hours long, with 91 participants, it was directed by Hewett's favourite director Rodney Fisher with assistance from Wal Cherry. Robyn Archer used two Hewett poems as lyrics for songs, excerpts from her plays were staged, the feminist protest singer Margaret Roadknight performed some of Hewett's folk songs, as well as a rendition of comic singer Bob Hudsen's 'Libel Song' to close the show, before a teary Dorothy got up to thank everyone.[21] Letters of support were sent from writers, actors and directors, including A. D. Hope, Graeme Blundell, Jim Sharman, David Williamson and Manning Clark. The benefit raised $1,200 towards the $6,000 paid. On 28 April 1977, South Australian parliamentarian Anne Levy read 'Uninvited Guest' into the South Australian record, under parliamentary privilege, which meant it was effectively released for publication in Hansard. The *Australian* reported that 'reading of the poem created an uproar, but Ms Levy said important issues affecting freedom of artistic expression were involved'.[22]

The storm was fuelled too by further legal actions from the Davies family. Because a substantial portion of the poem had been quoted in a review in the literary journal *Westerly*, its author Hal Colebatch, the editors of the journal and its publisher the University of Western Australia (UWA) were also charged with libel, this time with Jo, Lesley and David Davies only as plaintiffs. UWA's insurers also settled, for a separate $6,000. Actions continued—when Adamson issued a second printing of *Rapunzel in Suburbia* later in 1976, with a poem titled 'Envoi' substituted for 'Uninvited Guest', Davies issued another writ citing it, 'Re-Union' and other poems in charges of libel. 'Envoi' is explicitly about the 'Uninvited Guest' libel charge. Adamson published an apology and withdrew the new edition. The Currency Press–published version of *The Chapel Perilous* was the next subject of action, along with Hewett's more recent play *The Tatty Hollow Story*, which had been performed at The Stables in Sydney in August 1976, a month before the High Court case was due to be heard, and published by Currency Press with another earlier play later that year.

---

21   Rodney Fisher, 'A Tribute to Dorothy', *Theatre Australia* 1, no. 4 (1976): 38–39.
22   'Hansard Publishes "Libel" Poem', *Australian*, 29 April 1977.

As Davies describes it, *The Tatty Hollow Story* 'depicts an outrageously avant garde female poet—obviously an idealised Dorothy—who also had a maligned and ridiculed lawyer ex-husband'.[23] Davies issued a writ against Phillip Parsons, the publisher of Currency Press, requiring an injunction and damages, and this action was long and protracted, but the ultimate terms of settlement in 1978 prohibited the distribution or publishing of either publication in the State of Western Australia in the plaintiff's lifetime (Davies died in 2006). Red stickers reading 'Not for Sale in Western Australia' were applied to covers of circulating editions. When booksellers and distributors tried to sell *Rapunzel*, or publishers re-release 'Uninvited Guest', the Davies sent notifying letters. Declared Lloyd Davies: 'Clearly, for all the world to see, the libel had been an attack upon a husband and wife and their two young children in their private capacity. As such it was a violation not only of the law but also of Article 17 of the International Covenant on Civil and Political Rights [ICCPR]—to say nothing of the 9th Commandment'[24]—which is, of course, 'thou shalt not bear false witness against thy neighbour'.

The ICCPR, to which Australia is a state party, was endorsed by the United Nations in 1966 but came into effect from 23 March 1976. Notably, Article 17 mandates the right to privacy and states: 'No one shall be subjected to arbitrary or unlawful interference with his privacy, family, home or correspondence, nor to unlawful attacks on his honour and reputation'.[25] In September 1976, Australia had not yet ratified it, and the federal Australian Privacy Act was not passed until 1988. Nevertheless, in invoking the Covenant Davies was seeking to expand the offence at issue in the definition of libel in Australia to include not just the damage to any individual's public reputation (the defamation) but unwarranted ingress into privacy—announced as this ingress is in Hewett's title for her poem. The 'he' of the ICCPR definition in Article 17 is not accidental, moreover, neither for the UN nor for the Davies case—'his privacy, home, family', 'his honour and reputation'. The Covenant identifies the private sphere as an owned patriarchal space and a family as an extension of that singular man.

---

23   Davies, *In Defence of My Family*, 38.
24   Ibid., 26.
25   'International Covenant on Civil and Political Rights', Article 17, United Nations Human Rights Office of the High Commissioner, accessed 21 January 2019, www.ohchr.org/EN/ProfessionalInterest/Pages/CCPR.aspx.

The Australian Law Reform Commission (ALRC) undertook a review of Australian defamation and privacy laws, beginning almost immediately in the wake of the Davies–Lilley case, in late 1976, and published its report in 1979. As an issue of import for that moment, privacy was a legal concept under great strain. On the one hand, feminist and other liberationist critiques were exposing what political theorist Beate Roessler describes as 'the thoroughly conventional nature of the separation between public and private life', and the historical obsolescence of any 'natural' right to privacy.[26] On the other hand, a strong international trend towards the legal codification of exactly such a right was responding to the manifest expansion of the popular mediascape, in which public figures, especially politicians, were subject to far greater public exposure than had been the case. The all-male membership of the ALRC recommended 'significant change' to Australian law, to enable the Commonwealth to enact legislation protecting against not just defamation, or falsely implied damage to a person's reputation, but against the publication of what were termed 'sensitive private facts—whether they be true or false'.[27] These were defined as 'information relating to the health, private behaviour, home life, personal or family relationships of the individual, which, in all circumstances, would be likely to cause distress, annoyance or embarrassment to a person in the position of that individual'.[28]

This formulation reflected a perceived loss of what Deborah Nelson describes as a 'certain fantasy of privacy as a self-evident concept', which she presents as a formulation dependent on Cold War American patriarchal ideals of 'autonomy, freedom, self-determination and repose'. She argues that this concept broke down in the face of challenges such as those from confessional poetry, which showed that privacy could also mean 'isolation, loneliness, domination and routine'.[29] Women were contesting the terms of 'private behaviour', naming domestic violence and sexual harassment as issues of public, as well as political, concern, while the abolition of no-fault divorce in Australia with the passing of the Family Law Act in 1974 removed one notorious mechanism through which the

---

26   Beate Roessler, 'New Ways of Thinking about Privacy', in *Oxford Handbook of Political Theory*, ed. John S. Dryzek, Bonnie Honig and Anne Phillips, online edition (Oxford: Oxford University Press, 2009).
27   Australian Law Reform Commission, *Unfair Publication: Defamation and Privacy* (Canberra: Australian Government Publishing Service, 1979), xii.
28   Ibid.
29   Deborah Nelson, *Pursuing Privacy in Cold War America* (New York: Columbia University Press, 2002), xiii–xiv.

state enacted public judgement on such behaviour. The historical shift towards what Lauren Berlant conceives as 'public intimacy', with its overturning of social hierarchies of gendered experience, was driven as much by communication technologies and developments in the culture industry, as by political activity and targeted legal change.[30]

If we step back from barrister Lloyd Davies's extrapolation to the right to privacy from defamation, however, and notice the shift in the law's language in the late 1970s from the family to 'the individual', the interests of the other plaintiffs in this case move more clearly into view, while the gendered binary of the conflict also becomes complicated. Jo Davies, who married Lloyd in 1952, besides figuring most prominently in the poem, was a vocal and active participant in the first charges and writ and in the ongoing prosecution of their case, and those involved attest to her sustained anger, even fury, at the poem's characterisation of her and the children. Her own feminist activism also throws Hewett's position, and Lloyd's, into a different light: there is a feminist case to be made for her protection from the harmful public grievances of her husband's previous marriage. Lesley and David were adults by the time of the claim, furthermore, no longer mere dependents in the eyes of the law, while Jo and Lloyd's work as disability advocates on Lesley's behalf informed their stance in explicit terms too. For a case of defamation, the main defence historically is truth, though this was formalised in Australia only with the introduction of uniform defamation laws across all state jurisdictions in 2005. The misrepresentations in 'Uninvited Guest' are patent and multiple, however: this is why Hewett stood little chance in court. Where her position was exceptional, of course, was that the publication under question was a poem.

In responding to the first Statement of Claim against her, Hewett's defence team began from this position: that 'Uninvited Guest' is art and thus cannot be defamatory. The Statement of Defence issued in March 1976 denied the matters in the claim and 'further denies that any of the words in the poem ... are in *their ordinary and natural meaning* defamatory of any of the plaintiffs' (my italics).[31] There is no defence based on literary merit in Australian defamation law, however, as this phrasing reflects;

---

30   Cf. Lauren Berlant, *The Female Complaint: The Unfinished Business of Sentimentality in American Culture* (Durham, NC: Duke University Press, 2008), doi.org/10.1215/9780822389163.
31   'DAVIES Lester Lloyd; DAVIES Joan Gladys; DAVIES Lesley Annette and DAVIES David Clancy versus LILLEY Dorothy Coade', A12920, 17/1975, NAA.

rather, a text's meaning is stripped of any extraordinary, exceptional or figural reference. The original claim identified defamatory matter in the poem line by line, indicating to which member of the Davies family each matter referred: '(Second plaintiff): With her bare fat suffering feet/ with her head stuffed full of tranquilisers and her ovaries removed'.[32] In a later riposte to Dorothy's supporters, called 'Tit for Tatty' and published in response to the Adelaide fundraiser as well as articles that he felt assumed the truth of the poem, Davies identified and refuted individually what he characterised as the poem's 'lies'. 'My wife enjoys (and so do I vicariously) a well turned pair of pins and is particularly shapely of foot and ankle. Mutual acquaintances—both friend and foe—will testify she is much more slender in every way than Ms. Hewett.'[33]

The form or nature of poetic truth, or more exactly, truth in poetry, is a complex question, of course, but it is not a legal one in Australia, even though poetry's status as a special kind of speech or linguistic form is everywhere deployed in legal discourse. The ALRC's 1979 report on 'Unfair Publication' begins its section on privacy with a stanza from T. S. Eliot, one of Hewett's most frequently employed influences, and this could be read as a subtextual rebuke to her, given Davies's professional connections to the Commissioners:[34]

> There's a loss of personality;
> Or rather, you've lost touch with the person
> You thought you were. You no longer feel quite human.
> You're suddenly reduced to the status of an object—
> A living object but no longer a person.[35]

With that special status comes the contemporary assumption, as Rose Lucas articulates it discussing Sexton, that poetry has 'unique access to the personal and the so-called authentic',[36] and this is perhaps a legacy of the mid-century confessional lyric itself, besides Romanticism. Hewett's poem, with its caustic tone and calculated hurt, is nevertheless full of examples of what Sexton's poem, 'For John', cited earlier, calls a 'complicated lie'.

---

32 Ibid.
33 Davies, *In Defence of My Family*, 35–36.
34 See references in Davies, *In Defence of My Family*, 42–43.
35 T. S. Eliot's *The Cocktail Party*, Act 1, Scene 1, quoted in Australian Law Reform Commission, *Unfair Publication*, 109.
36 Rose Lucas, 'Gifts of Love, Gifts of Poison: Anne Sexton and the Poetry of Intimate Exchange', *Life Writing* 6, no. 1 (2009): 46, doi.org/10.1080/14484520802550312.

> And if you turn away
> because there is no lesson here
> I will hold my awkward bowl,
> with all its cracked stars shining
> like a complicated lie,
> and fasten a new skin around it
> as if I were dressing an orange
> or a strange sun.
> Not that it was beautiful
> but that I found some order there.³⁷

Itself addressing a critique very similar to Davies's of Hewett, 'For John, Who Begs Me Not to Enquire Further' locates its defence in art—'I will … fasten a new skin around it'—even if the poem's subject himself finds the words merely literal, without a 'lesson'.³⁸

'Uninvited Guest' has more expansive, less concentrated imagery, and locates both the poet and her subjects in a trajectory across the past, present and future, centred on a kitchen in which a green potato vine 'grows and covers the walls and ceiling/ a climbing, monstrous ganglia, green nerves, groping arms'. It seems to address Davies directly, calling on their shared memories ('Once you danced "L'Aprés-Midi d'une Faune" in a green garden/ With an ancient parrot swearing away like a stable hand'), and voices a wondering concern that seems to ask him to attend more closely to dangers haunting his family ('Where are you when your wife sits strangling in a great green vine in the kitchen … I want to cry after you, "Rip off those cataracts!"/ But haven't the heart').³⁹ The Daviese's Statement of Claim read these lines as directly defamatory: 'the defendant meant and was understood to mean that Mr Davies had no care for his wife and children and failed to show any responsibility for their physical and psychological condition'.⁴⁰ But the poem's literal mistakes—that there is only one Davies boy, no longer two; that the image of the 'delinquent boys piss[ing] over each other in bed' is impossible, and instead more likely to be sourced in Hewett's own children's behaviour;⁴¹ the casting of the Daviese's daughter as 'in a deep freeze, tranced out of hatred', rather than unhearing—these are the detritus of a greedily imagistic poem for

---

37 Sexton, 'For John', 26.
38 Ibid.
39 Hewett, 'Uninvited Guest', 14–15.
40 'DAVIES Lester Lloyd; DAVIES Joan Gladys; DAVIES Lesley Annette and DAVIES David Clancy versus LILLEY Dorothy Coade', A12920, 17/1975, NAA.
41 Cf. Tom Flood, interview by author, 20 October 2016.

which the real is perhaps beside the point. As her daughter Kate Lilley says, for Hewett, 'the stuff of poetry was everywhere: it was anywhere she was or could imagine, and everything was fair game to use or recycle, including her own earlier work'.[42]

By the mid-1970s, contemporary poetry was shifting its ground to encompass more obvious abstraction and linguistic play, via European post-structuralist critiques of the illusion of realism. Veronica Forrest-Thomson's *Poetic Artifice*, from 1978, articulated a full theory of poetic abstraction in which poetry is always fictive, arguing that it necessarily 'lifts meaning away from direct reference to a state of affairs' and makes it 'part of a thematic synthesis, where the external contexts are evoked only to be made fictional'.[43] And we can see the attraction of this kind of fabulation in much of Hewett's work, tipping as it does between the speaking confessional and the abstraction of the particular, or the thematisatio of such, and of everyday detail made representational, mythic. Forrest-Thomson would categorise Davies's reading—and that of the claim itself, the law's insistence on 'ordinary and natural meaning'— as an instance of what she terms 'bad Naturalisation', 'with its stress on external interpretation'.[44] Explicating the formal achievements of Sylvia Plath's 1962 poem 'Purdah', she describes such 'limited, external' reading: 'In its anxiety to get at the meaning *behind* the words it would overlook the meaning *of* the words'.[45]

Elizabeth Bishop, the highly influential mid-century American poet, was one of Hewett's favourites. Even though her work was never directly confessional, she was very close to Lowell, and her poems everywhere demonstrate a search for what she called 'accuracy'. As her biographer describes, by this she did not mean realism, but rather an emotional or subjective form of truth; an acute and formal way of inhabiting things, places, externalities through language, or linguistic image, to reflect on their subjective freight.[46] More than mere emotion, her poetry seeks in objects and nature, in observation of that which is other to the poet, states of understanding, not just feeling, that are not dependent on rationality.

---

42 Lilley, 'Introduction', 10.
43 Veronica Forrest-Thomson, *Poetic Artifice: A Theory of Twentieth-Century Poetry* [1978], ed. Gareth Farmer (Bristol: Shearsman, 2016), 19–20.
44 Forrest-Thomson, *Poetic Artifice*, 163.
45 Forrest-Thomson, *Poetic Artifice*, 163.
46 Brett C. Millier, *Elizabeth Bishop: Life and the Memory of It* (Berkeley: University of California Press, 1993), passim.

Sexton's poem voices this as a perception of 'order', distinct from beauty, that can work to hold complex significance, as she holds her bowl, which is also her head, herself. And we see something of this endeavour in Hewett's work too—an aim to render conceptually that which is felt and experienced, to bring such into language in a way that is grounded not on reference but on aesthetics, on the minimal techniques of poetic form, symbol and voice, as well as the more maximal reflexes of citation, imagery and story—even as it seems 'merely' to tell of her truths.

This kind of subjectivism, particularly confessionalism's dependency on a mimetic version of a self, even if a modernist abstracted or alienated form of such, gave way through the 1970s to a more thoroughly abstracted and experimental relation with language. But in the 1960s, confessional poetry was enacting a radical social impulse that had at its heart an attack on socially policed boundaries between public and private experience, and whose liberatory force for women was manifesting, by the early 1970s, in the exploration of self-identity, taboo-breaking and consciousness-raising as political acts. Confessional poetry actively trafficked in truth claims and as a gendered genre at once critiqued forms of authority and relocated it in performed versions of the self, often expressing taboo, traumatic or highly emotional aspects of life that were not customary parts of public discourse. Through the 1970s, feminist forms of autobiography and memoir took on this mantle, insisting not just on authenticity but on typicality and collectivity, testifying to women's experiences as at once true and representative, and transforming in profound ways what could be said about how people live.[47] This is the nature of the social and political work performed by such cultural production in these decades: literary texts could offer alternative bridges between public and private, political and personal, via pathways both more nuanced and expansive, as well as more ethically complex, than the laboured governmental and legal ones then being engineered.

Authenticity is precisely under abeyance in Hewett's poem, however, as both a legal and a literary concept, and, in as much as 1960s confessionalism has an aesthetic, this tension is characteristic. Paul de Man reminds us, moreover, of the function of guilt and shame in the act of confession, and warns that 'it is an epistemological use of language in

---

47 Rita Felski, 'On Confession', in *Women, Autobiography, Theory: A Reader*, ed. Sidonie Smith and Julia Watson (Madison: University of Wisconsin Press, 1998), 84–85.

which ethical values … are superseded by values of truth and falsehood'.[48] Hewett's 'Uninvited Guest' confesses only in so far as it slights and insults a present the speaker misreads through her own past; Davies was right to see the poem's rhetorical, generic claims to truth as its greatest threat. But perhaps in so far as 'Uninvited Guest' is a lie, it also reaches for the abstracted and fictive, and is not exhaustively referential; that is, perhaps it is not necessarily or always or only about the Davieses. Perhaps the poem's precise failure, even though it works well enough as a poem, is that it falls between these stools—it is neither a true enough confession nor a complicated enough lie. 'Put on dark glasses and a blind man's head', Hewett charges, in the poem's address to questions of experiential truth, to evidentiary seeing: 'A blind man's listening uneasiness'.

---

48   Paul de Man, *Allegories of Reading* (New Haven: Yale University Press, 1979), 279; cf. S. Rosenbaum, 'Confessional Poetry', in *The Princeton Handbook of Poetic Terms: Third Edition*, ed. Roland Greene and Stephen Cushman (Princeton: Princeton University Press, 2016), 54–56.

RE-GENDERING LANGUAGE, AUTHORITY AND CULTURE

CHAPTER 13

Changing 'man made language': Sexist language and feminist linguistic activism in Australia

Amanda Laugesen

'By the mid-seventies', wrote American feminist scholar Alette Olin Hill in 1986, 'there were many female voices being raised against the tyranny of patriarchal Loud Mouths. Language itself was being examined as both an instrument of oppression and as a possible tool of liberation'.[1] Language became a significant concern for the international feminist movement through the 1970s. Efforts were made to investigate the gendered nature of language, campaigns were waged to change popular understandings of sexism in language and, ultimately, style and usage guides were designed that aimed to transform language at the institutional as well as the personal level. Australia actively participated in this international debate about sexist language, and campaigns to change language usage were waged in Australia.

The feminist campaign to change language was a form of what linguist Deborah Cameron calls 'verbal hygiene' (Anne Pauwels uses the somewhat less loaded term 'linguistic intervention'): a way in which groups in society aim to monitor and censor language in ways that reflect their own social,

---

1   Alette Olin Hill, *Mother Tongue, Father Time: A Decade of Linguistic Revolt* (Bloomington: Indiana University Press, 1986), xvi.

political or cultural concerns.² It might be more useful—and this is the term I prefer to use in this chapter—to talk about these efforts as 'linguistic activism': an effort to change speech as part of a broader attitude to change cultural attitudes and from there to create social change and, in this case, to achieve greater equality for, and less discrimination against, women.

This chapter considers what I call 'feminist linguistic activism' in Australia in the 1970s and 1980s. I will firstly consider the international feminist and academic concern with the gendered nature of language. Some of the concrete efforts made to shape language use, through style guides and the use of titles such as 'Ms', will then be examined in an effort to assess what changes were made, or at least attempted, in terms of shaping official public language, such as the language of government. Finally, I will consider criticisms made at the time of such change, and the subsequent debates that continue to the present around so-called political correctness. These suggest a strong and continuing resistance and backlash to changes in language and usage.

Linguistic activism took place in a context of social, cultural and political change in Australia. The advent of the Whitlam Labor Government led to an increased concern with addressing the status of women at a legislative level, and a greater receptivity to the feminist agenda. The Whitlam Government ratified the International Labour Organization's convention on discrimination in employment, but although there was a move towards passing a federal Sex Discrimination Act, the dismissal of Whitlam's government in 1975 meant that such legislation would not be enacted until the 1980s.³ Nevertheless, the 1970s saw the beginnings of change in the status of women.

Language too, especially public language, changed rapidly through the 1960s, 1970s and 1980s. Major shifts in public language use began in the 1960s and were closely identified with youth culture and student activism.⁴ For student activists in the 1960s, the use of offensive language

---

2   Deborah Cameron, *Verbal Hygiene* (Abingdon: Routledge, 2012), x; Anne Pauwels, *Women Changing Language* (London: Longman, 1998), 92.
3   Marian Sawer, 'Women's Work Is Never Done: the Pursuit of Equality and the Commonwealth Sex Discrimination Act', in *Sex Discrimination in Uncertain Times*, ed. M. Thornton (Canberra: ANU E Press, 2010), 79, doi.org/10.22459/SDUT.09.2010.03.
4   Geoffrey Hughes, *Swearing: A Social History of Foul Language, Oaths and Profanity in English* (Oxford: Blackwell, 1991), 200.

was part of an attempt to 'shock and challenge authority'.⁵ Through that decade and the 1970s, there was a significant increase in obscenity in films in particular.⁶ This flowed through to other areas of popular culture. Popular culture became increasingly less subject to censorship, particularly in relation to language and depictions of sexuality. Swearing and offensive language became increasingly common in film and literature, and to a lesser extent on radio and television. Some censorship in the media continued: there were (and are still) guidelines in place that attempt to regulate acceptable content and language, especially at times that children might be listening or watching. But the 1970s was nevertheless a watershed decade in terms of changes in popular culture.

Feminists embraced opportunities to use language, including 'bad' language, in ways that matched their agenda of liberation. Feminists critiqued the gendered norms around swearing. Women were traditionally expected to refrain from using obscenity and were shamed for doing so; some feminists called for women to freely use obscenity as a form of power.⁷ Scholar of bad language Geoffrey Hughes has noted that despite this no distinctive vocabulary of abuse was developed by women.⁸ But women undoubtedly came to use bad language more freely in public,⁹ and for some women this could be a valuable form of empowerment.

Germaine Greer was probably the most notable feminist figure of the period to revel in using language as a means to shock and to call attention to women's liberation. Her use of four-letter words was deliberate—not just to shock but, as she said of one of them (unnamed in this *Australian Women's Weekly* interview, but probably 'fuck'), 'I'd like to take all the steam and violence out of that word. It's a factual word and it should be a gentle one'.¹⁰ Greer's notoriety for using 'shocking' language helped to call attention to women's use of language. A month after her interview in the *Weekly*, Greer was arrested in Auckland for using indecent language in a public place after saying the words 'bullshit' and 'fuck' at a public

---

5   Edwin L. Battistella, *Bad Language: Are Some Words Better than Others?* (New York: Oxford University Press, 2005), 82, doi.org/10.1093/acprof:oso/9780195172485.001.0001.
6   Ibid., 68.
7   Hughes, *Swearing*, 207, 210.
8   Ibid., 211.
9   Ruth Wajnryb, *Language Most Foul* (Crows Nest, NSW: Allen & Unwin, 2004), 124–25.
10 Kay Keavney, 'The Liberating of Germaine Greer', *Australian Women's Weekly*, 2 February 1972, 4.

lecture at Auckland University. When subsequently appearing before the magistrate, the court was protested by young people (including girls) chanting these words.[11]

While actions such as Greer's encapsulated the efforts of the women's movement to liberate women's use of language, especially in public, feminists also campaigned for what proved to be a much harder and longer fight: changing sexist and discriminatory language.

Gendered language and the call for change

A concern with the gendered nature of language, along with gendered stereotypes in the media and in children's books, was on the agenda of second-wave feminists in the 1970s and into the 1980s. Concerns ranged from debates over titles of address for women, to the negative connotations attached to many terms applied to women, to the sexist nature of language as demonstrated in, for example, job titles. The aim was not only to call attention to sexism in language, but also to agitate for change.

The gendered nature of language began to be actively investigated and debated within academia through the 1970s. Robin Lakoff's 1973 article 'Language and Woman's Place', and subsequent book of the same title, provided one of the first serious academic studies of the ways language was gendered. It had a significant impact in making language and gender an important field of study. In the article, Lakoff noted that 'linguistic discrimination' was part of how women were denied access to power.[12] She went on to describe various examples of women's distinctive linguistic behaviour; for example, how certain words, such as 'adorable', were more likely to be used by women.[13] However, Lakoff saw attempts to change certain usages—for example, the use of gendered pronouns—as ultimately futile, and she argued that it was better to focus on what could be changed.[14] She concluded that only social change could create language change, 'not the reverse'.[15]

---

11   '$40 Fine for Obscene Word', *Canberra Times*, 11 March 1972, 33.
12   Robin Lakoff, 'Language and Woman's Place', *Language in Society* 2, no. 1 (April 1973): 48, doi.org/10.1017/S0047404500000051.
13   Ibid., 51.
14   Ibid., 75.
15   Ibid., 76.

Australian feminist and writer Dale Spender also intervened into linguistic scholarship, but took a different view of the potential of feminist linguistic activism. She published the pamphlet *The Language of Sexism* in 1975, noting that there had been no systematic research to date into the language of sexism.[16] Her later book *Man Made Language* (1980) disputed what she regarded as Lakoff's 'acceptance' (that is, descriptive approach) of the gendered nature of language. Spender's book was a fierce attack on the sexist nature of language, arguing that a monopoly over language was one of the means by which men had ensured their own primacy. Her book went on to outline the various ways in which language was sexist and to call for ways in which women could have their voices heard.

Spender's contribution was, like many feminist works on language and sexism in this period, not just a study of the gendered nature of language but also a call to change language. Many feminists, although certainly not all, believed that changing language could help change attitudes and could be a way to empower women. Spender argued that 'changing both society and language were equally important tasks'.[17] Women could not rely on waiting for society to change so that language would change.[18] She argued that men had 'encoded' sexism into the language to maintain their superiority, and it was time for the feminist movement to challenge this by changing the language. Indeed, language was to be liberated. She declared: 'We need a language which constructs the reality of women's autonomy, women's strength, women's power'.

Spender's book was reviewed extensively at the time. Sarah Lawson in *American Speech* called the book 'fascinating and illuminating'; sharing Spender's feminist aims, she too called for the elimination of sexist words, and repeated Spender's call for consciousness-raising.[19] Verna Rieschild, an Australian linguist reviewing the book in the *Canberra Times*, saw the book as the product of both linguistic and feminist research, with 'an eventual feminist victory'. Victoria Green of the Women's Electoral Lobby was less concerned with the linguistic scholarship, seeing Spender's book as 'lucid, powerful and immensely entertaining'.[20]

---

16   Dale Spender, *The Language of Sexism* (Canberra: Curriculum Development Centre, 1975).
17   Dale Spender, *Man Made Language* (London: Routledge and Kegan Paul, 1980), 31.
18   Ibid., 30.
19   Sarah Lawson, 'More on Sexism and Language, Review of Dale Spender, *Man Made Language*', *American Speech* 59, no. 4 (Winter 1984): 371–72.
20   'Language, Gender and Power', *Canberra Times*, 3 October 1981, 14.

The view that changing language could change attitudes fitted into an intellectual perspective taking shape in the 1970s and 1980s that argued that knowledge was constructed and situated. Language was not 'natural'; instead it was possible to query and deconstruct language and construct new knowledge. The feminism of the 1970s was also concerned with the nature of power and how power governed human relationships.[21] An analysis of, and a call to change, language was part of this dissection and reimagining of power. Not all feminists agreed with this preoccupation and perspective, believing that the focus should be more on changing society—reiterating Lakoff's view: change society first and language will ultimately change. But as feminist linguist Anne Pauwels writes, looking back at the period from the perspective of the 1990s, many feminists believed that at the very least language needed a push in the right direction.

Campaigning against sexist language

One major way in which feminist linguistic intervention was enacted was through the push for a variety of guidelines and recommendations for usage. Much of this only happened in the 1980s, but were a direct product of the agitation and debates around language usage that began in the 1970s.

Influential early texts in the campaign included Casey Miller and Kate Swift's *Words and Women* (1976) and their *Handbook of Non-Sexist Writing for Writers, Editors and Speakers* (1980). Miller and Swift, who were both Americans, had already addressed the question of gender and language when their 1976 text, *Words and Women*, appeared. Both worked as freelance editors, and had come to be increasingly aware of the sexism inherent in the texts they edited, especially the common use of the generic pronoun 'he'. In 1971, they wrote an article for *Ms* magazine proposing new generic personal pronouns including 'tey', 'ter' and 'tem'. This article formed the basis of *Words and Women*, which was a broad study of gender and language. Miller and Swift discussed at length the various ways in which words and language could shape cultural assumptions, and pointed to what they called the 'double standard of linguistic behaviour'.[22]

---

21   Susan Magarey, *Dangerous Ideas: Women's Liberation—Women's Studies—around the World* (Adelaide: University of Adelaide Press, 2014), 30.
22   Casey Miller and Kate Swift, *Words and Women* (New York: Anchor Press, 1976), 55, 106.

While they acknowledged that by 1976 '[s]ignificant gains have been made in many areas', 'the transformation of English in response to the movement for human liberation has scarcely begun'.[23]

In both the *Ms* article and *Words and Women* Miller and Swift called for change, while also providing some basic guidelines on how writers and publishers could avoid sexism in their writing. These guidelines were expanded in the *Handbook* published three years later. The *Handbook* was published in American and British editions, and would have a significant influence on usage guides, including Australian usage guides. Miller and Swift wrote in their introduction in the British edition:

> What standard English usage says about males, for example, is that they are a species. What it says about females is that they are a subspecies. From these two assertions flow a thousand other enhancing and degrading messages, all encoded in the language we in the English-speaking countries begin to learn almost as soon as we are born.[24]

They went on to outline how users of the *Handbook* could start to change their linguistic and writing practices to address sexism. This included the use of the generic 'he'—again they called for a new gender-neutral pronoun to come into general use, proposing alternatives such as 'co', 'e' or 'tey'. They also noted that writers often made generalisations that excluded or denigrated women and distinguished women in a demeaning way; for example, referring to a female doctor as a 'lady doctor'.

A transnational print culture of language usage guides developed through the 1970s and into the 1980s, and complemented other efforts at transforming language, such as the publication of feminist dictionaries. Australian language usage guidelines were often adapted or drew from guides produced in the United Kingdom or the United States of America, including Miller and Swift's. Australian feminists embraced the campaign to change sexist language, and in particular called for new guidelines to help reshape usage. Numerous guides were subsequently published to help shape and guide language use in the public sphere—including and especially government agencies, publishing houses and editors, and

---

23   Ibid., 153.
24   Casey Miller and Kate Swift, *The Handbook of Non-Sexist Writing for Writers, Editors and Speakers* (London: The Women's Press, 1980), 4.

the media. Guidelines called attention to sexist usage and stereotypes, but could also help guide writers and others through providing viable alternatives.

The activism behind this activity was the product of the belief that language change and reform could have real-life consequences for women in terms of how they were depicted and treated. By implementing institutional change, community perceptions and ultimately behaviours could be changed. It was also driven and informed by, as Russell writes of feminist dictionaries, authority derived from personal experience.[25]

The first really influential set of guidelines reproduced in Australia was the *Guidelines for Equal Treatment of the Sexes in McGraw-Hill Book Company Publications* (1974).[26] McGraw-Hill was a major publisher of educational texts in the United States and globally, and the guidelines received extensive media coverage in the United States and elsewhere.[27] They were often cited in later language usage guides, and informed, for example, academic journal practices.[28] They also reflected an increasing willingness on the part of American publishers to address concerns over sexism in publications, and McGraw-Hill explicitly decided, after consultation with feminist groups, to develop guidelines to assist their editors.[29]

The McGraw-Hill guidelines were subsequently published in Australia in 1978 in a version edited by Edna (Edel) Wignell, an Australian children's author, and given the new title *Counter Sexist Guidelines*.[30] The Australian title explicitly suggested the activist function that Wignell saw the guidelines as having. The Australian version, as well as the US original, had an impact on Australian publishing practices, and informed many of the usage guides that followed.[31]

---

25   Lindsay Rose Russell, 'This Is What a Dictionary Looks Like: The Lexicographical Contributions of Feminist Dictionaries', *International Journal of Lexicography* 25, no. 1 (2011): 22.
26   A copy of the guidelines is available in *Elementary English* 52, no. 5 (May 1975): 725–33.
27   Miller and Swift, *Words and Women*, 144.
28   See, for example, 'Guidelines for Nonsexist Language in APA Journals: Publication Manual Change Sheet 2', *Educational Researcher* (March 1978): 15–17.
29   'Any Change in Sexist Texts? Feminist Press Staff Survey Education Publishers', *Women's Studies Newsletter* 2, no. 3 (Summer 1974), 10.
30   Edna Wignell, *Counter Sexist Guidelines* (Richmond, Vic.: Primary Education, 1978).
31   The original McGraw-Hill guidelines or Wignell's edition are cited as 'further reading' and in reference lists in many usage guides. Anne Pauwels in her 'Women and Language in Australian Society', in *Women and Language in Australian and New Zealand Society*, ed. Anne Pauwels (Sydney: Australian Professional Publications, 1987), 26n. 23, also attests to the influence of the guidelines in Australia.

The introduction to the guidelines—which stated McGraw-Hill's intentions in producing them—noted:

> We are endeavouring through these guidelines to eliminate sexist assumptions from McGraw-Hill Book Company publications and to encourage a greater freedom for all individuals to pursue their interests and realize their potentials. Specifically, these guidelines are designed to make McGraw-Hill staff members and McGraw-Hill authors aware of the ways in which males and females have been stereotypes in publications; to show the role language has played in reinforcing inequality; and to indicate positive approaches towards providing fair, accurate, and balanced treatment of both sexes in our publications.[32]

Acknowledging that 'the language of literature cannot be prescribed', the recommendations in the guidelines were intended 'primarily for use in teaching materials, reference works, and nonfiction works in general'.[33]

Counter Sexist Guidelines for the most part simply reproduced the American text, but included an annotated list of 'recent counter-sexist materials' that Wignell described as being a 'personal resource for teachers at all levels, parents, librarians, writers, discussion leaders, career advisers, [and] people concerned with breaking sexist language barriers'.[34] The American text contained a variety of instructions on usage, as well as content. For example, it suggested that feminine and masculine stereotypes should be avoided at all times. Women should never be 'typecast'; men should not be shown as 'constantly subject to the "masculine mystique" in their interests, attitudes, or careers'.[35] Beyond gender stereotypes, it was also recommended that all people should be depicted in ways that represented them as 'whole human beings'.[36] A 'patronizing or girl-watching tone' was to be avoided. They listed a number of examples of stereotypes to eschew: 'scatterbrained female', 'henpecking shrew', 'frustrated spinster', 'fragile flower'.[37]

---

32 Wignell, *Counter Sexist Guidelines*, 1.
33 Ibid.
34 Ibid., ii.
35 Ibid., 2.
36 Ibid., 4.
37 Ibid., 5.

The McGraw-Hill text also took up the issue of generic 'mankind', something that often featured in discussions of sexist language. It suggested a number of more inclusive, gender-neutral usages: 'mankind' should be replaced by 'humanity' or 'human race'; 'manmade' should be replaced by 'artificial', 'constructed', or other alternatives; 'manpower' should be replaced by 'human power' or 'human energy'.[38] While not advocating the use of a brand-new gender-neutral pronoun as Miller and Swift did, the guidelines did suggest either rewording prose so that gendered pronouns could be avoided, or alternating the use of 'he' and 'she' where possible. They conceded it may be difficult to avoid the use of 'he', but if it proved to be unavoidable, they called for 'emphatic statements' in the preface and wherever possible in the text 'to the effect that the masculine pronouns are being used for succinctness and are intended to refer to both males and females'.[39] Occupational terms ending in 'man', such as 'salesman' and 'chairman' were also to be replaced by gender-neutral alternatives.[40] Most later usage guides would include this as a standard suggestion; however, it would be one change that would continue to be criticised, as would the replacement of terms such as 'mankind'.

In addition, the guidelines devoted space to discussing what they called 'non-sexist and equal use of language'. This included making sure that men and women were referred to in parallel ways, and that women were referred to as individuals and not in terms of their marital status—an example used was to say 'Indira Gandhi' or 'Prime Minister Gandhi', rather than 'Mrs Gandhi'.[41] Job titles were to be non-sexist, and men should not always be first in order of mention.[42]

The impact of the McGraw-Hill guidelines on Australia pre-dated the publication of the Australian edition. Indeed, a notable moment in the campaign against gendered language in public and institutional discourse came as early as 1974. In November of that year, Australian United Nations delegate John McCarthy (who would go on to be an Australian ambassador) argued on the floor of the UN that the issue of

---

38   Ibid., 8.
39   Ibid., 9. It should be noted that while the changing of pronouns was largely dropped as an issue until very recently, when it has come back into debate due to the issue of how to include people of non-binary gender, a recent study concludes that the use of generic masculine pronouns continues to reinforce sexist assumptions and attitudes. See Megan M. Miller and Lori E. James, 'Is the Generic Pronoun He Still Comprehended as Excluding Women', *American Journal of Psychology* 122, no. 4 (Winter 2009): 483–96.
40   Ibid., 10.
41   Ibid., 11.
42   Ibid., 12.

sexist language should be addressed by the organisation. He was quoted as saying: 'My delegation would strongly suggest that such terminology be eliminated from all intra-secretariat communications'.[43] McCarthy also asked delegates to study the McGraw-Hill guidelines, copies of which he offered to them.[44]

Calls for changes to Australian workplace practice appeared in the middle of the 1970s, although they were generally dismissed. The ACT branch of the Administrative and Clerical Officers' Association, for example, called in 1975 for a motion to be passed on prohibiting the 'use of sexist words in all its correspondence, minutes, and other documents, wherever practicable'. This motion was at least in part inspired by the impact of the McGraw-Hill guidelines.[45] However, the branch council refused to even debate the motion, citing freedom of speech.[46] Language activism was also embraced by universities through the 1970s. For example, UNSW magazine *Tharunka* provided 'a guide to non-sexist writing' in 1978 (acknowledging the McGraw-Hill guidelines), and ANU student paper *Woroni* included a lengthy article on sexist language in 1979, which acknowledged Miller and Swift's *Words and Women*.[47]

Alongside usage guides, sexism in media and educational content was also debated through the 1970s. Feminists campaigned not just to change language but to change the substantive content of things such as school curricula and television programming. From the middle of the 1970s, a number of booklets were put out by the Curriculum Development Centre to address sexism in the public sphere.[48] Dale Spender's booklet on the language of sexism (mentioned above) was first published in this series in 1975; in the same year, a pamphlet on 'non-sexist curriculum' was also published. The latter was a background paper from a conference on International Women's Year where there was some discussion about how to avoid 'sex bias' in educational materials and media. The pamphlet noted that stereotypes were 'prevalent in the media' and such stereotypes 'may restrict the life options of students'.[49] It outlined how school

---

43   'Sexist Language at UN', *Canberra Times*, 21 November 1974, 5.
44   Ibid., 5.
45   'Publisher Tries to Equalise Sexes', *Canberra Times*, 4 March 1975, 7.
46   Ibid.; '"Bias" from ACOA', *Canberra Times*, 22 February 1975, 2.
47   'A Guide to Non-Sexist Writing', *Tharunka*, 25 September 1978, 10; 'The Hard Word', *Woroni*, 11 June 1979, 12. A further article on sexist language appeared in *Woroni* on 8 September 1980, 25.
48   The Curriculum Development Centre (CDC) was a government-backed statutory body established in 1974 and absorbed into the Department of Education in 1981.
49   *Non-Sexist Curriculum* (Canberra: Curriculum Development Centre, 1975), 3.

curricula should not present 'male' and 'female' courses; should provide sex education and the study of sexism; should include women's studies courses; and should address bias in educational materials.[50]

Another element of language that feminists took up in the 1970s was the use of the title 'Ms'. Pauwels suggests that feminists saw the use of the titles 'Miss' and 'Mrs'—the designation of women by their marital status—as a 'flagrant example of sexism in language'. Spender in *Man Made Language* observed that to insist on the title Ms was to 'undermine some of the patriarchal practices'.[51] Although usage guides only sometimes discussed titles as part of general language use, the issue is worth exploring here because of its importance within the feminist movement. As Pauwels argues, the quest for the adoption of 'Ms' as an alternative title for women was an integral part of women's rights and was the 'linguistic expression of women's concern to be recognized in roles other than that of "wife of"'.[52]

Pauwels's study of the adoption of the title in Australia suggests that the title only came to be adopted at a more widespread level in the early to mid-1980s. However, as she also points out, Ms became an *alternative* rather than a *replacement* (as had first been intended) for Miss and Mrs.[53] In a survey Pauwels conducted in the mid-1980s, only 20 per cent of her respondents used the title.[54] The survey revealed that most women at that point in time saw the title as being applicable largely to divorced or de facto women—that is, women whose marital status was not, by the standards of the day, conventional.[55] Some women also regarded the use of the title as 'an ideological expression'.[56] Those who did choose to use the title explained that they did so in order to obtain equal treatment with men. Reasons for not using it included those who thought it only applied if one was divorced or in a de facto relationship, but some simply thought it 'unaesthetic'.[57] Pauwels saw the title as being adopted slowly; to hasten its adoption, it was important that the title not be exclusively associated with marital status.[58]

---

50 Ibid., 4–5.
51 Spender, *Man Made Language*, 28.
52 Anne Pauwels, 'Language in Transition: A Study of the Title "Ms" in Contemporary Australian Society', in Pauwels, *Women and Language*, 132–33.
53 Ibid., 137.
54 Ibid., 143.
55 Ibid., 140.
56 Ibid., 142.
57 Ibid., 144, 146.
58 Ibid., 147, 152.

Changing official language: Usage guides in the 1980s

The 1980s saw the official adoption of non-sexist guidelines at an institutional level in Australia and this had an influence on public discourse, especially at the government level. This was reinforced by legislative changes such as the passing of state anti-discrimination laws and the Sex Discrimination Act under the Hawke Labor Government in 1984 that made gender-discriminatory job advertisements unlawful. In addition, Australia ratified the United Nations Convention on the Elimination of All Forms of Discrimination Against Women in 1983.[59] Despite opposition to these efforts, women finally were able to claim equal rights to employment opportunities.[60] Women would continue to battle for full equality in the workplace, but the passing of the Act was a significant milestone.

It is unsurprising then that the Hawke Government also saw a return to a focus on sexist language. The Office of the Status of Women (OSW), within the Department of Prime Minister and Cabinet, took up the issue. One of the first products of this renewed focus on discriminatory language was *Fair Exposure*. This was a pamphlet published by the OSW in 1983 that provided general guidelines for the non-sexist portrayal of women in the media. The foreword, written by the Minister Assisting the Prime Minister on the Status of Women, Susan Ryan, and the Shadow Minister responsible for Women's Affairs, Ian McPhee, argued that the media was 'a powerful determinant of attitudes' and that there was a need 'to reform media portrayal of women'. The guidelines in the booklet were an important first step, it was argued, in this reform process.[61] *Fair Exposure* included several pages of guidelines on language, as well as a detailed discussion of representation of women in advertising. It acknowledged both the McGraw-Hill and Miller and Swift texts in its compilation, and took up many of the same issues around language. For example, the section on language began with a discussion of male generics, suggesting

---

59 Pauwels, 'Women and Language in Australian Society', 22.
60 Sawer, 'Women's Work Is Never Done', 81.
61 Office of the Status of Women, *Fair Exposure: Guidelines for the Constructive and Positive Portrayal and Presentation of Women in the Media* (Canberra: Australian Government Publishing Service, 1983), ii.

that 'man' and 'men' could be avoided by the use of 'person', 'people' or 'human beings'.[62] After the publication of *Fair Exposure*, numerous official language usage guidelines were drawn up.

In 1984 the Australian Broadcasting Corporation (ABC) adopted their own non-sexist language guidelines, drawn up by the ABC Standing Committee on Spoken English. These guidelines suggested that broadcasters avoid the generic use of 'he', avoid 'irrelevant gender description' and 'unequal gender description', and avoid 'sexist stereotypes and demeaning language'. Arthur Delbridge, editor of the *Macquarie Dictionary*, who headed up the Standing Committee on Spoken English, noted that the guidelines were to 'remind broadcasters of the need … for communication to be achieved in words that are appropriate in meaning and style yet not needlessly or inaccurately discriminatory'. He pointed out, however, that the lists of examples provided in the guidelines were 'open-ended, and much is left to the judgement and good taste of the individual broadcaster'.[63]

Guidelines published by the Australian Council of Trade Unions (ACTU) were adopted in 1986, drawing on a number of publications including Spender's *Man Made Language* and the ABC's 1984 guidelines. The ACTU had launched its 'Action Program for Women Workers' in 1984, which had included prescribing the elimination of discriminatory clauses and sexist language in awards. The ACTU guidelines argued that trade unions had long fought for equality for women workers, but discriminatory day-to-day language was a more recent concern to be addressed. While acknowledging that some people saw language as a trivial matter, the ACTU argued that 'language is not a trivial matter, but a symbol of underlying attitudes, and it acts as a barrier to equality'. The guidelines were not just aimed at changing the language of awards, but also at systematically revising the 'terminology used in unions in many other ways, such as union titles, letter writing, rules, journals and day-to-day spoken language'.[64]

---

62   Ibid., 5.
63   'SCOSE Guidelines on Non-Sexist Language', *SCAN* (28 May – 10 June 1984): 8–9. Thanks to Tiger Webb of the ABC for providing me with a copy of this.
64   Australian Council of Trade Union, *Non-Sexist Language: Guidelines for Unions* (Melbourne: ACTU, February 1985), 2.

Like other guidelines, the ACTU text addressed issues such as masculine pronouns, and it recommended avoiding words that contained the word 'man', avoiding terms that relate to only one sex and avoiding patronising terms. It recommended that union publications be checked for language and for the content they contained (for example, making sure there were no sexist jokes or cartoons).[65] It also addressed some issues distinctive of the language of the union movement. For example, a section was devoted to letter writing. Letters to union membership were traditionally addressed 'Dear Brother' and signed off as 'yours fraternally'; the guidelines suggested addressing members 'dear comrade (or colleague, or member)' and signing off 'yours sincerely (or faithfully)'.[66]

The ACTU guidelines concluded with a general statement on the 'importance of the educative role that the provision of non-sexist worded awards can have on men and women workers and employers'. Undertaking such change would bring equal pay and equal opportunity and treatment for women closer; '[w]e thus consider that this exercise has far greater value than a mere token gesture and as such demands widespread support'.[67] 'It is not sufficient to dismiss as irrelevant changes to the award because women are not currently employed. The award in its language should accommodate and facilitate what is hoped to be changed occupational structures in the future.'[68]

Anne Summers, feminist, writer and public servant, was one of the key figures helping not just to develop usage guidelines, but also campaigning for a general acceptance of the need for such guidelines. This battle was never entirely won, but activists such as Summers helped to articulate (and continued to assert) why it was important that public language change. Summers was just one of a number of so-called 'femocrats'— feminists who entered the bureaucracy through the 1970s and especially in the 1980s, and who helped to guide and inform public policy, especially in relation to women's issues.[69] Their influence on shaping official language and usage was significant.

---

65   Ibid., 15.
66   Ibid., 14.
67   Ibid., 19.
68   Ibid., 20.
69   See Marian Sawer, *Sisters in Suits: Women and Public Policy in Australia* (Sydney: Allen & Unwin, 1990), 21–25. The term 'femocrat' was first used in 1983 and is an Australianism; see *Australian National Dictionary*, 2nd ed. (Melbourne: Oxford University Press, 2016), vol. 1, 600.

In 1986, Summers, then First Assistant Secretary with the Office of the Status of Women, addressed the Style Council on the new inclusive language chapter that was to be included in the *Commonwealth Style Guide*. The Style Council in the 1980s was a powerful body that helped to 'judge' appropriate language usage in the public sphere. Most notably, it helped in the production of the *Commonwealth Style Guide* that determined government usage and informed much public writing. Summers argued in her address that the chapter aimed 'to encourage the use of language which explicitly <u>includes</u> women and thereby acknowledges their existence and their contribution to our society'.[70] She also commented that '[w]e believe encouraging people to use different language will encourage them to think differently about women—including the way women think of themselves'.[71] Language as it existed at that point in time did not, she concluded, 'provide well enough for women to be described with dignity'.[72] Examples of language guidelines in the chapter echo those we have already seen. For government use, recommendations such as the use of 'chair' over 'chairman' and 'Ombud' rather than 'Ombudsman' had direct consequences for official government style and usage.[73]

Criticism and resistance

None of this linguistic activism and the attempts to reform usage occurred without significant resistance. Through the 1970s and 1980s (and beyond), plenty of arguments were raised, largely from conservative quarters, as to why all of this was unacceptable.

The conservative argument against language change was often couched in terms of arguing against the notion that language could be 'engineered'. This argument was often based on the idea that language was 'natural', and could not be artificially changed (and even if it could, this would be impractical and difficult). Much of this tied into a view that focused on using linguistic evidence to argue that language was inherently neutral. The most common example cited here was 'mankind', which many

---

[70] Anne Summers, 'Inclusive Language: Address to Style Council '86, Macquarie University, Sydney', 1–2, Papers of Style Council 1986, Australian National Dictionary Centre Archives. Emphasis in original.
[71] Ibid., 8–9.
[72] Ibid., 10.
[73] 'Draft of Inclusive Language Chapter for Commonwealth Style Manual', included with Papers of Style Council 1986, 3, 5.

argued was not gendered because of its long history of usage to refer to all of humanity. This overlapped with those who feared the dangers of change and who argued that non-sexist language often resorted to euphemisms and 'double-speak'. Language changed in the ways proposed would lack clarity. Some also argued that such change was meaningless: it could not actually change attitudes.

The 1984 ABC guidelines drew a variety of comments in the press that reveal some of the lines of argument. One editorial reported that one of the members of the ABC Standing Committee on Spoken English had found most members of the public were opposed to the guidelines. The editorial criticised the guidelines as 'a mixture of common sense and almost paranoid avoidance of "sexist" terms'. The usual objections were raised, such as the etymology and history of 'man' and 'mankind', and the fact that alternatives to sexist language were generally 'clumsy'.[74] Professor Ralph Elliott, an ANU English professor and regular reviewer for the *Canberra Times*, commenting on the ABC guidelines suggested:

> The cause of women is better served by a positive use of words which, wherever applicable, acknowledge their sex than by banning a large treasury of English words from the common vocabulary and prescribing colourless words of neutral, or neuter, connotation in their place.[75]

Both the editorial and Elliott's comments were challenged. Marian Sawer (then of the Women's Electoral Lobby) responded that the dropping of the generic use of 'man' was 'not engaging in the political manipulation of language—rather we are exposing it'.[76] Responding to Elliott's comments, two members of the ANU Women's Studies department, Dorothy Broom and B. Refshauge, argued for the value of guidelines such as the ABC's. They argued that both Elliott and the newspaper editorialist, in calling for more 'positive use of words', failed to specify what this language could actually be. They concluded that 'in the interest of accuracy as well as equity we should strive to avoid constructions implying that the male is the human norm from which the female is a diverting exception'.[77]

---

74   'The Neuter ABC', *Canberra Times*, 20 May 1984, 2.
75   Ibid.
76   Letter to the editor, *Canberra Times*, 4 June 1984, 2.
77   Letter to the editor, *Canberra Times*, 6 June 1984, 21.

Anne Pauwels was responsible for writing the chapter on inclusive language for the 1988 edition of the Australian *Style Manual* and recounts in her book *Women Changing Language* the backlash the chapter received. She summarises the range of criticisms thus: 'The guidelines were described as an attempt to de-sex language, to take sex out of language, to castrate language, to manipulate language, to can the man, to ban words, to outlaw words, to force manufactured words into usage'.[78] Some of the responses attest to the strong emotions that came into play, such as this letter to the editor in the *Australian*: 'This campaign is not only destroying our fine language ... but is designed to emasculate the virility characteristic of a young and enterprising country'.[79] The vitriol towards feminists was demonstrated by others, and the irrationality of the position is encapsulated in this letter: 'No wonder the Australian female cannot be taken seriously by males in their quest for equal opportunities when we are represented by dehydrated Mses with their psychotic dribbling of human eating sharks'.[80] Mainstream media also subjected the guidelines to ridicule. An opinion piece in the *Australian Financial Review* made fun of the change of job titles with 'man' in them and joked that his own name ('Waterman') would now have to change; indeed, 'person' was an inadequate substitute, he argued, all 'persons' should be 'perthings'.[81]

The move to condemn so-called 'political correctness' ignited from the late 1980s, and language guidelines have been favourite targets of conservative critics. John Howard's government in the 1990s, for example, attempted to bring back the use of 'chairman' in government publications and usage. A debate in federal parliament in 1997 over the use of 'chair' vs 'chairman' in the Productivity Commission Bill is indicative of the kinds of arguments posed by both sides. Senator Andrew Murray, an Australian Democrat, called for amendments to the Bill to change 'chairman' to 'chair'. He acknowledged that the Liberal Coalition was unlikely to support the amendments, but nevertheless stated that the use of chairman was 'demeaning, belittling and marginalising ... to many Australian women'.[82] Language was, Murray argued, 'a very potent force of both oppression and change. How we use language sends messages

---

78 Pauwels, *Women Changing Language*, 186.
79 Letter, October 13, 1988, quoted in ibid., 187.
80 Letter to the editor, *West Australian*, 11 October 1988, quoted in ibid., 188.
81 Peter Waterman, 'Newsperthing Bites Canberra-Speak', *Australian Financial Review*, 12 October 1988, 12.
82 Commonwealth, Parliamentary Debates, Senate, 1 September 1997, 6105, www.aph.gov.au/Parliamentary_Business/Hansard/.

about what sort of society we are'.[83] Murray expressed his disappointment that more women in the Coalition had not fought against the reversion to chairman. Michèle Asprey, a lawyer and plain language consultant, wrote in *Australian Style* (the newsletter of the Australian Style Council) later that year that Howard's push was, she believed, 'a disturbing symptom of the way the government is thinking about women more generally'.[84] Yet this commentary was met with a typical response from conservative quarters, with one man, Colin Taylor, writing to *Australian Style* to say that he was surprised to find the newsletter advocating non-sexist language, that made-up constructions such as 'chairperson' were unacceptable and that the 'pressure to disfigure the language to suit a vociferous minority' should be resisted.[85]

'Political correctness' became a common term of abuse used by the conservative wing of Australian politics (as it also became in the United States and the United Kingdom). As linguists Keith Allan and Kate Burridge argue, politically correct language is accused of being a form of euphemism, but in fact this is not always or commonly the case.[86] The debates over political correctness are too extensive to discuss here, but undoubtedly language and language change has been a major focus of criticism of so-called 'political correctness'.[87] This continues to be the case.

Two recent examples will suffice. The use of the term 'chairperson' continues to be contentious. In 2012, it was reported that Tony Abbott (then leader of the Opposition and a conservative) called the head of the Sydney University Student Representative Council a 'chair-thing' when she objected to being called a 'chairman'.[88] This reflects just one recent conservative complaint about the use of a gender-neutral alternative to 'chairman'. In 2016, the release of the Victorian Government's public service guidelines on inclusive language caused a furore in the press. In particular, the guidelines addressed the issue of language that could be properly inclusive of transgender and LGBTIQ people. The guidelines

---

83   Ibid., 6106.
84   Michèle Asprey, 'A Chair with No Leg to Stand On', *Australian Style* 6, no. 1 (December 1997), 2.
85   Colin Taylor, letter to the editor, *Australian Style* 6, no. 2 (June 1998): 5.
86   Keith Allan and Kate Burridge, *Forbidden Words: Taboo and the Censoring of Language* (Cambridge: Cambridge University Press, 2006), 96.
87   For further discussion of language and political correctness, see Sarah Dunant, ed., *The War of the Words: The Political Correctness Debate* (London: Virago Press, 1994).
88   Myriam Robin, 'Origin of the Species: Is "Chairman" a Gender-Neutral Term?' *Smart Company*, 19 October 2012; Howard Mann, 'Mansplaining the Word of the Year—and Why It Matters', 9 February 2015.

therefore revisited the use of gender-neutral pronouns, such as 'zie'. Critics rejected the guidelines, with one conservative academic, Jeremy Sammut from the Centre for Independent Studies, arguing that the guide was dictated by 'academics wielding their critical postmodernist theory of the world' who were 'determined to force [it] on the rest of us'. 'It's a totalitarian project dressed up as liberation theory', he concluded.[89]

Despite the ongoing debates over alleged 'politically correct' language change, is it possible to trace real change in sexist language, if not in attitudes? Pam Peters in her study of the power of usage guides to shape grammar and language has concluded that style manuals and usage guides have 'limited power … to dictate the paths of change against the tide of common usage'.[90] However, debates over sexist language have, arguably, helped to shift 'common usage'. Anne Pauwels writing in the 1990s concluded that real change had occurred. While it was difficult to assess an impact on spoken language, she argued that it was possible to trace an impact in written language. This was especially the case in institutional language, in education and in publishing.[91] Furthermore, ongoing debates around usage can, I would suggest, still raise awareness and influence our perceptions and practice around usage.

Language activism prompts much debate over whether it is proper to try and engineer language change. The feminist movement demonstrated that it was possible to go some way to changing attitudes by changing language, I would argue, but this was not done (and still is not done) without considerable resistance. In the current political climate where women's rights are under threat, and where we are seeing a populist surge that rejects so-called political correctness (and hence legitimises sexist and racist language), this may be an opportune time to learn from the story of feminist linguistic activism of the 1970s and 1980s.

---

89 'LGBTI's Guide to Safespeak', *Geelong Advertiser*, 17 December 2016, 21.
90 Pam Peters, 'Usage Guides and Usage Trends in Australian and British English', *Australian Journal of Linguistics* 34, no. 4 (2014): 597, doi.org/10.1080/07268602.2014.929082.
91 Pauwels, *Women Changing Language*, 204–13.

CHAPTER 14

'A race of intelligent super-giants': The Whitlams, gendered bodies and political authority in modern Australia

Bethany Phillips-Peddlesden[1]

Gough and Margaret Whitlam stood out as a political couple. 'When [Margaret] travels overseas with Gough', one woman told the *Sydney Morning Herald* after the December 1972 federal election, 'they'll be thinking Australians are a race of intelligent super-giants … [T]hey stand head and shoulders above the populace and I think this is one of the things that appealed to the voters. People like someone to look up to'.[2] The Whitlams' relationship was characterised as both a personal and political asset: 'The Prime Minister obviously sees Margaret as a person, not as an appendage of himself. Today the wife of a politician has a very important part to play and Margaret Whitlam is up to the task'.[3] The new prime ministerial couple were portrayed in the sympathetic press as harbingers of progressive politics, as the first modern political 'power couple', and Margaret Whitlam as an exemplar of the increasingly radical

---

1   I would like to gratefully acknowledge the assistance of the bursary which facilitated my participation in the Personal as Political confererence.
2   'Margaret Whitlam Leaves Men at a Loss for Words', *Sydney Morning Herald*, 8 December 1972.
3   Ibid.

demands of Australian women.[4] This reception reflected contemporary consciousness of women's changing roles and wider questioning of Australia's gender relationships, national character and international status.

Following his appointment as Australian Labor Party deputy leader in 1960, Whitlam waged a crusade to 'modernise' the party's organisational structures and policies. As parliamentary leader from 1967, he set about further rejuvenation, aimed at broadening Labor's electoral base to include progressive middle-class, professional and university-educated voters. This required a shift in the party's image, from a reputation as strategically, ideologically and structurally old-fashioned to one of contemporary relevancy. Cultivating and identifying with a mood for change, Labor's increasing political viability contrasted with the Liberal Party's seeming inertia and lack of an alternative vision for the future. Labor's electoral fortunes were enhanced by Whitlam's urbane performance of authoritative masculinity and the couple's perceived modernity.

Whitlam has been widely attributed with shifting the Australian political landscape through his impact on Labor institutions, and his eventful period as prime minister, 1972–75. Margaret Whitlam's reputation as a new type of political wife amplified this interpretation. The following focuses on the key role normalised ideologies of gender played in shaping the political images of both Gough and Margaret Whitlam. The reading of leadership is a gendered political statement, not a neutral or ahistorical process, even (or particularly) when men are compared with other men.[5] As gender theorist Michael Kimmel has noted, twentieth-century politicians 'have found it necessary both to proclaim their own manhood and to raise questions about their opponents' manhood',[6] including at the level of the body. Gender is thus revealed as an evaluative, explanatory and descriptive tool in politics.

Examining the history of male leaders' embodied practices in national contexts allows us to explore the shifting meanings of masculinity (and femininity) in Australian history. Theorists have increasingly revealed

---

4 Including Diane Langmore, *Prime Ministers' Wives: The Public and Private Lives of Ten Australian Women* (Ringwood: McPhee Gribble, 1992), 255; and Stephanie Peatling, 'Margaret Whitlam a Trailblazer', *Canberra Times*, 18 March 2012, 6.
5 Marilyn Lake, 'The Politics of Respectability: Identifying the Masculinist Context', *Historical Studies* 22, no. 86 (1986): 116–31, doi.org/10.1080/10314618608595739; Kate Murphy, 'Feminism and Political History', *Australian Journal of Politics and History* 56, no. 1 (2010): 25, doi.org/10.1111/j.1467-8497.2010.01539.x.
6 Michael Kimmel, 'Invisible Masculinity', *Society* 30 (1993): 28, doi.org/10.1007/BF02700272.

the importance of analysing the gendered processes of embodiment.[7] For example, American historian Kathleen Canning has noted how the political body is invoked to signify different class, race, ideological or political judgements and positions.[8] There has been significant work done on the marginalisation of female and non-white bodies in politics, but white hegemonic male bodies have not received substantial critical attention.[9] As I have argued elsewhere, we need to notice, and thus to denaturalise and historicise, the ways in which specific styles of embodied white manhood have been employed as markers of political legitimacy.[10]

Analyses of male political contests must remain conscious of the effects of these gendered constructions on women—political discourses naturalise a link between particular types of embodied masculinities and power.[11] Separate gendered spheres were constitutive of the way men, women and family life have been interpreted by contemporaries and written into (or out of) Australian political history. As such, Whitlam's modern image included the invocation of his 'private' roles as husband and father, and the public endorsement of his wife. The feminist ideas that would be embedded in Labor's welfare state were brought further into the mainstream by Margaret Whitlam's progressive pronouncements as a political consort. Yet her political capital also contributed to the election of a Labor Government with no female representatives in 1972.[12] An inherent tension thus existed between Margaret Whitlam's role as a women's liberation 'fellow traveller' and fulfilment of the expectations of prime

---

7   Including Judith Butler, *Gender Trouble: Feminism and the Subversion of Identity* (New York: Routledge, 1999); Fiona Webster, 'Do Bodies Matter? Sex, Gender and Politics', *Australian Feminist Studies* 17, no. 38 (2002): 191–205, doi.org/10.1080/08164640220147960; and Amanda Sinclair, 'Body Possibilities in Leadership', *Leadership* 1, no. 4 (2005): 387, doi.org/10.1177/1742715005057231.
8   Kathleen Canning, 'The Body as Method? Reflections on the Place of the Body in Gender History', *Gender and History* 1, no. 3 (1999): 505, doi.org/10.1111/1468-0424.00159.
9   A key Australian example is Julia Baird, *Media Tarts: How the Australian Press Frames Female Politicians* (Melbourne: Scribe, 2004).
10 Bethany Phillips-Peddlesden, '"A Stronger Man and a More Virile Character": Australian Prime Ministers, Embodied Manhood and Political Authority in the Early Twentieth Century', *Australian Historical Studies* 48, no. 4 (2017): 502–18, doi.org/10.1080/1031461X.2017.1323932.
11 Toby L. Ditz, 'The New Men's History and the Peculiar Absence of Gendered Power: Some Remedies from Early American Gender History', *Gender & History* 16, no. 1 (2004): 7, doi.org 10.1111/j.0953-5233.2004.324_1.x.
12 Lyndal Ryan, 'Feminism and the Federal Bureaucracy, 1972–1983', in *Playing the State: Australian Feminist Interventions*, ed. Sophie Watson (Sydney: Allen & Unwin, 1990); Margaret Thornton, 'Feminism and the Changing State', *Australian Feminist Studies* 21, no. 50 (2006): 151–72, doi.org/10.1080/08164640600731747.

minister's wife.[13] Despite Whitlam's progressive legislative agenda and the realities of Margaret Whitlam's liminal political positioning, gendered division remained in the interpretation of the couple's roles in the 'public' sphere. Gender continued to mark the boundaries of the political.

This chapter examines the continuities as well as the changes in the gendering of political culture and claiming of political authority during Whitlam's tenure. In what follows, the reforming, not revolutionary, nature of the Whitlams' gender politics is explored through a focus on the interpretation of Margaret Whitlam as a representative of modern Australian womanhood, and on the ways Whitlam's embodiment was implicated in his masculine political authority. I begin with a critical examination of the Whitlams in Australian historiography, recognising political history as a body of knowledge that (re)produces power relationships and gender norms. Next this chapter analyses masculine authority in contemporary contestations of political legitimacy. Whitlam legitimised his reforming political agenda by reproducing a respectable, middle-class masculine leadership model, as his physical stature was linked to his political and intellectual standing. This chapter then examines how the gendered logics and structures of the public/private divide were employed in Labor's 1972 election campaign. And, finally, I examine the interpretation of Margaret Whitlam as a new kind of political wife to explore the gendered political culture that shaped the possibilities of her public role. By re-examining key political sources (state archives, newspapers and published auto/biographical works), we can explore how gendered assumptions, language and political structures have shaped the way the Whitlams have been written into Australian history.

The Whitlams in Australian political history

Contemporary and historiographical assessments of Gough Whitlam's leadership focused on his substantial legacy, ego, marital relationship and stature. Labor's election has been commonly framed through a narrative of progress—a Whitlam-driven acceleration into modern Australia out

---

13   Susan Magarey, 'Women's Liberation Was a Movement, Not an Organisation', *Australian Feminist Studies* 29, no. 82 (2014): 380, doi.org/10.1080/08164649.2014.976898.

of the slow lane of the Menzies era.[14] The voluminous literature on Whitlam began contemporaneously, with political journalists publishing dissections of his rise, prime ministership and political demise.[15] The 1970s and 1980s saw a proliferation of such political biographies and histories in an expanding range of genres, including psychoanalysis, class, party organisations and political crises.[16] Partisan attempts to define an Australian story increasingly used historical portrayals of prime ministers to signify party meaning and national character, while Whitlam became a figure contemporary Labor defined itself against, and later reclaimed.[17] Enduring interest saw popular and academic scholarship on the Whitlam Government continue to be published during and beyond the interminable Howard years.[18] Yet the necessarily gendered nature of political leadership went unrecognised; the literature instead reflecting and compounding gendered interpretations of prime ministers by focusing on their wit, temperament and physical appeal, the acquisition and loss of power.

Whitlam was, and continues to be, portrayed in history as 'a man of commanding physical presence'.[19] Historians Robin Gerster and Jan Bassett have noted how his height shaped the language used to describe him and 'augmented his rhetorical gravity'.[20] Such historical readings of Whitlam's embodied political authority rest on a naturalised, rather than natural, association between physical stature and authority. Wallace Brown's

---

14 This narrative endures, particularly in popular history. However, a number of recent critical works complicate this reading, including Nick Cater, 'Hearts and Minds: The Meaning of "It's Time"', and Frank Bongiorno, 'Whitlam, the 1960s and the Program', in *The Whitlam Legacy*, ed. Troy Bramston, rev. ed. (Annandale: Federation Press, 2015); and Greg Melleuish, 'E G Whitlam: Reclaiming the Initiative in Australian History', in *Making Modern Australia: The Whitlam Government's 21st Century Agenda*, ed. Jenny Hocking (Melbourne: Monash University Publishing, 2017).
15 Including L. Oakes and D. Solomon, *The Making of an Australian Prime Minister* (Melbourne: Cheshire, 1973); Paul Kelly, *The Unmaking of Gough* (Sydney: Angus and Robertson, 1976); and Graham Freudenburg, *A Certain Grandeur* (Melbourne: Macmillan, 1977).
16 Including Allan Patience and Brian Head, eds, *From Whitlam to Fraser: Reform and Reaction in Australian Politics* (Melbourne: Oxford University Press, 1979); Michael Sexton, *Illusions of Power: The Fate of a Reform Government* (Sydney: Allen & Unwin, 1979); and James Walter, *The Leader: A Political Biography of Gough Whitlam* (St Lucia: University of Queensland Press, 1980).
17 See Carol Johnson, *The Labor Legacy: Curtin, Chifley, Whitlam, Hawke* (Sydney: Allen & Unwin, 1989); and Jenny Hocking and Colleen Lewis, eds, *It's Time Again: Whitlam and Modern Labor* (Melbourne: Circa, 2003).
18 Including James Curran, *Unholy Fury: Whitlam and Nixon at War* (Melbourne: Melbourne University Press, 2015); and Paul Kelly and Troy Bramston, *The Dismissal: In the Queen's Name* (Melbourne: Penguin, 2016).
19 James Walter, 'Gough Whitlam: Bursting Limitations', in *Political Lives*, ed. Judith Brett (Sydney: Allen & Unwin, 1997), 31.
20 Robin Gerster and Jan Bassett, *Seizures of Youth: The Sixties and Australia* (Melbourne: Hyland House, 1991), 169.

comparative analysis of Whitlam and his rivals is a representative example, arguing that 'all the symbolism and imagery was against McMahon': 'a tall, confident imposing figure versus an often nervous "Little Billy" with big ears'. The political contest was thus one sided: 'a witty and imperious Opposition Leader who knew his time was coming, versus the Liberals' last-choice Prime Minister ... the giant versus the dwarf'.[21]

As well as assessments of Whitlam's political legitimacy, historians have continued to re-examine his government's program in the context of contemporary debates over Labor's legacy and future. Into the 1990s, women remained at best peripheral in historical examinations of the period. Most analyses of the Labor Government's impact on gender relations have been contained within recent anthologies or in literature focusing on women in Australian history.[22] For example, the most recent monograph includes a chapter on a Whitlam government investigation of women's changing place in society.[23] Much of this scholarship has portrayed Margaret Whitlam's role and the couple's marriage as an illustrative example of Labor's progressive gender politics.

Early biographical works on Whitlam only briefly noted the couple's similarities in height and intelligence, and her supportive political role. Turn-of-the-century literature focused on Margaret Whitlam's 'modernity', forthrightness and life outside her marriage, and explored her auxiliary political role.[24] However, these works continued to employ gender tropes such as natural marital complementarity and conventional political history paradigms. Biographer Susan Mitchell's analysis is typical: Whitlam had 'innate feminism' while the couple were 'exact opposites in terms of personality and talents. These two opposites formed a great team'.[25] While these later studies went beyond trite references to wifely support, no historical work has provided a gender analysis of

---

21 Wallace Brown, *Ten Prime Ministers: Life among the Politicians* (Double Bay: Longueville Books, 2002), 101. Also, Mungo MacCallum, *The Whitlam Mob* (Melbourne: Black Inc., 2014), 142.

22 Including Marian Sawer, 'Reinventing the Labor Party? From Laborism to Equal Opportunity', in Hocking and Lewis, *It's Time Again*; and Carol Johnson, 'Gough Whitlam and Labor Tradition', in Bramston, *The Whitlam Legacy*.

23 Michelle Arrow, 'An Enquiry into the Whole Human Condition? Whitlam, Sexual Citizenship and the Royal Commission on Human Relationships', in Hocking, *Making Modern Australia*.

24 Langmore, *Prime Ministers' Wives*; Susan Mitchell, *Margaret Whitlam: A Biography* (Milson's Point, NSW: Random House, 2006); Jenny Hocking, *Gough Whitlam: A Moment in History* (Melbourne: Melbourne University Press, 2008); Jenny Hocking, *Gough Whitlam: His Time*, updated (Melbourne: Miegunyah Press, 2014).

25 Susan Mitchell, *Margaret and Gough: The Love Story That Shaped a Nation* (Sydney: Hachette, 2014), 122, 141, 317.

their political images and impact. Yet the Whitlams' important role in Australian political history needs to be contextualised within the longer history of the gendered construction of political office.

'A towering and commanding figure': Embodiment and political authority

Arthur Calwell, following his own removal from Labor leadership, despaired at the party's new direction and composition. Writing with some bitterness to the widow of former prime minister John Curtin in 1970, Calwell argued that, under his successor Whitlam, the party had changed beyond recognition, or repair:

> The Labour Party [sic] today has too many academics and long-haired and mini-skirted people in its ranks, and I am afraid that some of the top people in this party will do us as much harm as ever Billy Hughes did if ever they get the chance.[26]

This pointed questioning of Whitlam's class loyalty reflected the discomfort socially conservative, working-class Labor elements felt with the party's new style, class composition, priorities and changing gender relations. Suspicion of Whitlam's lack of working-class credentials was often articulated through a focus on his authoritative body, as his physique, dress, mannerisms and leadership style were read as evidence of his class (dis)loyalty and political character. Personal domination, oratory and control of policy direction were central to Liberal Party leadership.[27] Bruce Grant has argued that Whitlam had an ambivalent relationship with conservative politicians, holding 'them in disdain while sharing their style'.[28] His leadership attitude and middle-class appearance were therefore the focus of internal challenges to his legitimacy as a Labor leader.[29] Advocates attempted to counter this unease through reference to Whitlam's intellectual qualities and policy vision, his commitment to promoting equality of opportunity and, crucially, his growing political legitimacy and thus potential ability to win government.[30]

---

26 Arthur Calwell, letter to Elsie Curtin, 15 January 1970, 'Personal Letters from Elsie Curtin', series 21, box 73, Arthur Calwell Papers, MS 4738, National Library of Australia, Canberra.
27 Judith Brett, *Australian Liberals and the Moral Middle Class: From Alfred Deakin to John Howard* (Melbourne: Cambridge University Press, 2003), doi.org/10.1017/CBO9780511481642.
28 Bruce Grant, 'Introduction', *The Whitlam Phenomenon*, 3.
29 Troy Bramston, 'The Whitlam Ascendency', in Bramston, *The Whitlam Legacy*, 1.
30 Elizabeth Riddell, 'Whitlam: The Fashionable New Look in Labor', *Sydney Mirror*, 20 March 1960, 43.

Figure 14.1: A towering figure on the world stage. Gough Whitlam and Margaret Whitlam with the Emperor and Empress of Japan, 1973.
Source: National Archives of Australia: A6135, K16/11/73/69.

By the late 1960s, television had become a key medium for political communication.[31] This new visibility, in combination with an increased focus on party leaders and new advertising techniques, intensified the significance of an authoritative image.[32] The Whitlams proved adept at generating positive public exposure and cultivating a strong political image. Gough Whitlam quickly developed a reputation as 'a Colossus', in the words of a fellow Labor member, who described him as 'a big man in every sense who helped all of us and our country walk taller'.[33] Contemporary political commentary made almost universal reference to Whitlam's height and appearance, depicting his body as a political asset on a national and international stage. He was described by colleagues and the press as 'imposing', a 'towering and commanding figure' whose dominance in parliament was due to his 'eloquence, his erudition … [and] his witty

---

31 Gerster and Bassett, *Seizures of Youth*, 169.
32 Bridget Griffen-Foley, *Party Games: Australian Politicians and the Media from War to Dismissal* (Melbourne: Text Publishing, 2003); Sally Young, 'Selling Australian Politicians: Political Advertising 1949–2001' (PhD thesis, University of Melbourne, 2003); Stephanie Brookes, *Politics, Media and Campaign Language: Australia's Identity Anxiety* (London: Anthem Press, 2017).
33 Mike Rann, 'Gough Whitlam', *Round Table* 103, no. 6 (2014): 600, doi.org/10.1080/00358533.2014.988029.

and sometimes devastating repartee, allied to his commanding stature'.[34] As a national leader, Whitlam was also seen to embody the Australian nation in gendered ways—he was a representative of national *manhood*. Whitlam's physique, hair and sartorial style were described in evaluations of his electoral attractiveness and ability to engender the necessary gravitas of prime ministerial office. His body was overwhelmingly appraised as authoritative and sufficiently masculine for the necessary stamina, belligerence and assertion of will needed to succeed in politics.

The frequent commentary on Whitlam's masculine physique reveals the link made between the masculinities of leaders and political legitimacy in Australian political culture. Whitlam was measured against alternative Liberal Party leaders (as well as potential Labor rivals). In contrast to the frequent references to Whitlam's physical stature and attractiveness, his 1972 Liberal Party rival, William McMahon, was consistently found wanting. This reflected the ascendency of a dominant leadership style, personified by Robert Menzies and later practised, with mixed success, by Whitlam. In contrast, colleagues and opponents rhetorically linked McMahon's weak leadership to his diminutive physique, reading his body as an externalisation of personal and political character. For example, in a litany of diminutives Liberal Cabinet colleague Paul Hasluck associated McMahon's small stature with deficient morals and political illegitimacy. He was 'a contemptible creature', a 'sorry little person … extremely sensitive about his lack of manly qualities', a perpetual liar, a 'sneak', a 'tick', a 'puny little fellow', a treacherous and 'dirty little bastard'.[35]

From the late 1960s, a political culture that valued authoritative masculine leadership had increasingly normalised a strategy of belittling politicians through reference to inadequate physical and verbal performances.[36] Historians including Robert Manne have argued that Whitlam and the press utilised this 'politics of derision' against their Liberal rivals, including mocking McMahon's body, oratory and leadership.[37] However, they have not recognised the specifically gendered nature of this derision.

---

34 Alan Reid, *The Whitlam Venture* (Melbourne: Hill of Content, 1976), 1; Gareth Evans, 'The Build Up to 1972', *The Whitlam Phenomenon* (Melbourne: McPhee Gribble/Penguin, 1986), 177; Ralph Willis, 'A View from the Backbench', in Bramston, *The Whitlam Legacy*, 122.
35 Paul Hasluck, *The Chance of Politics* (Melbourne: Text Publishing, 1997), 184–94.
36 Gerster and Bassett, *Seizures of Youth*, 169.
37 Including Robert Manne, 'The Whitlam Revolution', in *The Australian Century: Political Struggle in the Building of a Nation*, ed. Robert Manne (Melbourne: Text Publishing, 1999), 181; and James Carleton, *The Wit of Whitlam* (Melbourne: Melbourne University Press, 2014), viii.

John Gorton was undermined by his detractors, including Whitlam's supporters, for his inability to speak clearly and forcefully, like a proper man.[38] For McMahon, the focus of derision was on his inability to embody masculine political leadership qualities, including eloquence, a forceful will and a virile body: 'With his puny stature, his high-pitched voice, his ageing playboy demeanour and his apparently outmoded views, McMahon was constructed by the media as a comical figure of a bygone age'.[39] His anachronistic qualities were exaggerated through comparison to the more youthful Whitlam (and Sonia, McMahon's much younger wife). McMahon's political authority was thus challenged by emasculating references to his aged, diminutive, unassertive, insufficiently masculine body, and even his sexuality.[40]

Furthermore, in the wake of Prime Minister Holt's death in 1967, Gorton and then McMahon were unable to consolidate their party leadership. This allowed Labor to disseminate the idea that the Liberals weren't modern but instead remained anchored to the past by the weight of Robert Menzies's influence. It also meant that Whitlam was implicitly (and often explicitly) compared with Menzies.[41] The language used to describe Whitlam echoed that of Menzies: he too had a forceful, masculine presence that revealed, even conferred, political dominance.[42] The similarities in the aggression, wit and bodies of Menzies and Whitlam were mobilised to promote the latter's political skill and leadership potential.[43] Whitlam's physical dominance, ascendency in parliament, biting wit, erudition and respectable middle-class appearance therefore supported his claim to political legitimacy in modern Australia.

---

38   Alan Reid, *The Gorton Experiment* (Sydney: Shakespeare Head Press, 1971).
39   Manne, 'The Whitlam Revolution', 181.
40   In discussing rumours about his sexuality, McMahon attempted to prove his heterosexual virility: 'when I was single, it could have been charged that exactly the opposite was true of me'. Interview in Ray Aitchison, ed., *Looking at the Liberals* (Melbourne: Cheshire, 1974), 15.
41   Paul Strangio, Paul 't Hart and James Walter, *The Pivot of Power: Australian Prime Ministers and Political Leadership* (Melbourne: Miegunyah Press, 2017), 89, 116.
42   Katharine West, *Power in the Liberal Party: A Study in Australian Politics* (Melbourne: Cheshire, 1965), 255; Don Whitington, *The Rulers: Fifteen Years of the Liberals* (Melbourne: Landsdowne Press, 1964), 101; Pat Farmer, *Menzies: Man and Myth* (Kenthurst: Kangaroo Press, 1983), 228.
43   Craig McGregor, *Profile of Australia* (Ringwood: Penguin, 1966), 204.

'Winning the female vote!' The Whitlams, gender and the 1972 federal election campaign

While Menzies and Whitlam were very different politicians, not least in political longevity, they shared style and personality traits, and flaws. Both developed reputations as cold and arrogant, which both attempted to soften by demonstrating an affiliation with normal Australians' concerns. One of the main vehicles of each man's endeavour to change his image was an extensive political advertising campaign. Menzies's costly 1949 campaign was designed by the Hansen Rubensohn Company. Featuring an innovative use of radio, it aimed to 'promote the softer side of Menzies' personality' and portray him as a 'man of the people'.[44] Similarly, the perception of Whitlam as aloof was addressed in part through a campaign emphasising his 'private' relationships as husband and father, and the foregrounding of his wife.

Labor's 1972 election campaign promoted not only the party but also, more specifically, Whitlam as leader. The 'It's Time' campaign has received historiographical attention for its public relations and marketing research innovations, political strategies and emphasis on political image.[45] Yet there has been no critical analysis of the link made between the highlighting of Whitlam's 'private' life and his political viability. Examining the public relations recommendations and political strategies reveal the gendered assumptions and masculinist political structures that shaped Labor's campaign, and the ways the ambiguous relationship between the 'private' and the 'political' was exploited by men in politics.

---

44   Julian Fitzgerald, *On Message: Political Communications of Australian Prime Ministers 1901–2014* (Canberra: Clareville Press, 2014), 222.
45   Including Glenn Kefford, *All Hail the Leaders: The Australian Labor Party and Political Leadership* (North Melbourne: Australian Scholarly Publishing, 2015), 70; Murray Goot, 'It's Time: Spectrum's Market Research, Modern Campaigning, and Whitlam's Mandate', in Hocking, *Making Modern Australia*, 295, 303; Robert Crawford, 'Modernising Menzies, Whitlam and Australian Elections', *The Drawing Board: An Australian Review of Public Affairs* 4, no. 3 (2004): 139; Vicky Braund, 'Timely Vibrations: Labor's Marketing Campaign', in *Labor to Power: Australia's 1972 Election*, ed. Henry Mayer (Sydney: Angus and Robertson, 1973), 19, doi.org/10.1080/00323267308401315; Stephen Mills, *The New Machine Men: Polls and Persuasion in Australian Politics* (Melbourne: Penguin, 1986), 134; and Young, 'Selling Australian Politicians', 321, 621.

In the postwar period, the Liberal Party had proved adept at appealing to women through their domestic identities, while Labor continued to frame Australian politics around issues of class and the concerns of male breadwinners. By the late 1960s, this perspective shaped Labor's reputation as old-fashioned, masculine and undemocratically trade-union dominated. Yet gender progressiveness was increasingly linked to modernity, and Whitlam wished to modernise the party. In 1971, Labor hired Spectrum International Marketing Services to research the party's image, and public relations company Hansen-Rubensohn-McCann-Erickson to devise their federal election campaign. Spectrum's initial report contained a key conclusion: Margaret Whitlam was a potential political asset, perceived as intelligent, warm and down-to-earth.[46] This was welcome news, as another major finding was that Labor, and Whitlam, had an image problem, especially with women. In order to address the gender imbalance in voting intentions, the marketing consultants urged Labor to 'soften' Whitlam's image and increase his presence on platforms favoured by women.[47] But their key recommendation was to use Margaret Whitlam to promote her husband, and Labor, to women. This strategy became a central plank in the proposal submitted by Hansen Rubensohn McCann Erickson in December 1971.[48]

While Labor's 1972 election platform did not elaborate policies specifically relating to women, strong lobbying by groups such as the Women's Electoral Lobby (WEL) and female Labor members saw them given more attention.[49] Labor candidates generally scored better in the WEL surveys conducted to determine politicians' attitudes to feminist concerns such as equal pay and abortion. Yet this focus did not just reflect the influence of WEL. It was also a sincerely held conviction by many newer Labor members, including Whitlam. Furthermore, the public relations surveys independently highlighted Labor's need to attract women.

---

46   'Political Parties, Leader & Issues: A Pilot Study of Voters' Attitudes', Report for the Australia Labor Party by Spectrum International Marketing Services, 11 August 1971, item EGW 44043, box 0205, The Whitlam Institute, Sydney (Whitlam Institute).
47   They made no mention of developing *policies* that would appeal to women.
48   'It's Time' Proposal from Hansen-Rubensohn-McCann-Erickson, 7 December 1971, Copy 1, Whitlam Institute.
49   Marian Sawer, *Making Women Count: A History of the Women's Electoral Lobby* (Sydney: UNSW Press, 2008); Ann Curthoys, 'Doing It For Themselves: The Women's Movement Since 1970', in *Gender Relations in Australia: Domination and Negotiation*, ed. Kay Saunders and Raymond Evans (Sydney: Harcourt Brace Jovanovich, 1992), 425–47.

'It's Time' was an innovative campaign, particularly the celebrity-laden television advertisements, which foregrounded Whitlam's place in a family.[50] The campaign, and Margaret Whitlam's prominent role within it, were designed to show 'one of our primary target groups that the Leader is not a political automat, but has a wife and a family. Additionally, it will show that the Whitlam family is a tight-knit unit, a factor which most women will support'.[51] The importance of 'Winning the Female Vote!' was thus reiterated to Labor.[52] The party responded quickly, cultivating Margaret Whitlam's public presence, including on television and radio.[53] These appearances gained positive coverage in the print press. The *Sydney Morning Herald* noted in March 1972 that 'Mrs Whitlam's charm, intelligence and willingness to comment on a wide range of subjects is a considerable electoral asset to Gough Whitlam'.[54]

Yet a focus on Labor's new policies and innovative campaign in 1972 has overshadowed continuity in the message and delivery. Politicians' families have long been used to reinforce their position as advocates of normal family values. The efficacy of promoting a politician as a family man reflected the mutually reinforcing male power in both 'private' and 'public' spheres. Similarly, Margaret Whitlam's interpretation as 'the best public relations agent Gough could have' reflected a conventional narrative in political circles, including an assumption that wives were ciphers of their husbands' politics.[55] Her appeals were mainly targeted to other women, who were seen as a discrete, special interest group. The view that Margaret Whitlam could improve her husband's political legitimacy also rested on an assumption of complementary gender roles in marriage, with husbands as intellectual, rational, authority figures and wives as emotional, supportive figures. According to feminist scholar Charlotte Adcock, within this gendered logic, political wives could be deployed as 'cultural reference points for the promotion or judging' of their husbands' political parties and leadership. Wives therefore 'constituted sites for the

---

50 Cater, 'Hearts and Minds', 51.
51 'It's Time' Proposal, 18, 53–55.
52 'Political Party, Leader and Issues'; Peter Shenstone, Letter to Gough Whitlam, 2 June 1972, item EGW 44060, box 0205, Whitlam Institute. Emphasis in original.
53 Graham Freudenberg, Letter to John Ducker, 5 October 1971, item MEW 47946, box 0287, Whitlam Institute.
54 'Mrs Whitlam: Women's Link with Labor', *Sydney Morning Herald*, 16 March 1972.
55 *Daily Telegraph*, 9 November 1972. See also 'Putting in a Word for Gough', *Herald*, 8 June 1972, 21.

playing out of a wider cultural and sexual politics'.[56] Margaret Whitlam's public role thus influenced public perception of the Labor Government's gender politics and her husband as a man and leader.

'A thinking woman': Margaret Whitlam as a modern prime minister's wife

Margaret Whitlam was understood by many contemporaries as a new type of prime minister's wife because she spoke her mind, including on controversial subjects, before and during her husband's terms in office. Her outspokenness was also interpreted as further proof that Whitlam, and Labor, held progressive gender values. Once in power, Labor had enacted an impressive range of reforms affecting women, including the adult minimum wage, the Family Law Act, and the appointment of a federal advisor on women's affairs.[57] Margaret Whitlam became personally involved with one Labor initiative, the programs developed around International Women's Year. She even attended the International Women's Year conference held in Mexico in June 1975 as a delegate. This was the first time a prime minister's wife had travelled overseas to represent her country at an event independent of her role as political consort. Her public presence also extended beyond tradition in other ways, such as her 'My Day' newspaper columns and appearances on television and radio shows.

In light of the new feminist movement, it was becoming more acceptable, even expected, for political wives to be politically engaged and visible. The *Daily Telegraph* argued in 1972 that 'with Australian women at last beginning to become politically aware, Margaret Whitlam—well-educated … well-travelled and with a mind of her own—fits well with the ALP's election slogan, "it's time"'.[58] She espoused many progressive views and was seen as modern and intelligent.[59] As one article argued, as a 'thinking woman', Margaret Whitlam would be an 'asset to her husband'.[60]

---

56   Charlotte Adcock, 'The Politician, the Wife, the Citizen and Her Newspaper: Rethinking Women, Democracy and Media(ted) Representation', *Feminist Media Studies* 10, no. 2 (2010): 146.
57   Susan Ryan, 'Women of Australia', in Bramston, *The Whitlam Legacy*, 206; Hester Eisenstein, *Inside Agitators: Australian Femocrats and the State* (Philadelphia: Temple University Press, 1996).
58   *Daily Telegraph*, 9 November 1972.
59   *Sunday Australian*, 1972, quoted in Hocking, *Gough Whitlam*, 384.
60   'Margaret Whitlam Leaves Men at a Loss', *Sydney Morning Herald*.

Yet her outspokenness and attempts to make a meaningful position as prime minister's wife were also met with resistance.[61] Praise turned increasingly to criticism, as detractors attempted to police the supposedly apolitical and supportive nature of her role.[62] It is illuminating that those wanting to delegitimise Margaret Whitlam's authority attempted to undermine her femininity—like the *Sunday Mail*'s derisive reference to her height in an article about her 'illegitimate' acceptance of payment for a position on the Commonwealth Hostels Board.[63] Margaret Whitlam was aware of the fraught nature of the role she played: both supporting her husband and party while remaining publicly 'apolitical'. She wrote of frustrating invitations 'given because of one's husband's political position and yet there is often the spoken fear that one might make a political comment and thus pollute the minds of those attending a "social" occasion!'[64]

Here we see the fundamental paradox in the auxiliary role given to political wives. Margaret Whitlam was building a public presence, at least in part, to assist her husband's career. Her activities were thus linked to her position as prime minister's wife.[65] This is not to undermine her agency—Margaret Whitlam had a longstanding interest in journalism—but to recognise the social and structural factors at play in expectations of her as a political consort. For example, despite the new governmental 'advisor on women's affairs', she was still widely interpreted as a representative of Australian womanhood, a position consistently attributed to prime ministers' wives while no women sat in parliament. She played this role in a way some felt modern Australian women could be proud of, with one arguing that 'it's the greatest thing that has happened … to have a really intelligent spokeswoman who knows what she's talking about'.[66]

Historian Susan Magarey has argued that unlike Margaret Whitlam, previous prime ministers' wives have 'seen their role merely as an extension of their existing roles of wife and mother'.[67] Yet a number of earlier Labor prime ministers' wives also attempted at times to expand or challenge the expectations placed on them as political consorts. Elsie Curtin argued

---

61 Susan Mitchell, *The Matriarchs: Twelve Australian Women Talk about Their Lives* (Ringwood: Penguin Books, 1987), 22.
62 Langmore, *Prime Ministers' Wives*, 244.
63 'Big Purse for Big Marg', *Sunday Mail*, quoted in Mitchell, *Margaret and Gough*.
64 Republished as Margaret Whitlam, *My Day* (Sydney: Collins, 1973), 73.
65 Coulston, 'Women's Rights and the Whitlam Program', 13.
66 'Margaret Whitlam Leaves Men at a Loss', *Sydney Morning Herald*.
67 Magarey, 'Women's Liberation Was a Movement', 190.

repeatedly that she should be viewed as separate from her husband.[68] Furthermore, interpretations of Margaret Whitlam as a new kind of prime ministerial wife ignore the precedent set by Enid Lyons in the 1930s.[69] Lyons was integral to her husband's populist appeal and a household name with a prodigious public presence, including writing articles for newspapers.[70] And as Diane Langmore has noted, unlike Lyons, Margaret Whitlam 'was not closely involved in the political affairs of her husband's term of office ... her attractiveness to the media was due more to her readiness to speak and write uninhibitedly on a wide range of subjects'.[71] Yet Lyons has largely been dismissed as a figure deserving of historical study because of her social conservatism and maternalist rhetoric.

Like her husband, Margaret Whitlam's popularity as a modern public figure was partly based on a longer political lineage. The couple's politics were fundamentally reforming, not revolutionary. Their politics reflected a modern outlook and new feminist challenges, including Margaret Whitlam's advocacy for an expanded role for prime ministers' wives and Labor's support for women's emancipation. Yet they contained less of an immediate challenge to men's position in politics.

The structural, political and personal constraints on women's roles and men's continuing hold on political power thus remained. This is clear in Margaret Whitlam's dual roles in the Labor Government as both a symbol of women's expanding voice in society and as 'private' evidence of Whitlam's credentials as a normal family man. The difference between Whitlam's progressive policies and gendered divisions of labour in his own marriage and office reflected a widespread reality of the period's sexual revolution.[72] As political scientist Rosemary Whip has shown, the expectation of the free labour of politicians' wives, the 'two person single career', continued into the 1980s and beyond, a situation 'based not on necessity but on convention, on convenience from the point of view of the husband and the invariably male-dominated employing institution'.[73] This maintained a political culture that, both on a personal

---

68   Curtin argued that 'you do not represent your husbands, I don't see why I should represent mine'. 'What Is Happening in Your Home State', *Army News*, 2 October 1944, 2.
69   *The Herald*, 5 December 1972; Langmore, *Prime Ministers' Wives*, 227.
70   With a few exceptions that do little more than mention the precedence in passing.
71   Langmore, *Prime Ministers' Wives*, 227.
72   Hocking, *Gough Whitlam*, 239, 284.
73   Rosemary Whip, 'The Parliamentary Wife: Participant in the "Two Person Single Career"', *Australian Journal of Political Science* 17, no. 2 (1982): 42–43.

and individual, as well as political and systemic level, continued to take advantage of political wives' physical, emotional and social labour while minimising its relevance to the political world it enabled.

Conclusion

The Labor Government's shift away from socialism and incorporation of the demands of the women's movement under Whitlam facilitated and reflected a commitment to the more inclusive 'equality of opportunity'.[74] The three years of the Labor Government were thus transformative in many ways. Yet masculinity continued to be a benchmark for political performance, a key political dynamic that shaped and reflected political discourses in Australia during the 1970s. While women's concerns gained more traction in the state, they remained atypical politicians, their ability to embody leadership complicated by gendered assumptions of political behaviour. Women representatives remained a minority and white men continued to be represented as neutral political actors. This obscured a key similarity, sex and a key tool and marker of political contestation and hierarchisation, gender.

Claiming political authority is a relational and performative process, (re)producing historically specific knowledges about the nature of political power that have enduring political effects. In 2012, the first female prime minister, Julia Gillard, responded to a parliamentary attack with an excoriation of Opposition leader Tony Abbott's gender politics.[75] Her powerful speech gained positive international coverage, but was dismissed by large sections of the Australian media as 'playing the gender card'.[76] Conservative media commentator Miranda Devine was particularly virulent:

> Playing the gender card is the pathetic last refuge of incompetents and everyone in the real world knows it ... [Abbott] asks whether men might have innate advantage ... For instance, voice is important to demonstrate authority. Men with a booming

---

74 Carol Johnson, 'Gough Whitlam and the Re-imagined Citizen-Subject of Australian Social Democracy', in Hocking, *Making Modern Australia*.
75 Julia Gillard, House of Representatives, Hansard, 9 October 2012, 11581.
76 See A. Worth, M. Augoustinos and B. Hastie, '"Playing the Gender Card": Media Representations of Julia Gillard's Sexism and Misogyny Speech', *Feminism & Psychology* 26, no. 1 (2016): 52–72, doi.org/10.1177/0959353515605544; Marian Woodward, 'Ditch the Witch: Julia Gillard and Gender in Australian Public Discourse' (Honours thesis, University of Sydney, 2013).

baritone command attention. Height is another issue. Men are usually taller than women, and height generally correlates with high office.[77]

This construction of what constitutes political authority 'in the real world'—what it looks, acts and sounds like—has been remarkably resilient in Australian politics. If this is to change, we need to pay critical attention to the historically specific, and therefore contingent and mutable, enactments of masculinity and femininity on which Australian political leadership is based.

77　Miranda Devine, 'Gender Card is a Loser for Gillard', *Sunday Telegraph*, 14 October 2012.

CHAPTER 15

Cleo magazine and the sexual revolution

Megan Le Masurier

> I am a scripture teacher in a girls' school and spend a lot of time trying to teach my girls the value of chastity and clean living. But with publications such as yours writing so frankly about things which, to my mind, ought to be kept private, it is no wonder that young people today think of nothing but sex, sex, sex.[1]

In November 1972 a new women's magazine was launched in Australia that popularised many of the ideas of the sexual revolution and women's liberation. *Cleo* was the brainchild of publisher Frank Packer at ACP Magazines and editor Ita Buttrose, influenced by the success of *Cosmopolitan* magazine in the United States and a determination to corner the younger women's market before the Australian version of *Cosmo* launched in March 1973. Buttrose's aim, as she wrote in her 1985 memoir, was to bring to everyday women—not those actively involved in the women's movement—a confronting directness about both women's and sexual liberation. 'We equipped the rebels with knowledge and thus stoked the fires of revolution.'[2]

Sexual liberation and women's liberation were entwined in the early years of second-wave feminism. This connection began to unravel as second-wave feminists contested the meaning of the sexual revolution for

---

1   Mrs J.W., Brisbane, *Cleo*, December 1972, 146.
2   Ita Buttrose, *Early Edition* (South Melbourne: Macmillan, 1985), 151.

women throughout the 1970s in what became known as the 'sex wars'.[3] For *Cleo*, however, the two remained entwined and became the cornerstone of the magazine's editorial philosophy. The gender politics of sex were explored in its pages in the language of equal rights: women had a right to the freedoms and erotic pleasures it seemed men had always had, and they had a right to knowledge about their bodies that could make such ecstasy possible. It was the sexual politics of the fair go. Informing women about the sexual potential of their bodies and providing a regular source of sex education was framed as feminist practice, what I have termed elsewhere as 'popular feminism'.[4]

What becomes apparent in *Cleo*'s repetitive discussion of sex is the encouragement of an active approach in women's sexual behaviour with men. *Cleo* attempted to break down one of the oppressive polarities of traditional understandings of heterosexuality and gender—of masculinity as active and femininity as passive. This was quite a radical position at the time and was surprisingly evident in *Cleo*'s feature journalism and in the readers' responses on the letters pages. For many readers, embracing the new practices of active female sexuality involved a struggle against shame and ignorance. There was a baseline lack of knowledge about women's bodies and the sexual pleasures they were capable of. As Michael Warner explains so well: 'The more people are isolated or privatised, the more vulnerable they are to the unequal effects of shame. Conditions that prevent variation, or prevent the knowledge of such possibilities from circulating, undermine sexual autonomy'.[5] While Warner is writing here about sexual practices that are not considered 'mainstream' or 'normative', shame via isolation and privatisation of sexual knowledge and experience was operative within heterosexuality too, especially in this period and especially for women. There was a lot of sex work to do, especially by and for those women who were isolated from social formations where sexual liberation or feminist discussion groups were active.

---

3   See, for example, Kath Albury, *Yes Means Yes: Getting Explicit about Heterosex* (Crows Nest, NSW: Allen & Unwin, 2002); and Ellen Willis, 'Villains and Victims: "Sexual Correctness" and the Repression of Feminism', in *Bad Girls, Good Girls: Women, Sex, and Power in the Nineties*, ed. Nan Bauer Maglin and Donna Perry (New Brunswick, NJ: Rutgers University Press, 1994), 44–53.
4   Megan Le Masurier, 'My Other, My Self: *Cleo* Magazine and Feminism in 1970s Australia', *Australian Feminist Studies* 22, no. 53 (2007): 191–211, doi.org/10.1080/08164640701361766.
5   Michael Warner, *The Trouble with Normal: Sex, Politics, and the Ethics of Queer Life* (Cambridge, MA: Harvard University Press, 2000), 12.

15. *CLEO* MAGAZINE AND THE SEXUAL REVOLUTION

This chapter will establish the inadequacy of sex education in Australia at the time and the role *Cleo* played as one of the primary popular sites for teaching women about their bodies and their potential for sexual pleasure. As much as *Cleo* relied on sexperts, theirs were not the only voices to be heard in this intimate public sphere. In the reader letters and questions to advice and doctor columns we hear stories of women certainly anxious to know what 'normal' means in a time of dramatic social change and the wake of the sexual revolution. But we also hear stories of women's struggles and triumphs in finding sexual pleasure and the refusals of their bodies to do what experts, be they doctors, sexologists, advisors or feminists, said they should. In *Cleo*'s chaotic sexo-babble of experts and amateurs, the varieties of sexual pleasures women experienced were all valued. 'Normal' female heterosexuality expanded beyond containment as the decade unfolded in *Cleo*'s pages, but a stubborn unshiftable opposition between male as active/strong/desiring and women as passive/weak/desired is not what we hear. The meaning of the 'mainstream' of female heterosexuality was under noisy reconstruction.

Looking back at the decade of the 1970s in an article for *Cleo*, Bettina Arndt, a sexual therapist at the time and editor of the Australian edition of *Forum* magazine, wrote: 'In the early 1970s, sex was a topic which abounded in mythology'.

> Most people knew very little about sex and what they thought they knew was often wrong. It was widely assumed, for instance, that most women had very little interest in sex—and those who did were regarded as nymphomaniacs. Female orgasm had rarely been heard of and the clitoris was quite uncharted territory.[6]

In a study of sex in Australia published as *The Sex Survey of Australian Women* in 1974, Professor Robert Bell interviewed 1,500 women. He concluded that there had been a sexual revolution in Australia in terms of attitudes but the behaviour was 'lagging behind'. Writing in *Cleo* he explained: 'The revolution has been towards greater sexuality as a right for both women and men … [but] the conservative forces governing sexual morality continue to be strong'. The greatest failure, wrote Bell, was that Australian society 'provides little in the way of reliable information about sex as a human experience. It is not provided in the schools and there is

---

6   Bettina Arndt, 'Did the Earth Move for You? 10 Years That Shook the Bedrooms of the World', *Cleo*, November 1982, 176.

little available written material'.[7] A review of current practices and trends in sex education in Australia by the Australian Council of Social Service (ACOSS) in 1974 revealed that sex education was not taught as a separate subject in any school, and that the little sexual information on offer was subsumed into science courses or religious instruction.[8] Sex education was a subject of public debate in the 1970s. There was ambivalence about what should be taught, how the information should be presented, by whom and where. In schools? At home? The church? By doctors? It was noted that 'apprehension' best described the issue of educating teenagers about sex.

The usual source of information about sex, apart from ill-informed friends, came from a one-off Family Life Movement of Australia mother/daughter, father/son evening. The nine guides produced by the Family Life Movement sold an extraordinary 1.25 million copies in 1969 alone and 'probably did more than any other individual or organisation to distribute sex education information among Australians of the post-war generation'.[9] The content of the guides, however, was Christian-inspired and highly conservative. Readers were told that masturbation would bring guilt and shame and risk the development of homosexuality; avoidance of the practice was 'character building'. Homosexuality was a perversion for both men and women. Sex was for marriage and pre- and extra-marital sex were sinful and psychologically scarring, and contraception was not discussed. Using the guides as an aid, the primary responsibility for sex education lay with parents. Parents, however, were embarrassed and often ill-informed themselves. In *The Female Eunuch*, Germaine Greer had written about the ignorance of both mothers and daughters:

> When little girls begin to ask questions their mothers provide them, if they are lucky, with crude diagrams of the sexual apparatus, in which the organs of pleasure feature much less prominently than the intricacies of tubes and ovaries.[10]

In a *Cleo* feature about the importance of sex education for girls, the complaint was the same. Mothers' ignorance and shame was being passed onto their daughters: 'Many mothers unwittingly bombard their

---

7 Robert Bell, 'Sex and the Australian woman', *Cleo*, April 1974, 92.
8 ACOSS, *Sex Education: A Review of Current Practices and Trends. Background Paper* (Sydney: ACOSS, 1974), 17.
9 Rosemary Auchmuty, 'The Truth about Sex', in *Australian Popular Culture*, ed. Peter Spearritt and David Walker (Sydney: Allen & Unwin, 1979), 182.
10 Germaine Greer, *The Female Eunuch* (London: Flamingo, 1999 [1970]), 44.

daughters with negative and damaging information about sex'.[11] The story, as is usual for women's magazine features, is filled with anecdotes from ordinary women who spoke of the guilt-ridden messages about sex received from their mothers. One woman said: 'I remember her saying when I was about 16: "If you ever feel tempted, just see my face before you". It was tantamount to having the bone pointed at you'.[12]

The female readers of *Cleo* had been raised on respectability but were being hailed on many fronts in the media by popular discourses of sexual and women's liberation. The clash produced much anxiety and confusion, evident in the doctor and advisor pages. By default it seems, throughout the 1970s *Cleo* became one of the most important regular sites for the provision of explicit and non-judgemental sexual information for young women (and men) in Australia. Australian women's magazines had simply not covered this territory before. And while another new magazine for women, *Pol*, certainly wrote *about* the sexual revolution and *about* women's liberation as social phenomena, it didn't provide women with the gritty 'how-to' technical and biological details. *Cleo* adopted the tradition of the service guides, the 'trade' manuals of feminine work that had defined mainstream women's magazines, and applied sex to the format. As did *Cosmopolitan* magazine in the United States under the editorship of Helen Gurley Brown from 1965 and the Australian version of *Cosmo* when it launched in March 1973.

In a special *Dear Cleo Doctor* booklet inserted in the magazine in 1976, the editors commented about the 'staggering' number of letters that arrived each month and the ignorance of young women about their bodies. 'They are too embarrassed to seek medical advice—and even after they consult a doctor they are quite ignorant of their condition and the treatment they are receiving.'[13] The booklet provided a list of questions to ask doctors and encouraged women to be more assertive and demanding. The 1975 *Cleo Advisor Booklet*, based on the 'hundreds of letters' that were sent to the magazine's advice column every month, was critical of the standard of information available to young women. The editors advised that women should avoid male doctors and go to Women's Health Centres or to the Family Planning Association clinics.[14]

---

11 Patricia Johnson, 'Can You Ruin Your Daughter's Sex Life?', *Cleo*, January 1977, 84.
12 Ibid., 84.
13 *Dear Cleo Doctor* (insert), *Cleo*, July 1976, 60.
14 *Cleo Advisor Booklet* (insert), *Cleo* July 1975, 42.

It was not that Australian women were *completely* without resources when it came to finding information about sex. An Australian edition of *Forum* magazine, the international journal of sex research, was available in selected newsagencies. And by late 1972, just as *Cleo* launched, Australians could begin to buy the mainly American-authored books of popular sexology such as David Reuben's *Everything You Wanted To Know About Sex (But Were Afraid to Ask)* (1969), J's *The Sensuous Woman* (1969), Inge and Stan Hegeler's *The ABZ of Love* (1971) and, of course, Alex Comfort's *The Joy of Sex* (1972). These books were the start of an avalanche that was to roll through the 1970s and provided *Cleo* with much of its feature material. Every new book released seems to appear in excerpt form in *Cleo*'s pages.

Feminists had begun to wrench sexology from the hands of male experts, medical and psychological. Through meetings of consciousness-raising groups, the Boston Women's Health Collective produced the first edition of *Our Bodies, Ourselves* in 1969, which circulated in various forms in Australia and was available as a book from 1973. When *Our Bodies* was released in September that year, *Cleo* ran a long excerpt with an introduction explaining its feminist origins and women's frustration with 'condescending doctors'.[15] The excerpts *Cleo* chose were about genital self-examination in groups; the explanation of the clitoris; the individuality of sexual response and orgasm; children by choice; shared contraceptive responsibility and the double messages about sex being dirty, virginity being saved for true love and the pressures of a commercialised sexual 'liberation': 'What really has to be confronted is the deep, persistent assumption of a sexual inequality'.[16] Sexual frustration or non-responsiveness was explained in social terms, the result of a 'male dominated culture [which] imbues us with a sense of second-best status … the men we sleep with are never as interested in our orgasms as they are in their own'.[17]

Cleo readers knew the story about male selfishness already. 'Men and the Female Orgasm' was a feature in the fourth issue based on a small focus group of men and a female journalist. Shelley Summers fired the questions. 'How important is it to you that a woman has a climax?' 'Peter', a doctor in his early 30s, replied, 'If she is a one-night stand I don't give a

---

15   Boston Women's Health Collective, 'Our Bodies, Ourselves', *Cleo*, September 1973, 10.
16   Ibid., 11.
17   Ibid., 10.

damn whether she does or not—why should I? I don't really expect her to under those circumstances anyway'. 'Michael', another doctor in his 30s, seemed confused:

> I find most birds who have trouble climaxing are pretty demanding. That is about the only thing wrong with the liberated woman— she is not happy with anything but what she calls a vaginal orgasm and that takes a lot of determination from a man.

'John', a divorced solicitor in his 30s, thought some women were 'getting too aggressive' when it came to sexual liberation and becoming a 'sexual threat' to men. Peter, the doctor, was convinced that liberated women had a lot more neuroses and that they could never have the same attitude to sex as men. 'Men are going to suffer', he said prophetically.[18]

Men's responses to the challenges of women's sexual liberation became a running theme in *Cleo*. They were, after all, almost one-third of the readership (if not the buyers) according to the McNair Anderson survey in 1974.[19] Journalist Jan Smith answered 'The Burning Question: Have We Demanded Too Much from Men?' with irony. It was a long article about how men had now become unnecessary and sex was much better with the varieties of vibrators now available:

> It's all just too much trouble and hardly a week goes by without articles on the bliss of living alone. Vibrators and masturbation may not be specifically mentioned in the nicer type of publication. The more militant journals may be advocating homosexuality or even celibacy. But the whole point is that having a man around actually means more frustration than not having one around.[20]

There is a final twist, however. Smith wonders whether women have tried too hard. After all of that 'deconditioning, Masters and Johnsoning and consciousness raising', perhaps women expected too much? 'Of course we haven't', railed S.B from Canberra on the letters pages:

---

18 Shelley Summers, 'Men and the Female Orgasm', *Cleo*, February 1973, 114–17.
19 McNair Anderson Associates P/L 1974, *Print Readership Survey. National Magazine Readership, 1974* (Sydney: McNair Anderson Associates, 1974).
20 Jan Smith, 'The Burning Question: Have We Demanded Too Much from Men?' *Cleo*, August 1976, 19.

> If men are going to sink into their water beds and refuse to take up the challenges issued by the New Women, then I say let them sink. Any man worthy of the name will not wilt at the prospect of a woman who wants him to be aware of the needs of her body and mind. Men have been asking the same thing of women for centuries and look what happened. Women became so resourceful in meeting men's demands that they eventually became strong enough to meet their own. Perhaps if men try to satisfy the New Woman they will go through the same evolution until they too liberate themselves. The way is forward, not backwards.[21]

In exploring their potential for sexual pleasure, the readers/writers of *Cleo* were being encouraged to become *active* sexual beings. This didn't necessarily mean having sex with more men, it meant women learning about their bodies, taking control of their own pleasure and their right to orgasm, with men or without them.

Orgasm became the symbol of women's sexual liberation in *Cleo*, as it had in some of the early writings and discussions of second-wave feminists. Anne Koedt, in her famous pamphlet 'The Myth of the Vaginal Orgasm', had insisted on the primacy of the clitoris for the 'feminist' orgasm.[22] Greer by contrast had insisted on women's active engagement with the whole cunt as a means to erotic pleasures and liberation as yet unknown in her theory of 'cuntpower' that embraced vaginal penetration and women's active movement during sex.[23] *Cleo* tried not to take sides and explored as many varieties of female sexual pleasure as it could with an underlying belief that women had not been getting a fair go when it came to sex with men. In 1974 this connection was clearly made to *Cleo*'s readers. 'For centuries pleasure in sex was regarded as reserved for men only', wrote staff writer Anne Woodham. 'Now women see their own needs and want men to know.'[24]

If the clitoris had become the feminist truth of female sexuality in the 1970s, with the regulatory and disciplinary powers that accompany such truth claims, especially when bound up in identity politics, the magazine format created a far more democratic space for the multiple 'truths'

---

21 *Cleo* Letters, October 1976, 226.
22 Anne Koedt, 'The Myth of the Vaginal Orgasm', in *Radical Feminism*, ed. Anne Koedt, Ellen Levine and Anita Rapone (New York: Quadrangle Books, 1973 [1970]), 198–207.
23 Megan Le Masurier, 'Resurrecting Germaine's Theory of Cuntpower', *Australian Feminist Studies* 31 no. 87 (2016): 28–42, doi.org/10.1080/08164649.2016.1174925.
24 Anne Woodham, 'What Women Wish Their Men Would Remember', *Cleo*, December 1974, 15.

of female orgasms to gain representation. One of the unsung powers of the intimate style of sex journalism in women's magazines is that its reliance on the voice of the sexpert *as well as* the anecdotal voice of the amateur inevitably results in a picture of the pluralities of female sexuality. There is just too much to be said and too many voices. The democratic generosity of a popular journalism reliant on readers' voices, as well as experts and journalists, can open up the possibilities of female sexuality and the popular orgasm—not shut them down. It is a feminist effect, indeed a feminist desire, all enacted without too much direct mention of feminism at all.

Cleo didn't stop—couldn't stop—running features on the orgasm. Editorial choices were often made in response to readers' questions that kept pouring in to the *Cleo* Doctor and Advisor columns. With each repetition of the orgasm story, following the journalistic requirement of the fresh angle, different inflections on sexological research and personal anecdote were building a highly complex picture of female sexuality. Sexologists, psychologists, doctors, sex counsellors, feminists—all the experts quickly took up residence in *Cleo*'s pages. But so did readers. Through these voices of everyday women—the voices of anxiety and disappointment alongside the testimonials of pleasure and demands for validation—a space was created to represent the multiplicity of sexual pleasures women were experiencing through sex with men, and without them. In an attempt to explain the female orgasm in response to 'the hundreds of letters we receive from women asking about orgasm', journalist Katrina Petersen, like Koedt, blamed Freud for diverting women away from the clitoris towards the sexually mature orgasm of the vagina. 'Thousands of women since have been given psychoanalysis directed at achieving what is in fact a biological impossibility.'[25] In a feature on the popularity of vibrator attachments, Anne Woodham took issue with 'rubber sheaths with lumps and bumps [which] pander to the myth of the vaginal orgasm'. There was no point to these devices if the clitoris was 'the real key to female orgasm'.[26]

The first *Cleo* Doctor, a male gynaecologist, had been running quite a different line in his column. Writing to the Doctor, one reader chastised him for 'perpetuating the old Freudian myth of the vaginal orgasm' and sent him a leaflet for his feminist sex education. The doctor was cross. 'The Myth of the Vaginal Orgasm by Anne Koedt leaves me cold',

---

25 Katrina Petersen, 'The Female Orgasm: What Is It Really Like?' *Cleo*, November 1974, 25.
26 Anne Woodham, 'The Aids of Living', *Cleo*, June 1974, 99.

he replied in his column. 'Utter rubbish.'[27] There were readers who agreed with him. Responding to an article asserting "'out with Sigmund Freud's vaginal orgasm, in with the clitoral orgasm'",[28] 'Freud Forever', as the reader described herself, wanted to take issue with the feminist 'experts' and demanded public recognition of the existence of the vaginal orgasm:

> there has been mention in previous issues of 'the myth of the vaginal orgasm'. I feel I must let the women readers of *Cleo* know that I can have both clitoral orgasm and vaginal orgasm.

In 1981, 'The Little Man in the Boat' was billed as 'the story every man must read!'[29] Lisa Southern wrote personally about her orgasmic journey, her faking of orgasms before D-day (1969 and 'the discovery of the clitoris'), her experience of lesbianism and clitoral orgasms, her return to men and political refusal to fake vaginal orgasm with them. 'After making futile attempts to bring me to orgasm, men would give me little-boy hurt looks or accusing glares as they recounted their orgasm-producing exploits with other women.' For their ignorance and false pride, Southern held other women responsible for keeping men in the clitoral dark. Her tips for 'what women really want' were graphic:

> Women had faked vaginal orgasms so well that men were confident that there was nothing like good old-fashioned penetration to produce a climax. The clitoral orgasm was just some new-fangled feminist con … men felt incredibly threatened by the revelation that they had probably never brought a woman to a genuine climax.[30]

'The response was staggering', wrote *Cleo* later in its review of the year. The article was 'probably the most talked-about sex article of 1981'.[31] The letters in response in the May 1981 issue expressed gratitude, relief and identification: 'It is framed and hung next to my bed'; 'I've a mind to post photocopies of it to all the males in Australia'; 'It was a weird feeling to read an article written about me by someone I've never met'.

---

27 *Cleo* Doctor, *Cleo*, March 1974, 83.
28 Sandra Hall, 'Commonsensuality', *Cleo*, July 1974, 91.
29 Lisa Southern, 'The Little Man in the Boat', *Cleo*, February 1981, 28.
30 Ibid., 27.
31 Wendy Taye, 'The Best of *Cleo*', *Cleo*, November 1982, 141.

Just as *Cleo*'s readers seemed to be finally settling in to the clitoral truth of female orgasm came the truth-exploding news of the G-spot in the June issue in 1981. 'Was Freud right after all?' asked Jack Jardine and Ruth Austen as they explained the history of sexology, Masters and Johnson, the refusals of experts to believe in women's stories of deep and different orgasms within the vagina and their tales of female ejaculation. With the rediscovery of the G-spot it turned out that the vaginal orgasm may not be a myth after all.[32]

In the following October issue a reader from Bondi thanked *Cleo* for 'enlightening' her that 'those wonderful experiences were not figments of my imagination':

> I for one have experienced many vaginal orgasms through stimulation of the G-spot. I used to find it hard to achieve orgasm … We stumbled upon this hidden pleasure purely by accident when we were experimenting with different positions to try to increase my sexual response by means other than oral stimulation.[33]

In the same issue, Chris from WA was relieved to find an explanation that her ejaculations during G-spot orgasms were not urination and happy to share the news with *Cleo*'s readers. 'I have experienced this ejaculation three times in all, with numerous vaginal orgasms (also clitoral) until now I have not known what was responsible.'[34] Priscilla from NSW was grateful for the article. In the letters pages she also decided to share some of her own sexpertise with *Cleo*'s readers:

> *Cleo*'s article omitted one vital piece of information; the truly devastating effect of achieving both the clitoral and G-spot orgasm at the same time. Quite often I would break down and cry afterwards in massive relief. It was as if my soul left my body and I could fly …[35]

By the end of *Cleo*'s first decade it became apparent that a singular truth of orgasm and female sexual pleasure kept slipping out of everyone's grasp. The detailed sexual intimacy of these letters would have been inconceivable in mainstream women's magazines before the 1970s, and

---

32 Jack Owen Jardine and Ruth Austen, 'Introducing the G Spot or, a Funny Thing Happened on the Way to Orgasm', *Cleo*, June 1981, 32.
33 *Cleo* Letters, *Cleo*, October 1981, 248.
34 Ibid. 248.
35 *Cleo* Letters, *Cleo*, November 1981, 250.

utterly impossible to print in newspapers. In this eruption of popular sexpertise any clear meaning of 'normal' female sexuality dissolved. And *Cleo*'s popular sex journalism provided the public space for contending truths to circulate.

Orgasm and sexual expertise became 'lifestyle' signifiers of the new woman. She aspired to be good at sex, she knew about orgasm, her magazine proudly shouted about sex on its covers. The movement from ignorance to knowledge, from pre- or non-orgasmic to orgasmic, signified participation in the imagined liberated community of *Cleo*'s new women. And writing about the orgasm, reading about it, having or struggling to have it, allowed her to participate in that community. Sex without shame had become a marker of 'the good life', even a sign of cultural capital. At the same time, this legitimation of women's right to sexual pleasure and the repetition of stories about sexual experimentation and orgasm could also lead to feelings of shame and anxiety among those readers who could not manage to reach the heights of such 'liberation'. The difficulty for some in engaging in the expanding repertoire of normal heterosexual practice are constants in the readers' letters. An exchange on the letters pages in December 1977 over oral sex illuminates the emotional complexity of engaging with the practices of sexual liberation. J.H. of NSW had found a feature discussing oral sex 'disgusting, unclean and revolting … I nearly threw up … I couldn't believe what I read. How any woman can put her mouth near a penis or a man put his mouth near a vagina is beyond me'.[36] The response from other readers the following March was one of shock. One reader responded: 'My boyfriend and I had to take another look at the issue's date to make sure it wasn't December 1947!'

Penelope George wrote a first-person account of her frustration in having an orgasm. She had to take the matter into her own hands. It took days to find the courage to go to a sex shop, but she did. Then went into her room and got to work:

> The vibrator hummed for over half an hour … Suddenly, my mind snapped, my surprised body exhibited all the textbook signs of a good orgasm and I was, truly, gut boggled. I laughed, the sensation was extraordinary. Relief settled on me like winter sunshine.[37]

---

36   *Cleo* Letters, *Cleo*, December 1977, 240.
37   Penelope George, 'Oh, for a Big O', *Cleo*, September 1979, 198.

In fact, she suggested that vibrators were so good at providing better, more reliable orgasms that women might be tempted to dispense with male partners altogether.

The journey to sexual liberation and orgasm through the use of a vibrator was a difficult pleasure for some. One reader, who had been uncertain and embarrassed about buying a vibrator, and especially from a sex shop, had been reassured and given explicit directions by another on the letters page in May 1974, bypassing the expert altogether. S.D. suggested she buy a massager from a department store and use the smooth button. 'Excellent for masturbation', said S.D.[38] Another reader writing to the *Cleo* advisor wanted to try a vibrator but was concerned that her husband found the idea threatening. 'He thinks it means something is wrong with our relationship if we do. I don't have a problem with orgasm but I admit I'm curious about vibrators.' Wendy McCarthy, *Cleo*'s avowedly feminist 'agony aunt' from 1978 to 1984, sympathised that the man could be anxious about being replaced by a machine and very sensibly suggested: 'Why not buy a general massage vibrator and try it on your husband so he feels comfortable with it. You could then begin to use it together in your lovemaking'.[39]

A sisterly atmosphere was created in the pages of *Cleo* for women to share their stories of sexual fantasies, 'still one of the most taboo subjects'.[40] It was another way the magazine encouraged women to explore the range of their sexuality and alleviate shame. As Michael Warner argues, 'Isolation and silence are among the common conditions for the politics of sexual shame. Autonomy requires more than civil liberty; it requires the circulation and accessibility of sexual knowledge'.[41] Talking about sexual fantasies in public was framed by discourses of liberation, equality and progress. In an interview with Nancy Friday upon the publication of *My Secret Garden* in Australia in 1976, Camilla Beach confronted the myth that 'nice girls don't have sexual fantasies':

---

38 *Cleo* Letters, *Cleo*, May 1974, 81.
39 *Cleo* Advisor, *Cleo*, May 1982, 31.
40 Polly Wilson, 'Female Fantasies', *Cleo*, January 1973, 15.
41 Warner, *The Trouble with Normal*, 171.

> In the bad old days before *My Secret Garden* hit the American bestseller list, women who openly confessed to sexual fantasising were popularly pronounced either mentally sick or over-sexed. Consequently many such women unnecessarily suffered feelings of guilt.

Friday spoke of the reception to her book. 'People get scared to death ... they simply cannot understand that women have erotic lustful fantasies and desires just as men do.'[42]

In *Cleo*'s pages, female heterosexual desire was represented as a force that could not easily be trained or constrained by sexological truth, by moral dictates or by feminist theory. It kept erupting uncontrollably. This desire would not be faithful[43] and would not stay interested in its chosen partner.[44] It got bored[45] or it wanted more than its lover could provide.[46] It persisted in attaching itself to the wrong men,[47] couldn't align itself with lasting love,[48] and wanted to sleep with strangers or friends.[49] It wanted sex without love[50] and sex without the double standard foiling its plans.[51] Female 'heterosexual' desire even wanted sex with women.

In an extraordinary story, 'Woman to Woman', a 'happily married woman' wrote in the first person about an experience that allowed her to discover more about her sexuality. At 35, the author makes love to her friend Amelia, also a married woman. The husband Ken is in bed with them. He fades out of the picture fairly quickly. 'Much to Ken's disappointment, neither Amelia nor I felt the need of a penis.' The reader is taken on a highly descriptive tour of both women's bodies. 'Almost a year later,' she writes, 'we find neither of us has become lesbian. I still prefer a male partner but would never discount the possibility of another experience

---

42 Camilla Beach, 'A Woman's Secret Garden', *Cleo*, March 1976, 116.
43 'Men—and Sex Outside Marriage', *Cleo*, January 1975, 126–29; 'Who Wants to be a One Man Woman? I Don't', *Cleo*, September 1977, 58.
44 'Is There Sex after Marriage?', *Cleo*, April 1978, 52–55; 'After Sex…What Next?', *Cleo*, November 1977, 254–55.
45 'The Big Freeze. Does Sex Send You to Sleep?' *Cleo*, October 1979, 16–19; 'Single Life in a Double Bed', *Cleo*, October 1976, 105–8; 'Could You be Happy with One Man After Sleeping with a Lot?', *Cleo*, July 1978, 17–21.
46 *Cleo* Advisor, *Cleo*, June 1973, 17.
47 'Men Are Proper Bastards', *Cleo*, November 1972, 14–17.
48 *Cleo* Advisor, *Cleo*, March 1983, 21.
49 'Sex with Strangers? Sex with Friends?' *Cleo*, May 1977, 12–14; 'The Sexual Etiquette of Brief Encounters', *Cleo*, October 1976, 73–79.
50 'Sex Without Love', *Cleo*, January 1979, 62–64.
51 'True Lust and Real Love', *Cleo*, February 1984, 52–56.

with a woman.' There was no guilt or shame and the experience had made her a better lover. The author discovered a new empathy for men. 'I know how difficult it can be … If a woman doesn't tell him what she likes or wants, how on earth is the man to ever know?'[52] Lesbian readers saw the article as a step towards the acceptance of gays by straights[53] and were writing in for back issues years later. And straight readers who responded to the story expressed relief that their sexual experiences with women meant they were *not* lesbian.[54] From another reading, *Cleo* was suggesting how women could explore their sexual assertiveness and curiosity without worrying about labelling their sexuality at all.

A singular definition of 'normal' female heterosexuality had completely dissolved over this decade in *Cleo*. What remained normative was the presumption that women *should* be interested in sex as part of their newfound liberation and independence. Sex with men, however, was not represented as something to be exchanged or endured for a meal ticket or social mobility, nor was it represented as something extracted from women as unwilling victims of phallic domination. Women were encouraged to lose their shame and embarrassment about sex. They were being provided with the techniques and attitudes to *do* sex—not have it *done to* them. Doing sex didn't even necessarily mean sex with men. Women could do it alone, with machinery, in fantasy, or with other women.

Cleo can be read as an historical document of everyday women's struggle in the 1970s (and beyond) to become actively sexual and knowledgeable in the name of gender equality. The struggle was clearly represented as one of women's as much as sexual liberation. And for many of *Cleo*'s female readers, the result was revolutionary. As Penelope George wrote, 'I was not frigid … My life must surely change'.[55]

---

52 'Woman to Woman', *Cleo*, November 1979, 75.
53 *Cleo* Letters, *Cleo*, May 1980, 264.
54 *Cleo* Letters, *Cleo*, February 1980, 144.
55 George, 'Oh, for a Big O'.

CHAPTER 16

Male chauvinists and ranting libbers: Representations of single men in 1970s Australia

Chelsea Barnett

In September 1970, the magazine *Pix* published the following reader's letter:

> Pity the poor victimised bachelor. He's overtaxed, pays high rent for a room or flat, does his own laundry, cooking and household chores. He has to take out girls, even if only for his own sanity. But, unless he's well off—and not many are—how can he save enough money to marry and settle down?[1]

For the letter-writer—dubbed 'Fed Up', from Mt Gambier in South Australia—the life of the single man deserved pity, sympathy. Expectations of marriage lingered, as did those of financial security; a man had to be 'well off' to even contemplate marriage, 'Fed Up' reckoned. Read on its own, the letter reveals something of the uncertainty that shaped the lives of single men in the Australian 1970s. We might recognise the 1970s as a period in which the transformations of the 1960s continued to unfold with increasing visibility, but for 'Fed Up', at least, more conventional ideas about masculinity continued to burden unmarried men.[2] The publication of the letter suggests a complex gender order operating in the 1970s, particularly as it functioned outside the continuing legitimacy of marriage.

---

1   Letter to the editor, *Pix*, 19 September 1970, 23.
2   Michelle Arrow, *Friday on Our Minds: Popular Culture in Australia since 1945* (Sydney: UNSW Press, 2009), 141.

Yet when read in the broader context of *Pix* (which would become *Pix/People* in 1972) in the 1970s, a more complicated image of single men emerges. True, that the letter was even published suggests that 'Fed Up' was speaking to a sympathetic audience. But 'Fed Up' was ultimately an anomaly in the pages of the magazine. Far from appearing as a figure requiring pity or sympathy, *Pix* and *Pix/People* charged the single man with asserting and maintaining a masculinism that both produced and was contingent upon a subservient femininity.

The 1970s continue to be remembered, in popular memory at least, as a decade of upheaval and change. Indelibly linked to these lingering memories is former Labor prime minister Gough Whitlam; upon his death in 2014, the statesman was eulogised as '[coming] to embody a period in Australian history which, for better or worse, was one of rapid and unparalleled change'.[3] While Whitlam's prime ministerial term was both the product of and catalyst for social change, cultural shifts were also unfolding—particularly in relation to the Australian national ideal. In this chapter, I argue that we see these shifts in *Pix* and then *Pix/People* magazine. I am particularly focusing on the periodical from 1970 to 1976, before it again changed its name to *People with Pix* and became more explicitly involved in reporting celebrity gossip—this change foreshadowed its eventual transformation to *People* magazine (and, simultaneously, the change to a magazine intended for both men and women). In these first seven years of the decade, *Pix* and *Pix/People* was a men's lifestyle magazine that, in its coverage and discussion of politics, current affairs, gender and sex, articulated a particular masculinist vision of Australia in response to the increasing visibility of the women's liberation movement in the 1970s. This chapter will explore the ways in which *Pix* and *Pix/People* linked particular understandings of femininity with a masculinist national ideal—and, thus, the ostensible threat to that ideal posed by the contemporary women's liberation movement—before identifying how the magazine called upon unmarried men to adopt and embody the label of the 'male chauvinist' in response to this supposed challenge. More than just furthering a trite 'battle of the sexes', *Pix* and *Pix/People* mobilised a particular image of unmarried men to articulate an idealised, masculinist nationalism that left no space for femininity as posited by second-wave feminism.

---

3   Emma Griffiths, 'Obituary: Former Prime Minister Gough Whitlam Dead at 98', *ABC News*, October 2014, www.abc.net.au/news/2014-03-10/gough-whitlam/3945026.

This chapter works within, and adds to, complex bodies of scholarship on Australian gender and Australian weekly periodicals. Betty Friedan may have, in 1963, positioned women's magazines as 'the purveyors of [a] cloak of darkness from which women had to escape', yet historians have, to some extent, recognised the importance of such cultural texts in their articulation of gendered ideals and expectations in twentieth-century Australia.[4] The *Australian Women's Weekly* has received much of this scholarly attention—perhaps unsurprisingly, given that it became the most popular Australian women's magazine by the end of the 1930s (its first decade of circulation), attracted hundreds of thousands of readers in World War Two despite printing restrictions and then came to represent the 'popular face of Australian femininity' in the middle of the century.[5] Megan Le Masurier has argued that *Cleo* in the 1970s created a public domain through which Australian women could access and engage with second-wave feminism.[6] Yet although other scholars have acknowledged magazines' liberatory potential—Katie Holmes and Sarah Pinto, for instance, note that women's magazines in the early years of the twentieth century 'enabled some women to imagine autonomy'—deep engagement with magazines other than *Cleo* and the *Weekly* is rare.[7]

These gaps in the scholarship are only amplified when we turn to men's magazines. Historians interested in Australian men's magazines have most commonly looked to *Man*, published from the 1930s to the 1970s, and its place in the academic conversation has unfolded since the end of that decade.[8] More recently, Madeleine Hamilton and Julie Ustinoff have both understood *Pix* as a harbinger of conventional hegemonic masculinity; however, they were not only looking at the magazine before it explicitly claimed to be 'entertainment for men', but they also explored its

---

4   M. J. Le Masurier, 'FAIR GO: *Cleo* Magazine as Popular Feminism in 1970s Australia' (PhD thesis, University of Sydney, 2004), 12.
5   Jeannine Baker, *Australian Women War Reporters: Boer War to Vietnam* (Sydney: UNSW Press, 2015), 48; Sue Sheridan, with Barbara Baird, Kate Borrett and Lyndall Ryan, *Who Was That Woman? The Australian Women's Weekly in the Postwar Years* (Sydney: UNSW Press, 2002), 56.
6   Le Masurier, 'FAIR GO'.
7   Katie Holmes and Sarah Pinto, 'Gender and Sexuality', in *The Cambridge History of Australia*. Vol. 2, *The Commonwealth of Australia*, ed. Alison Bashford and Stuart Macintyre (Port Melbourne: Cambridge University Press, 2013), 309, doi.org/10.1017/CHO9781107445758.044.
8   See Richard White, 'The Importance of Being *Man*', in *Australian Popular Culture*, ed. Peter Spearritt and David Walker (North Sydney: George Allen & Unwin Australia, 1979), 145–68; Ross Laurie, 'From Bodybuilders to Breadwinners: Depictions of Masculinity and Gender Roles in Popular Magazines in Australia during the 1950s' (PhD thesis, Griffith University, 1995); and Chelsea Barnett, '*Man*'s Man: Representations of Australian Post-War Masculinity in *Man* Magazine', *Journal of Australian Studies* 39, no. 2 (2015): 151–69, doi.org/10.1080/14443058.2014.1001422.

representations of, respectively, femininity and homophobia rather than masculinity.[9] Beyond this, engagement with Australian men's magazines is scant. Yet in her work on contemporary British men's magazines, Bethan Benwell has identified such texts as both producing representations of masculinity and, simultaneously, functioning as 'a site within and around which meanings of masculinity circulate and are negotiated or contested'.[10] Benwell's approach to the scholarly engagement with men's magazines is a productive one, and I share with her the belief that men's magazines, like popular culture more generally, both shape and are shaped by gendered meanings. This chapter's focus on *Pix* and *Pix/People* accordingly works to contribute to scholarship on Australian weekly periodicals as well as shed light on Australian meanings of masculinity in the 1970s.

In turning my attention to the representation of single men in *Pix* and *Pix/People* in the 1970s, I am interested in the ways in which masculinity functioned outside the confines of the heterosexual marital relationship, and so seek to establish the single man as an historical figure through which historians might understand the changing gender order over time. The unmarried man has lingered on the periphery of Australian historians' interrogation of masculinity. Marilyn Lake has hinted at 'bachelordom' being a way of life rather than an indication of a man's marital status, in her acknowledgement that the nineteenth-century Australian bushman, 'whether married or not, enjoyed the pleasures of "bachelordom"'.[11] More recently, Catharine Coleborne has located the unmarried man in the insane asylums of late colonial Australia and New Zealand.[12] Bart Ziino's work on enlistment in World War One has identified the ways in which expectations of men's enlistment were often shaped by their

---

9   Madeleine Hamilton, '"A Girl Cannot be Beautiful Unless She is Healthy": Nationalism, Australian Womanhood, and the *Pix* Beach Girl Quests of World War II', in *Historicising Whiteness: Transnational Perspectives on the Construction of an Identity*, ed. Leigh Boucher, Jane Carey and Katherine Ellinghaus (Melbourne: RMIT Publishing in association with the School of Historical Studies, University of Melbourne, 2007), 234–43; Julie Ustinoff, '"Hit Him with Your Handbag!" Homophobia in Australian Magazines of the 1960s', in *Homophobia: An Australian History*, ed. Shirleene Robinson (Sydney: Federated Press, 2008), 128–47.
10   Bethan Benwell, 'Introduction: Masculinity and Men's Lifestyle Magazines', in *Masculinity and Men's Lifestyle Magazines*, ed. Bethan Benwell (Oxford: Blackwell, 2003), 8, doi.org/10.1111/j.1467-954X.2003.tb03600.x.
11   Marilyn Lake, 'The Politics of Respectability: Identifying the Masculinist Context', *Historical Studies* 22, no. 86 (1986): 117, doi.org/10.1080/10314618608595739.
12   Catharine Coleborne, *Insanity, Identity and Empire: Immigrants and Institutional Confinement in Australia and New Zealand, 1873–1910* (Manchester: Manchester University Press, 2015), 114–38.

marital status.[13] And Zora Simic has noted that single migrant men in postwar Australia were a source of concern for their ability to elicit both fear and desire, in turn recognising the specific anxieties produced at the intersection of gender and race.[14] Yet this recognition has done little to ignite broader interest in the single man; this is especially unlike the unmarried woman, whom scholars have recognised as eschewing and challenging conventional expectations of femininity.[15] A focus on the cultural articulation of unmarried men, then, might reveal new ideas about gender in the 1970s, and suggest new ways to think about the 1970s themselves.

Australian historians have keenly investigated the ways in which the cultural landscape of the 1970s understood and articulated masculinity. This scholarship has focused most heavily on 'ocker' masculinity as depicted in the flourishing cinematic landscape of the decade, although others have identified this ockerism in contemporary music and advertising as well.[16] The ocker functioned along particularly nationalist lines in this era. Stephen Crofts notes that the imagined figure 'asserted an Australian self versus its British other more virulently than was possible before or after'.[17] Michelle Arrow further links the ocker on screen to the nation-building project unfolding in the Oz Rock scene of the period. 'Pub rock', she writes, 'articulated an aggressively masculine popular nationalism …

---

13 Bart Ziino, 'Enlistment and Non-enlistment in Wartime Australia: Responses to the 1916 Call to Arms Appeal', *Australian Historical Studies* 41, no. 2 (2010): 217–32, doi.org/10.1080/10314611003713603; Bart Ziino, 'Eligible Men: Men, Families and Masculine Duty in Great War Australia', *History Australia* 14, no. 2 (2017): 202–17, doi.org/10.1080/14490854.2017.1319739.

14 Zora Simic, 'Bachelors of Misery and Proxy Brides: Marriage, Migration and Assimilation, 1947–1973', *History Australia* 11, no. 1 (2014): 153, doi.org/10.1080/14490854.2014.11668504.

15 On Australian unmarried women, see Katie Holmes, '"Spinsters Indispensable": Feminist, Single Women and the Critique of Marriage, 1890–1920', *Australian Historical Studies* 29, no. 110 (1998): 68–90, doi.org/10.1080/10314619808596061; Marilyn Lake, 'Female Desires: The Meaning of World War II', in *Gender and War: Australians at War in the Twentieth Century*, ed. Joy Damousi and Marilyn Lake (Cambridge: Cambridge University Press, 1998), 60–80; and Kay Whitehead, 'The Spinster Teacher in Australia from the 1870s to the 1960s', *History of Education Review* 36, no. 1 (2007): 1–17, doi.org/10.1108/08198691200760001.

16 See Tom O'Regan, 'Australian Film in the 1970s: The Ocker and the Quality Film', *Culture & Communication Reading Room*, wwwmcc.murdoch.edu.au/ReadingRoom/film/1970s.html; Lisa Jacobson, 'The Ocker in Australian Drama', *Meanjin* 49, no. 1 (1990): 137–47; and Stephen Crofts, '*The Adventures of Barry McKenzie*: Comedy, Satire and Nationhood in 1972', *Continuum* 10, no. 2 (1996): 123–40, doi.org/10.1080/10304319609365744; and Robert Crawford, '"Anyhow … Where D'yer Get It Mate?" Ockerdom in Adland Australia', *Journal of Australian Studies* 31, no. 90 (2007): 1–15, doi.org/10.1080/14443050709388105; Arrow, *Friday on Our Minds*, 112–16, 122–26.

17 Crofts, '*The Adventures of Barry McKenzie*', 123.

The ocker, it seemed, was alive and well and enjoying his Angels gigs'.[18] Much like the ocker on the big screen and in local pubs, the single man in the pages of *Pix* and *Pix/People* was engaged in a nationalist project, responding to the women's liberation movement of the 1970s through affirming, and maintaining, a masculinist nationalism.

'Sex and love: The most talked about subject on earth'[19]

Pix was first published in January 1938, and began as a weekly lifestyle magazine for both men and women. The magazine did not explicitly state its imagined or intended audience, but with coverage of celebrity affairs and human interest stories situated alongside that of the spectre of another world war, it certainly catered to a wide (imagined) audience in its early issues.[20] Ustinoff notes that the periodical attempted to appeal to the 'broadest possible readership consisting of both men and women from predominantly a working-class background'.[21] By the 1970s, however, the magazine openly targeted a male readership. Nude or scantily clad women graced the magazine's covers in the early years of the decade; when, in 1972 and 1973, covergirls were indeed covered by a tiny bikini, an open vest or a strategically placed towel, the audience demanded a return to the more revealing images. In doing so, readers like 'Happy Medium' explicitly articulated that the magazine was produced for men:

> I was disappointed when Pix/People discontinued nude pictures, due to the selfish few who are not content to have most magazines in a prudish form but want them all that way. If they find such harmless things offensive, there is a large range of women's magazines which should fulfil their needs. I, and many others would like to enjoy more of the old Pix/People.[22]

---

18   Arrow, *Friday on Our Minds*, 128–29. See also Jon Stratton, 'Nation Building and Australian Popular Music in the 1970s and 1980s', *Continuum* 20, no. 2 (2006): 243–52, doi.org/10.1080/10304310600641778.
19   'Do Hormones and Alcohol Help?', *Pix*, 7 March 1970, 14.
20   See 'Shirley Temples: Hollywood Has Them by the Carload', *Pix*, 29 January 1938, 36–37; 'He's 34 Stone on the Hoof', *Pix*, 29 January 1938, 24–25; and 'Children for War and War for Children', *Pix*, 29 January 1938, 8–11.
21   Ustinoff, '"Hit Him with your Handbag!"', 129.
22   Letter to the editor, *Pix/People*, 12 December 1972, 12.

16. MALE CHAUVINISTS AND RANTING LIBBERS

While it was not clear whether 'Happy Medium' was a man or a woman, the editor's brief response indicated that they, at least, understood the letter's author to be a man, confirming that 'Happy Medium can be sure we will not disappoint him'.[23] Sure enough, 'Happy Medium' would soon be pleased. The nude covergirls returned in early 1973, only months after the letter was published in December 1972.

In voicing their displeasure at the magazine's supposed 'prudish form', 'Happy Medium' articulated a distinction between women's and men's magazines. Clearly, for this particular reader, *Pix* and *Pix/People* was a magazine that, in catering for a male readership, was thus obligated to represent 'the beauty and appeal of the female nude from an artistic point'.[24] By the time this letter had been published, the magazine had already introduced the tagline 'For Men' on its covers; the more enduring tagline, 'Entertainment For Men', was adopted in December 1972 (albeit discarded in July 1975).

Despite this explicit recognition of its male audience, *Pix* and *Pix/People* continued to cater to women through the 1970s. Indeed, while the magazine continued to cover human interest stories, current events and celebrity natter as it did in the 1930s, more titillating material was also discussed, and the magazine functioned as a site in which issues of sex and gender could be discussed by men and women, young and old. One reader thanked the magazine for its 'thought-provoking and generally enlightening' coverage of sex, adding: 'At my age (33) I find my education in these matters left a lot to be desired, and I wish my parents had had courage and the knowledge to inform me much sooner'.[25] Women who wrote requesting the inclusion of male nudes, to be on par with the magazine's male readers, were rewarded with posters of barely clad men.[26] While editors deemed full-frontal views impractical because 'retailers wouldn't sell them', they also saw no harm in providing 'beefcake bonanza … strictly for the girls'.[27] Whether these letters were genuinely sent in by readers is less important than the comments being '*presented* as the

---

23 Ibid.
24 Ibid.
25 Letter to the editor, *Pix*, 21 November 1970.
26 'Men for Walls', *Pix/People*, 26 October 1972, 20–21.
27 Ibid., 20; Editorial, *Pix/People*, 26 October 1972, 41.

work of readers ... [to] give readers a sense of agency and project a feeling of communality'—and, ultimately, to suggest a community of readers engaged in a dialogue with each other, and with the magazine.[28]

Understanding the relationship *Pix* and *Pix/People* had with their imagined or intended readership is important, because it is clear that the magazine was articulating ideas around gender, sex and marriage to both men *and* women. The magazine did acknowledge female sexuality and sexual agency outside of marriage, with the yoga column 'SEXercises with Swami Sarasvasti' encouraging women to exercise their pelvic muscles:

> which are so important for childbirth and enjoying your sex life. Well-toned muscles add to a girl's femininity ... You can get the man you want and keep him as long as you want him to stay with you.[29]

Overwhelmingly, however, *Pix* and *Pix/People* advocated a conventional femininity that was both subordinate to masculinity and bound by marriage. Other 'SEXercises' columns noted that 'a clever woman will always keep her man happy by dressing to please him ... A really sexy woman is feminine all the time, whether she is dressed up to go to a ball or is simply doing her housework'.[30] Married women were advised to reignite the spark with their husbands 'after she's sent the children to her mother's, and cleaned the house and made some good steaks'.[31] More generally, it was only within the marital relationship that women's sex was represented as legitimate at all. One woman asked regular columnist 'Dr Pix' for advice: her boyfriend was requesting she wear 'see-through gear', but she was a 'bit too timid'. Dr Pix's advice? Not to worry until after marriage, for 'see through gear is essentially designed for the bedroom after the nuptial deal has been sealed, signed and delivered'.[32] Another 16-year-old girl was worried about getting carried away with her boyfriend, for 'anything's liable to happen after that'. Dr Pix's suggestion was, again, to wait: 'Keep your passion under control until the wedding bells toll. Then get on "The Pill" (or what) and your problems will vanish'.[33] Furthermore, married women who *had* access to the pill were advised to reconsider their

---

28　Bridget Griffen-Foley, 'From *Tit-Bits* to *Big Brother*: A Century of Audience Participation in the Media', *Media, Culture & Society* 26, no. 4 (2004): 540, doi.org/10.1177/0163443704044216.
29　'SEXercises with Swami Sarasvasti', *Pix*, 23 January 1971, 31.
30　'SEXercises with Swami Sarasvasti', *Pix*, 26 December 1970, 22.
31　'What I'd Like to Tell my Husband about Sex', *Pix/People*, 26 June 1972, 18.
32　'Dr Pix', *Pix*, 29 August 1970, 24.
33　'Dr Pix', *Pix*, 30 May 1970, 22.

usage should it 'wreck' their sex life and produce 'disastrous, marriage-destroying symptoms'.[34] While acknowledging that sex was an important (and even essential) component of married life, *Pix* and *Pix/People* was clearly committed to an ideal femininity that could mobilise sexual agency and desire sexual pleasure only within the bounds of marriage.

'I want one who recognises her own subservience'[35]

Through its articulation of feminine sexuality circumscribed by marriage, *Pix* and *Pix/People* was engaged in a broader cultural conversation that was grappling with changing meanings of gender and, by extension, changing ideas of the Australian nation. That the nation is a gendered institution is widely accepted by scholars of gender; others similarly recognise that nationalism, and Australian nationalism in particular, has been constructed by and through 'masculinized memory, masculinized humiliation, and masculinized hope'.[36] Gail Reekie, for instance, notes that it is through the exclusion of the experiences of women that Australia has 'retained its masculine integrity'.[37] As such, while the idealised Australian nationalism has relied upon 'the celebration of a particular style of white masculinity', feminist historians have emphasised that this nationalism 'could come into conflict with a feminist interest in the rights of women'.[38] Accordingly, the continued rearticulation of the dominant, masculinist national ideal was dependent upon a subservient femininity, which the women's liberation movement of the 1970s sought to dismantle.

Certainly, women's liberation made significant strides to bring about social change in this period. The establishment of 'refuges, women's centres, rape crisis centres, Women's Studies units in institutions of tertiary education', as well as campaigns against sexist advertising, for equal pay and for safe

---

34 'The Pill is Wrecking My Sex Life', *Pix*, 9 January 1971, 10.
35 Hugh Schmitt, 'The Girls Said: "Bring on the Piggies"', *Pix/People*, 12 July 1973, 7.
36 Cynthia Enloe, *Bananas, Beaches and Bases: Making Feminist Sense of International Politics*, 2nd ed. (Berkeley: University of California Press, 2014), 93; Mrinalini Sinha, 'Gender and Nation', in *Women's History in Global Perspective*, ed. Bonnie G. Smith (Urbana & Chicago: University of Illinois Press, 2006), 230.
37 Gail Reekie, 'Contesting Australia: Feminism and Histories of the Nation', in *Images of Australia: An Introductory Reader to Australian Studies*, ed. Gillian Whitlock and David Carter (St Lucia: University of Queensland Press, 1992), 145.
38 Patricia Grimshaw, Marilyn Lake, Ann McGrath and Marian Quartly, *Creating a Nation*, 2nd ed. (Perth: API Network, 2006), 2.

and legal access to abortion, signalled 'second-wave feminism at work'.[39] But a significant component of this feminist project unfolded in cultural terms, particularly regarding the relationship between Australian women, and Australian femininity, and the nation. While Susan Magarey, for instance, notes the complex relationship between women's liberation and the government, emphasising that both entities (the movement and the state) and their relationship changed over time, she also acknowledges 'the overwhelming desire unleashed in Women's Liberation for an order of transformation unimaginable in conjunction with any kind of government we know'.[40] Patricia Grimshaw, Marilyn Lake, Ann McGrath and Marian Quartly point out that second-wave feminists, 'armed with a university education and the pill', aimed for liberation, and not equality, upon realising that dominant assumptions of the national political economy 'worked against women'.[41] Elsewhere, Lake has emphasised women's 'sense of profound alienation from the nation' in the 1970s.[42] The second-wave-feminist quest to liberate women from 'the orbit of their mothers' produced not only the possibility of a femininity that functioned beyond the 'oppressive and stifling' expectations of marriage, motherhood and domesticity, but also produced the possibility of a feminist national imaginary.[43] However, it was this very possibility that threatened the gendered conventions advocated in *Pix* and *Pix/People*.

It is important to acknowledge that the women's liberation movement was not exclusively derided or panned in *Pix* and *Pix/People*. Readers' letters advocating equality, for example, found space in the weekly feature. Miss S. Angus went so far as to declare that she wouldn't marry a man 'for the world': 'Women should have double [men's] pay', she argued. 'They earn it.'[44] Beyond readers' contributions, however, feminism found an interesting ally in Ormsby Wilkins, a weekly columnist in the decade's early years. Wilkins lauded the increasing divorce rate of the early 1970s as 'quite a healthy sign', arguing it signalled that 'more women are finding the means to get out of their unhappy marriages and, maybe,

---

39   Susan Magarey, 'Women's Liberation Was a Movement, Not an Organisation', *Australian Feminist Studies* 29, no. 82 (2014): 378, doi.org/10.1080/08164649.2014.976898; Holmes and Pinto, 'Gender and Sexuality', 324.
40   Magarey, 'Women's Liberation Was a Movement, Not an Organisation', 379.
41   Grimshaw et al., *Creating a Nation*, 294, 298.
42   Marilyn Lake, 'Women and Nation in Australia: The Politics of Representation', *Australian Journal of Politics & History* 43, no. 1 (1997): 48, doi.org/10.1111/j.1467-8497.1997.tb01377.x.
43   Grimshaw et al., *Creating a Nation*, 294.
44   Letter to the editor, *Pix*, 27 June 1970, 46.

try again'.⁴⁵ But although Wilkins's support was articulated in numerous columns, it seemed that even he recognised the movement's limits.⁴⁶ One particular column, entitled 'Bachelor Bliss', expressed Wilkins's difficulties navigating household chores as a single man and his sense of pride at having completed the tasks but, so too, a final concession:

> It's time somebody started a Men's Lib movement to prove that at least when it comes to housekeeping, men are just as good in every way as their female counterparts. Mop in hand and saucepan under my arm I'll join and defy any woman to do better. Yet deep down inside me I know that I do need a woman if ever my house is going to be in perfect order again, try as I may to deny it.⁴⁷

Even the most ardent male supporters of feminism were ultimately shown to rely upon women to maintain their expertise in all things domestic. More than just reinforcing the notion of women's 'roles', however, the emphasis on Wilkins's unmarried status suggested it was single men who were ultimately responsible for resisting the social and cultural changes that second-wave feminism produced.

Despite *Pix* and *Pix/People* publishing positive ideas around women's liberation, these favourable representations did little to challenge the magazine's overwhelmingly negative position on the movement. The whole world was ostensibly 'in fear' as the 'Women's Lib "monster" [ran] amok', and although one reader conceded that 'Australia is behind the world in some aspects of the Women's Lib beast', the editors dryly noted their gratitude: 'and thank heavens for that'.⁴⁸ The same reader expounded their opposition to the movement on religious grounds, noting that: 'The Good Book says women should serve their husbands, and although the Bible is criticised by many people today, few (men at least) could argue with it in this case'.⁴⁹ Largely driving the general opposition to the increasing visibility of second-wave feminism in *Pix* and *Pix/People* was a broader discontent with the movement's challenge to conventional expectations of femininity. Reporting on what it deemed a 'backlash' to the women's liberation movement, the magazine asked if women had 'lost more than

---

45   Ormsby Wilkins, 'Our Sex Laws Made by Old Men!', *Pix*, 3 October 1970.
46   See, for example, Ormsby Wilkins, 'Women Get a Raw Deal', *Pix*, 21 November 1970, 23; and Ormsby Wilkins, 'Laugh's on Women's Lib.', *Pix*, 3 April 1971, 26.
47   Ormsby Wilkins, 'Bachelor Bliss', *Pix*, 18 September 1971, 22.
48   Letter to the editor, *Pix/People*, 8 March 1973, 14.
49   Ibid.

they [had] gained?'[50] Further, what of the social effects? Feminists had reportedly '[deserted] their families', making children suffer.[51] Concerns about women 'out of control' permeated the magazine's contents, as contributing authors and readers alike looked to the ostensibly dangerous precedent set by American feminists. *Pix* and *Pix/People* warned that '[m]any Australians living in the US fear the backlash of the women's liberation movement will soon be felt back home', and spoke to an Australian woman living in Miami with her husband who cautioned her female compatriots:

> Australian women are blindly following what the American women's libbers say they should do … I want men to open doors for me. At the same time if I do equal work I'd like equal pay. But this equality cannot be general because I generally can't do the work of a man.[52]

Others lamented the extent to which American feminism had grown recalcitrant: 'Americans created the Women's Lib monster—now they are searching grimly for ways to control it'.[53] These continual references to the state of women's liberation in the United States reveal concerns for the unruliness that could potentially unfold in Australia, as incredulous readers demanded:

> What do women want from liberation now? They've got the vote, are less sexually restricted, are no longer slaves in the kitchen … So what's the bellyache about by women's liberation movements? They're only malcontents or militants who are just plain bossy types wanting to exercise tyranny.[54]

Pix and *Pix/People* thus quite explicitly advocated for the maintenance of conventional femininity and sexual norms that would maintain masculine superiority and, by extension, a masculinist national vision. Sophie Robinson's work on men's engagement with second-wave feminism argues that while Australian masculinity was, in the 1970s, being confronted by both feminism and the gay liberation movement, 'it was feminism which was the most challenging to late-twentieth century Australian masculinity and politics'.[55] The magazine represented

---

50   Colin Dangaard, 'Women's Lib Backlash', *Pix/People*, 5 April 1973, 5.
51   Ibid.
52   Ibid., 4.
53   Letter to the editor, *Pix/People*, 8 March 1973, 14.
54   Letter to the editor, *Pix*, 16 January 1971, 35.
55   Sophie Robinson, 'The Man Question: Men and Women's Liberation in 1970s Australia', *Outskirts* 31 (November 2013), www.outskirts.arts.uwa.edu.au/volumes/volume-31/sophie-robinson.

the relationship between Australian men and feminism along these lines; it was reported that men '[resented] women's domination', which was said to '[gall] his masculine pride'.[56] Contributing authors undermined feminism and feminists by interviewing women who generally resented the movement: one woman advised women's libbers to 'honestly [ask] themselves if they want to be equal with men'.[57] Said another: 'I don't care what the libbers say, a pair of strong arms around me is as much of a turn-on as you can get'.[58] This negative representation of feminists aligns with broader media portrayals of the movement in the 1970s. Susan Sheridan, Susan Magarey and Sandra Lilburn note that early accounts of the women's liberation movement 'attracted a good deal of intrigued, though rarely sympathetic, reportage'.[59] But as the decade wore on—and 'the novelty wore off'—feminism and feminists were more generally depicted in ways that were 'less than friendly'.[60] Recruitment efforts for the 'short-lived Women's Liberation Movement' in Adelaide were reported to be unsuccessful, as 'potential recruits … indicated that they would remain the objects of men's desire, and like it'.[61] And one letter-writer, dubbed 'Anti-lib', succinctly expressed the general opposition to the cultural transformations wrought by women's liberation:

> Women's Liberation is a lot of rot. What is happening to feminine women? Women can be powerful without being liberated?
>
> I, for one, don't like the idea of liberated females running the world. In a woman's own little world, the order of significance is usually, husband, children, then herself.[62]

How, then, might the conventional gender order—and with it, a masculinist Australian nationalism—be maintained and rearticulated in the 1970s? While Orsmby Wilkins's 'bachelor bliss' implied that unmarried men were responsible for the continuation of a femininity subordinate to a dominant masculinity, *Pix* and *Pix/People* adopted more explicit measures as well. In particular, *Pix* and *Pix/People* turned to unmarried men whom the magazine called, and who self-identified as,

---

56 '16 Truths About Men', *Pix/People*, 17 October 1974, 32.
57 Colin Dangaard, 'Women's Lib Backlash', *Pix/People*, 5 April 1973, 5.
58 'Why Girls Go for Macho Men', *Pix/People*, 23 September 1976, 13.
59 Susan Sheridan, Susan Magarey and Sandra Lilburn, 'Feminism in the News', in *Feminism in Popular Culture*, ed. Joanne Hollows and Rachel Moseley (Oxford & New York: Berg Publishers, 2006), 25.
60 Ibid.
61 'It's Slavery, Said the Lady', *Pix*, 25 April 1970, 26.
62 Letter to the editor, *Pix/People*, 16 August 1973, 18.

'male chauvinists'. This was a label that was not only to be embraced and embodied as a badge of honour, but also functioned to represent the antithesis of second-wave feminism. Key to this male chauvinism was the dominance of men over women, of masculinity over femininity, which would in turn ostensibly secure the masculinist nationalism that the women's liberation movement sought to demolish. Indeed, if this legitimate Australian nationalism functioned as incompatible with feminist claims for women's rights, then a continued subservient femininity was an essential component of a masculinist Australia.

Pix and *Pix/People* called upon single men to embrace male chauvinism, rather than their married peers, because it was in their sexual relationships with women outside of the bonds of marriage that men could most forcefully assert their dominance. Attached or married men were not in a position to remind women of their inferiority. In such relationships, the magazine warned its readers, men needed to become accustomed to losing arguments, to receiving criticism, to becoming sexual and emotional equals: 'it's getting to know her body so well that you don't have to ask and she doesn't have to tell'.[63] Single men faced no such burdens. On the contrary, in claiming the male chauvinist label, men were *required* to be 'aggressive, active and extroverted' in order to remind women how they 'should' be acting, and what they 'should' be doing.[64] One author recommended that single men make themselves sexually 'irresistible' in order to tame uncontrollable women. Women were, the article explained, 'by nature devious', but had it in them 'to be loving, exciting, skilful and sensual. All they [needed] was a man who [could] bring out these qualities, using his knowledge, intuition and intelligence to select the right approach'.[65] The magazine here deemed self-confidence to be 'the most attractive quality a man can have'; elsewhere, *Pix* and *Pix/People* extended this assertion, assuring men that 'millions' of women '[yearned] for the strong individual who is the personification of what the ranting libbers dislike most: the man who takes charge in any male-female relationship'.[66]

More than just appealing to other women than the 'ranting libbers', *Pix* and *Pix/People* charged male chauvinists with being 'macho' (which, it explained, was 'Spanish for masculine') to remind women of the

---

63 Eleanor Williams, 'Sharing a Bed is Not Sharing a Life', *Pix/People*, 18 July 1974, 17.
64 Tim Leach, 'You Don't Have to be an Athlete', *Pix/People*, 20 July 1972, 54.
65 Robert Wimpole, 'The Irresistible Male', *Pix/People*, 17 August 1972, 38.
66 'Why Girls Go for Macho Men', *Pix/People*, 23 September 1976, 12.

benefits of a 'strong man'.[67] In the 'silence' that had followed the 'first explosions of women's lib … many girls [remembered] it's pretty good to have a masculine man who opens doors for them, gives them a shoulder to cry on, and has a mind of his own'.[68] This was the 'gutsy guy, also known as a male chauvinist pig'—a label not to be baulked at:[69]

> So if you're considered a tough guy by some ladies, if you've been called a male chauvinist pig because of your attitudes, if you're the type who is the aggressor in a male-female relationship, don't change. You're probably making out better than the rest of us.[70]

Readers approved the magazine's advocacy for this masculine type:

> Your article on macho men … proves what I have been saying all along. Women don't want small, snivelling men. They want real men who can push them around when necessary and show them who rules the roost.
>
> This 'mother instinct' seems to be fine for a week or so, but sooner or later any woman wants her man to show her what he's made of.
>
> Underneath the women's lib facade these women want real men.[71]

For this male chauvinist, dominance over women included physical strength; '[pushing] them around' was an acceptable means of reminding women 'who ruled the roost'. But male chauvinists also 'loved women', and *Pix* and *Pix/People* mobilised a particular romantic ideal to appeal to potential or untapped male chauvinists. One interviewed man, a 43-year-old divorcé, was a self-confessed male chauvinist who claimed to 'love women', and accordingly '[resented] having to treat some of them like men, just because they claim to be equal'.[72] He continued:

> I love to be kind and considerate with a woman. If I am denied this pleasure, which is the trend these days, then my enjoyment is not what it used to be.
>
> Many men I know feel the same way. I'm proud to be a male chauvinist.[73]

---

67 Ibid.
68 Ibid.
69 Ibid.
70 Ibid., 13.
71 Letter to the editor, *Pix/People*, 11 November 1976, 2.
72 Colin Dangaard, 'Women's Lib Backlash', *Pix/People*, 5 April 1973, 5.
73 Ibid.

But male chauvinist claims of loving women were limited to very specific notions of femininity. Male chauvinists clearly did not seek out feminists on whom to lavish their attention. Rather, these men sought women who would let them 'pull out chairs, open doors, extend old-fashioned graces ... Women should be kissed and cuddled, hugged and pampered and cherished. They should be put on pedestals, smell sweet and be well scrubbed at all times'.[74] Male chauvinism thus depended upon, and celebrated, a subservient femininity that was driven by particular beauty standards—something against which feminists had been actively campaigning since the emergence of the second wave in the United States.[75]

Accordingly, and unsurprisingly, interaction between male chauvinists and women involved in second-wave feminism did not unfold smoothly. *Pix* and *Pix/People* continued to affirm the necessity of single men embracing male chauvinism by reporting on its increasing visibility in Australian society. In doing so, the magazine emphasised the belief that male chauvinists could push back against any progress achieved through the women's liberation movement. The magazine reported on a 'Student Sex War' unfolding between feminists and members of the Male Chauvinist Society in operation at the Western Australian Institute of Technology (WAIT). Describing the conflict as 'a full-scale, bomb-throwing battle [that] flared up as the women fought for liberation and the men for their chauvinism', *Pix* and *Pix/People* claimed to be 'male chauvinists at heart'.[76] The magazine thus supported the claim made by the president of the Male Chauvinist Society that 'male strength will drive [feminists] into submission', and applauded the society's slogan: 'Keep 'em barefoot and pregnant'.[77] Over a month after this first report was published, author Hugh Schmitt returned to report on a debate that unfolded on the WAIT campus between three feminists and two members of the Male Chauvinist Society: outgoing president Tim Robinson and his incoming replacement Peter Woodward.[78] Woodward criticised women's liberation for being 'violently sexist, a case of the so-called oppressed becoming oppressive', and stated that '[w]omen should learn

---

74 Ibid.
75 Michelle Arrow, '"It Has Become My Personal Anthem": "I Am Woman", Popular Culture and 1970s Feminism', *Australian Feminist Studies* 22, no. 53 (2007): 214, doi.org/10.1080/08164640701361774.
76 Hugh Schmitt, 'Student Sex War', *Pix/People*, 31 May 1973, 8–9.
77 Hugh Schmitt, 'The Girls Said: "Bring on the Piggies"', *Pix/People*, 12 July 1973, 6.
78 Ibid., 6–7.

to live the role they've been born to'.[79] Similarly, Robinson was interested in the prospect of marriage, but only conditionally; he wouldn't marry, he said:

> until females start to change back to what they were before Women's Lib came along. I don't want a dumb bird, but I want one who recognises her own subservience—and with expertise on housework.[80]

While the Male Chauvinist Society was located only at WAIT at the time the article was published, Robinson hoped that branches would open at other universities and technical colleges; they were needed 'to straighten out the women of Australia who have gone the wrong way'.[81] Women who had 'gone the wrong way'—who had embraced feminism—threatened the Australian vision in which male chauvinists were invested. While WAIT's feminist women were adamant that they had 'destroyed' the Male Chauvinist Society, Robinson was equally forceful: '[t]hey can't laugh us off'.[82]

Conclusion

Five years after 'Fed Up' asked the readers of *Pix* to '[p]ity the poor vicitmised bachelor', the magazine published another reader's letter calling for sympathy for unmarried men. Mrs CLE of Wollongong, New South Wales, declared that she detested the expression 'Male Chauvinistic Pig', which she acknowledged had 'only existed during the last decade'.[83] It was an ill-fitting label, she argued, because:

> the expression does not aptly describe what it is supposed to describe—smug, superior, female exploiting males. Until this woman's [sic] liberation movement started men treated women like ladies, and only females who allowed themselves to be exploited were exploited. Women's Liberation is something each woman must battle on her own, subtly. The present form adopted only gets the fellows' backs up; and rightly so.[84]

79 Ibid., 6.
80 Ibid., 7.
81 Ibid.
82 Hugh Schmitt, 'Student Sex War', *Pix/People*, 31 May 1973, 9.
83 Letter to the editor, *Pix/People*, 7 August 1975, 2.
84 Ibid.

For Mrs CLE, men were undeserving of such a label; women who required liberating needed to work alone, and discretely. While her dislike of the label 'Male Chauvinistic Pig' sat at odds with the magazine's own enthusiastic embrace, the responsibility she placed on women to navigate women's liberation without troubling men aligned more closely with its own engagement. Indeed, while *Pix* and *Pix/People*'s representation of the women's liberation movement was not homogenous, the threat that it posed to men—and, more broadly, particular ideals of masculinity—was of particular concern to the periodical throughout the 1970s.

In emphasising and advocating male chauvinism, *Pix* and *Pix/People* represented single men as functioning with a particular power in the face of cultural and social transformations. If, by imagining a new agenda for women's rights and thus a new femininity, second-wave feminists were challenging masculinist Australian nationalism, then *Pix* and *Pix/People* charged single men, through an embrace of male chauvinism, with maintaining that national vision. This tension that unfolded in the cultural sphere of the 1970s reveals not only the necessity of understanding the single man as a historical figure, but also that cultural transformations did not unfold in the 1970s as easily as popular memory suggests.

Index

Page numbers in **bold** indicate an image; a comment in a footnote appears as e.g. 86n2.

Abbott, Tony 259, 277
abortion 5, 127, 156, 272, 304
activism 25, 46, 60
    arts 100
    culture in feminist 8, 200, 201
    feminist in education 15, 37, 46, 124
    feminist in employment 23
    feminist linguistic 19, 242, 245, 256, 260
    language 251, 260
    needlework 103, 107, 111, 120
    publishing as 122–23, 131
    Women's Domestic Needlework Group 113
Adams, Jude 89, 119
Adams, Kathryn 125
Adams, Phillip 189
Adamson, Robert Sydney 227, 230
Adcock, Charlotte 273
affirmative action 30, 31, 33
Affirmative Action Agency 27
Affirmative Action in Training 29, 31
Ahmed, Sarah 192
All That False Instruction 152
Allan, Keith and Burridge, Kate 259
alternative lifestyles 63–82, 146
    see also Earth Garden; *Grass Roots*
alternative technologies *see* appropriate technologies
Altman, Dennis 2, 163

Amazon Acres 4, 15, 69–70
Anderson, Jessica 150
Angelides, Stephen 6
Ansara, Martha 220
Antolovich, Gaby 176
appropriate technologies 75, 76, 79–80
Archer, Robyn 230
Arndt, Bettina 281
Asprey, Michèle 259
Astley, Thea 150
Atwood, Margaret 124
Austen, Ruth 289
Australian Broadcasting Corporation (ABC) 12, 116, 146, 254
Australian Council of Trade Unions (ACTU) 254
Australian Labor Party (ALP) *see* Hawke/Keating Government; Whitlam Government
Australian Law Reform Commission (ALRC) 232, 234
Australian Schools Commission 39
    report, *Girls, School and Society* 15, 40, 50–51
Australian Women's Broadcasting Cooperative 219

back-to-the-land movement 64, 72–80

Bail, Murray 151
Baker, Elizabeth 87
Bandler, Faith 137
Barry, Kay 187
Bartlett, Alison and Henderson, Margaret 112, 201
Bassett, Jan 265
beat sex 6, 18, 186, 196–97
beats 186, 189–90, 192–98
Befriending Group 172
Behind Closed Doors 220–22
Bell, Robert 281
Bellamy, Suzanne 3, 86n2, 127, 153
Benwell, Bethan 298
Berlant, Lauren 233
Berlant, Lauren and Warner, Michael 184, 198
Bishop, Elizabeth 236
Blonski, Annette 206
Blundell, Graeme 230
Bongiorno, Frank 5
Bonsall-Boone, Peter 168
  see also Phone-A-Friend
Boston Women's Health collective 284
Brennan, Bernadette 141–42
Brett, Judith 141
Brisbane, Katharine 228
Brophy, Kevin 141, 146, 148–49, 156, 158
Broude, Norma and Garrard, Mary 89
Brown, Diane and Hawthorne, Susan 132
Brown, Rita Mae 124
Brown, Wendy 198
Budden, Frances *see* Phoenix, Frances
Burridge, Kate 259
Butler, Elaine 34
Buttrose, Ita 279

Calwell, Arthur 267
Cameron, Deborah 241–42
CAMP (the Campaign Against Moral Persecution) 17, 163–82
  telephone counselling 164, 165
  see also *CAMP Ink* magazine; Gays Counselling Service; Homosexual Guidance Service; Phone-A-Friend
CAMP Ink magazine 166, 172, 176
  see also CAMP
Campaign Against Moral Persecution see CAMP; Gays Counselling Service
Canning, Kathleen 263
Carey, Gabrielle *see Puberty Blues*
Charlton, Susan *see Behind Closed Doors*
Chicago, Judy 89, 90, 114–16
Christian Homesteading Movement 78
Clark, Jocelyn 170, 175, 182
Cleo magazine 7, 9, 12, 19, 166, 279–93, 297
Clohesy, Mike 166–67, 172–73
Coleborne, Catharine 298
Comer, Lee 211
Comfort, Alex 284
'coming out' 2, 163, 173, 176
The Coming Out Show 116, 219
Commonwealth Schools Commission see Australian Schools Commission
conferences
  Confest 70, 71
  Corcoran Biennial in Washington DC 86
  First International Gay/Lesbian Health Conference 175, 178
  International Women's Year 274
  Mt Beauty feminist theory conference 153
  National Homosexual Conference 170
  Women and Labour Conference 135
  Women in Print movement 130

consciousness-raising 2–3, 8, 72, 85–86, 90, 100–1, 108, 109, 110, 112, 124, 150, 158, 173, 188, 219, 237, 245, 284–85
  groups 2, 72, 100
  reading as vehicle for 123–24, 143, 150
  refuges and rape crisis centres 164
  sex 284, 285
  use in production of art 85, 86–93, 100, 108
  use of methods for social reform 188
  Women's Art Movements 90
  writing 150, 158
Conway, Ronald 148
Corris, Peter 148, 155
Couchman, Peter 191
  see also Stokes–Turner case
counter-culture 4, 9, 75, 81, 113, 145, 147–48, 152, 219
Creswell, Rosemary 156
Croft, Brenda L. 97–98
Curtin, Elsie 267, 275–76

Dalton, Derek 193, 197
Davies, Jo 18, 225, 233
Davies, Lesley and David 227, 233
Davies, Lloyd 18, 223, 225
Davies family
  in poem 226–27
  see also Lilley–Davies case
de Beauvoir, Simone 124
de Man, Paul 237–38
de Waal, Peter 168, 177, 181
  see also Phone-A-Friend
de-schooling 38, 59
defamation *see* Lilley–Davies case
Delbridge, Arthur 254
democratic art 91
democratic rights 18
democratic schooling 38, 42, 59
Devine, Miranda 277–78

direct action 3, 201
Dixson, Miriam 124
d'oyley *see* doily
doily 16, 110–13, 116–20
  D'oyley Show 111–13
  see also Phoenix, Frances, *Kunda*; Women's Domestic Needlework Group
domestic (sphere) 88–89, 96, 99
  linking with/exploration in art 16, 89, 98, 105
  personal-political/women's movement critique 99, 103, 106, 304
  as place of confinement for women 104, 304
  see also Women's Domestic Needlework Group
domestic chores 2, 57, 73, 77–78, 305
domestic craft 16, 103, 105, 108, 109
domestic violence 18, 205, 213–19
  see also gendered violence
Dowse, Sara 150
Dunn, Irina 148

Earth Garden 15, 63–79
Earthworks Poster Collective 213
Edelman, Lee 197
Edgar, Suzanne 154
education 15
  feminist reform 9, 29, 41
  sex difference 39
  sex education 8, 19, 145, 281, 282
    as feminist practice 280
  utopian elements 45
educational materials
  avoiding sex bias in 251–52
educational reform 37–38, 39
  see also Karmel Report; Royal Commission on Human Relationships
Edwards, Professor Allan 226
Eliot, T. S. 234

Elliott, Professor Ralph 257
Elliott, Stephan 12
Ellison, Jennifer 141
Elsie women's refuge 203, 204, 209
empowerment, women's 14, 28, 54, 57, 243, 245
Engels, Friedrich 2
Eveline, Joan 33
Eveline, Joan and Butler, Elaine 34

Fallon, Kathleen Mary 135
Family Life Movement of Australia 282
Family Planning Association clinics 283
Farr, Cecilia Konchar 123, 125
Featherstone, Lisa 5, 183n2
Fellowship of Australian Writers meeting 229
feminism *see* second-wave feminism; Women's Liberation movement
see also consciousness-raising
femocrat 3, 47, 255
Ferrier, Carole 129, 142n8
film 7, 12, 200, 219–22
    Australian film industry 7, 219
    Behind Closed Doors 221–22
    censorship/classification 7
    impact of *Cruising* 191–92
    increase in obscenity in 243
    Monkey Grip 144, 146
    We Aim to Please 220
film-making 8–9
    as feminist activism 8–9
    gay and lesbian 10
Firestone, Shulamith 2, 124
Fisher, Rodney 230
Fiske, Pat *see Behind Closed Doors*
Flannery, Kathryn 122
Flood, Joe 225
Flood, Les 225, 226
Forrest-Thomson, Veronica 236
Forster, Laurel 127

French, Marilyn 143, 150
Friday, Nancy 291–92
Friedan, Betty 124, 297
    on women's magazines 297

Garner, Helen 139–59
    see also Monkey Grip
Garrard, Mary 89
Gay Liberation 179
    counselling 170
gay liberation movement 1, 2, 13, 17, 19, 20, 163, 177, 183, 188, 306
Gay Mardi Gras *see* Sydney Gay and Lesbian Mardi Gras
Gay Pride Week 169
Gays Counselling Service 164–66
Gemmel, Judy 215–16
gender-based violence 60
    1974 Commission 203
    artistic representation/interpretation 18, 199–200, 213–14
    'battered body' 205
    history of feminist response 201
    refuges as escape from 203–4
Genovese, Ann 200, 205
George, Penelope 290, 293
Gerster, Robin 265
Gertsakis, Elizabeth **96**, 97
Gibbs, Anna and Tilson, Alison 135
Gibson, Sarah *see Behind Closed Doors*
Gilbert, Kevin 154
Gilbert, Pam 154–55
Giles, Barbara 147, 148
Gillard, Julia 277
Gillard Government 24
Goldsworthy, Kerryn 141, 147, 156
Gorton, John 270
Goulden, Terry and Hay, Bob 175, 178, 180
    see also Phone-A-Friend
Grant, Bruce 267

Grass Roots 63–82
   first women's issue 71–75
Green, Victoria 245
Greenaway, John 181
Greer, Germaine 2, 127, 145, 243–44, 282, 286
Grenville, Kate 150
Gribble, Diana and McPhee, Hilary 137, 144
   see also McPhee Gribble (publishers)
Grimshaw, Patricia 304
Grounds, Joan 107, 213
   see also Women's Domestic Needlework Group
Group Apprenticeship schemes 30
Group Training Companies 31

Hacking, Ian 185, 185n8
Halley, Janet and Brown, Wendy 198
Hamilton, Madeleine and Ustinoff, Julie 297–98
Harker, Jaime 123, 125
Hasluck, Paul 269
Hawke/Keating Government 28
   legislative changes 253
Hawthorne, Susan 132
Hay, Bob 175, 176, 177–78
Hazelhurst, Noni 144
Hecate 126, 129
Hegeler, Inge and Stan 284
Henderson, Claire 47
Henderson, Margaret 11
   feminism and material culture 112–13
   on histories of the Australian women's movement 201
   women's movement as a cultural avant garde 7–8
Hess, Thomas and Baker, Elizabeth 87
heteronormativity 99, 184, 194
heterosexual desire, female 292
heterosexual masculine culture
   dominance of 9, 20

heterosexual relationships 7, 142, 158, 198
   critique of 216
   legality of versus homosexual 187, 190, 192
heterosexuality 5, 6, 7, 192, 280, 281, 293
   as orientation 192, 192n36
   'normal' female 281, 293
Hewett, Dorothy 223–38
   poetry 224, 225–26
   'Uninvited Guest' 225, 226–27, 230, 231, 233, 235, 238
Hewett, Rene 225
Higgins (later Sheridan), Susan 157
Higgs, Kerryn (under the pseudonym Elizabeth Riley) 152, 153
   see also Riley, Elizabeth
Hill, Alette Olin 241
Hinch, Derryn 191
   see also Stokes–Turner case
Holmes, Katie 299n15
Holmes, Katie and Pinto, Sarah 297
Holt, Harold 225, 270
Homosexual Electoral Lobby (later Homosexual Law Reform Committee) 189
Homosexual Guidance Service (HGS) 170
Homosexual Law Reform Committee 189
homosexuality 1, 2, 5, 6, 17–18, 163, 167–68, 170, 173, 183, 185, 189
   see also Stokes–Turner case
Hope, A.D. 230
Horne, Donald 5
housework, 2, 4, 76, 127, 215, 311
   communes 81
Howard, John 259
Howard Government 29, 258
Hubbard, Phil 197
Hudsen, Bob 230
Hughes, Geoffrey 243

Industrial Revolution 63
International Covenant on Civil and
    Political Rights (ICCPR) 231
International Women's Year 8, 129,
    274

Jam Factory 93
Jardine, Jack and Austen, Ruth 289
Jaynes, Garry 196
Jeffries, Janis 106–7
Jennings, Kate 11, 145, 215
    Mother I'm Rooted 124, 145,
    215–16, **217**
Jennings, Rebecca 3n7, 4n8, 77,
    173–74, 188
Jolley, Elizabeth 150

Karmel Report 39
Kerr, Joan 88
Kimmel, Georgie 31
Kimmel, Michael 262
Kirby, Sandy 213
Kirby, Sandy and Mayhew, Louise 206
kiss-in 18, 184–87, 192, 197
Koedt, Anne 286, 287
Kokoli, Alexandra 118
Kristeva, Julia 95–96
Krone, Bernadette 107
    see also Women's Domestic
    Needlework Group

Labor Government *see* Hawke/
    Keating Government; Whitlam
    Government
Labor Party *see* Hawke/Keating
    Government; Whitlam
    Government
Lake, Marilyn 202–3, 298, 304
Lakoff, Robin 244, 245, 246
Lambert, Susan 220, 221
    see also *Behind Closed Doors*
Langmore, Diane 276

language
    counter-sexist guidelines 248–50
    feminist use of swearing /
        offensive language 242–44
    gendered 244–45, 258–59
    non-sexist guidelines 250, 253,
        254–55
    personal pronouns, generic 246,
        247, 250, 252, 260
    political correctness 242, 258–60
    resistance against changes 256–60
Larkin, John 147
Laurie, Robin 220
Lawson, Louisa 125
Lawson, Sarah 245
Lessing, Doris 142
Letray, Kathy 107
    see also Women's Domestic
    Needlework Group
Lette, Kathy 151
    see also *Puberty Blues*
Levine, Cathy 116
Levy, Anne 230
Levy, Bronwen 151, 157
LGBTIQ 11, 60, 165n6, 259
Lifeline 167
lifestyles
    alternative 15, 66, 71, 146
    see also *Monkey Grip*
Lilburn, Sandra 307
Lilley, Dorothy 227
    see also Lilley–Davies case
Lilley, Merv 226
Lilley–Davies case 227–28, 231–34
    further legal action 230–31
Lindberg, Brian 171
Lip magazine 108–9
Lippard, Lucy 88, 90
Llewllyn, Kate 218
Lowell, Robert 225, 236
Lucas, Rose 234
Lyons, (Dame) Enid 276

Mabel: Australian Feminist Newspaper 126, 128, 209, **210**
  origin 128
Mabel the mechanic **28**
Mackinolty, Chips 213, **214**
MacLeod, Mary 211
Madsen, Jane 220–21
Magarey, Susan 7, 8, 11, 201, 304, 307
magazines, men's 298
  see also Pix and *Pix/People* magazine
magazines, women's 203, 211, 297, 304
  see also Cleo; *Hecate*; *Lip*; *Mabel*; *Vashti's Voice*
Maines, Rachel 109, 117
male chauvinist 20, 154, 296, 307–10
Male Chauvinist Society 310–11
Manne, Robert 269
Mardi Gras *see* Sydney Gay and Lesbian Mardi Gras
marriage 71, 233, 295, 302, 303, 304, 311
  effect of social change on 202–3
  gender roles in 273, 311
  as political 266, 273, 276
  same-sex survey 11
  sex in 282, 302
  sex outside of 308
Martin, Jean 39
Masters, Olga 150, 285, 289
Matthews, Jill 157
Mayhew, Louise 206
McCarthy, John 250–51
McCarthy, Wendy 291
McDiarmid, David 10
McDonald, Patricia 107
McGrath, Ann 304
McKee, Alan 7
McKemmish, Jan 135
McLaren, John 154
McLean, Kath 133
McLeod, Amanda 77–78

McMahon, Marie 95–96, 104, 107–8, 109, 114–15
  see also Women's Domestic Needlework Group
McMahon, Sonia 270
McMahon, William 19, 266, 269–70
McNair Anderson survey 285
McPhee Gribble (publishers) 143, 150–51
McPhee, Hilary 137, 144
  see also McPhee Gribble
McPhee, Ian 253
Melbourne Gay Liberation 169, 175, 182, 188n21 189
Melbourne Gay Liberation Front (GLF) 170, 182
Menzies, Robert 269, 270–71
  era 265
Mercer, Jan 124
Migalka, Peter 170, 171
Miller, Casey 246, 247, 250, 251, 253
Miller, David and Meg 65
Millett, Kate 2, 42, 124, 212
Mitchell, Juliet 124
Mitchell, Susan 266
Modjeska, Drusilla 149, 152
Monkey Grip 17, 124, 139–59
  as feminist novel 150–54
  feminist response 154–58
  publishers 141, 144, 150–51
  reviews 147–49
  success 146, 154
Moore, Clive 6, 188
Morgan, Lesley 155, 158
Morgan, Robin 123
Mother Earth News journal 64, 65, 79
Mother I'm Rooted see Jennings, Kate
Ms (title) 4, 242, 252
Ms magazine 126, 130, 246, 247
Murray, Andrew 258–59
Murray, Simone 131
Murray-Smith, Stephen 229

319

Nash, Margot 220
Nash, Megan 221–22
National Book Council Award 141, 146, 152, 154
Native Title Act 1994 98
Nearing, Helen and Scott 63–64, 79
needlework 16, 73, 103–20
    elevation as art 111–13
    expression of activism 107, 120
    source of resistance against feminine ideals 107, 109, 113
    upholding ideology of femininity/ symbolising relation with domestic sphere 105–6, 110, 113
    see also Women's Domestic Needlework Group
Nelson, Deborah 232
Newmarch, Ann 87, 91, **92**, **94**, 95, 213, 216, **217**
Nicholson, Joyce 154
Nochlin, Linda 15, 86, 87, 104–5
Nussbaum, Martha 194

Oakley, Ann 124
'ocker' 19–20, 299–300
Office of the Status of Women (OSW) 253
orgasm, female 20, 281, 284, 286–90
    clitoral versus vaginal 285, 287–89
    G-spot 289
    as sexual liberation 286, 290
    and vibrators 290–91
O'Sullivan, Deirdre 152–53
O'Sullivan, Kimberly 6

Packer, Frank 279
    see also Cleo magazine
Parker, Rozsika 105
Parramatta Factory 207
Parsons, Phillip 231
Parsons, Talcott 43

Pauwels, Anne 241, 246, 248n31, 252, 258, 260
    personal is political 16, 88, 97–98, 129
Peters, Pam 260
Petersen, Katrina 287
Phoenix (nee Budden), Frances 16, 93, 104, 107, 108–9, 114–16
    The Dinner Party 114–16
    Kunda 16, 116–20
    see also Women's Domestic Needlework Group
Phoenix, Frances and McMahon, Marie 107, 108, 109, 114, 115
Phone-A-Friend (PAF) 165, 167–72, 181–82
Piercy, Marge 124
Pinto, Sarah 297
Pitman Hughes, Dorothy 126
Pix and *Pix/People* magazine 20, 295–324
Plath, Sylvia 225, 236
Plum Farm Women's Land near Adelaide 74
poems
    'FINISHED' Kate Llewllyn 218
    'For John, Who Begs Me Not to Enquire Further' Anne Sexton 226, 234–35
    'Into the Sun' Judy Gemmel 215
    'Refractory Girl' 207
    'Witch Poem' Chris Sitka 216
    see also Hewett, Dorothy; Eliot, T. S.
poets 145, 147, 206
poetry 93, 201, 215–19, 224, 237
    see also Lilley–Davies case
Poland, Louise 131–32, 135
'politics of derision' 269
popular culture 7, 13, 243, 298
Pride History Group's 100 Voices project 168
print media
    feminist press 125, 131

printing press 122–29, 131–33, 138, 150, 215
  see also publishers, feminist
privacy/private sphere 18
  as concealment, shame stigma 193, 224
  changing definition 223
  equality as alternative 190
  feminist critique of 18, 224, 232
  gendered access 173
  as oppression 184n3
  as patriarchal space 231
  reform 232
  see also International Covenant on Civil and Political Rights; Wolfenden Report
Puberty Blues 151
  TV series 12
publishers, feminist, 8, 8n28, 16–17, 121–38, 150
  Artemis Publishing 137
  Everywoman Press 133
  Sisters Publishing 137
  Spinifex Press 137, 138
  Sugar & Snails 132–33
  Sybylla Co-operative Press/ Sybylla Feminist Press 133–35, **136**
  Tantrum Press 137
  Virago 131
  The Women's Press 131
  Women's Redress Press 137
  see also printing press
publishing 121
  difficulties publishing feminist content 124
  feminist 121–23

Quartly, Marian 304

race 129, 299
Race, Kane 185
Raj, Senthorun 194
Ramsay, Janet 203–4
Reddy, Helen 8
Redgate, Jacky 97
Reekie, Gail 303
reform, educational 37–38, 48, 51, 52, 55, 58, 61
  feminist 40, 43, 45, 46, 51, 59–60
  Whitlam Government instituted 39
  see also Australian Schools Commission; Karmel Report
reform, legal 163, 178, 185, 187, 190–91, 193–94, 196, 205
  campaign for 163, 186–89
  see also Australian Law Reform Commission; Homosexual Law Reform Committee
reform, linguistic 248, 253, 256
reform versus revolution 179, 188, 276
Refractory Girl 8, 129, 130, 133, 153, 207, **208**, 211, 218
Reid, Elizabeth 8, 47, 87
Reynolds, Robert 173, 183
Rich, Adrienne 124, 225
Rieschild, Verna 245
Riley, Elizabeth 124, 152
  see also Higgs, Kerryn
Roadknight, Margaret 230
Roberts, Violet and Bruce 199, 205
  banner **200**
  release campaign 220
Robertson, Toni 86, 200, **200**, 212, 213, **214**
  see also Earthworks Poster Collective; Tin Sheds Collective
Robinson, Sophie 6, 306
Robinson, Tim 310, 311
Roessler, Beate 232
Romantic movement 63
Romanticism 234
Rooney, Brigid 143

Rowbotham, Shiela 131
royal commissions
    Royal Commission on Human Relationships vii, 37–38, 156–57, 171, 224
    Woodward Royal Commission 79

Sammut, Jeremy 260
Save Our Sons 225
Sawer, Marian 24, 257
Schmitt, Hugh 310–11
schools
    1970s changes 38, 39
    absence of sex education in 281–82
    role in education about jobs in trades 26, 31, 32
    second-wave feminism in 41, 59–60, 251–52
    sexual inequality in 39–40
    as socialising agents 42
    see also Australian Schools Commission, report *Girls, School and Society*; de-schooling; education; Karmel Report
Schwarz, Veronica 156
second-wave feminism 27, 42–44, 47, 48, 103, 106, 111, 114, 122, 143, 144, 244, 279, 286, 296, 297, 304–6, 308, 310, 312
    critique of privacy 224
    and culture 11, 85–90, 126
    in education/schools 40–46, 59, 61
    and employment policies 34
    and film-making 8n28, 219–22
    gendered nature of language and stereotypes 244
    hierarchical organisation in 114
    linguistic activism 19, 242, 245, 247–48, 256, 260
    magazines see *Cleo*; *Vashti's Voice*
    politics and needlework 103, 106, 109, 112
    popular feminism 280
    as print media movement 125, 138
    reading and writing 121, 123–24, 141
    see also Women's Liberation movement
self-sufficiency 64–81
sex education 145, 281–82
sex role 37, 42–44, 46, 51, 56–58, 60, 76, 156
sex-role stereotyping 30, 42, 46, 47, 50, 52, 55
sexology 284
Sexton, Anne 225–26, 234, 237
sexuality 5, 10, 14, 18, 60, 91, 119, 171, 203, 280
    in back-to-the-land movement 75
    education 37
    female 281, 286–87, 290, 291, 293, 302
    feminist writing on 122
    history in Australia 5
    in *Monkey Grip* 144
    in popular culture 243
    studies 121
    teenage 6
    see also heterosexuality; homosexuality
Seymour, Sally and John 64, 79
Sheridan, Susan 222, 307
Short, Penny 130
single men 295, 296, 298
Sitka, Chris 216 (poem)
Smaal, Yorick 6
Smith, Irene 71, 79
Smith, Jan 285
Smith, Judy 76
Smith, Keith Vincent and Irene 64–65, 71
    see also *Earth Garden*
Smith, Louisa 36

Smith, Mr C. H. 228
Society Five 188
Spare Rib magazine 126
Spender, Dale 245, 251, 252, 254
Spongberg, Mary 129, 207–9
Stahl, Chris 167, 174
Steinem, Gloria 124, 126
Stokes, Terry 187
    see also Stokes–Turner case
Stokes–Turner case 187, 188, 190, 191, 198
Stuart Mill, John 224
Summers, Anne 123–24, 154, 204, 255, 256
Summers, Shelley 284–85
Supporting and Linking Tradeswomen (SALT) 26
Sutherland Harris, Anne 87
Swift, Kate 246, 247, 250, 251, 253
Sydney Gay and Lesbian Mardi Gras 10, 11, 12, 163, 180
Sydney Star gay newspaper 177
Sydney University Fine Art Workshop see Tin Sheds Collective

TAFE 26, 28–29
    harrassment at 35
Taylor, Noela 107
Theobald, Jacqueline 203
Thompson, Denise 176–77, 179, 182
Tilson, Alison 135
Tin Sheds Collective 213
Tomasetti, Glen 124, 151
Tomsic, Mary 206, 219, 220
Tourvis, Dina 97
trades, male-dominated 14
    efforts at encouragement 28–29
    lack of change 25, 31–32
    reasons for 30–31, 32–36
    women's entry into 14, 23–36
tradeswomen 26, 27, 35
Tranter, John 215
Trebilco, Peter 164n4, 175

True Blue 99–100
Turner, Darren 187–88, 190–91, 197, 198
    see also Stokes–Turner case

Ustinoff, Julie 297, 300

Vashti's Voice/Vashti magazine 8, 126, 139–40, 145, 158, 218–19
Vickery, Anne 206, 215
Victorian Apprenticeship Commission 30
Victorian Premier's Literary Award 135
Vieceli, Loretta 107, 213n27

Wakoski, Diane 142
Walker, Alan 167, 168
Walker, Alice 124
Ward, Peter 93
Ware, John 170
Warner, Michael 184, 198, 280, 291
Watson, Lex 176
    see also CAMP
Whip, Rosemary 276
Whitlam era 48
    impact of subsequent conservative backlash 178
Whitlam, Gough 19, 39, 262, 269–71, 296
Whitlam, Gough and Margaret 261–78, **268**
Whitlam Government 39, 79, 128, 141, 156, 242
    dismissal 128, 134, 156, 242
    educational reform 39
    equitable access to higher education 48
    It's Time campaign 271
    social policies and reform 156
    see also royal commissions, Woodward Royal Commission

Whitlam, Margaret 1, 19, 261–62, 274, 276
Whitlock, Gillian 150
Wignell, Edna (Edel) 248, 249
Wilkins, Ormsby 304–5, 307
Willessee, Mike 191
   see also Stokes–Turner case
Willett, Graham 169, 186
   see also Phone-A-Friend
Williams, Joan 227
   see also Lilley–Davies case
Williams, John 99
Williamson, David 230
Wills, Morgan 80, 81
Wills, Sue 170, 174, 176
   see also CAMP
Wilson, Sue
Winton, Tim 151
Witig, Monique 152
Wolfenden Report 170, 190, 194, 224
Women Behind Bars 200, 205
Women's Art Movements 89–90, 93, 95, 213
Women's Art Register 213
Women's Commissions 203–4
Women's Domestic Needlework Group 103–4, 107–16
Women's Electoral Lobby 126–27, 189, 245, 257, 272
Women's Health Centres 283
Women's Liberation Halfway House Collective 204
Women's Liberation movement 3, 16–18, 20, 85, 87, 90, 122–23, 132, 150, 159, 296, 300, 303–8, 310, 312
   and art 16, 87
   crossover with gay and lesbian liberation 10
   and film 219–22
   links to publishing industry 127, 132–33
   newsletters and journals 128–29, 139, 203–4
   see also *Cleo*; *Mabel*; *Hecate*; *Vashti's Voice*
   relation to government 304
   response by men's literature 20, 296, 300
Women's Movement Children's Literature Cooperative Ltd 132
women's refuges 3, 164, 202–5, 212, 219, 303
   history in Australia 203–4
   role 204–5
   women in 221–22
   see also Elsie women's refuge
Women's Theatre Group 145
women's writers see Anderson, Jessica; Astley, Thea; Atwood, Margaret; Brown, Rita Mae; Dixson, Miriam; Dowse, Sara; Garner, Helen; Greer, Germaine; Grenville, Kate; Jennings, Kate; Jolley, Elizabeth; Masters, Olga; Mercer, Jan; Piercy, Marge; Rich, Adrienne; Riley, Elizabeth; Summers, Anne; Tomasetti, Glen; Walker, Alice
Woodham, Anne 286, 287
Woodward, Brian 168–69
Woodward, Peter 310–11
Woodward Royal Commission 79
working-class trades see trades, male-dominated
Wright, Clare 144

Young, Stacey 122

Ziino, Bart 298–99

www.ingramcontent.com/pod-product-compliance
Lightning Source LLC
Chambersburg PA
CBHW042042240426
43667CB00048B/2958